Kulanu:
All of Us

A Program and Resource Guide for Gay, Lesbian, Bisexual, and Transgender Inclusion

Revised and Expanded

Rabbi Richard F. Address, D.Min.;
Joel L. Kushner, Psy.D.; and Rabbi Geoffrey Mitelman
Editors

URJ Press
Department of Jewish Family Concerns
Union for Reform Judaism
New York, New York

All rights reserved. No part of this book may be reproduced, stored in a retrieval system, or transmitted without express written permission from URJ Press.
This excludes brief quotations used only for the purpose of review.

For permission to reprint, please contact URJ Press at:

URJ Press
633 Third Avenue
New York, NY 10017-6778

(212) 650-4124
press@urj.org

Library of Congress Cataloging-in-Publication Data

Kulanu: all of us: a program and resource guide for gay, lesbian, bisexual, and transgender inclusion / edited by Richard F. Address, Joel L. Kushner, and Geoffrey Mitelman. — Revised and expanded ed.
    p. cm.
  ISBN 978-0-8074-0612-0
 1. Homosexuality—Religious aspects—Judaism. 2. Reform Judaism—United States—Doctrines. 3. Jewish gays—United States. 4. Jewish lesbians—United States. I. Address, Richard F. II. Kushner, Joel L. III. Mitelman, Geoffrey.
  BM729.H65K85   2007
  296.8´34108664—dc22

2007020426

Printed on acid-free paper
Copyright © 2007 by URJ Press
Manufactured in the United States of America
10 9 8 7 6 5 4 3 2 1

Kulanu:
All of Us

Contents

Permissions	ix
Statements of Purpose	**xi**
A Statement from Rabbi Eric H. Yoffie	xiii
A Statement from Rabbi David Ellenson	xiv
A Statement from Rabbi Harry K. Danziger and Rabbi Steven A. Fox	xv
Introductions	
Introduction by Rabbi Richard F. Address, D.Min.	xvii
Introduction by Joel L. Kushner, Psy.D.	xviii
Introduction by Geoffrey Mitelman	xix
***Hineini*: Personal Stories**	
Introduction	1
Ten Lessons Learned from Our Role as Parents and Educators, *Bobbi and David Fishback*	3
A Gay Jewish Divorce, *Neil Spencer Welles*	9
Exiled, *Laura Wolfson*	11
A Traditional Jewish Lesbian Wedding, *Inbal Kashtan*	13
"I Now Belong to a Clan of the Mystery People . . .": On Being Gay and Gray, *Harriet Perl*	19
The Voice of a Wandering Jewish Bisexual: An Update, *Rebecca Gorlin*	27
Whose Side Are You On? Transgender at the Western Wall, *TJ Michels and Ali Cannon*	29
The Journey of Congregational Inclusion	
Introduction	41
The World's Original Gay and Lesbian Synagogue: Why There Is (Still) a Place for Us, *Rabbi Lisa A. Edwards, Ph.D.*	43
What Makes a Congregation Welcoming?, *Bernard Schlager, Ph.D.*	47
Welcoming GLBT Jews into Our Synagogues: A Congregational Self-Study Guide, *Rabbi Margaret Moers Wenig; updated by Joel L. Kushner, Psy.D.*	49
Gays and Lesbians in Mainstream Congregations: A Case Study of Temple Beth-El of Great Neck, New York, *John E. Hirsch, Ph.D.*	57
Chambers Filled with Riches: Some Thoughts for Those Who Work on Outreach, *Seth W. Goren*	63

Mazal Tov on Your New Rabbi!, *Rabbi Victor S. Appell*	67
The Role of URJ Regional Offices in Promoting Inclusion of GLBT Jews, *Rabbi Richard F. Address, D.Min., and Rabbi Geoffrey Mitelman*	71
Angling for Alliances, *Rabbi Burt Schuman*	75
Creating Welcoming Classrooms and Inclusive Lesson Plans: Ten Dos and Don'ts, *David Shneer, Ph.D.*	79
Out at School, *David Shneer, Ph.D.*	83
Know the Heart of the Stranger: A Curriculum on Combating Assumptions and Stereotypes, *Rabbi Geoffrey Mitelman and Joel L. Kushner, Psy.D.*	93
What Does Biphobia Look Like?, *Lani Ka'ahumanu and Rob Yeager*	109
Understanding Your Bisexual Congregants (Colleagues, Friends, Family Members . . .), *Rabbi Jane Rachel Litman*	112
Beyond Stick Figures: Why Congregations Should Be Concerned with Transgender Inclusion, *Rabbi Elliot Kukla*	119
Making Your Community More Transgender Friendly: Guidelines for Individuals and Congregations, *Reuben Zellman*	123
Transgender 101: A Curriculum on Gender Diversity in Judaism, *Rabbi Elliot Kukla and Reuben Zellman*	129

Marriage Matters

Introduction	145
A Curriculum on Reform Jewish Views on Same-Gender Marriage, *Rabbi Geoffrey Mitelman and Joel L. Kushner, Psy.D.*	147
What Rabbis Should Do to Help Protect Legal Rights in Same-Sex Couples, *Rabbi Arthur Gross-Schaefer and Robert Dixon*	167
Premarital Counseling for Same-Sex Couples: Highlights for Rabbis and Cantors, *Rabbi Nancy H. Wiener, D.Min.*	177
Working Together: Rabbis, Congregations, and Same-Gender Marriage, *Rabbi Sharon L. Sobel*	183
Enfranchising the Monogamous Homosexual: A Legal Possibility, A Moral Imperitive, *Rabbi Bradley Shavit Artson*	191

Blessings and Texts

Introduction	205
Reflections on Liturgy, Ritual Texts, and Innovations by the GLBT Community, *Rabbi Richard N. Levy*	207
Union Ceremonies for Same-Gender Couples, *Working Group on Same-Gender Officiation, Central Conference of American Rabbis*	211
Document of Separation, *Rabbi Denise Eger*	227
Adoption/Hebrew Name-Taking Ceremony, *Rabbi Yoel Kahn, Ph.D.*	229
A Coming-Out Prayer for Lesbian, Gay, Bisexual, and Transgender People and Those Who Love Them, *Congregation Sha'ar Zahav*	231
A Blessing for Transitioning Genders, *Rabbi Elliot Kukla*	233
Liturgical Resources	235

History of the Reform Movement's Positions on GLBT Issues

Introduction	239

Tribute to Rabbi Alexander M. Schindler (1995), *Rabbi Margaret Moers Wenig*	241
Including Gay and Lesbian Jews (1989), *Rabbi Alexander M. Schindler*	245
Resolution of the Women of Reform Judaism National Federation of Temple Sisterhoods 25th Biennial Assembly, 1965: Homosexuality	247
Resolution Adopted by the 45th General Assembly of the Union of American Hebrew Congregations Biennial, 1977: Human Rights of Homosexuals	249
Resolution Adopted by the Central Conference of American Rabbis 88th Annual Convention, 1977: Rights of Homosexuals	251
Resolution Adopted by the National Federation of Temple Youth, 1983: Homosexuality	253
Resolution Adopted by the 59th General Assembly of the Union of American Hebrew Congregations Biennial, 1987: Support for Inclusion of Lesbian and Gay Jews	255
Resolution Adopted by the 60th General Assembly of the Union of American Hebrew Congregations Biennial, 1989: Gay and Lesbian Jews	257
Report of the Ad Hoc Committee on Homosexuality and the Rabbinate of the Central Conference of American Rabbis Annual Convention, 1990	259
Resolution Adopted by the National Federation of Temple Youth, 1991: Homosexuality	265
Resolution Adopted by the National Association of Temple Educators, 1991	267
Resolution Adopted by the Women of Reform Judaism National Federation of Temple Sisterhoods 38th Biennial Assembly, 1991	269
Guide for Advocacy and Action by the Women of Reform Judaism National Federation of Temple Sisterhoods Implementing Resolutions Adopted in 1991 at the NFTS 38th Biennial Assembly: The Rights of Gay Men and Lesbian Women	271
Statement Adopted by the Convention of the American Conference of Cantors, 1991: Homosexuality in the Cantorate	273
Resolution Adopted by the Commission on Social Action of Reform Judaism, 1991: Eliminating Discrimination against Gays and Lesbians in the Military	275
Resolution Adopted by the Executive Board of the Central Conference of American Rabbis, 1992: The Boy Scouts of America	277
Resolution Adopted by the Executive Board of the National Federation of Temple Youth, 1992–1993: The Boy Scouts of America	279
Resolution Adopted by the 62nd General Assembly of the Union of American Hebrew Congregations Biennial, 1993: Recognition for Lesbian and Gay Partnerships	281
Resolution Adopted by the 62nd General Assembly of the Union of American Hebrew Congregations Biennial, 1993: Responding to Anti–Gay Rights Referenda	283
Resolution Adopted by the Central Conference of American Rabbis 104th Annual Convention, 1993: Convening in States Denying Legal Protection of Civil Rights for Gays and Lesbians	285

Resolution Adopted by the 63rd General Assembly of the Union of
American Hebrew Congregations Biennial, 1995: Promoting Equal
Employment and Leadership Opportunities for Lesbians and Gays
in the Reform Movement ... 287
Resolution Adopted by the Central Conference of American Rabbis 107th
Annual Convention, 1996: Gay and Lesbian Marriage ... 289
CCAR Responsum on Marriage after a Sex-Change Operation (1978) ... 290
CCAR Responsum on Homosexual Marriage (1985) ... 295
CCAR Responsum on Conversion and Marriage after Transsexual Surgery
(1990) ... 297
CCAR Responsum on Homosexual Marriage (1996) ... 301
Resolution Adopted by the 64th General Assembly of the Union of
American Hebrew Congregations Biennial, 1997: Civil Marriage
for Gay and Lesbian Jewish Couples ... 327
Resolution Adopted by the Central Conference of American Rabbis 111th
Annual Convention, 2000: Same Gender Officiation ... 329
Same Gender Officiation: A Statement by Rabbi Eric Yoffie (2000) ... 331
Resolution Adopted by the Executive Board of the Commission on
Social Action of Reform Judaism, 2003: Support for the Inclusion
and Acceptance of the Transgender and Bisexual Communities ... 333
Countering the Family Values Monopoly, *Rabbi David Ellenson* ... 335
NER-CCAR Passes Resolution in Support of Marriage Ruling; Opposes
Efforts to Undermine Equality for Same-Sex Couples ... 337
Resolution Adopted by the Executive Board of the Commission on
Social Action of Reform Judaism, 2004: The Proposed Federal
Marriage Amendment to the United States Constitution ... 339
Resolution Adopted by the Central Conference of American Rabbis 115th
Annual Convention, 2004: Proposed Federal Marriage Amendment
to the United States Constitution ... 341
Excerpt on Same-Sex Marriage from Rabbi Eric H. Yoffie's Regional
Biennial Speech, 2004–2005 ... 343

Glossary ... 345

Resources ... 355

General GLBT Internet Links ... 379

Biographies of Contributors ... 381

Biographies of Editors ... 387

Permissions

Every attempt has been made to obtain permission to reprint previously published material. The authors gratefully acknowledge the following for permission to reprint previously published material:

BRADLEY SHAVIT ARTSON: "Enfranchising the Monogamous Homosexual: A Legal Possibility, a Moral Imperative," *S'vara: A Journal of Philosophy, Law and Judaism* 3, no. 1 (1993). Used by permission of Rabbi Bradley Shavit Artson.

BISEXUAL RESOURCE CENTER OF BOSTON, MASSACHUSETTS: "What Does Biphobia Look Like?" by Lani Ka'ahumanu and Rob Yeager. Based on conversations with Gerard Palmeri, Danielle Raymond, Loraine Hutchins, and Cianna Stewart Portions. Adapted from material by the Rape Crisis Center of West Contra Costa County, CA; the Boston Lesbian Task Force; and Building Bridges. Used by permission of Bisexual Resource Center of Boston, Massachusetts.

CENTRAL CONFERENCE OF AMERICAN RABBIS, DENISE EGER, AND YOEL KAHN: *Kiddushin Service for Same Gender Group.* Used by permission of Central Conference of American Rabbis, Rabbi Denise Eger, and Rabbi Yoel Kahn.

CONGREGATION BET SIMCHAT TORAH: *A Coming-Out Prayer for Lesbian, Gay, Bisexual, and Transgender People and Those Who Love Them* adapted by Yehuda Berger from *Gates of Prayer.* Used by permission of Congregation Bet Simchat Torah.

JEWISH JOURNAL OF GREATER LOS ANGELES: "Countering the Family Values Monopoly" by Rabbi David Ellenson. Used by permission of the *Jewish Journal of Greater Los Angeles* and Rabbi David Ellenson.

ELLIOT KUKLA, MARGARET MOERS WENIG, AND REUBEN ZELLMAN: "People and Labels," by Rabbi Margaret Moers Wenig and Reuben Zellman, edited and revised by Rabbi Elliot Kukla for Kulanu 2006. Used by permission of Rabbi Margaret Moers Wenig, Reuben Zellman, and Rabbi Elliot Kukla.

REFORM JUDAISM MAGAZINE: "Angling for Alliances" by Rabbi Burt Schuman. Used by permission of *Reform Judaism* Magazine and Rabbi Burt Schuman; "Exiled" by Laura Wolfson. Used by permission of Reform Judaism Magazine and Laura Wolfson.

BERNARD SCHLAGER: "With Open Arms: Gay Affirming Ministries in Bay Area Faith Communities" by Bernard Schlager, Ph.D. Used by permission of Bernard Schlager.

SIMON & SCHUSTER: Reprinted with the permission of Simon and Schuster Adult Publishing Group from WHY MARRIAGE MATTERS: "America, Equality, & Gay People's Right to Marry" by Evan Wolfson. Copyright © 2004 by Evan Wolfson.

TAYLOR AND FRANCIS: Copyright © 2002 "Breaking Ground: A Traditional Jewish Lesbian Wedding" by Inbal Kashtan, in *Queer Jews*, ed. David Shneer and Caryn Aviv. Reproduced by permission of Routledge, a division of Taylor & Francis Group; Copyright © 2002 "Whose Side Are You On? Transgender at the Western Wall" by TJ Michaels and Ali Cannon in *Queer Jews*, ed. David Shneer and Caryn Aviv. Reproduced by permission of Routledge, a division of Taylor & Francis Group: Copyright © 2002 "Out at School: A Queer Jewish Education in Queer Jews," by David Shneer, in *Queer Jews*, ed. David Shneer and Caryn Aviv. Reproduced by permission of Routledge, a division of Taylor & Francis Group.

W.W. NORTON & COMPANY: The lines from "Phantasia for Elvira Shatayev" in *The Dream of a Common Language: Poems 1974–1977* by Adrienne Rich. Copyright © 1978 by W.W. Norton & Company, Inc. Used by permission of the author and W.W. Norton & Company, Inc.

NANCY WIENER: "Pre-Marital Counseling for Same Sex Couples: Highlights for Rabbis and Cantors" by Nancy Wiener. Used by permission of Nancy Wiener.

REUBEN ZELLMAN: "Making Your Community More Transgender Friendly: Guidelines for Individuals and Congregations." Used by permission of Reuben Zellman.

Statements of Purpose

Fall 2006

Dear Friends:

I believe that gay, lesbian, bisexual, and transgender Jews in our midst—our children, our relatives, and our friends—are in great need, as are we all, of spiritual support. It is the responsibility of our clergy, educators, and lay leaders, therefore, to create synagogues whose message of Torah is so inspiring, whose spiritual energy is so transforming, and whose web of kinship and caring is so embracing that no one who enters their gates, regardless of sexual orientation or gender, will ever consider forsaking the holy communities that they provide.

It is my hope that within the gates of our synagogues, gay, lesbian, bisexual, and transgender Jews will be exposed to the authenticity of our worship, the profundity of our Torah study, and the vitality of our social justice work. More important, however, they, and indeed all who enter our religious homes, need to find an environment in which they feel safe, comfortable, and connected. They need congregations where they are supported in the deep experiences of life; where other people are there for them as they are there for others; where notice is taken when they are missing and trouble is taken to find out why; and where they never face a crisis alone.

Loving, permanent, same-gender relationships, once difficult to conceive, are now recognized as an indisputable reality. Indeed, from a Jewish perspective, we strive for loving, monogamous, long-term relationships—regardless of orientation—for it is in these unions that God and holiness are sure to be present. To do less than to be *anshei chesed*—doers of goodness and purveyors of kindness—by welcoming Jews in such relationships with enthusiasm, enfolding them within our synagogue communities, and working to achieve full equality for them and for all gay, lesbian, bisexual, and transgender individuals in our society at large is to forsake our commitment as Reform Jews.

Sincerely,

Rabbi Eric H. Yoffie
President
Union for Reform Judaism

Fall 2006

Dear Friends:

It gives me great pleasure to offer words of introduction and greeting to this publication of *Kulanu*. As the Hebrew word indicates, *Kulanu* signifies "all of us." This compendium speaks to that end and provides our Union for Reform Judaism congregations and our membership with printed resources and texts that help to facilitate our communal-religious goals of inclusion and self-respect for all human beings. The URJ is to be applauded for this and for so many other efforts in the fight to achieve social and religious equality for our gay, lesbian, bisexual, and transgender sisters and brothers. I am honored to be a member of a Jewish religious denomination that has so consistently been in the forefront of struggles to secure the basic human rights that are the legitimate birthright of every individual—gay or straight.

As president of Hebrew Union College–Jewish Institute of Religion, I have had the opportunity to raise my own voice in this arena on several occasions and am proud that the College-Institute long ago affirmed the rights of GLBT Jews to study at HUC-JIR and complete all our programs. I am also delighted about the roles our Institute for Judaism and Sexual Orientation and our Jeff Herman Virtual Resource Center on Sexual Orientation Issues in Congregations and the Jewish Community play in this ongoing battle for human dignity. It is a great *z'chut* (privilege) for the College-Institute to support the URJ and our Reform Movement in their efforts in these ways.

On a personal level, as a heterosexual male enjoying a position of privilege and comfort, I must confess that for many years I never even considered the issues that this volume raises. However, as a young professor teaching at the College-Institute in the early 1980s, my many conversations with a number of my gay and lesbian students and friends made me realize the intolerable pain of exclusion and the unjust lash of discrimination they suffered in so many parts of their lives. I would like to thank them for educating me and allowing me to see them in their fullness as the human beings they are. I will always be appreciative of the empathy and identity they evoked in me. I hope that others who read the pages of this work will be similarly moved so that the messianic dream of inclusion and justice that animates our Jewish tradition will be further realized.

With friendship, gratitude, and all best wishes,

David Ellenson

Rabbi David Ellenson
President
Hebrew Union College–Jewish Institute of Religion

CENTRAL CONFERENCE OF AMERICAN RABBIS
FOUNDED 1889

Fall 2006

Dear Friends:

We are delighted to learn of this revision of *Kulanu*, our Movement's primary resource guide for programming in the area of gay, lesbian, bisexual, and transgender persons in our community.

As you know, the CCAR has for decades supported the principle that all Jews, indeed all people, are religiously equal regardless of their sexual orientation. For more than thirty years we have supported vigorously all efforts to eliminate discrimination in housing and employment, we have called upon states to legalize same-gender ceremonies as legitimate weddings, and we have expressed our support for rabbis who officiate at same-gender unions. We therefore applaud the fine work of the URJ Department of Jewish Family Concerns to offer programs and materials to fully integrate all Jews into the life of the community.

Now ten years since the first edition of *Kulanu* opened new areas of synagogue support and understanding, we anticipate that this revision will continue to raise our consciousness, our skills, and our programming in this important area of Jewish life.

With every good wish,

L'shalom,

Rabbi Harry K. Danziger
President

Rabbi Steven A. Fox
Executive Vice President

Central Conference of American Rabbis

Introductions

Shalom. In the years since the original *Kulanu* was published, there has been great progress in the way the Jewish community in general and the synagogue community in particular has welcomed gay, lesbian, bisexual, and transgender Jews. It is to the credit of the Reform Movement, its congregations, clergy, and leaders that this not always quiet revolution has emerged. The success of the first edition of *Kulanu* is testimony to the desire on the part of the community to open the doors of inclusion.

The revised edition of *Kulanu* reflects much of the change that has taken place. This document is indebted to the pioneering work of Rabbi Alexander M. Schindler (z״l) under whose presidency the Reform Movement raised the issue of sexual orientation and equality. Likewise, we would be remiss if we did not remember the pioneering work of Rabbi Julie Spitzer (z״l), a talented colleague who was taken from us all too soon. Her gifts and spirit still impact our work.

The revision of *Kulanu* owes a debt to the work of Mike Rankin and Rabbi Burt Schuman. They spearheaded the project in its infancy and designed the basic format. Together with several members of the Department of Jewish Family Concerns, they helped edit and strengthen the content. Much of the work and thought that went into the visioning of *Kulanu* rests with Dr. Joel Kushner of the Institute for Judaism and Sexual Orientation of the Hebrew Union College–Jewish Institute of Religion. Dr. Kushner has created a wonderful partnership with the Union for Reform Judaism's Department of Jewish Family Concerns, and his attention and care for the project is evident in this document. Likewise, thanks to our rabbinic intern, Geoffrey Mitelman, who worked diligently in the summer of 2006 organizing and editing the final drafts of *Kulanu*, as well as writing two original curricula. We thank him for his dedication and enthusiasm and wish him well as a newly-ordained rabbi.

We hope that you find use and meaning in the contents of this book. We dedicate the impact of *Kulanu* to the memory of Rabbis Schindler and Spitzer and to the examples of commitment and love of Rabbi Erwin and Agnes Herman.

Rabbi Richard F. Address, D.Min.
Director, Department of Jewish Family Concerns
Union for Reform Judaism

Shortly after becoming the director of the Institute for Judaism and Sexual Orientation (IJSO) at Hebrew Union College–Jewish Institute of Religion, I discovered the original *Kulanu*. As the IJSO is dedicated to training students about GLBT inclusion in the Jewish world, I was excited to have such a resource and used it often. Later, I wondered if there was an updated version that incorporated the developments of the past ten years. I discovered that Rabbi Richard Address was already active on the project, and I am so thankful to him for allowing the IJSO and me to take on a leadership role in the creation of this important book.

Geoffrey Mitelman, a fifth-year rabbinical student and an amazing ally, has put incredible time, energy, and soul into this project. We thank him for all his work. The new *Kulanu* could not have been developed without him.

I have been fortunate to meet and learn from some of the pioneering people who have helped our movement in this process of inclusion: Rabbi Erwin Herman and his wife Agnes, who have supported GLBT causes since 1969; Alan Bennett, the first rabbi to officially come out in 1977; Rabbi Yoel Kahn, who wrote groundbreaking CCAR documents supporting the inclusion of gay and lesbian Jews in the Reform Movement; and founding congregants at Congregation Beth Chayim Chadashim, the first gay and lesbian synagogue in the world, founded in 1972. There are, of course, many pioneers in the Reform Movement, all across the country, both straight and GLBT, who have been quietly and not so quietly doing their part to foster GLBT inclusion in the Jewish world. They have done this work far longer than I, without the benefit of any guide or even much support. Thank you for all the sacred work that you have done for this cause.

In this revision of *Kulanu*, we have tried to provide those who are just starting out on this journey, along with those who have been doing it for a long time, new tools, new inspirations, and even higher aspirations for lesbian, gay, bisexual, and transgender inclusion. This is a book for all congregations as well as the rabbinic, cantorial, education, and Jewish communal service students I help train at Hebrew Union College–Jewish Institute of Religion. The vision found here will be a stretch for some, and others will say that we have not gone far enough. Whatever your position, we hope that this book will help you reach the goal that all Jews, regardless of sexual orientation or gender identity, are welcome and celebrated in our Jewish home, the synagogue, and that it is a home where each person can contribute their unique gifts and talents. We will be a richer Jewish community for it.

Joel L. Kushner, Psy.D.
Director
Institute for Judaism and Sexual Orientation
The Jeff Herman Virtual Resource Center for Sexual Orientation in the Jewish Community
Hebrew Union College–Jewish Institute of Religion

For decades, two principles have guided every Reform Movement resolution on gays and lesbians:

1. The ideals of social justice demand civil rights for gays and lesbians.
2. Every synagogue should ensure it is a welcoming and inclusive community for gay and lesbian Jews.

Today, almost every Reform Jew would accept the above statements, and yet there are several areas where challenges still arise:

- What do synagogues need to *do* in order to be a "welcoming and inclusive community for gay and lesbian Jews"? How do we move from including "gay and lesbian Jews" to including "gay, lesbian, bisexual, and transgender Jews"? What can the synagogue do to welcome bisexual and transgender Jews?
- How do we make sense of same-gender marriage, when traditional Judaism, societal norms, legal issues, and a sense of social justice sometimes point in entirely different directions?
- With the first generation of openly GLBT Jews now aging, how do we engage older GLBT Jews?
- How do we reduce prejudice against those who are GLBT?
- How do we create a safe space in our schools for students to feel comfortable in their own sexual identity?
- How do we take traditional Jewish blessings and texts and transform them so they are meaningful and relevant for GLBT Jews?

This edition of *Kulanu* seeks to address these topics. It provides clergy and congregations with the following:

- Personal stories and journeys of GLBT Jews
- Concrete steps for clergy and congregants to improve GLBT inclusion in their synagogue
- Educational resources for reducing prejudice against those who are GLBT
- A curriculum on Reform Jewish views on same-gender marriage
- Reform Jewish blessings and texts on topics relevant to GLBT Jews
- A collection of historical documents from the Reform Movement on GLBT issues (up through 2006)

While this book is far from exhaustive in terms of what congregations can do to better include GLBT Jews, we hope this new version of *Kulanu* will give all Reform Jews the knowledge and the tools to fulfill the words of the prophet Isaiah:

כִּי בֵיתִי בֵּית־תְּפִלָּה יִקָּרֵא לְכָל־הָעַמִּים׃

For My house shall be called a house of prayer for all peoples. (Isaiah 56:7)

Geoffrey Mitelman
Hebrew Union College–Jewish Institute of Religion, Class of 2007

Hineini: Personal Stories

Inclusion and welcoming is first and foremost about understanding individual people. Thus *Kulanu* begins with personal reflections from gay, lesbian, bisexual, and transgender (GLBT) Jews, who say, "*Hineini*—Here I am." Once we know someone, it becomes much harder to hate, harass, joke about, turn a cold shoulder to, or ignore that person. There are other important compendiums that include the personal stories of GLBT Jews, but we believe that it is important in this volume on congregational inclusion and welcoming that the included stories be heard.

The experiences of these Jews can be used as jumping-off points for discussions, examples for congregations on what are (and are not) effective paths to GLBT inclusion, or simply journeys to understand and appreciate. Without understanding personal histories—the struggles, the emotions, the joys—it is impossible for congregations to be truly effective in creating a community that encompasses *kulanu*, "all of us."

Ten Lessons Learned from Our Role as Parents and Educators

Bobbi and David Fishback

Our story is not atypical for parents of gay children. We are the proud parents of two sons, two and a half years apart in age, both of whom happen to be gay. Each realized his attraction to other boys at the age of ten, during the fifth grade of elementary school. They both suffered alone and in fear of their own humanity for many years.

Even though both of our sons were fortunate to be able to excel academically in school, their middle and high school years presented each of them with a far more difficult journey as compared to other boys their age. In high school, both of our sons dated the most beautiful girls in their class, hoping that perhaps they would be attracted to them and prove to themselves that what they were experiencing was just a stage of life that could be outgrown. But these efforts were to no avail.

With respect to our younger son, at age fifteen, he reached the point where he felt he had to either commit suicide or like himself just the way he was. Fortunately, he chose the latter. After he confided his secret to a friend at school, he learned that word had gotten back to his brother. When he approached his brother at home to discuss the secret that he had kept so well for so long, he was surprised to learn that his older brother, too, had been keeping the same secret. At that point our sons cried for the pain that each knew the other had endured. They also cried over the realization that we, their parents, might never be blessed with grandchildren. Out of that love for us, they planned that our younger son would "come out" to us first, and he did so that summer after planning for the appropriate moment.

Our older son, who was eighteen and getting ready to graduate high school, remained in the closet, both because he was not at all ready to tell anyone else his secret and because he knew that we would not be able to handle the shock of finding out at the same time that both of our beloved sons were gay. He finally came out to us, and then, slowly, to the rest of his world, in his junior year of college.

For more information about how your synagogue and religious school can be more aware of GLBT issues, see the two articles by Dr. David Shneer, and "Creating Welcoming Classrooms and Inclusive Lesson Plans" (pages 91–93) and "Out at School" (pages 95–103).

After our sons came out, we saw in each of them a true metamorphosis. They went from lives filled with fear and shame to lives of fulfillment and happiness. Our younger son distinguished himself as a columnist for his college newspaper, winning national and local awards, and is now a writer and performer in New York City, where his work, among other things, shines a light on issues affecting the gay community and encourages young gay teens to break through stereotypes. Our older son decided to become a middle school teacher. He came out to his students; he discussed this coming-out in a book about GLBT teachers and in a national publication for educators. With dignity and courage, he helps children to appreciate themselves and each other in all their diversity.

Below are ten lessons we have learned from our journey with our two sons, and we hope that rabbis, congregations, friends, and family members will find these helpful on their own paths.

Lesson 1. **Rabbis need to show clear signs that they are supportive advocates for GLBT issues. This can be demonstrated by topical sermons, creating a congregational statement of inclusiveness that welcomes GLBT people, placing GLBT books on their tables or bookshelves, or exhibiting rainbow symbols in their offices.** At the times we learned our children were gay, we did not turn to our rabbi for support. Although our rabbi had reached out to congregants with respect to other family matters, we had never received a specific signal about what our rabbi's feelings were on gay issues. Much later, when we finally spoke to our rabbi about our family's journey, he became our strongest advocate for GLBT inclusion in our temple. In retrospect, we are sorry that we did not seek his counsel when we needed it, but there is a lesson here for rabbis. If rabbis do not show that they are supportive and available to congregants specifically on this issue, congregants who are in most need of support might not seek them out.

Lesson 2. **Share your story, and find or create supportive networks.** By creating a "*Kulanu* group" in our synagogue, we were able to send the signal that Jews of all sexual orientations were considered a part of our Jewish community. By presenting ourselves publicly as parents of gay children, we also offered ourselves as a resource for congregants in similar situations. Many fellow synagogue members have come to us with stories of a gay child, a gay sibling, a gay aunt or uncle, or a gay friend. As we found that we were not alone, we discovered and reaffirmed the oneness of our Jewish community—indeed, of the entire human community. The simple act of deciding not to be in a closet as parents of gay children or as a GLBT opens the minds and hearts of those around us.

Lesson 3. **Don't live in fear or ignorance. Educate yourself about GLBT issues.** There is an increasing acceptance and understanding of sexual orientation in our society, and the findings of every mainstream medical and mental health association support the facts that homosexuality is not a disease or mental disorder and is not something that people "choose." Still, learning that your child is gay can be difficult. Educating yourself is one important way to help you understand and clarify your own expectations and those of your child. Upon realizing our children were gay, we searched for information that would support and help us to understand our children better.

We found that information through a therapist we sought out, through the organization Parents, Families and Friends of Lesbians and Gays (PFLAG), and by visiting the gay and lesbian bookstore in our city. Don't be afraid to seek out a therapist to get support. You are not the only one asking for help. Seeing a therapist helped give us support at a difficult time. The PFLAG meetings were also very helpful as an ongoing support. Visit http://pflag.org/ to find a PFLAG chapter near you.

Lesson 4. **Create inclusive spaces, and educate others too.** When we became active in creating an inclusive atmosphere in our congregation, one of the first things we did was to establish a bookshelf in our synagogue library with a variety of books dealing with gay and lesbian issues, including books for those seeking to "come out" to parents, as well as supportive books for parents to help them understand the process of their child's "coming-out." We also included a number of books that look at homosexuality in a positive Jewish context, something that we, unfortunately, did not have available to us during our journey.

Lesson 5. **Be aware of your language and the underlying expectations it conveys.** One of our sons' most telling comments was that throughout those years of suffering alone and in fear, they never doubted for a moment that we, their parents, would always love them unconditionally. One reason they hid their secret from us was the fear of disappointing us. As we think back on each time we carelessly used the phrase "bring home a nice Jewish girl" during their formative years, we now realize how we were literally torturing the children we hold so dear. It would serve a congregation well to have frank discussions with parents of school-age children to be mindful of how they inadvertently communicate expectations to their children, and specifically, the expectations of "bringing home a nice Jewish girl or guy."

Lesson 6. **Match education with age-appropriate information.** The previous point brings us to the question of how we should deal with the subject of homosexuality in our religious schools. In our synagogue's confirmation class, a class session is set aside for discussing the issue of homosexuality. Our older son was asked to lead that session, and he did so when he lived nearby. The classes were exceptionally well received.

Our synagogue was fortunate to have our son so near, but there are groups in many communities that will be able to help provide or recommend discussion leaders, such as PFLAG or the local gay and lesbian center. Some religious schools start these discussions in the *b'nei mitzvah* year. What should be clear is that by the teen years, the discussion of homosexuality is part of a larger discussion about sexuality and identity in general—all, of course, in a Jewish context.

The issue of how we approach the topic of homosexuality with the youngest children in our religious schools is a more delicate one, and one where good people may disagree. One of the best resources we found is the award-winning documentary called *It's Elementary*, which is geared to be shown to and discussed by educators. It sensitively demonstrates how even the very youngest among us can understand "homosexuality" not in the context of "sex" but in the context of love, respect, and appreciation of diversity. The documentary is a valuable resource to be shown to religious school staff and school boards. See http://www.womedia.org/itselementary.htm.

Early education on family diversity and sexual orientation is vital because the synagogue is a moral and spiritual center of our lives. If children are taught, from the very beginning, that this diversity exists and enriches our community, then they are less likely to fall prey to the homophobic views that still are present in the wider world. This education is important for all our children: for straight kids with straight parents, for those who are from families headed by same-sex couples, for those who have gay family members, and for those who will later discover that they are GLBT. With respect to the last, it is important to note that our sons, like many gay men, recall that their first same-sex attraction was when they were ten years old. Therefore, we believe that it is critical for religious schools to deal with this subject long before puberty.

Lesson 7. **Don't make assumptions. Let children become who they are meant to be, and allow for new constellations of family.** Reform Judaism teaches the importance of marriage as a key Jewish life-cycle event, but the teaching, in our experience, assumes that this event applies only to heterosexual couples. While the Union for Reform Judaism and the Central Conference of American Rabbis have now come to recognize the sanctity of same-sex unions, our religious schools have not necessarily expanded their teaching in parallel. Our own synagogue religious school, like many others, not only has children who will someday identify themselves as being GLBT, but also children in families headed by same-sex couples. It is important for them, as well as for all of our straight children with opposite-sex parents, that our religious school expands its teaching so that all Jewish life-cycle events apply to all Jewish congregants, without exception.

One opportunity for many religious schools to expand the application of marriage to same-sex couples is during a mock wedding, which students often participate in as part of their study of ritual observances. Our sons have commented to us that if just the mention of gay couples had been included in this one aspect of their study, it would have gone a long way to lessening their pain. Teachers should be the ones to mention the possibility that two men or two women can also get married, and they should address the responses from students that may follow that statement in an educational and nonjudgmental way. It is not the responsibility of the gay child or the child of a same-gender couple to raise this issue.

Lesson 8. **Build connections, and reach out into the community.** As mentioned above, the mission of our synagogue's *Kulanu* group is not only in-reach (supporting, educating, and celebrating the diversity of all of our members), but also outreach. With this in mind, we have partnered with a local gay and lesbian synagogue downtown. When their congregants would have trouble getting downtown for Shabbat services during inclement weather, we invited them to come spend Shabbat with us. In addition, we have been in touch with the *Kulanu* groups of other Reform congregations nearby to share programming ideas and resources and to develop a safe and inclusive network in our area.

Early on, we asked members of our *Kulanu* group what they thought would be effective ways to reach out to GLBT Jews in the community at large, which we have now been doing for a few years. They suggested things like running a notice in the religious calendar section of the local gay newspaper and having a booth at the local Pride Festival in June.

The gay couple who suggested the booth idea remarked that having a Jewish religious presence at the Pride Festival would not only attract possible members, but would also send a significant signal to those in the GLBT community that there are many religious houses of worship, including Jewish synagogues, that would welcome them.

Lesson 9. **Create a "welcoming congregation," share it, and see how deeply it affects people.** Our *Kulanu* group's annual participation in the Pride Festival has been extremely rewarding, and we are now joined each year by other Reform congregations with whom we have networked. A few years ago, as we were sitting at our booth in front of our Temple Emanuel banner, we were approached by a lovely middle-aged woman wearing a large Star of David around her neck. She was weeping as she described to us how she had celebrated her bar mitzvah at a Temple Emanuel in New York, where she grew up as a boy. She had not returned to a synagogue since her transition to being female, and she had been estranged from her family for just as many years. She said that she was overwhelmed to see our banner and the familiar name "Temple Emanuel" scrawled across it. She told us that, although she has always considered herself Jewish, she never thought she would be welcomed in a synagogue again. She was brought to tears at the possibility that she would be welcome now to come "home."

Lesson 10. **Be "out and proud."** When we began our *Kulanu* group, we placed a small article in our synagogue newsletter about the group and its mission to reach out to the GLBT community. It was, in effect, our family's "coming-out" notice. Afterwards, we were thrilled to receive several warm and wonderful notes from friends, and we marveled at how supportive our congregation was. There was only one negative response that was sent to our rabbi, who forwarded it to us. The congregant angrily denounced the formation of our *Kulanu* group, arguing that by attracting "these people" to our synagogue we would be harming our children. We answered him by relating our family's personal journey and closed by explaining that "these people" are our children.

Our family traveled this journey with the help of many family members and friends. While it seems nearly incomprehensible to us now, we once thought we would never be truly happy again following our sons' coming-out. How wrong we were. The fact is, when you look into the eyes of your children who are no longer burdened by a secret identity, but are true to who they are and free to enjoy the fullness of life, there can be no greater happiness.

A Gay Jewish Divorce

Neil Spencer Welles

During the spring of 2004, our relationship of almost nineteen years had come unraveled. We had done far too little, far too late to repair it. There was no acrimony between us, just much sadness and many regrets. Harlan and I accepted the fact our separation was inevitable, and we planned for it in a manner that took into account the feelings of our family and friends. Most importantly, because we had always lived our lives together Jewishly, we knew we wanted to end our union with appropriate Jewish sanctification.

To be sure, we had had many happy years together. Harlan and I had joined Temple Micah, in Washington, D.C., as a family, in 1988. There had never been a question as to our inclusion as such. In 1995, to celebrate our tenth year together, we had decided that we wanted the sanctification of a *kiddushin*, regardless of the fact that we had no legal right to marry. Our rabbi, Dan Zemel, was delighted when we approached him about the ceremony. He declared to us that it would be a mitzvah to marry us and that he had always wanted to perform a gay union. So on November 5, 1995, ours was the first *simchah* to be held in Temple Micah's newly dedicated building. We had a beautiful Reform Jewish ceremony under the chuppah. Only a few words of the liturgy needed to be changed to allow for a same-sex union. And, of course, two glasses were broken at the conclusion. We celebrated joyously with family and friends. Two grooms were atop the wedding cake.

We had always been discreet about our family matters, so few of our friends or family members were aware during spring 2004 that we were separating. Finally, after we had amicably settled all matters between us, we made an appointment to meet with Rabbi Zemel in June. He was quite taken aback when we explained to him that we wanted the Reform Jewish equivalent of a *get*, the traditional Jewish divorce. After an in-depth discussion, our rabbi agreed to perform the divorce. He said he would need a week to prepare. He stated to us that, indeed, divorce is a life-cycle event. We set another appointment with him for June 22, five weeks after what would have been our nineteenth anniversary.

We had no idea what to expect that Tuesday afternoon when we returned to the rabbi's study. After all, most straight, modern Jewish couples obtain civil divorces. We thought of a *get* as anachronistic and the traditional Jewish divorce ceremony, blatantly sexist. In our view, only religious Jews still availed themselves of a *get*. What would be offered to us?

For more information about Reform Jewish separation rituals for GLBT Jews, see "Document of Separation" by Rabbi Denise Eger (page 227).

As it turns out, Reform Judaism does have a dignified and compassionate separation ceremony, though it is not called a *get*. It is entitled a *Seder Peridah*, a "Ritual of Release," and it is especially important for separating gay and lesbian Jewish couples to be aware that this option is available to them. With the exception of Vermont, Massachusetts, and New Jersey, civil marriages (or unions) and civil divorces are not available to us in the United States at the time of this publication.

When we entered Rabbi Zemel's study, he was ready to proceed. He asked us a few questions so he could complete the Documents of Separation that he had prepared for us in both English and Hebrew. He then asked us to stand, and he asked each of us if we wanted to be released from our vows. In tears, we each answered affirmatively.

He then read to us the brief ceremony, the words of which admonished us not to speak ill of one another, and asked us to try to remain friends. We were reminded that we would now be leading separate lives and were no longer responsible for one another. The liturgy reflected our feelings exactly and comforted us. We continued to love one another, and we remained best friends, though we no longer could live together. We were beginning new lives.

We slipped off our wedding bands and placed them in special boxes that Harlan had brought to the ceremony. Finally, we signed the Documents of Separation. It was over. A few days later, we sent out an e-mail, sensitively composed by Harlan, to friends and family, apprising them of our divorce, and of our continuing friendship.

Upon reflection, this little-known Reform Jewish ritual brought us closure and peace. Rabbis would be performing a mitzvah by making their congregants aware of its existence.

Exiled

Laura Wolfson

In December 2003, after nine years of living in a committed, loving relationship with my Jewish partner, I was finally able to be married in a synagogue with both Jewish and Canadian legal sanction. Tish and I were among the ranks of thousands of Canadian gay and lesbian couples who have walked down the aisle following the landmark 2003 court rulings instructing municipal licensing offices in the provinces of British Columbia and Ontario to issue marriage licenses to same-sex couples—but with one significant difference: few of these weddings have taken place in synagogues. Ours was only the third to be celebrated in a synagogue—but, sadly, not in our own.

Let me explain. My partner and I had discussed marriage with our rabbi some years ago, but he was unwilling to officiate. Accustomed to waiting for others to become more comfortable with us, we decided to wait until he was ready. After much study and reflection, he said yes, but our congregation's lay leadership said no. Exiled, we sanctified our marriage in the presence of our family, friends, community, and our rabbi at a Reform synagogue in another city that is more than an hour's drive from our home.

While my partner and I are accustomed to waiting for others to become comfortable *with* us, waiting for acceptance is not comfortable *for* us. We are active contributors to the Jewish community, and I am a respected community leader. When others sit in judgment, debate the legitimacy of our "lifestyle," and determine whether the Jewish community should recognize it, we feel something akin to the indignation, fear, and rage that public expressions of anti-semitism evoke in us and in all Jews worldwide—only it's more personal.

Like most Jewish parents, we want our two-year-old daughter, Hannah, to feel connected to the Jewish people. If she someday learns that our synagogue refused to affirm the sacred union that binds her parents together and forms the basis for her family, will Hannah still feel that she belongs? And will she find it incongruous—even hypocritical— that our synagogue has accepted an openly lesbian Jew as a congregational leader, accepted our money, and was willing to celebrate her *Brit bat* by welcoming both her mothers to the *bimah*—all the while refusing to embrace us fully as a family?

Being a religious Reform Jew is at the very core of my identity; it informs each decision I make and everything I do. Being rejected hurts, but as an adult I understand that change takes time. My preschool daughter, though, has no such patience or understanding. It would break my heart if someday she were to abandon the Jewish community because the congregation in which she grew up had not fully accepted her family.

Laura Wolfson, "Exiled," *Reform Judaism* 33, no. 1 (Fall 2004): 88.

Can the Jewish people risk losing even one Jew? As a Jewish educator who has dedicated her life to strengthening our community by helping children and families improve their ability to live Jewishly, I say no. We cannot afford to lose even one Jew. And as a mother, I weep at the thought that my own daughter could be that Jew.

A Traditional Jewish Lesbian Wedding

Inbal Kashtan

Kathy and I had a sense before, during, and after our wedding that we were making history—breaking ground in positioning lesbian weddings within traditional Judaism. We wanted to record this history, and so along with our thank-you cards, we sent out a request for guests to write us a note about their experience of our wedding. We received numerous responses, most from people who were deeply moved by the ceremony and who felt in some way transformed by it. One of our guests, a heterosexual modern Orthodox woman, wrote:

> I was quite impacted by my sense of the courage it required of you both to stand so boldly in your love and commitment to one another. It seemed to me, given the innovative and "untraditional" nature of your "traditional" wedding, that there were few places for the two of you to hide.

Another friend expressed his difficulty in grappling with the image of two women in a traditional Jewish ceremony. He wrote: "The lesbian piece shook me up a little. It was just totally new to see a traditional Jewish wedding [in which] my eyes kept seeing . . . two dresses, two pairs of breasts . . . A challenging new image." Another heterosexual friend, who had been a vocal supporter of gay and lesbian rights for years, understood the event differently from how she expected to. "I get it now," she wrote. "It wasn't just a wedding; it was a political rally." And a relative wrote: "Your wedding was truthfully one of the deepest and most beautiful I've seen. Every little bit of exposure I get to gays and lesbians expands my vision of what is 'normal.'"

In different ways, each of these responses captured something of the essence of our traditional Jewish wedding. The first two responses reflected the dichotomy of tradition and innovation, the shock of "two pairs of breasts" at the most traditional locus of heterosexual union. The third response grasped the radical political statement still inherent in the act of lesbian and gay marriage. The fourth response and a number of others like it attested to the way our wedding resonated for Jews—many of an older generation—connecting it with their own heterosexual experience. All of these responses confirmed that our attempt to create a recognizably "normal" Eastern-European Jewish wedding had succeeded; these people

---

Inbal Kashtan, "Breaking Ground: A Traditional Jewish Lesbian Wedding," in *Queer Jews*, ed. David Shneer and Caryn Aviv (New York: Routledge, 2002), pp. 148–55.

were able to resonate with the sacredness and power of the day in a way that profoundly affected their understanding of the meaning of a "lesbian" and a "Jewish" wedding.

In creating a traditional Jewish lesbian wedding, Kathy and I joined a generation of Jews who are seeking a more meaningful relationship with Judaism. Many contemporary Jews are seeking to connect to Judaism by turning to older traditions, ancient texts, and spiritual practices. However, our unique relationship to Judaism as queer Jews presents a poignant paradox: the deeper we delve into tradition, the more it seems to reject our sexualities, our loves, our unions, our families.

How, then, do we struggle with this seeming rejection and still fulfill our yearning for tradition and connection to Judaism? Kathy's and my response to this question was to stake our relationship at the center of Jewish ritual by creating a wedding utterly grounded in Jewish tradition, yet boldly asserting our queerness. For us, this meant taking a traditional Orthodox wedding and wrestling with every ritual and text that we could uncover, taking our wedding beyond the realm of a "political rally" and squarely into the sphere of cultural transformation. Choosing any framework other than traditional Judaism for our wedding was unthinkable for us, because the particular rituals of our tradition are the ones we find most meaningful for marking our important life-cycle events.

One of the reasons that our lesbian wedding resonated so powerfully for our mostly heterosexual guests is that it took them not only into their own experience but, more profoundly, *beyond* their experience, touching on their own yearning for a spiritual connection with Jewish tradition. Our wedding looked like an Orthodox wedding—aside from the two pairs of breasts. Yet because it was a wedding of two women, it was an inclusive Orthodoxy, one that held a promise to queer *and* straight Jews of the possibility of finding themselves in the tradition.

Figuring out how to create a traditional Jewish lesbian wedding was a bittersweet challenge. We struggled with how to capture in the texts of the ceremony two of the deep truths about the day. First, that this was a wedding like the countless weddings that had gone before it in the history of our people, in the sense that it publicly expressed, in Jewish idiom, a commitment to a life together. Second, that this wedding was something new and different and radical and traditionally inconceivable.

Originally, the *halachic* requirements that made a wedding Jewish were simple: "the bride accepts an object worth more than a dime from the groom, the groom recites a ritual formula of acquisition and consecration, and these two actions must be witnessed."[1] The other rituals familiar to most Jews, such as the wedding canopy (*huppa*), having a rabbi officiate, and even breaking the glass, are customs that developed over centuries, and that varied between locations and times, suggesting that the tradition has been flexible and open to interpretation and modification. We relied on this understanding of the imperative to interpret texts and make them relevant to contemporary Jews in the design of our wedding.

Our interpretive work varied with each element of the traditional Jewish wedding. Some texts we were able to keep with very few changes, some required a great deal of work to make them both relevant to our particular situation and still clearly resonant with the original text. The text of *Birkat Erusin* (engagement blessing), for example, praises God for creating marriage as a vehicle for intimacy, but also records the teachings regarding forbidden marriages

---

1. Anita Diamant, *The New Jewish Wedding* (New York: Simon & Schuster, 1985), pp. 18–19. While the book's title suggests a break from tradition, Diamant convincingly argues that customizing the tradition is in fact part of the traditional Jewish wedding.

(such as those between siblings). We chose to abbreviate the text slightly to emphasize the delight over the very existence of rituals to sanctify a relationship, and cut completely the section on forbidden marriages. This was one of the easiest choices for us.

One very brief yet key text we changed was the spoken formula during the exchange of rings, the key text marking the union: "You are hereby sanctified unto me, with this ring, *according to the religious law of Moses and Israel.*" Kathy and I wrestled with the question of whether we can, with full integrity, claim this wedding as falling within our people's explicit legal framework. We ended up deciding that we could not make such a claim, and so we changed the wording to reflect what we felt we could claim. We said to each other, and wrote in our ketubah, the wedding contract: "You are hereby sanctified unto me, with this ring, *in the tradition of the Jewish people.*" This was the one choice we made that we later regretted. In retrospect, we wished we had made the claim of legality, because our wedding was so profoundly an expression of Jewish life and tradition that it made more clear to us the imperative to chart a path toward making it legal. As our rabbi and friend Rona Shapiro said at the wedding, it marked the direction that Jewish law *should* follow:

> If *halachic* principles, followed strictly, yield unjust conclusions, then it is our duty according to *halacha* to exercise civil disobedience. At such times brave individuals and communities must be willing to stand in front of the *halacha*, to walk as Abraham did in front of God, and to say, "this is where we're going," trusting that *halacha* will catch up with us. We stand on the edge of a *halachic* limb and assert stubbornly that this limb is part of the tree. We say, *this* is *halacha*, *this* is Torah, and we wait for the rest of the community to join us.

Other texts presented different challenges. We almost entirely rewrote the text of the ketubah. Written in Aramaic (Jews' lingua franca when the text was being formulated in the early centuries C.E.), the ketubah was essentially a legal contract in which the woman's dowry and her monetary settlement in case of divorce or the death of the husband were specified. The different branches of Judaism have devised alternate, more egalitarian ketubot; some couples create their own. Since we could not find great meaning in the original text, we did not want to use it as a base for creating a same-sex ketubah. Instead, we chose to retain the text's framing structure while constructing a new document composed of quotations from Jewish texts. The first paragraph follows the traditional text stating the facts of the marriage—with an embellishment at the end. The second paragraph begins as a quotation from the last of the wedding ceremony's seven blessings, while our commitments to one another are primarily amended quotations of verses from the books of Hosea and Ruth. And in keeping with the Jewish tradition of not making explicit vows—as well as with our own understanding of human nature—we stated our commitments as intentions rather than promises. The text of the ketubah follows:

> On Monday, the fourth of Elul in the year 5756, August 19, 1996, in Berkeley, California, Katherine Grace Simon, daughter of Anna, of blessed memory, and Jerome, and Inbal Kashtan, daughter of Rivka and Mordechai, of blessed memory, entered into a covenant of kiddushin, according to the traditions of the Jewish people, and as is the practice of lovers in all the nations of the world.

In joy and happiness, gladness and delight, love and companionship, mindfulness and seriousness, Inbal and Kathy committed to one another to do their utmost to continue cultivating their shared and unique paths, deepening their love, and renewing their relationship.

Inbal and Kathy said to one another: You are hereby sanctified unto me, with this ring, in the tradition of the Jewish people. I sanctify you unto me for life; I sanctify you unto me in justice and righteousness, in loving kindness and compassion; I sanctify you unto me in faithfulness. Where thou goest I will go, where thou dwellest I will dwell.

All this was done and said under God's wings and with the support and presence of family and friends.

All this is valid and binding.

A pastiche of biblical and rabbinic verses and framed by the traditional structure of the ketubah the text is more *midrash*, or textual interpretation, than contemporary marriage agreement.

Unlike the ketubah, which we crafted ourselves, the text of the Seven Blessings we were able to retain almost entirely, struggling principally with producing a clear translation and gleaning the different blessings' themes. We asked seven different people to "bless" us by reading the texts. Most simply, where the blessings traditionally speak of "the bridegroom and the bride," we used alternate constructions. Other changes reflected more theological and political concerns. In order to highlight God's many manifestations, we used alternate names for God in addition to the traditional, "Lord, our God, King of the Universe." After much discussion, we replaced "the cities of Judah" with "the cities of Israel and the hearts of the world" to acknowledge our sadness about continued Israeli occupation of Palestinian land in the Judean Hills and our wishes for peace and joy for all peoples.

In addition to the original blessings, we also suggested a theme that the people giving each blessing might use as the basis of a brief personal blessing for us. We derived these themes from traditional commentaries, which explain why these particular blessings are used at wedding ceremonies, as well as our own interpretations:

First blessing
Blessed are you, Adonai our God, ruler of the universe, creator of the fruit of the vine.

Theme: Abundance, sweetness, joy.[2]

---

2. Kathy's father gave us this blessing, which many of our guests found particularly moving. He said:
In trying to think of what I could say to bless the two of you on the theme of abundance, sweetness, and joy, it finally occurred to me that the most sincere and deepest thing I could say to you is to remind you that I, in my lifetime, was blessed with marriage with two wonderful people. And I enjoyed with each of my wives the sweetness and the abundance and the joy in such measure that if I could wish it for you, it would be the most wonderful thing of all. And that's what I wish for you.

Second blessing
Blessed are you, Shchina, creator of the universe, who created all for your glory.

Theme: Creating relationships adds to the glory of creation.

Third blessing
Blessed are you, source of life, creator of the first human beings.

Theme: A new relationship is like a fresh creation of humanity.

Fourth blessing
Blessed are you, spring of life, who created human beings in her image, humanity in the image of divinity, and patterned for humanity the perpetuation of life. Blessed are you, spring of life, creator of humanity.

Theme: The divinity in human beings, and the ability to give life through procreation and nurturing.

Fifth blessing
May the barren one rejoice in the ingathering of her children in gladness and peace. Blessed are you, righter of the world, who brings Tzion joy in her children.

Theme: Hope that those who are separated will come together and unite in peace and joy, and that we may return to a whole relationship with the earth.

Sixth blessing
Delight these beloved companions as you delighted your creations in the Garden of Eden of yore. Blessed are you, heart of the world, delighter of beloved companions.

Theme: This union is a little glimpse of the delight of the Garden of Eden

Seventh blessing
Blessed are you, embracer of the world, who created joy and happiness, bride and bride, mirth, merriment, gladness, delight, love and companionship, peace and partnership. Quickly, embracer of the world, may there be heard in the cities of Israel and in the hearts of nations, the voice of joy and the voice of happiness, the voice of the bride and the voice of the bride, the mirthful shouts of beloveds under their *huppas*, of young women and men feasting and singing. Blessed are you, Adonai our God, delighter of the beloved companions.

Theme: Through the union of loving people, the possibility of joy and healing in the world is increased.

We framed the ceremony with rituals that also reflected the melding of tradition and radical innovation. We appropriated the custom of a *tish*, in which (traditionally) the groom takes a few minutes before the ceremony to speak some words of Torah, known as *dvar Torah* (with his male guests seated with him around a table—*tish* in Yiddish).

Traditionally, too, the groom is nervous, and not much in the mood to teach, so his friends interrupt his talk with teasing and song. At our wedding, we declared ourselves teachers and transmitters of Jewish tradition by having two separate *tishes* (we were separate so as not to see each other until the ceremony began), where we each gave a *dvar Torah* and were each joyously interrupted. After the ceremony, our wedding turned into a raucous celebration, with guests partaking in the traditional Eastern European *freilakh*—lifting us up in chairs, dancing in whirling circles, and sitting us down to watch mirthful acrobatics, a rap song, a rhyme on our relationship, and impromptu merry-making.

As Jews who grew up disconnected from traditional Judaism because of our sexual orientation, we have the challenge of making our connection to Judaism meaningful and personally authentic. In order to build a significant and meaningful relationship with traditional Judaism we had to wrestle with the tradition. What we saw at our wedding was that, although as queer Jews, we are *forced* to struggle with tradition, every Jew who wishes to engage with Judaism, to make meaning out of Judaism *should* struggle, because the tradition does not lend itself readily to our modern sensibilities. Many Jews feel alienated by their tradition, and queer Jews have the tools to make it meaningful for *everyone*. The gift some queer Jews have is that we come into this engagement with Judaism from a feminist and queer critical awareness. We have experience with teasing meaning out of history that has traditionally felt exclusive and alienating to us. If we can harness this awareness with an impulse for finding connection, love, and meaning in these traditions and texts rather than abdicating what is uncomfortable to us, we can actually find the threads of dissent and internal critique. Our tradition has been built on interpretation and multivocality. And therein lies the true paradox: the more we delve into a tradition that seems to exclude us, the more we find embedded within it the principles and voices we can use to transform it. Daniel Boyarin, an Orthodox professor of talmudic culture, writes:

> My endeavor is to justify my love [of rabbinic texts and culture], that is, both to explain it and to make it just. . . . I cannot . . . paper over, ignore, explain away, or apologize for the oppressions of women and lesbigay people that this culture has practiced, and therefore I endeavor . . . to render it just by presenting a way of reading the tradition that may help it surmount or expunge—in time—that which I and many others can no longer live with.[3]

As queer Jews who wish to participate in Judaism's ritual traditions, we must engage in cultural transformation. Through our endeavor we forge a path for other Jews seeking to make their relationships to Judaism fully engaged and meaningful. Mining our tradition for meaning—contemporary, relevant, and deeply rooted—we open it up to all Jews who do not see themselves reflected in an unexamined Judaism.

---

3. Daniel Boyarin, *Unheroic Conduct: The Rise of Heterosexuality and the Invention of the Jewish Man* (Berkeley: University of California Press, 1997), p. xvii. For more on the multivocality of talmudic Judaism, see his *Intertextuality and the Reading of Midrash* (Bloomington: Indiana University Press, 1990), and *Carnal Israel: Reading Sex in Talmudic Culture* (Berkeley: University of California Press, 1993).

"I Now Belong to a Clan of the Mystery People...": On Being Gay and Gray

Harriet Perl

Old age is a solitary journey through uncharted territory. Its destination, admitted or not, is death. Sooner or later every really old person recognizes that. Depending upon circumstances, the journey may be an adventure, a nightmare, or simply a continuation of the usual, with increasing variations. Although individual psychology has a big role, it is possible for outside influences to make the journey less solitary and more pleasant, and to keep thoughts of the destination at bay. I hope to suggest those ways by which Reform synagogues can be good friends to the elders in their congregations, with particular attention to gay/lesbian elders.

Who are our elders? In today's youth-obsessed culture, old age seems to begin with the first gray hair or the tiniest wrinkle, even if they show up well before forty. But when I say old age or elder here, I am referring to people who really are old, never mind the standards of our culture. Seventy is only the beginning, but it is a decided start. Seventy-five is getting there, and at eighty, one is truly entitled to say, "I am old." And in a decent society, one could say it with pride at any of those ages.

Those who do reach and acknowledge old age may find themselves in a new world, different from what they once knew. Friends and relatives are gone, the body is behaving in unexpected, worrisome ways, and ordinary activities become problematic. Some elders will recognize themselves in these midnight thoughts of mine: *I now belong to the clan of the mystery people. We are the old ones living alone, whose daily and nightly lives are unknown to all who think they know us. The outsiders never ask; they don't think to do so. So we on the inside have our routines, our comforting rituals, our scares, our concerns—all the pills, what's that pain, how much longer can I drive, will the money hold out? We also have our pleasures—all too often these are solitary ones, like reading something interesting, watching amusing TV, eating something good (probably forbidden, though), even going to bed. They wouldn't seem like pleasures to others, but we cherish what we can. We are truly unknown; others see only what they choose to know.*

For example, the media is quick to praise and feature an older person who has achieved a remarkable goal that defies the ordinary expectations of old age. We read about a centenarian who lives alone, a seventy-year-old running a marathon, or Mike Wallace at age eighty-eight finally cutting back a little on his duties on *60 Minutes*. The unfortunate result is an increase of uneasiness among the other, ordinary old people and the wrong expectations among the young in their relationships with the old. Those extraordinary ones who show up in the media are just that, extra-ordinary; they must not be considered a standard for others to live up to. Yes, they deserve praise, but it is misplaced adulation if it results in their contemporaries being in effect punished for not being themselves.

Cut a little slack for the old; do not expect them to perform miracles. All that we know about human life and health tells us that things do slow down in old age; the old tire sooner, are more susceptible to whatever germs are going around, take more trips to the doctor, the dentist, the optometrist than when they were younger. Tactfully follow the lead of the elders you know when offering help; maybe they really can't manage the stairs in a theater or the walk from the parking place to the restaurant. The elder may hesitate to tell you things like that; it is embarrassing to one who once could all but leap over tall buildings! Just keep your expectations at the level apparently comfortable for the elder. Not quite incidentally, the cliché that "you are only as old as you feel" is simply a lie. Old age is real, not something imaginary to be sent packing by a cheerful attitude. Being old is a real condition; denying it only makes it painful.

There are, however, pockets of decency in our youth-oriented culture, and one of them can be the synagogue. In that special society, elders can be not just accepted but truly valued; their pride can be protected, many of their needs largely met, and their solo journey given company. When I walk into my synagogue, half a dozen people near the entrance greet me by name. It is the only place left to me where that happens, and I cherish it. That doesn't mean I am friendless, only that the synagogue holds the concentration of my friends. Once upon a time, the workplace had that characteristic; long before then, it was school. But at eighty-five, those places are gone from my life and the lives of most of us who have reached old age, and synagogue takes their place.

The Gay or Lesbian Elder: Similarities and Differences with Their Heterosexual Counterparts

How does the synagogue fit into our lives, and how can it specifically fit into the life of the gay/lesbian elder? To begin, the not-yet-old should recognize that there are similarities and differences among their elders. The common stereotype is of a grandparent, often still married to a lifetime spouse, surrounded by children and grandchildren, who, in varying degrees, love and attend to their elder. Physical weaknesses are acknowledged, but the popular assumption is that the elder is still functional on most levels and, indeed, is expected to provide for such family occasions as seders and birthday celebrations.

That may be a reasonably accurate picture of the straight elder, but it probably does not apply to the gay/lesbian one. For example, I did not marry, and most of the gays and lesbians I knew also were unable to reconcile their sexuality with traditional marriage. My generation discovered their forbidden sexuality in the 1940s or earlier, a time when the word "gay" was not in common use; a time when society in general considered homosexuality a psychological illness at best and a criminal perversion at worst; a time when homosexuality could mean the loss of a one's job, status, family, and sometimes life.

The odds are that the truly old gay or lesbian elder, like me, has lived through and survived a period in life when just about everyone, including relatives and almost certainly employers and professional colleagues, believed that homosexuality was a punishable aberration, that the homosexual person was disgusting and a law breaker. Add to that the fact that today's gay/lesbian elders lived through the worst of the AIDS epidemic—we saw friends and lovers get terribly sick and die. Confusion, ignorance, fear, and bigotry traumatized an entire generation.

The Ramifications of Being Hidden

Forced to hide our deepest affections and to disguise our living arrangements, I and the gays and lesbians I knew were deprived of much of the social life enjoyed by our straight friends; but most of all, we lost out on the feeling of comfortably belonging amid friends and relatives. To hide one's very nature, to go through contortions to keep a lover secret, to lie and lie and lie, to pretend to be someone else (to laugh at homophobic jokes, to drag a willing friend of the opposite sex to a business or social event, and above all, to hide from one's own family), all of this hurt and hurt badly. No matter how hard the gay/lesbian person tried to make peace with the whole thing, real tranquility came only to the rarest of the few. The rest of us simply coped, and our scars sometimes show, still. When I attend an ordinary social event, I wonder how I would be received if my sexuality were as visible as my gender. The gay/lesbian elder can carry such uneasiness into his or her first contacts with a new synagogue experience, as well.

Perhaps the most serious scar carried by today's gay/lesbian elders can be the one those like me bear: no children, no grandchildren. At our advanced age, we have fewer and fewer blood relatives. That leaves us dependent on friends for social life as well as for the kind of help that everyone needs on occasion. These deprivations take a toll on personality and living conditions, and thus the psychology of the gay/lesbian elder may not be the same as that of the elder surrounded by loving family. *Relatives matter.*

Gay and lesbian elders have the same needs for affection and friendship as everyone else; we just can't meet those needs as easily. Among the gay and lesbian people I knew, the lucky ones found a lover; the super lucky formed relationships that lasted. For many, if not most, there were successive relationships, lasting only until varying pressures felled them—and there were no marriage counselors for them then. And for some, for a while, promiscuity was a reasonable response. At least there could be some companionship; more than that remained an unreachable goal for far too many. Some did marry. That was one way of coping: it silenced the family, made one look respectable in the professional world, and led to the presumption of heterosexuality by the outside world. It also provided some of the satisfactions that seem to be inherent in our species: children, stability, "fitting in." Nevertheless, there was an inner sense of self-betrayal, of masquerading instead of living fully. All of this in our personal histories can make it difficult for us to show ourselves for who we are and can make it uncomfortable to find our place in a synagogue.

Synagogues and Their Gay and Lesbian Elders

Despite all that I have said, remember that gays and lesbians are not a separate species. Our life experiences have been both similar to and different than those of most heterosexuals. I have focused on one aspect, that older gays and lesbians are now without the customary full support of relatives to help them meet their needs and gain their pleasures.

This is where the synagogue steps in. What follows is sort of a guideline to help that role become definite. Most of these ideas apply to all elders, but recognizing the special circumstances of the gay or lesbian elder will call for some differences.

It would be natural here to ask, "How does one actually know a person is gay or lesbian?" You don't, unless the person tells you. All the stereotypes are misleading to various degrees, and the person you think is gay may not be and vice versa. It is best simply not to ask. For the gay/lesbian elder, there may still be the haunting fear that began so long ago, the knowledge that they belong in a category that still, today, is denied many of the ordinary civil rights that the rest of the congregation takes for granted. Long habits of clinging to a necessary privacy sometimes interfere with making friends. The ordinary introductory questions about marriage and children are possible land mines, capable of setting off feelings of hurt and invaded privacy. How can the conscientious congregant cope with that situation? By indicating an understanding and acceptance of gay and lesbian people in general, you may learn the orientation of the person you are wondering about—but the fact is, you also may not. Leave it up to the person to come out or not.

1. **Public statements are important.**
   - The rabbi, as the spiritual spokesperson of the congregation, must speak openly about the pleasure the congregation takes in having members who are gay/lesbian.
   - The rabbi or the president of the congregation should make public statements to the media about the synagogue's policy and its goal to serve a diverse congregation.
   - An occasional article in the synagogue's newsletter will help all members to know and understand that there are gay/lesbian elders in the congregation and that the congregation welcomes them.

   Such public commitments not only strengthen the synagogue's policy, but attract new members, and not just gay/lesbian ones, but all who believe in the basic principles of Reform Judaism and its inclusiveness.

2. **Celebrate those gay and lesbian elder couples who would welcome it.** If the congregation is fortunate enough to have some gay/lesbian couples—pairs who have survived together and are in a lasting relationship—celebrate them. Like any couple who is so fortunate, they deserve admiration. Above all, their relationship needs to be recognized in the synagogue: invitations go to them as a pair, anniversaries are noted, and so on. There may also be some lucky gay/lesbian elders who are actively dating. Such people and their dates, if brought to synagogue, should be greeted and treated exactly as heterosexual couples are—with smiling acceptance and no tactless inquiries.

   A common complaint among people who have trouble accepting homosexuals is that "they flaunt it." You may have heard someone say, "I don't mind their being what they are, I just don't want to have to see it." When two people show their affection, the rest of us are usually pleased to see such signs of caring and are indulgent toward them. It really does not matter whether the couple is heterosexual or homosexual—the two people care for each other, and that is good.

   Incidentally, one hears a lot about the "gay lifestyle" today. Be assured, there is no such thing. At every age, gay/lesbian people have lifestyles that suit them under whatever circumstances they are living. They are neither more nor less sexually active or promiscuous than comparable straights. And the gay/lesbian elder lives more or less the way straight elders do.

3. **Congregations should include gay and lesbian elders and do whatever is possible to make those elders a true and active part of the congregation.** An elder who had a career, as is the case with almost all gays and lesbians, has more to offer than may be immediately recognized; a wise rabbi, executive director, or president will seek out those people and learn what skills and experience they have. For example:

   - Invite the elder to participate in various temple projects and rituals.
   - Don't limit them to lighting Shabbat candles or stuffing envelopes. Gay and lesbian elders may know people of importance, have organizing skills, be experienced writers or speakers, and so on.
   - Don't wait for volunteers; seek out the elders and ask them for help.

   They will be pleased to be thought of, because common to almost all elders is the need to be useful and the fear of being a burden. We can argue that both feelings should be unnecessary, since a life of having been useful deserves time off now, and a beloved person should never be thought of as a burden. But that "should" is, unfortunately, observed in the negative all too often, and the elder's fear is probably at least somewhat realistic. The congregation's attitude can do much to relieve it.

4. **Invite the gay and lesbian elder to Shabbat services, special events, and simple everyday meals at your home.** Kind congregants usually see to it that single elders or couples are invited and taken to Shabbat services and special events, such as Erev Rosh HaShanah meals, the Yom Kippur break-fast, and nonreligious major occasions, such as Thanksgiving. That is wonderful, but what happens in the times in between those events? Being alone, the single elder, gay or straight, struggles against loneliness, a feeling of ghostliness, and simply being unnoticed for periods of time. The surest antidote to this situation is a phone call and/or an invitation, not to anything special, but just to join you when you go to a movie or sit at your family table for an ordinary meal. The phone call is the easiest way to counteract the loneliness of the single elder; it doesn't have to be about anything important, and it shouldn't be too directly zeroing in on "How are you?" which only underlines the negative aspect of the elder's life. All you have to do is maintain the same kind of contact you have with your other friends.

5. **The highest goal of the congregation can be to provide a surrogate or extended family for the gay/lesbian elder. Make friends with your gay and lesbian elders.** When friendship has developed between a congregant, individual, or family and the elder, it can grow into a close relationship, approximating that of a family. The participants can even claim a lighthearted "adoption" and consider themselves bonded on a really close level. The members count on each other in the same way that blood-related family does, with the same comfortable results. Most ordinary coupled people give little thought to the solitary state of the gay/lesbian elder. In fact, many lead such busy lives that they may actually envy the quiet life of the unrelated person. Family gatherings, birthdays to celebrate, children and grandchildren to get to school, and other activities, not to mention career and ordinary household obligations, all take time and effort and leave many just plain frazzled. If the gay/lesbian person has been thought of as an adopted or surrogate grandparent, he or she can be included in many of those family

activities, to the mutual advantage of everyone. Just spending an evening with a family watching TV or engaged in ordinary conversation can be a treat for the person who has no family, and the addition of one more person is not likely to create a problem.

6. **Gay and lesbian elders have special gifts to offer.** Gifts come in all sizes and shapes, from the benefit of seventy-plus years of experience to the lost art of how to make a home-cooked meal. On the practical side, the women have usually cooked for themselves all their lives and can provide cookies or kugel if allowed. (These elders can still produce old-time favorites now hard to find in original form. My chopped liver has won me invitations!) And many gay men of that generation learned to cook for themselves and can surprise you with their gourmet creations. However, gay and lesbian elders have more than food to offer: their memories of other times can be and usually are of interest to their hosts.

Once upon a time, long ago, society moved so slowly that elders had skills, knowledge, and wisdom to pass on to the young. Today, the workplace and culture generally have changed so radically that many of the older generations may be out of touch or at least will not have many skills that are still a part of the workplace. Yet, there are some that have turned their teaching, engineering, or investment skills into second or third careers or volunteer work. Regardless, it is the wisdom gained from having worked a lifetime, and done so under much tougher circumstances than are likely to apply today, that is always available for the asking. Their memories bring history to life for children, a benefit not otherwise available. The elders should not preach, of course, nor will the younger ones sit at their feet in awe; that would be unpleasant for everyone. But in the course of conversation, the elder may offer some moments from past experience that will resonate with the present. Everyone profits.

Something for the young to think about: in conversation or appearance, the gay and lesbian elder may not always be "with it," but friends should remember that it was not always that way. While active professionally (and romantically), the gay and lesbian person was not only in tune with his or her culture, but may well have been avant-garde. Those who are old now were young during some exciting times. They may have been active in the beginning of the gay liberation movement, in feminism, or in various unusual political campaigns. They experienced the Depression, World War II, and all the following wars. They lived through changes in popular music, and they wore clothes that were stylish in their time. They survived McCarthy and all the anti-gay laws. That means they have plenty to remember and talk about, of a time when they were in the middle of what was going on, not sidelined as they may feel themselves to be now. They can be forgiven, one hopes, for not caring about hip-hop and preferring the big bands that they danced to so long ago. They may still dress more formally than some of the younger congregants, a holdover from the time when they wore suits and ties, white gloves and girdles. Or they may not: they may embrace the comparative freedom of dress that today allows. In either case, they are entitled to their opinions, and these opinions and experiences are the basis for good conversations.

7. **A caution on invitations.** Oddly, it is possible for an eager congregation to overdo the invitations. When they come in too fast and often, the elder is in the difficult position of not wanting to turn down something pleasant, but knowing at the same time that too much is being expected. Worse, refusing an invitation may bring on an anxious "Are

you OK?" from the well-meaning friend, who assumes that every invitation will be immediately accepted. It is a tricky business, and the only way to keep it comfortable for all involved is for everyone to be honest and up front. For many elders, one "event" per day is enough, and "event" can mean grocery shopping as well as something more dramatic. When that is understood, it is easier for the invitations to be accepted or not and will not stir bad feelings. While moderating expectations of the elder's physical activity, it is good to remember he or she used to be more active and might feel embarrassed about his or her current limitations. The elder may be apologetic or may try to do more than is comfortable or healthy. An easy acceptance of what appears to be pleasant is the best response.

8. **Offer a helping hand as the infirmities of age approach.** Sooner or later the elder stops driving, usually in stages—first no driving on high-speed freeways, then no driving at night, and so on. Again, when there are no relatives to ask or to depend upon, it is up to a welcoming congregation or congregants to see that offers are made to take the elder to synagogue, to arrange for market assistance, and to help establish links with social services. Too many elders become prisoners in their own homes because they can't drive and public transportation is not available or safe. But again, the offer must be made. Don't wait to be asked.

Congregants who have maintained a friendship with the elder will have access to his/her home and can assess—quietly, inconspicuously—whether there is evidence of trouble. Are there signs of confusion, neglect, or shortages of important things like heat and food? If serious problems are discovered, it may be time for clergy or others with information to assess the situation and see if referral to a social agency may be needed. Jewish Family Service (JFS) is available in large cities, and other social agencies may be available if JFS is not. However, for the gay or lesbian person, the ordinary answers to the problem may not be suitable; if the city has a gay and lesbian community, consultation with someone of authority in it may be more helpful. A lot depends upon how the gay and lesbian elder has lived and who his or her friends are. To go into the usual kind of old-age facility without grandchildren to brag about, children to visit, or companions around one who have an idea of what having lived as a gay or lesbian means can be a nightmare, not a blessing.

I hope that I have not given the impression that the synagogue is a kind of social service agency. It certainly is not. But it may very well be the first responder to a situation that will eventually call for the help of such an agency. The JFS can take over when there is a referral from a synagogue. If there is no JFS, there very well may be some other agency that can, at the very least, advise the synagogue leadership on how best to provide the needed help for the gay or lesbian elder. Basically, all that is being suggested is that the synagogue act as an extended family and that congregants offer real friendship for all of its elders, and especially for the gay and lesbian ones, who are less likely than others to have a support system of relatives automatically in place.

Conclusion

In its simplest form, the goal of the synagogue should be to welcome gay and lesbian elders and integrate them lovingly into the congregation. This can take many forms but should include providing positions of worth in the congregation for the gay and lesbian elders, including them often socially, forming friendships with them, and keeping an eye on their welfare. Essentially, that means doing for them what every synagogue hopes to do for all its members, the difference being that the gay/lesbian elder may have both a greater need for attention and the possibility of a unique contribution, different from what is usually expected of elders in our culture.

The Voice of a Wandering Jewish Bisexual: An Update

Rebecca Gorlin

When I think of being bisexual, I am reminded of my Jewish ancestors who, kicked out of different countries, tried to find a place to call home. I, too, have wandered, in the gay and straight worlds, Jewish and not, feeling kicked out and alienated.

We've both built our own communities, straddled several worlds, and survived enormous oppression. Millions of Jews as well as gay and bisexual people were killed in Nazi concentration camps. In more recent times, many more bisexual and gay men (and fewer bisexual and lesbian women) have died of AIDS. Being Jewish or bisexual is not something that can be seen just by looking at us. If I am walking down the street with my same-sex spouse, I am automatically assumed by gays and heterosexuals alike to be a lesbian. If I were to walk with a male partner, everyone would think I'm heterosexual. By the same token, everyone assumes I am Christian.

Over many years, I have done plenty of soul-searching. I began to understand what being a Jew means to me and to gain a sense of Jewish pride. I had no Jewish education growing up and wanted to learn more about Jewish history, rituals, and customs. I have read a lot about Jewish women and feminism. I sang with the Zamir Chorale of Boston and learned about Jewish choral music. Since college, I've been a member of Am Tikva, an LGBT Jewish group. In 1999, I had an adult bat mitzvah. The more I learn, the more at home I feel as a Jew. As bisexuals, we too must go through a learning process in order to feel at home and to gain bisexual pride and visibility and power for ourselves and as a community.

The first years of this search during my adolescence included my struggle to develop a proud lesbian, then bisexual, identity. Identifying as a lesbian for seven years made me see how much I love women and began my awareness of homophobia and heterosexism. When I realized that I was still attracted to men and fell in love with one, I came out again as a bisexual. Being with a man again, I had to deal with male-female differences, sexism, and heterosexual privilege. Fortunately, I was able to talk about these issues in a lesbian-to-bisexual group called the Hasbians.

What I want most is to integrate my bisexual and Jewish identities. This has not been easy because, as a bisexual, I feel alienated from both the heterosexual and homosexual Jewish communities. I do not go to certain straight Jewish functions to avoid getting sucked into a sexist and heterosexist community that will only accept me if I'm with a man and do not discuss my "other side." I do go to most "lesbian and gay" events because my feelings and politics are queer-identified. It is important for me to be there with my lesbian sisters and gay brothers because homophobia is the main oppression and we all have to work together to fight it. Putting up with biphobia and bisexual invisibility among lesbians and gay men is minor in comparison to mainstream society's homophobia that results in violence and lack of civil rights.

Am Tikva works on the issues of sexism and heterosexism, but not much on biphobia. There are other bisexuals in Am Tikva, as well as transpeople, and except for a token topic in an occasional discussion group, our issues are almost never addressed. Although the name of "the group for lesbian and gay Jews" was changed to include bisexuals and transgendered people, the group is still very gay- and lesbian-oriented.

As bisexuals, we have got to come out in Jewish circles whenever possible. Am Tikva and other gay- and lesbian-oriented Jewish groups need to recognize our presence and be more inclusive in their actions, not just change the description of their name. Discussions on bisexuality would be a good start. I want to participate in these groups without having some people barely tolerate me or have an uptight tone in their responses to my coming out as bi. Lesbians and gay men have worked hard for recognition in heterosexual Jewish groups; they need to remember those struggles to help them understand our situation as bisexuals and Jews.

In their Summer 1989 issue, *Lilith*, a Jewish feminist magazine, had an article about the particular difficulties experienced by Jewish lesbians and gay men coming out to their families because of the Jewish traditions of family and having children. I was annoyed to find no mention of Jewish bisexuals. (There's been nothing about us in the years since, in *Lilith* or in other Jewish magazines that I have read.) We, too, face homophobia when we come out to our families. Like lesbians and gays, we are sometimes seen as unlikely to have children if we are with our same-sex partner. If we have children with an opposite sex partner, we are seen as a traditional family, when in fact we are not.

In addition, there are the heterosexual biases. Our opposite-gender partners are celebrated, while our same-sex partners can be denied or devalued. Many people do not realize that bisexuals get beaten up, lose custody of their children, and face other homophobic reactions just as often as lesbians and gay men, because the larger world is only interested in two categories, heterosexual or not. The media, when they do acknowledge that we exist and even use the B-word, love to portray us as swingers, violent killers, AIDS vectors, or, in the case of bisexual women, as a straight man's sexual fantasy.

As bisexuals, we have to come out and challenge biphobic stereotypes and attitudes whenever we experience them in the straight and queer media and at secular straight and queer groups. Am Tikva and other synagogues need to include and value us and be willing to participate in education and awareness programs. Gaining this recognition takes a strong and united bisexual front. It will not happen unless we demand it. Concurrently, in non-Jewish circles, be they bisexual, gay, lesbian, or heterosexual, we have to be proud and come out as Jews and challenge any anti-Semitism we encounter, as one prejudice affects the other. If we do not, biphobia and anti-Semitism will go on, and we will be invisible. When we can stand up and be proud of our Jewish bisexual selves, then we will find a place to call home.

Whose Side Are You On? Transgender at the Western Wall

TJ Michels and Ali Cannon

> Blessed are You, Adonai our God, Ruler of the Universe,
> for having created me according to Thy will.
> —Morning Brachah

The Western Wall in the Old City of Jerusalem, where the First and Second Temples once stood, unequivocally represents Judaism's holiest site.

It is a site where the religious wrap *tefillin* and fulfill their *mitzvot*, where secular tourists stuff prayers into its weed-filled cracks, and where the diaspora focuses its collective emotional attention, even thousands of miles away.

But it is a site where males and females do not mix, where 13-year-old boys vibrantly rejoice in reading the Torah for the first time, where girls the same age are expected to contain their prayers to near whisper, where women have been heckled and had eggs, chairs, and feces hurled at them by men incensed they dare to don *tallisim* and conduct Torah services in public religious space.

And it is a site where two queer Jews, a transgender man, and a transgender butch, independently faced life-altering experiences—exhilarating and painful respectively—as they descended upon it, where two people traversed the confines of gender and blurred the boundaries the *mechitzah* seeks to maintain.

It is a site where they each problematized their gender, or gender problematized them, and where they prayed, most significantly, as Jews.

We first met after TJ, an editor at a Jewish newspaper, interviewed Ali for a story on his involvement in a queer Jewish performance ensemble. In the course of the conversation, we learned we both had transformative experiences at the Western Wall: Ali spoke of the poems he wrote, about passing on the men's side of the Wall. TJ had struggled to pen an article on visiting the men's side—after being refused entry on the women's side.

TJ Michels and Ali Cannon, "Whose Side Are You On? Transgender at the Western Wall," in *Queer Jews*, ed. David Shneer and Caryn Aviv (New York: Routledge, 2002), pp. 148–55.

TJ later agreed to write on the juxtaposition of gender and religious identity using the Kotel incident as a launching pad for this essay. She invited Ali to collaborate, evolving into this dialogue.[1]

Our goal is twofold: To posit the compelling, but often contentious, butch/female-to-male transgender discussion—what Gayle Rubin first coined as "frontier fears," later inspiring Judith Halberstam and Jacob Hale's "butch/FTM border wars"—in a Jewish context.[2] We feel it both necessary and urgent to explore where and how we connect and diverge vis à vis our respective locations, but seek to avoid replicating the combativeness of earlier community debates. The few works to elaborate on the various nuances of masculine gender identifications primarily originating within lesbian communities are seminal. However, we know of few that specifically address regulatory notions of Jewish masculinity.[3]

Secondly, we wish to carve a space for transgendered people within Jewish tradition, and vice versa, by paying particular attention to how our queer sexualities and trans locations challenge and intersect with our spiritual and cultural identities. Combining subjective and analytic discourses, it is our hope to demonstrate that with the same indefatigability that has preserved the Western Wall and the continuity of our people, so too will our struggles transform our traditions and communities.

TJ: We're beginning this dialogue at an interesting cultural juncture: when transgender is just starting to click in the queer world and queer is beginning to register in the Jewish world. Using our respective experiences at the Wall—this holy site fraught with symbolism and metaphors—we're two transgender Jews talking about being and living as transgender Jews. I'm hoping we can illuminate areas of overlap as well as departure. Both of us participate at the same synagogue and are heavily invested in various dyke and trans communities, but we currently occupy different locations on the gender/sexual continuum. I have not transitioned in the "typical" sense: hormonally and/or surgically. I guess transgender butch or boy are the most intelligible ways within queer culture to describe myself, for now.

Ali: While "transition" has historically been used by psychiatrists and surgeons to describe the moment in which one makes a medical intervention in the gendering of their body—sex reassignment surgery—I think that the modern transgender movement is challenging

---

1. A quick note on pronouns: TJ has not, at this point, transitioned in medically—or, for the most part, socially—validated ways. The use of third-person feminine pronouns in no way is intended to suggest that surgical and/or hormonal transition is the requisite for linguistically conforming to the gender of one's choice. However, for various reasons beyond the scope of this essay, TJ is not discomforted by use of them. That notwithstanding, she is uncomfortable being attributed to feminine constructs of gendered nouns, such as, girl, lady, woman. For more on this, see TJ Michels, "Rants of a Label Whore," www.gay.com. As an FTM, Ali has transitioned socially and hormonally, and is referred to in masculine terminology. It would be inappropriate to do otherwise.

2. Gayle Rubin, "Of Catamites and Kings: Reflections on Butch, Gender, and Boundaries," in *The Persistent Desire: A Femme-Butch Reader*, Joan Nestle, ed. (Boston: Alyson, 1992) and Judith Halberstam and C. Jacob Hale, "Butch/FTM Border Wars: A Note on Collaboration" in *GLQ, A Journal of Lesbian and Gay Studies*, Vol. 4, No. 2, 1998.

3. See, for instance Rubin, Hale & Halberstam, and Halberstam, *Female Masculinity* (North Carolina: Duke UP, 1998). Additionally, Naomi Scheman's "Queering the Center by Centering the Queer: Reflections on Transsexuals and Secular Jews" in *Feminists Rethink the Self*, Diane Tietjens Myers, ed. (Boulder: Westview Press, 1997), pp. 24–162, does raise separate issues of Judaism and transsexuality as they conflict with social normalizing apparatus. However, her intent was not to explore transgender Jewish identity. See also Danya Ruttenberg's "Blood Simple: Transgender Theory Hits the Mikveh" in *Yentl's Revenge: The Next Wave of Jewish Feminism* (Seal Press, 2001). We are encouraged by and pleased to be in the company of other transgender Jewish contributors to this anthology.

the narrow assumption of those definitions. In the six months since I made the big decision to start testosterone, I have not been viewed as a woman, except for once or twice over the phone because my voice is still changing. But I began my transition more than two years ago, when I first started living as a man.

I'm really interested in exploring, as a trangender man, our experiences in terms of how we differently identify along the butch-trans spectrum. I think it's important for both of us to tell our specific stories to engage Judaism in a new type of conversation about what we mean when we say gender and gender identity.

TJ: And how Israel played a role in our identity formation specifically.

Ali: Right. I'll start by describing my experience in Israel in 1999.

As background, I should mention that I came out as a lesbian in 1982, two years before I "came out" as a Jew, as was true for many of the dykes of the "nice Jewish girls" generation.[4] As Evelyn Torton Beck argued, many of us didn't have the tools to overcome internalized anti-Semitism until we first chipped away at our internalized homophobia.

But I've spent much of the past 17 years claiming a strong Jewish identity that was not part of my childhood. And taking my first trip to Israel was definitely a spiritual journey for me.

By the time my girlfriend Jessica—who's now my wife—and I were preparing for our trip that summer, my sense of self was shifting. I was, in a very limited way, starting to identify as transgendered. I didn't know exactly what that meant for me but I knew that it meant something.

After we got the tickets to go to Israel, I still had to apply for a passport. I filled out the application, checked the female box—I had not legally changed my gender from female to male—and submitted the form along with my female birth certificate and my head shot. And my passport came back from the federal government with an "M" on it! In the words of Irena Klepfisz, an important mentor of mine, this was *bashert* to happen to me; it was something I had to pay attention to on many levels. Essentially I went to Israel with a passport that said I was male, so I practiced going into men's bathrooms and prepared myself to live as a man for some period of my stay.

TJ: That's amazing. You realize, Ali, that you may very well be the first FTM to be recognized as legally male, according to a federal document, long before getting the restroom thing down pat? I almost feel compelled to say a *shehechiyanu!* Can you talk a bit about how a religious site became the catalyst for a queer epiphany?

Ali: Going to the Wall was a specific site of gender identity formation and resistance for me as a Jew and as a nascently identified transgender person. Israel is a more markedly gendered place. There are gender police at every religious site. Throughout the trip, we'd gone to various religious sites, and I never was given the modest clothing for the women to wear. And I don't have a flat chest! *No one* ever noticed that I had breasts, which is weird for me because as a butch, and now as a transgendered man, I'm very conscious of the fact

---

4. Evelyn Torton Beck, ed., *Nice Jewish Girls* (Watertown, MA.: Persephone Press, 1982). The publication of Beck's anthology marked an emergence of theory and activism that sought to make lesbian Jews visible agents of change within lesbian feminist communities, and to some extent, broader mainstream Jewish communities.

that I have breasts. So to claim my male identity at that holy place was to affirm my right to seek the deepest sense of myself as a Jewish man in the making.

Of course, walking down that path to the Wall, I knew that I was crossing the great binary divide of Jewish law and regulated social religious space; as a born woman, I was also aware that I was not "supposed" to be there.

This excerpt from one of the poems I wrote about going to the Wall expresses some of what I am talking about:

in the day light
I wrap the large cream tallis
With dark blue stripes
to honor the heavens
around my body
the most sacred aloneness
that Judaism allows

bowing at the Kotel, rocking back and forth
like a million Jewish men before me
I write prayers for the transgendered
Ask that the Jewish people
become less binary
less misogynist
but this is too technical
I am here at the Wall
and this is where I belong

a man in a black coat comes up to me asking for money
without tzedaka I am not worth his time

I leave this holy site of men
still a man on these streets
not even my passport betrays me[5]

TJ: It sounds like the way you experienced Israel and the Wall was something of a metaphoric Bar Mitzvah, both a Jewish rite of passage and "becoming a man."

Ali: By the time I went to the Wall, there were a lot of questions coming up. It was both "This is rite of a passage," and "Is this really a rite of passage?"

It's important to note here that my close friends who lived in Jerusalem thought I was going to the men's side of the Wall as a butch dare, to see if I could pull off passing as a man. But Nicole and Ruti didn't know that I was experiencing Israel as a man instead of a dyke. I had mentioned, nonchalantly, that my passport had an "M" on it, but that was it. So, they didn't really get it, because I didn't talk about it—because I was afraid to talk about it.

---

5. From "My Visit to the Wall: The Lesbian Friends' View" by Ali Cannon, 1999.

I knew that going to the Wall was a rite of passage for me as a Jew and as the man I was becoming, but it was somewhat private. The issue for me centered on how much of my trans identity I was claiming. I knew that I wanted to go to the men's side. Even in my young trans identity I wasn't interested in going to the women's side. However, had I been in a different place in my identity, I would have wanted to go to the women's side. I had hardly ever been in communities with men. Yet I was able to take our lesbian friends' three-year-old son up to the Wall, aware that as a man, I was responsible for sharing this experience with him within the prescribed boundary of male space and generational time.

I even went back to the Wall to pray again—still not out to my close friends—and so the journey was also mediated by that fact. Regardless, that act of going to the Wall and living as a man for three weeks in Israel catapulted me into a sense of urgency; I had to seek out the FTM community when I came back to the States. I had to reconcile that rite of passage because I had claimed something most sacred about myself as a man before those ancient stones. I was left to come to terms with my trans identity for the year and a half following that important trip to Israel.

What was your experience of going to the Wall, TJ? How did that impact your sense of gender identity and your identity as a Jew?

TJ: To give you some background, my agenda for going to the Western Wall was simple: to pray to God. And that was huge; powerful enough for me to "forget" that what, or who, I would pray *as* could very well come into play.

Before this trip, I had returned to Judaism after several lapsed years—not surprisingly, the period of time between my Bat Mitzvah and coming out as a dyke. Whereas I never felt the need to "come out" as a Jew—I enjoyed both (ostensibly) egalitarian Reform and Conservative environments growing up—I had only recently acknowledged my belief in God. This dramatically tilted my identity from passive to active: I was shifting from the cultural Jew who "felt" Jewish to a more observant Jew who has a felt need to engage with Judaism and God.

I'm sure I viewed it as a rite of passage; gone were the days of shul daydreaming during the Amidah. I had it in my head that I would come to know the *kavanah* of prayer and that God is somehow "closer" there. I wouldn't say that today, but at the time, I suppose some sort of Zionist socialization had seeped its way in.

Complicating matters, though, was I didn't have this warm, fuzzy "Jew among Jews" feeling in Israel as I had anticipated. I could almost taste the bitter division between the religious and the secular. It's a dichotomy that's foreign to most American Jews, because our communities in the United States are so pluralistic.

Ali: This clearly was a spiritual journey for you, then. You weren't checking out the gay scene?

TJ: Somewhat in Tel Aviv, but the Old City is a whole other animal. I was with my sister, Mindy, and her partner, Melissa. We're a trio of queers. Given that we were in the Middle East, none of us particularly wished to stand out, but with my baggy shorts, T-shirt, and shaved head peering from underneath a baseball cap, I guess I didn't do the best job of camouflaging myself.

To get to the Wall, we entered through the Dung gate instead of the Jewish quarter tunnel, meaning we had to go through a set of metal detectors and security turnstiles marked women's or men's entrance. Without much thought, I followed my sisters. As long as I don't bind my breasts, which I generally don't, I operate under the assumption that my sex will be read as unambiguously female; my gender pegged as some version of dyke. And when I do pass—I owe it all to the military cut and hairy legs—it tends to be momentary, with considerable embarrassment on the part of the other. Since I had forgotten to pack long pants in my knapsack, I was a bit nervous the groundskeepers would make me put on one of those horrendous skirts to cover my bare calves. Luckily, nobody stopped me, and I figured I was in the clear.

As we stepped onto the plaza, I could feel myself getting intensely emotional with a good hundred feet before the stone itself. I told my sisters to go on ahead. I needed to be alone.

I began to slowly make my way, until a uniformed officer stopped me in my tracks. I didn't speak enough Hebrew to know what he was saying, but he was very, very agitated. Damn, I thought, all this fuss because he can see the few inches of skin between my knees and my workboots. I could see a box of those raggedy *shmatas* out of the corner of my eye so I pointed over to them, to indicate I would put one of them on, however humiliating. But that didn't seem to change his mind, which confused the hell out of me. By now, he was yelling and gesticulating wildly. My heart was racing; I felt completely intimidated and at a loss for what his problem was. Finally, he pointed to the other side of the plaza.

In other words, this soldier—or was he literally the gender police?—figured he was on to me; he suspected I was a guy trying to sneak into the women's side.

Ali: That must have felt entirely disorienting.

TJ: It knocked the wind out of me. I assumed I'd be viewed with suspicion for rejecting femininity, but I hadn't expected to pass per se. You and I both have probably garnered considerable skill in the gender attribution game. I know that when I'm read as male, I replay every detail in my head: What kind of space was I in, what was I wearing, who was I with, my demeanor and disposition? Alternatively, when I perform gender in unconvincing ways, I mentally analyze the endless particulars that may seem absurd to non-trans folks. By virtue of being non-normatively gendered, I believe many of us become acutely aware of—that's code for "obsessed with"—how we are being perceived. That said, in a foreign land I don't have the context to assess people's perceptions of gender.

Ali: Which at home allows us to perform gender in ways meaningful to our culture. Neither of us had a point of reference to expect we would be treated as men as readily as we were. I may have been forced into thinking about it in advance of the trip. Because of the passport issue, I feared for my safety if I *didn't* pass. But I was shocked that it took absolutely no effort—and it sounds as if you were operating under the assumption that Israel was an inappropriate place to make the effort.

TJ: It didn't occur to me to attempt the men's side from the get-go, not that it felt "right" to go to the women's side. The divider itself is incredibly problematic on multiple levels. As Jewish feminists have noted, the *mechitzah* doesn't just separate women and men: It keeps the women *away* from men. But from a transgender critique, the *mechitzah* functions much like the binary gender system that says there are two, and only two genders, which must be congruent with one's sex, in other words, genitals.

Not to mention that in Israel, especially the Old City, I was almost entirely in "Jew mode," the first time in my adult life that queerness ever took a backseat. By way of some epistemic inheritance, I "just knew" this holy, historical setting coursed through my bloodstream by birthright or some such *meshugas*.

Though I have constructed my Jewish identity in consciously chosen ways as an adult, being a Jew is the one constant that has at least *felt* essential to my existence; inexplicably, it is who I am. But the hegemonic power of the Orthodox had forced me to take pause in Israel. How did I know myself to be a Jew when these black-hatted sorts were the "real" thing?

This impression already had me emotionally overcome before this male soldier, whose language I don't share, began to verbally attack me. Fearing for my safety, I backed away from him, to advance toward the men's side.

But paralysis stopped me dead. In my mind, I was devoid of any option. Even if I walked over to the men's side, someone would surely notice my breasts, yell at me or kick me out, or worse. I had no access to the women's side *or* the men's side—and no recognizable gender. Long before Israel, I had stopped identifying as a woman, but here I couldn't even "count" as one. Being considered among the men, in this context, made just as little sense.

So in that moment, I phenomenologically vanished. I had absolutely no identity to reasonably cling to, my body was rendered meaningless. What I had once clung to as a fundamental truth—I am a Jew—not only had been called into question, but became a casualty, too, as my gender ceased to be intelligible.

In the past few years, hanging out in the margins had somehow, paradoxically, become this comfortable place for me to loiter. But no amount of gender anxiety has before prevented me from passing, as *possessing* a gender. It must be horrifying for people who are absolutely gender ambiguous or at an awkward stage of transitioning. Most people don't know how to interact with transgender people because our culture remains so preoccupied with trying to figure out if you're a man or a woman. This was that kind of debasement—I just was utterly indiscernible. There was no space for me.

Ali: What you're saying about feeling debased, your body rendered meaningless, seems to be at the core of something incredibly painful. What's different about my experience is that I was starting to recognize that I no longer could be in that margin of having my gender be ambiguous; I just couldn't survive from there. So what ended up being your next move?

TJ: I had to pull myself together because I was intent on *davening*. From behind my sunglasses, tears were streaming. I made my way to the men's side. There was all this commotion and jubilation. Men were dancing around the Torah and Bnai Mitzvah. Admittedly, it was quite spectacular to be that close to it all. And in their preoccupation, no one noticed me. But as I neared the actual Wall, I took a glance to my right, toward the *mechitzah* that separated the men from the women. I could see all these women struggling to look over it: It was their sons and grandsons and nephews that had just read from the Torah, who were being elevated in chairs by their elder patriarchs. The women could only experience these celebrations from behind the divider.

And there were Mindy and Melissa, pining to catch a look, to snap a photo. I stood there, facing them perpendicularly. It was chilling. My sisters, my first feminist dyke mentors, were being kept from what should have been accessible to all. Guilt-ridden, I felt a wave of unwanted privilege, and it made me incredibly uncomfortable. I tend to feel at most ease being among men—well, within fag space—but not as a means to acquire privilege. Passing had always been such a thrill, a validation. But this? I didn't want it.

It took being in Jerusalem, on the men's side of the Wall, for me to realize that years of gender dysphoria—all the things that I wanted to reject about my own body—had at times lodged itself as femme phobia, or even a form of sexism. I resented having feminine characteristics attributed to me, to have the "fact" of my sex feel at odds with my gender. Given that so few people can read the fiction of it all, I've had moments of anger that I've projected onto those who embody femininity.

So here came another epiphany, which I transformed into a choice: either be the oppressor or be the oppressed, which really isn't a choice at all. I had to get over to the women's side where I "belonged," and I had to get past that guard.

I headed back over and sure enough, he got in my face. Mysteriously, he spoke to me in English this time. I still remember the timbre of his voice, his manner of questioning me in a slow deliberate grunt. "Are . . . you . . . a *woman?*" And I paused because it's almost never something I answer affirmatively. I had to say yes. He took a step back, looked me up and down, and had this "you're despicable" look on his face. With a deep breath, I headed up to where the women were gathered, and it is on that side of the Wall that I prayed. Sobbing, I asked God to guide me, with patience, to become a better Jew.

Ali: As transgender people, our bodies hang in the balance—to be found out, scrutinized, made unwhole by outsiders' perception of us. You had so much taken away from you by that gender-policing guard. He challenged your right to define your gender on your own terms.

But I am curious to hear you say more about how being on the men's side made you feel like being on the side of the oppressor. This speaks to me about the issues of transitioning and the accusation of "betraying" women.

TJ: That reaction does seem a bit extreme now, but mind you at the time, my agency and autonomy had been challenged by that guard, flooding me with a sense that I had turned my back on feminism the moment I came out as trans. And I'm willing to concede this emotion; this guilt comes despite the arsenal of logical defenses many of us built up against those who accuse us of betraying "the sisterhood." Like you said earlier, you were afraid at first to share with Nicole and Ruti that you were experiencing, not to mention enjoying, Israel as a man. These kinds of fears, I think, are almost presupposed when you're socialized in the lesbian-feminist world.

There were few environments for me to confront that until I went to Israel and witnessed firsthand how pervasively patriarchal Judaism can be.

But I think you're touching on something crucial here. Within the queer world, we hear a lot about, and fall prey to, the anxieties surrounding that fuzzy, discursive overlap between lesbian, butch, boydyke, transgender, FTM, and so on. So often the people who challenge and "cross" gender boundaries by transitioning have been, and still are accused of, betraying the lesbian community. And in Jewish lesbian communities, the issues become even more complicated. Jewish feminists have long complained about how sexist Judaism's customs can be, and have constructed an entire body of knowledge and ritual to reclaim an egalitarian Judaism. The notion that someone born female would want to become party to male privilege raises suspicions and hostility, unfortunately, but I think this is misguided. Your experience testifies to that. Appropriating masculinity via a trans trajectory—and all the discrimination that comes with that—is not necessarily synonymous with appropriating the misogyny of paradigmatic men.

Ali: The whole notion of betrayal to me is an avoidance of looking at the complex notions of gender that transgender folk call into play. Betraying women, betraying feminism, for being transgender, for wanting to be seen as a man, for feeling like a man, for living as a man—these are big things that disrupt certain boundaries feminist theory has constructed in the hopes of creating justice for women. I feel like most people who conform to conventional gender categories are not walking around in their bodies the way you and I are walking around in our bodies. Normatively gendered people can't theorize about who we are from their own personal experience, and therefore, what right do folks have to accuse us of betrayal? There's a dangerous tendency among non-trans academics (in other words, most of academia) to theorize *us*, and that is part of the silencing of our voices, bodies, and self-identifications.[6] Of course, that's happening in the Jewish lesbian community too.

A recent example of this occurred the night you attended Chutzpah: A Queer Jewish Show, where I read my poems about the Wall at Luna Sea, a women's theater and performance space. The annual show originated as a Jewish dyke ensemble, but expanded to include FTMs and bi women.

A well-known Jewish lesbian writer shared the stage with me. She read a poem named something to the effect of "Butch Resisting the Pressure to Change Genders." The content of the poem—which included the line "is this what we fought for?"—was even more hurtful than the title suggests. One FTM walked out. Another, a friend of mine who formerly identified as butch, was in tears. This writer refused to engage in a dialogue about her piece in a talk-back with the audience. Later, I was accosted by one woman who asked me what right I had, as a man, to be performing.

As a newly out transgender man, it was difficult to be up against that betrayal, on stage, in a primarily Jewish lesbian context. I'm proud to say that the theater, the cast, and most of the audience supported and celebrated trans inclusion in this location. However, that I was exposed to this hostility is not necessarily an anomaly.

TJ: I think one of feminism's failures is its desperation to maintain this seamless category of "women." The first thing we learn as we become budding radicals is that biological sex and gender are not the same thing. Imagine if we—that is, all women and genderqueers—let this feminist mantra really take us somewhere, instead of locking the door because it appears it might hit us on the way out.

---

6. The most infamous of these is Janice Raymond, whose *The Transsexual Empire: The Making of a She-Male* (Boston: Beacon, 1979) became a work that stood as "the" lesbian-feminist critique of transsexuality long after its publication and gave rise to another, more recent separatist tirade: Sheila Jeffreys, *The Lesbian Heresy: A Feminist Perspective on the Lesbian Sexual Revolution* (Melbourne: Spinifex, 1993). Other examples coming from the queer theory/gender studies camp that tend to trivialize or deny transgender agency: Marjorie Garber, *Vested Interests: Cross Dressing and Cultural Anxiety* (New York: Routledge, 1992); Elizabeth Grosz, *Volatile Bodies: Toward a Corporeal Feminism* (Bloomington: Indiana UP, 1994); and Bernice L. Hausman, *Changing Sex: Transsexualism, Technology, and the Idea of Gender* (Durham, NC: Duke UP, 1995).

For one thing, many of us who no longer identify *as* women nonetheless identify *with* women.[7] Our consciousness, histories, and life experiences involve considerable investment among queer, dyke, and women's communities. Hence, many FTMs and transgender butches' self-constructions still embody or pay historical debt to dyke nomenclature.[8]

Ali: I will always feel connected to the life I lived as a lesbian. My former self informs who I am in so many ways: the way I make love, the centrality of lesbians in my life, the anti-oppression models I've learned and still adhere to. I can't imagine a time in my life in the future when I wouldn't still make proud reference to my former dyke identity. That will always be something I am walking around with and that lends itself to much of my consciousness as a feminist transgender man who opposes gender-based discrimination of any kind.

TJ: Gender oppression, to me, is this culture saying there's two, and only two, things you can be. If you're not a man, you're a woman, period. Sure, there's more room to deviate presentation nowadays, but at times it feels like it's merely some androgynous vortex—Gap-mentality consumerism—that has sucked us all in. I'm much more interested in broadening our gender imaginations, not merely blending what's already in front of us, nor calling for a third gender, which really only winds up reinforcing the hegemonic two.[9] And at the same time, not feel forced to abandon the tradition and rituals, in our case Judaism, that contribute such richness and spiritual meaning to our lives.

Ali: I think we learned from our respective visits to the Wall and this discussion that we can begin to carve a space for transgender people within our culture. My wife and I did exactly that by having a huge Jewish wedding.

A lesbian Reform rabbi married us—a transgender man and a bisexual woman. Jessica and I were married under *a chuppah* created by our family and friends. We circled one another seven times, exchanged rings, and recited the Hebrew declaration of commitment: "Behold you are sanctified to me with this ring in keeping with the traditions of Moses, Miriam, and Israel before our God and this community."[10]

We felt it was a radical act to use the same words Jewish brides and grooms have been saying for centuries, even though our union would not have been previously sanctioned by Jewish law.

Our parents held our ketubah and passed it to us, symbolizing the blessing of the generations, and they wrapped us in my tallis. Honored members of our community blessed us, based on themes of the Sheva Brachot.

---

7. Hale, "Tracing a Ghostly Memory in My Throat: Reflections on FTM Feminist Voice and Agency," in *Men Doing Feminism*, Tom Digby, ed. (New York: Routledge, 1998), pp. 101–103.
8. While there are multiple formal and informal community sources for this, one of the earliest documented accounts of FTMs on their butch and lesbian affiliations is in Deva, "FTM/Female-to-Male: An Interview with Mike, Eric, Billy, Sky and Shadow," in *Dagger: On Butch Women*, Lily Burana, Roxxie, and Linnea Due, eds. (San Francisco: Cleis Press, 1994).
9. Halberstam, "An Introduction to Female Masculinity," p. 26.
10. The addition of the biblical matriarch Miriam was added to the traditional declaration at Ali and Jessica's wedding to denote female representations within the People of the Book.

Our ceremony was transformative for us, for those in attendance, for Judaism itself. We claimed our right to have all the deep elements of a Jewish wedding, before God, and we made them our own. By doing so, under the *chuppah,* with the blessing of our rabbi, we insisted upon the inclusion of our love within the Jewish tradition.

TJ: Wow, Ali, it's beautiful to hear how you and Jessica have updated our customs in ways meaningful to you both, while preserving the sanctity of their origins.

I'm also trying to strike the balance between transformation and tradition. We both participate in the same lesbian, gay, bisexual, and transgender synagogue. But who doesn't notice the dominance among gay men first, then lesbian women? It seems as if bisexual and transgender Jews, as is the case with many community institutions, are erased. It is up to these individuals, not the congregation as a whole, to make efforts to fit in or not, educate others, or keep quiet.

I nonetheless find myself uncomfortable with all the tweaked passages, prayers, and melodies of the synagogue's siddur. Admittedly, there are times that I, and several of my friends, are annoyed that the neutralization of Hebrew has gone so overboard that the familiar Judaism we were raised with is no longer recognizable. Understandably though, the amended wording is highly significant to many congregants, mostly women, alienated by the original text.

So in addition to our progressive synagogue, I have alternatively sought out a more traditional place of worship that would welcome me as openly queer: namely, a neighborhood Chabad-Lubavitch house. While this young rabbi and rebbetzin have embraced me from the start, as Chassids, they observe *halachic* sex roles. Recently, while celebrating Simchas Torah there, I knew the rabbi sensed my disappointment at the need to have two separate circles of dancing. To avoid confrontation, it was, of course, vital that I locate myself among the women. But it was also strategically necessary for me to become one: the *mechitzah* has become a call for me to ally myself with those oppressed by it. Interestingly, as the rabbi proceeded to offer rounds of *l'chaim* to the men, he poured shots of whiskey for his butch guest, too, opening the access of partaking in this particular *mitzvah* to all in attendance. Additionally, he has made it quite clear to me that I may bring whomever I please to his Shabbos table, and so I have.

To varying degrees, I apply pressure as well as applaud progress at both settings—be it the LGBT Reform congregation, where I was initially welcomed because of my queerness, or the ultra-Orthodox shul, where I was initially welcomed because of my Jewishness. Undoubtedly, as I flitter back and forth, I reinforce my location as an inhabitant of fluctuating margins. It is much easier to live in this body as a construction that I've carved out, rather than as a set of identities that were pushed out.

Judith Halberstam has suggested that "butches and FTMs alike think carefully about the kinds of men or masculine beings that we become and lay claim to: alternative masculinities, ultimately, will fail to change existing gender hierarchies to the extent that they fail to be feminist, antiracist, antielitist, and queer."

A Jewish FTM friend of mine likens Halberstam's *tikkun olam*–like call as embodying all that it means to be a mensch. Throughout our struggles, I think it would serve us well individually and as a community to keep this in mind as we continue to participate in our shuls, at our Shabbos tables and simchas, before God, as Jews. Just as we seek to interpret the positive values within our texts, so too, should we embody progressive definitions of our genders.

I would like to think that we each had a nascent version of Halberstam's vision, conscious or subconscious, when we each went to the Wall, motivating us to act accordingly, in ways truest to ourselves and our communities, given the constraints.

Ali: I think we each challenged the gender hierarchy that exists at the Wall by going there as transgender Jews while in a place of inventing ourselves. Our conversation has made connections in a way that no longer isolates our transgressive experiences in Israel. I'm hopeful about the manner in which we are bringing our trans selves to Jewish institutions, the way we are bringing Jewish identity into the transgender fold. Overall, the act of having this dialogue helps mediate the possibility of differently gendered understandings within the Jewish community, within Judaism itself.

The Journey of Congregational Inclusion

One of the greatest strengths of the Reform Movement is its openness to a variety of different types of Jews, whether by birth (by matrilineal or patrilineal descent) or by choice. Through the missions of outreach and inclusion, thousands of Jews who would have otherwise remained unaffiliated have entered our synagogues' doors and felt welcomed. What they have brought to our communities—their passion, their knowledge, and their skills—have enriched the Reform Movement beyond measure. Indeed, by ensuring that our communities are welcoming and inclusive, we are creating strong and vibrant congregations.

The importance of inclusion and welcome for gay, lesbian, bisexual, and transgender Jews has long been a commitment of Reform Jewish policies. Starting in the mid 1980s and greatly supported by UAHC (now known as URJ) president Rabbi Alexander Schindler (z"l), who spoke out and said that mainstream congregations must take active steps to welcome gay and lesbian Jews, synagogues have had a charge to welcome GLBT Jews into their congregations and allow them to bring their unique contributions to the community. This section explores how congregations can begin the journey of inclusion and ultimately make their communities a safe and welcoming place for GLBT Jews to share *their* passion, *their* knowledge, and *their* skills.

Among other topics, this section includes the following:

- Several articles outlining concrete steps for congregations to create an open and welcoming atmosphere for GLBT Jews
- Classroom- and school-based educational resources on ways to reduce prejudice against those who are GLBT
- Information on ways the URJ Regional Offices can help promote GLBT inclusion in synagogues

The World's Original Gay and Lesbian Synagogue: Why There Is (Still) a Place for Us

Rabbi Lisa A. Edwards, Ph.D.

In 1972, it was simple enough: few gay and lesbian Jews felt welcome in Judaism or in most synagogues. Rejection by families and clergy had caused many lesbian, gay, bisexual, and transgender Jews to drift away (or be driven away) from the communities in which they grew up. Such departures, however, did not mean these folks no longer felt a need for a spiritual home.

In the late 1960s and early 1970s, several gay Jews began to attend a "rap group" with the Reverend Troy Perry, founder of the first gay and lesbian Christian congregation, Metropolitan Community Church (MCC), in Los Angeles. Though most welcoming, Reverend Perry also encouraged his Jewish friends to form a synagogue and helped them garner the support of Rabbi Erwin Herman, then director of the Pacific Southwest Region of the Union of American Hebrew Congregations (UAHC; now Union for Reform Judaism [URJ]). In 1972, the Metropolitan Community Temple (MCT) became an official Jewish congregation, and two years later, in 1974, with Rabbi Herman's help, MCT became BCC—Beth Chayim Chadashim (House of New Life). When BCC became a member congregation of UAHC in 1974, it was the first gay and lesbian congregation ever to be voted in as a member organization of *any* mainstream religious organization.

From their inception, the gay and lesbian synagogues that sprung up across the United States were radical change agents. In 1974, BCC pioneered the first gender-sensitive prayer book. The very existence of the congregation also helped inspire new liturgy and rituals. For example, Savina Teubal's *Simchat Hochma* (Joy of Wisdom) ceremony, marking her transition from adult to elder, took place at BCC in 1986 and brought with it the creation and premier of Debbie Friedman's now famous song "L'chi Lach." In the early years of the AIDS crisis, BCC and other gay and lesbian synagogues developed new "caring community" models and created healing services that are now widespread in the Reform Movement.

More than three decades later, much has been accomplished, but much still remains to be done. Despite the 1990 decision by the Central Conference of American Rabbis (CCAR) to welcome GLBT Jews into rabbinical and cantorial programs, and despite verbal support from the URJ to invite GLBT people and their families into our congregations, many

GLBT people still find a gap between the public words of support and everyday inclusion. I have been BCC's rabbi since 1994, and every time I begin to think progress toward actual inclusion is being made, something will come along to remind me "not yet."

These reminders come when I'll get a call from a gay colleague whose contract was not renewed or learn of a same-gender wedding ceremony banished from the synagogue's sanctuary. Sometimes it's just a subtle remark in private or at a board meeting, such as, "Why do you have to be so open about your private life? People don't care." "Why don't they care?" I ask. They seem to care whether straight rabbis are happily married. But of course, that's not exactly what they meant.

At the congregational level, even today there are few mainstream synagogues with GLBT membership above a token number, and even fewer where same-gender relationships are afforded the open respect and celebration that straight couples receive. Imagine the isolation of the children of these couples. For that matter, imagine the isolation of the "mainstream" membership whose own gay children, whether adolescent or adult, experience rejection from their parents' synagogue community.

It is not insignificant that the heads of Hebrew Union College–Jewish Institute of Religion (HUC-JIR) and the URJ are speaking out loudly for marriage equality. However, the proportion of GLBT members at "pluralistic" congregations will remain below the proportion of GLBT Jews in any given area until groups of congregants become proactive in their own communities to educate themselves about GLBT culture, figure out what they can genuinely offer to prospective GLBT members, and maintain open and ongoing dialogues with each other and their GLBT members about feelings, perceptions, and needs. Believing that GLBT Jews are fundamentally not different from other Jews can only come from action. "We will do and we will understand"—*naaseh v'nishma*—say the Israelites in response to God's commandments given at Mount Sinai (Exodus 24:7). Sometimes it takes doing the work, acting a certain way, before we come to understand what it means to do so.

Why do GLBT Jews choose GLBT synagogues? For me it is still pretty simple: I want my congregation to be my center, the center from which I can go out into the world and help change it, using Jewish values and ethics, which I continually study and practice at home with my community. If I have a choice between a congregation that will go out into the world with me and one in which I'll spend a lot of time needing to work on changes right there, I choose the former.

The Reform Movement has continued, for over thirty years already, to be leaders in the acceptance of GLBT people. In his 2004–2005 address to the URJ regional conferences, URJ president Eric Yoffie gave a rousing and relatively lengthy declaration of support for GLBT people and against the religious right in this country (see pages 343–44). And yet, despite his call to action that very morning, at the regional conference that I and 500 other Reform Jews attended, only 10 people attended the workshop about making synagogues GLBT inclusive. Today, more than ever, Reform Jews feel and voice their support of equality for GLBT people, but only in small numbers do they seem willing to make equality a priority for their own work of *tikkun olam*.

Lack of full acceptance by the mainstream is hardly a reason for GLBT congregations to succeed and thrive, but thrive we do. Several years ago, an anthology was published with the marvelous title *Twice Blessed: On Being Gay or Lesbian and Jewish*. The title continues to remind me of what it means to be in a GLBT Jewish community: It implies being part of a community of people doubly aware of how it feels to be "other" and of what it is like to be rejected or suspect or oppressed. It also implies, consequently, a community of people more determined than your average "pluralistic" Reform congregation to be inclusive, to embrace diversity, to give voice to all its members, to actively seek members different from our "mainstream," to be vigilant about creating a welcoming and caring community for all who seek to join us, to continually challenge each member to be out in the world doing good works, and to create a place where our children learn through our examples what it means to live a Jewish life. Does this sound harmonious? Does it sound simple? Not always, of course, but we nonetheless stand by our commitment to be a place of safe haven, spiritual sustenance, and a value-laden Jewish community for all.

What Makes a Congregation Welcoming?

Bernard Schlager, Ph.D.

1. Meaningful integration of LGBT people into congregational membership and leadership
2. Sponsorship of dialogue between LGBT people and others on a variety of topics
3. Committees devoted to LGBT persons and their concerns
4. Educational opportunities for LGBT persons and their allies
5. Ministry to LGBT persons inside and outside the religious community
6. Involvement in larger religious LGBT causes and/or movements
7. Development of theological statements of welcome and inclusion for LGBT persons
8. Production of sermons, pamphlets, and other materials pertaining to LGBT persons and their concerns
9. Advocacy of debate and positive change within larger religious organizations (e.g., denominations, national or regional alliances) re: LGBT persons and LGBT-affirming ministries
10. Congregations display remarkable degree of openness to contemporary ideas and trends
11. Congregations place high value on work/service focused outside the synagogue/church
12. Congregations emphasize "an activist approach to social action" vs. more traditional approaches which leave social action up to individual congregants' initiative

---

This list is taken from a 2004 report entitled "With Open Arms: Gay Affirming Ministries in Bay Area Faith Communities" by Bernard Schlager, Ph.D. The report, funded by the Evelyn and Walter Haas, Jr. Fund, examined how Bay Area religious communities developed supportive congregations for LGBT people; it also outlines strategies to further promote gay-affirming congregations and increase dialogue about LGBT issues within larger denominational groups. Bernard Schlager, "With Open Arms: Gay Affirming Ministries in Bay Area Faith Communities," Center for Lesbian and Gay Studies in Religion and Ministry, http://www.clgs.org/5/open_arms.html (accessed October 13, 2006).

Welcoming GLBT Jews into Our Synagogues: A Congregational Self-Study Guide

Rabbi Margaret Moers Wenig; updated by Joel L. Kushner, Psy.D.

Truly welcoming lesbian, gay, bisexual, and transgender Jews into our synagogues means appreciating their gifts, allowing them and their concerns to be visible, and eliminating heterosexual biases.

Bernard Schlager writes:

> Any process of welcoming means that the congregation at large will necessarily be transformed by the GLBT people who are invited to live as "out" members of the congregation. Those congregations that fear such transformations are not ready to incorporate in any meaningful way GLBT people who bring unique gifts, talents, and needs to the community-at-large and perhaps even challenge their non-GLBT coreligionists in ways that may make some of them profoundly uncomfortable. To welcome GLBT people into congregations of faith is risky business precisely because it is an invitation that involves change on the part of those who have the power to do the welcoming.[1]

To begin a process of congregational self-reflection, Rabbi Wenig offers the following guide that addresses specific areas in congregational life. It asks direct questions about

---

This article was first prepared for a workshop at a UAHC regional biennial. It was subsequently published in "Welcoming Lesbian and Gay Jews into Our Synagogues," *New Menorah*, Spring 1991; then reprinted in "A Guide for *Kehillot Mekablot* (Welcoming Congregations)," in *Homosexuality and Judaism: A Reconstructionst Workshop Series*, ed. Rabbi Robert Gluck (Wyncote, PA: Reconstructionist Press, 1992); and again in "Kaafikim Banegev: A Manual for Rabbis to Engage their Communities," in *Embracing Lesbian and Gay Jews*, ed. Sara Paasche, David Rosen, and J. B. Sacks (for the 1994 convention of the Rabbinical Assembly of the Conservative Movement). Her second checklist, "Beyond Acceptance: Meeting the Needs of Your Lesbian and Gay Congregants" was included in the first edition of *Kulanu* in 1996. This current version has been updated by Joel L. Kushner, Psy.D., for this edition of *Kulanu*, with permission from the author, Rabbi Margaret Moers Wenig.

1. Bernard Schlager, "With Open Arms: Gay Affirming Ministries in Bay Area Faith Communities," Center for Lesbian and Gay Studies in Religion and Ministry, http://www.clgs.org/5/open_arms.html (accessed October 13, 2006).

concrete items such as application forms as well as asking more philosophical questions about attitude and behavior. The answers to these questions do not end with a response of "yes" or "no." Rather, the answers are a launch point for ongoing discussion over time that should involve increasingly larger numbers of people in the congregational community. Engaging in such a reflection process takes both courage and patience. It cannot be done as a short-term fix, and it cannot be done without enlisting support and partnership among the clergy, staff, and members of the actual community.

Clergy and Lay Leadership

Sermons

Is the presence of GLBT people in our congregation/community/families ever evident in the word we hear from the pulpit?

Do sermons ever address (directly or in passing) events/issues of concern to GLBT people (e.g., marriage equality, adoption rights, discrimination against homosexuals in the armed services, positions of politicians and nominees for judicial appointments, Lesbian and Gay Rights March on Washington, AIDS)?

Do the rabbi's sermons presume that all Jews have been, are, or want to be married or to bear children? Or, are words such as "committed relationship" and "raising children" used instead, as not all same-gender couples can get married or bear children?

Liturgy

Is the clergy comfortable incorporating and using new liturgy and rituals that address the life-cycle events of GLBT people? Do they know where to find such liturgy (e.g, union ceremonies, coming-out prayers, transitioning blessings, rituals of separation)?

Do we invite people to add names of lovers/partners/husbands/wives to the *Mi Shebeirach* list? And, do we say "John, lover of our member David" or "Sarah, wife of our member Joan"?

Do we include people with AIDS, "whose names we are not free to mention," in our *Mi Shebeirach* prayer for those who are sick, along with those whose names we can mention?

Do we invite people to add the names of close friends to the *Mi Shebeirach* list? Inherent in this, do we recognize that many GLBT people have created a family of choice that is equal in their eyes to the biological family they may no longer be connected to?

Do GLBT couples receive joint *aliyot* and anniversary blessings?

May GLBT couples celebrate *kiddushin* (Jewish holy union) in our sanctuary? Will our rabbi or cantor officiate?

May GLBT families name children (born by artificial insemination, surrogacy, or adopted) in our sanctuary?

When a child is named and we say, *K'shem shenichnas lab'rit, kein yikaneis laTorah, ul'chuppah ul'maasim tovim* (Just as he/she has entered the covenant, so may he/she be introduced to Torah, chuppah, and deeds of loving-kindness), how is *chuppah* translated? As "marriage"? If so, since Reform Jews have the option to have a *kiddushin* ceremony but civil marriage is not yet allowed for all Jews (in the United States), one might say instead, "So may he/she be introduced to Torah and deeds of loving-kindness, and may he/she someday find her/his love," thus eliminating a heterosexist bias with the focus on marriage.

In our Yom HaShoah service, if victims other than Jews are mentioned, are gay men included?

In our home and congregational seders and in our printed Haggadot, when oppressed groups other than Jews are mentioned, are lesbian, gay, bisexual, and transgender people included?

If contemporary poetry, readings, and musical compositions are ever included in our liturgy, are works by GLBT authors/composers included?

Could our congregation celebrate Lesbian and Gay Pride Shabbat or a Pride Seder in June during Gay Pride Month?

When the Song of Songs is read on the intermediate Shabbat of Pesach, might a woman read/chant passages that speak of love for a woman, and a man read/chant passages that speak of love for a man?

When the love between God and Israel is described liturgically, is it always put in heterosexual terms? When the love between Israel and Shabbat is described liturgically, is it always put in heterosexual terms? What other language could we use?

Pastoral Care

When a supposedly "single" member is sick or dies, is the rabbi sensitive to the possibility that there may be a surviving same-gender partner/spouse? Does the rabbi ask the patient about the important relationships in his or her life? Does the rabbi remain in contact with the partner/spouse during the member's illness? Does the rabbi consult with that person in the preparations for the funeral and eulogy?

If our synagogue ever distributes, or publishes in the monthly bulletin, information about legal issues such as living wills or funeral planning, does that information presume heterosexuality or does it also include information for GLBT people? Does the bulletin or program include information on domestic partnerships, wills, cohabitation agreements, co-parent agreements, and advanced directives? If recommendations are being given, does the information include a list of attorneys who specialize in helping GLBT people gain these needed protections?

Does our congregation arrange shivah minyans for members who have lost lovers/partners/husbands/wives or siblings/equivalents? (As noted, often GLBT people establish families of choice and become as sisters and brothers to each other, especially when they have been estranged from their biological families. One can grieve over an "adopted" sister or brother just like a biological one.)

Visibility

Are GLBT Jews in visible positions of leadership in our congregation as trustees, committee chairs, lay service leaders (e.g., Torah readers, shofar blowers), teachers, youth advisors, administrative staff, clergy?

Are lesbian, gay, bisexual, or transgender people ever invited to speak to the congregation as guest lecturers, scholars in residence, keynote speakers, and so on? (Or do we give the impression that all "experts in their field," all politicians, historians, psychologists, educators, etc., are heterosexual?)

Has our congregation ever given an award to or testimonial dinner for a GLBT person?

Are GLBT couples able to feel comfortable to hold hands in our synagogue? Or, is it only okay if they come to services as long as they don't touch each other?

When our children leave for college and beyond, if they turn out to be lesbian/gay/bisexual or transgender, will they feel comfortable bringing their girlfriend/boyfriend home for the weekend and to synagogue on Friday night? Will they feel free to hold hands and kiss each other "*Gut Shabbes*" in public?

Will our GLBT children consider a *kiddushin* ceremony? Will they feel comfortable asking our rabbi to officiate?

Social Action

Are there GLBT people on the social action committee?

Are GLBT concerns reflected in the work of the social action committee and in the educational programs sponsored by the committee?

Remember: fighting for GLBT rights in America is not a onetime project but an ongoing struggle, conducted on numerous fronts, and in response to specific crises as they arise.

Sisterhood

Are lesbian, bisexual, or transgender women in our Sisterhood invisible? Do they feel welcome as they are, or do they feel that to be involved in the Sisterhood they must remain in the closet?

Are issues of concern to lesbian, bisexual, or transgender women on our Sisterhood's agenda?

Are our Sisterhood meetings accessible to single and working mothers? Is child care provided?

Brotherhood

Are gay, bisexual, or transgender men in our Brotherhood invisible? Do they feel welcome as they are, or do they feel that to be involved in the Brotherhood they must remain in the closet?

Are issues of concern to gay, bisexual, or transgender men on our Brotherhood's agenda?

Are our Brotherhood meetings accessible to single and working fathers? Is child care provided?

Religious School and Youth Group

Does our application say "parent 1, parent 2" and with room for more to support co-parenting families as well as families with divorced parents, or do our forms still say "mother and father"?

What about our permission forms for trips and other documents requiring signatures?

Are letters to home addressed to parents or to "moms"?

Do our textbooks, teaching materials, community presentations, and hands-on projects render GLBT people invisible or betray a heterosexual bias?

When family is referred to verbally or portrayed in photographs, is it always a heterosexual family?

Does our school library have books for all age levels that reflect diverse families and life stories?

How would a child of gay co-parents, a child of a single lesbian mother, or a child with a transgender dad and a straight mother feel in our school? Would he/she feel comfortable talking about his/her family? Are his gay co-parents listed as co-parents in religious school address lists? Are both invited to events for parents?

Does our synagogue provide any support for the children of GLBT parents? Could our synagogue host a local chapter or invite a presentation by COLAGE (Children of Lesbians and Gays Everywhere)?

How would a teenager in our school or youth group who is struggling with his/her sexual identity feel at social events? In discussions of Jewish sexual ethics? In discussions about contraceptives? Is safe sex, in the context of loving monogamous relationships, discussed without disparaging comments being made about same-gender couples?

Are our youth group events safe and accessible for queer and questioning teenagers (e.g., dances, support groups)?

How do the adults and teachers respond when they hear kids call each other "fag," "gay," "sissy," and so on?

Does the school do annual training for teachers on tolerance, bullying, and/or GLBT issues?

Does our synagogue provide any support for the parents of lesbians and gay men? Is there a need for a parents' group? Could our synagogue host a local chapter of PFLAG (Parents, Families and Friends of Lesbians and Gays)?

Do we expose our children to any positive lesbian and gay role models (in teachers, clergy, fictional/movie/theater characters)?

Social Events

Would a lesbian/gay couple or single GLBT members or prospective members feel welcome at our social events?

Could people of the same gender dance together?

Could gay folks dance with straight folks?

Can GLBT people talk freely about their work/lives at the *Oneg Shabbat* or the Brotherhood breakfast?

If, in our community, there is no GLBT community center and no lesbian or gay bars, restaurants, or places to meet, talk, and dance, could our synagogue rent space to GLBT people for social or communal events (as synagogues often rent space to AA, Scouts [another issue for the congregation to discuss], or other groups)? Could our synagogue sponsor social events for single GLBT Jews (e.g., speed dating, potluck supper, trip to the Jewish museum)?

Administration

Employment

Does our congregation have a written policy of nondiscrimination on the basis of sexual orientation and gender expression? Do search committees make that policy explicit when seeking placement assistance from the NATE (National Association of Temple Educators), NATA (National Association of Temple Administrators), CCAR (Central Conference of American Rabbis), or ACC (American Conference of Cantors) and when interviewing applicants? Or do employees and prospective employees feel they must remain in the closet?

Does our congregation extend "spousal benefits" to the partners of our employees? Is the health insurance we provide for a GLBT person with a partner an individual or a family policy? Does our congregation provide paid leave days for an employee to care for a sick "partner" or to mourn his/her death?

Does our congregation invite "partners" to events for employees and their families (e.g., Teacher Appreciation Shabbat)?

Membership

Do our membership conditions/materials presume heterosexuality or discriminate against lesbians, gays, bisexuals, and transgender people and their families?

If we have family memberships, do they apply to GLBT couples?

Does our application say "member 1 and member 2" and then ask "relationship," or does it say "husband and wife"?

Do we ask about marital status on our membership application? (Remember, lesbian and gay couples are not allowed to marry in most states.) Do we list another category besides "married" or "single"? Or, can we just ask the person to fill in the relationship?

When we ask, "Would you like the name of a family member included on our *yahrzeit* list?" do we also invite GLBT members to name deceased partners/spouses and close friends (who may have been the emotional equivalent of a brother/sister)?

Publicity

Do we have an official statement of welcoming and inclusion for GLBT people? Where is it published? On our Web site, in our promotional materials, in our newsletter, on the table at the entrance to the synagogue office along with all our other materials?

Have we joined the Institute for Judaism and Sexual Orientation (www.huc.edu/IJSO) or the World Congress of GLBT Jews—Keshet Ga'avah (www.glbtjews.org) or other such Jewish GLBT organization as a sign of our welcome? Is that membership noted in our materials and on our Web site?

Is the presence of GLBT Jews in our community/congregation visible in our publicity? Will we announce same gender-marriages and births/adoptions in the *simchah* section of our synagogue newsletter?

Do notices of events for "couples" make explicit that same-gender couples are welcome?

Do notices of events for "families" make it explicit that lesbians and gay men (as single parents or as co-parents) are welcome with their children? (Or is the parent/toddler group called "Mommy, Daddy, and Me"?)

In which publications does our synagogue advertise its activities? Could we list our activities in publications read by GLBT people (such as *Frontiers*, *The Native*, or travel guides such as *Places of Interest* and *The Women's Traveler*, both of which list places of worship)?

As a sign of solidarity and welcome, can our synagogue march with a temple banner in the local gay pride parade? Or can we have a booth, along with other religious organizations, at pride festivals in our area, that share who we are and our welcoming community?

Gays and Lesbians in Mainstream Congregations: A Case Study of Temple Beth-El of Great Neck, New York

John E. Hirsch, Ph.D.

Background

By the time of the 1987 Union of American Hebrew Congregations (UAHC) Biennial in Chicago, four congregations in Los Angeles, San Francisco, Chicago, and Miami with special outreach to gays and lesbians had been admitted to the Union. While some thought that including these congregations was enough of an outreach to gays and lesbians, some of us brought to the floor of the plenary a resolution to admit and welcome gay men and lesbians into "mainstream" congregations. At the urging of Rabbi Alexander Schindler, president of the UAHC, a second resolution was presented at the 1989 Biennial in New Orleans welcoming gays and lesbians into congregations not merely as individuals, but as couples and families. Subsequent Biennials saw additional resolutions, including one calling for civil recognition of same-sex marriage.

Temple Beth-El of Great Neck, New York, was one of the first—and is still one of the strongest—congregations to actively welcome gays and lesbians into the community. This article gives some examples of what Temple Beth-El did to include GLBT Jews and illustrates some of the steps the synagogue took to help create this inclusiveness. It shows how the welcoming of GLBT Jews had a positive impact on the congregation as a whole and provides several specific steps any "mainstream congregation" can take to promote GLBT inclusion.

Temple Beth-El of Great Neck Gay and Lesbian Inclusion Committee

The Gay and Lesbian Inclusion Committee was originally formed as a standing committee of Temple Beth-El of Great Neck in 1991 as the Gay and Lesbian Inreach Committee (GLIC). At that time, the committee consisted of a few gay members of the congregation and three sets of parents who were members of the congregation with gay or lesbian adult children. It was formed for the mission of educating the congregation about the gay and lesbian issues that had been identified by the UAHC and to make it clear to closeted gay members and closeted member families with gay or lesbian adult children that Temple Beth-El was truly inclusive. In this process, the committee also reached out to gay and lesbian nonmembers. However, after some years, the first mission seemed to have been accomplished, with the Committee firmly entrenched at the congregation, and the words "gay" and "lesbian" were no longer a surprise in sermons, bulletin articles, and programming. The outreach into the larger Long Island community of gays and lesbians became a more prominent mission, and a change of name seemed appropriate. Nearly a decade later, when its mission of "inreach" had clearly shifted to inclusion, the committee became the "Gay and Lesbian *Inclusion* Committee."

Over the years, the committee formed coalitions with other arms of the synagogue for special projects or events. These coalitions have been with, among others, the Caring Community Committee, the Social Action Committee, and the Brotherhood/Sisterhood. Because members of GLIC saw opportunities to work with these organizations toward mutual goals, members of GLIC have served on both the Caring Community Committee and the Social Action Committee. Indeed, the founder of GLIC had been one of the founders of the Caring Community of Temple Beth-El of Great Neck in the 1980s.

Here are several examples of what GLIC was able to do in conjunction with other synagogue committees:

- GLIC's fifteen-year-old December holiday toy drive to benefit children infected with or affected by HIV/AIDS has expanded to a major synagogue-wide drive, with GLIC organizing and leading the way. Every year, GLIC has been able to provide a truck filled with new toys, games, and books for a major hospital's HIV/AIDS Program—enough to last them from one Chanukah to the next. In December 2005, when GLIC announced its annual drive, the chair started receiving calls from various synagogue arms: first was the Caring Community, then the director of education in the religious school, then the director of the Early Childhood Development Center, then Sisterhood. They all were asking if they could help collect toys. Finally, a member of Brotherhood offered his truck to help transport the collection to the hospital. In the "old days," GLIC had to seek out these coalitions; now they come knocking.
- The Social Action Committee has been a natural for a coalition with GLIC, with opportunities to present topics of special interest to gay and lesbian members of the synagogue as well as to the larger community. GLIC found, from its earliest days, that gays and lesbians are interested in many of the same issues as their Social Action counterparts: politics, Israel, local government, and health care. For the last several years, Social Action has presented evening roundtable discussions with guest speakers on a variety of topics. Not only were gay and lesbian topics such as marriage and gay rights on the program, but gay and lesbian members of the committee were instrumental in creating and facilitating these roundtables.
- Several times, when the Sisterhood and Brotherhood were planning a social event, they called upon GLIC to participate. My favorite example was a Saturday evening country western square dance and dinner. No one was surprised at men dancing with men, women dancing with women, and even men dancing with women.
- For a number of years, during "Gay Pride Month" in June prior to the Long Island Gay Pride March, a picnic and fair were held in a series of Long Island parks. Various groups

participated by setting up tables advertising their organizations, such as PFLAG (Parents and Friends of Lesbians and Gays), DIGNITY (a national gay Catholic group), various AIDS care groups, the Unitarian Universalists, and of course, Temple Beth-El of Great Neck, with banners, brochures, and volunteers to describe the outreach of the synagogue. As a result, GLIC currently has a mailing list of over 300 people—young, old, gay, lesbian, bisexual, transgender, straight, members, nonmembers, residents of Great Neck, and residents as far away as Westchester, New Jersey, and the Hamptons.

- Every year since its founding, GLIC has also hosted three holiday celebrations for the gay and lesbian community of Long Island. These three events—a Sukkot potluck supper, a Chanukah party, and a Pesach supper—are open not only to synagogue members (straight and gay) but to friends and family members as well. Appropriate holiday music is provided by the cantor, and one or more of the rabbis attend, contributing interesting information about the specific holiday or a brief ceremony.

GLIC is also proud that through its outreach, several people have been drawn to Temple Beth-El and have become Jews-by-choice. We consider this among our most important contributions, not just for the congregation, but for the entire Jewish people. While neither Temple Beth-El nor GLIC have actively sought converts to Judaism from among the GLBT community, the congregation's reputation for inclusiveness as exemplified by GLIC and its outreach to gays and lesbians has created an atmosphere of welcome. Several of those converts have been in longtime partnerships with born Jews, some have come to us prior to their same-sex marriages to Jews, and one of the most remarkable has been one person without family ties to Judaism who has chosen to join us. Many of those who attend our Sukkot potlucks, Chanukah parties, and Pesach suppers are not Jewish. Our invitations always state that we are open "to gay and lesbian Jews, their families and friends"—we check no one's credentials at the door. As we all understand from the very ceremony of conversion, like all other converts to Judaism, these special Jews add strength to *K'lal Yisrael*.

It should be noted that a major reason why Temple Beth-El has been able to be so active in gay and lesbian issues is that its rabbis have championed GLBT causes and have been leaders in the fight for same-sex marriage, officiating at numerous ceremonies not only outside of the facility, but in its Rabbi Jacob Philip Rudin Chapel and its main sanctuary as well. The temple's senior rabbi, Jerome K. Davidson, was one of the leaders at the Central Conference of American Rabbis (CCAR) to press for its acceptance of the right of Reform rabbis to officiate at same-sex marriages. At Temple Beth-El of Great Neck, babies of same-sex couples have been named publicly in the same ceremonies as the children of heterosexual couples. Anniversaries of same-sex couples are publicly acknowledged along with those of heterosexual couples. Also, in one of the most moving shows of support, in 2000, Rabbi Davidson arranged for a waiver from the state of Vermont permitting him to officiate at a same-sex civil union and Jewish wedding ceremony. He traveled five and a half hours each way to officiate at this civil union and marriage in Brattleboro, Vermont.

GLIC has now been completely integrated into the larger congregational community. Two weeks before Shavuot in 2006, several members of the congregation congratulated me on the decision to show the film *Trembling Before G-d*, a film about gay and lesbian Orthodox Jews, at the annual *Leil Shavuot* program. I was amused to inform them that neither GLIC nor I had a hand in the decision, and it was the first I had heard about it. It was a hugely successful program planned totally by the rabbis, even outpacing the cheesecake served.

Today, an openly gay man and a lesbian serve on Temple Beth-El's Board of Trustees—not so much representing the GLBT communities, but as active and fully participating members of the congregation. They and others serve in various leadership capacities and are recognized for their contributions to the well-being of Temple Beth-El of Great Neck.

What Synagogues Can Do

Here are some basic steps that can be imitated for a congregation wanting to implement GLBT inclusion following in the footprints of Temple Beth-El of Great Neck:

- **Form an ad hoc committee of GLBT people and family members of GLBT people.** Having as broad a base as possible will benefit the effort. A person with a "fire in the belly" can work wonders. The more we worked and were visible in the congregation, the more people with close family members who were gay or lesbian felt comfortable to "come out" to us—they were our unseen constituency. Over the years, there have been a number of synagogue members who have been empowered by this visibility to have the confidence to discuss their concern and to seek advice about their own questioning teenage or younger children.
- **Examine the congregation's bylaws to see if there is any impediment for inclusion.** The bylaws of some congregations, for example, identify "family" in an old-fashioned, noninclusive way—husband, wife, and children. Similar issues may need to be addressed. The ad hoc committee should have a plan of action with answers to possible questions. A congregation cannot begin to welcome GLBT Jews in the larger community if only second-class membership is offered. Using terms such as "adult 1 and adult 2" or "member 1 and member 2" is preferable to "husband and wife"; likewise, "parent 1 and parent 2" on nursery or religious school forms is preferable to "mother and father."
- **Be prepared.** Take a carefully planned proposal to the board of your congregation. Ask for board action such as a formal resolution. It can be as simple as one to recognize or implement the URJ resolutions about the subject. Lobby, lobby, lobby for these very important changes. People of goodwill do not wish to be seen as discriminatory. The ultimate argument is that this is "good for the synagogue," since it could bring in members and make members already there feel more comfortable.
- **Start a process of education.** Talk with your rabbi, since rabbinic support is very important. Plan educational programs for the board and then for the congregation, the religious school committee and/or faculty, and possibly the larger community. At this point, coalitions with congregational committees such as caring community, social action, and the like should be formed.
- **Visibility is important.** GLBT couples should feel comfortable to kiss or hug one another at the conclusion of Shabbat services and other appropriate times just as straight people do. This includes dancing together at congregational social events and holding hands with their partner. Form a speakers bureau. Organize a contingent to participate in gay pride marches, carrying the synagogue banner. Host a pre–pride march brunch.

Bulletin articles and presentations should always use the "GLBT words"—gay, lesbian, bisexual, and transgender as appropriate. This will help make the congregation comfortable. Use these words often and in a variety of contexts and venues. Advertise programs widely in the larger community; the local press is a good idea.
- **Plan events appropriate to the particular synagogue and community.** Temple Beth-El used holidays (Sukkot, Chanukah, and Pesach) for event planning, as we found that religiously based or educational events were a better first start than purely social events; those can come later. Be inclusive in these events—creating a congregation within a congregation is not the best way to become welcoming and inclusive.
- **Begin to utilize the coalitions formed in the synagogue.** Invite the social action committee to work on a GLBT social action project. Offer to cosponsor the Sisterhood/Brotherhood fall square dance (making sure that the gays and lesbians attending will be made comfortable to dance). Help plan, prepare for, and implement the event. It never hurts for the GLBT committee to become dependable and indispensable.
- **Work with the clergy and congregational staff.** Begin to have public life-cycle events in the synagogue such as baby namings, anniversary acknowledgments, and weddings.
- **Do not be obnoxious, but be assertive and even pushy if you have to be.** Equality is not given, it is demanded.

Our tradition teaches us that our congregations should be "Houses of God for all people." Those who come to our events see quite clearly that Temple Beth-El is a truly inclusive place because they see the way we treat everyone—members and strangers alike. Temple Beth-El's Gay and Lesbian Inclusion Committee has evolved from Inreach to Inclusion; from educating of the congregation to full acceptance; from caution from the Beth-El Board of Trustees to expectation of full participation; and most of all, from the unknown to the ordinary. We have been called to do this work, and with perseverance over the years, it has been very successful. We hope that our story will also help you on your journey.

Chambers Filled with Riches: Some Thoughts for Those Who Work on Outreach

Seth W. Goren

> A house is built by wisdom and established by understanding.
> Its chambers are filled with knowledge and all its riches are deep and pleasant.
> —Proverbs 24:3–4

The past several decades have borne witness to incredible and dramatic changes in how the Union for Reform Judaism addresses issues of particular importance to GLBT Jews. From endorsing antidiscrimination laws to advocating for same-sex civil marriage, the URJ religious and lay leadership has been at the forefront of the political fight on behalf of GLBT rights. On a parallel front, the URJ has undertaken a concerted effort to embrace GLBT Jews and make our congregations and organizations more welcoming to those of us who have been shut out of the Jewish mainstream for so long.

As much as this effort has been resolute and concerted, progress has been far from uniform. While some congregations have undertaken serious efforts to welcome GLBT Jews into their midst, others have made few conscious attempts to modify their communal stances and attitudes on GLBT issues. As an additional wrinkle, congregational personalities defy the stereotypes we tend to gravitate toward; there are communities situated in rural, conservative areas that have made strides toward GLBT inclusion, while the outlooks of some otherwise liberal suburban and urban congregations have remained unchanged. As a result, URJ congregations and organizations cover a good part of the spectrum on GLBT issues.

This diversity within the URJ makes it imperative for a person engaging in outreach to be aware of the views of the particular group of people he or she is addressing. It goes without saying that the temperature of a given URJ audience as a whole may be anywhere on the continuum. Moreover, there may well be a great deal of variation among the individuals in attendance. As a result, the first step of any successful outreach meeting is to actively listen to those who have invited us into their spiritual home to speak to their community. This necessarily involves ascertaining how they feel about GLBT issues, where these feelings flow from, and what concrete actions, if any, they have taken as a community to welcome GLBT Jews. By understanding where those present stand, we will be better able to work with them as they open their communities to serve the entire Jewish community.

Gaining a sense of an audience allows us to meet people where they are emotionally, psychologically, spiritually, and intellectually, wherever that may be. Most people lack a safe space in which they can ask questions they feel to be embarrassing or ignorant or make "mistakes" in talking about GLBT issues; the ongoing nature of work, family, or social relationships often precludes discussing GLBT issues for fear of saying the "wrong" thing. Such individuals' mere presence at a meeting on GLBT outreach indicates an inclination to become more open-minded, regardless of their initial positions. The overwhelming majority have the best of intentions, even if their words do not display the level of sensitivity we may be used to. What we may hear as an offensive statement may be the speaker's attempt to offer support in the best way he or she knows. By keeping an open mind and an open ear, we can develop insight into a speaker's vantage point and craft new and creative comments to which he or she will be more responsive.

For those engaging in outreach, it is important to keep an eye on the overall goal of opening congregations to GLBT members of the community. Thus, before making any comment or posing a question, it is worthwhile for each of us to consider how the statements we formulate relate to the overall goal of outreach. Does a given remark flow from a desire to open a listener's eyes to the need to build a welcoming home for Jews, regardless of sexual orientation and gender identity? Is it phrased in a way that the listener will feel comfortable and understand the point being expressed? Or is the comment anchored in an internal desire to express frustration in a way that will release anger, but put the listener on the defensive?

There is no doubt that many of us engaging in outreach will find ourselves in situations where people pose what we see as being very elementary questions; we may repeatedly face provocative inquiries like whether homosexuality is a choice or if there is a connection between homosexuality and pedophilia. While there will be some who may not have the most benevolent objectives, most of these people will be acting out of a desire to learn. Instead of reacting with anger, as we ordinarily might be inclined to do, we should approach the question as an opportunity to teach. Furthermore, even if the questioner is acting out of malice, having a calm demeanor is bound to have an impact on the other people in attendance.

Perhaps the most difficult members of a given audience will be those who perceive themselves to be stalwart supporters of GLBT rights. Many of those who consider themselves liberal and progressive will be unable to see the ways in which they themselves hold heterosexist beliefs. Such people may resent the implication that they have work to do on GLBT issues. This combination makes them potentially the strongest allies and the most challenging members of a congregation or organization. An effective method to help them become allies may be by talking with them to discover the root cause of why they are championing GLBT causes. Is it because they have a friend or family member who is GLBT? Is it because they support progressive causes in general? As with any other member of the community, the critical piece is simply trying to understand where this prospective supporter is coming from.

In addition to recognizing the makeup of the audience, it is important to keep an eye on how people are reacting as the discussion unfolds. Some listeners will be able to absorb a significant amount of new information, while others may have the capability to take in only so many changes to their worldview in a certain period. Pushing listeners beyond their capacity for learning may undermine the overall effectiveness of a presentation. For this reason, having an ongoing awareness and understanding of the people to whom we are speaking is invaluable.

Returning to the selection from Proverbs quoted above, by bringing our own wisdom and experiences to a given congregation or organization, we can help build strong and supportive communities. At the same time, each of us is most persuasive when we attempt to understand the people we are trying to reach. It is only when our synagogues are established and built through mutual understanding and appreciation that they will be filled with the most precious gift of all: a warm and open community that welcomes all Jews, regardless of their sexual orientation or gender identity.

Mazal Tov on Your New Rabbi!

Rabbi Victor S. Appell

Mazal tov on your new rabbi, who happens to be gay!

It is a major step for a congregation to have a rabbi who is gay or lesbian joining the clergy staff. Such a congregation demonstrates a desire to live up to the highest ideals of Reform Judaism. While most congregants will be very comfortable with their new rabbi, a congregation may have some congregants who will need some time to adjust to a rabbi who is gay or lesbian.

1. **Create a transition committee.** Your first concern is making your new rabbi feel comfortable and welcome and providing your congregants with an opportunity to get to know their new rabbi. While rabbis are entitled to their privacy, it is natural for congregants to want to get to know their rabbi by getting to know about him or her. A transition committee is the perfect vehicle for navigating this process. Like any committee, this one should constitute a diverse range of members. Be sure to have a parent of young children and an older member on the committee. If you have any GLBT congregants, ask one to be on the committee. If you do not know of any such members, perhaps a congregant with a lesbian or gay relative might be a good choice.

    Many rabbis have the opportunity to visit their new communities before beginning their position in order to find housing and meet with gay leaders. This is a perfect time for the transition committee to meet with the new rabbi. Together, they can anticipate some of the questions that congregants might bring up.

    Congregants will want to be assured that their new rabbi is a rabbi who happens to be gay or lesbian, rather than a "gay rabbi." They will want to know that the rabbi understands the concerns of the congregation and shares a similar set of values. Parents might want to be assured that the new rabbi will be a good role model to the children in the congregation. Parents of younger children may want some assistance in explaining to their children what the words "gay" and "lesbian" mean.

    Members of the transition committee can be very valuable in helping frame the discussion about the rabbi's personal life that congregants will naturally be curious about.
    - Is the rabbi comfortable being asked if he or she is dating?
    - Is the rabbi comfortable talking about being gay or lesbian?
    - Will both the rabbi and the congregation be comfortable with the rabbi self-identifying as a member of the GLBT community from the bimah or in the newsletter?

- On the synagogue's Web site, are there bios of the clergy? If so, do they include personal information, and what personal information will be included about the new rabbi?

2. **Determine the rabbi's comfort level in discussing personal issues.** While both the rabbi and the congregation need to find the right level of comfort, it is always important for the congregation to express pride in their rabbi and not feel as if the rabbi's sexuality is something that cannot be made public.

   Congregants might want to know if they can discuss issues about being lesbian, gay, bisexual, or transgender with their new rabbi. They may want to know if they can talk to their rabbi about a relative or friend who is a member of the GLBT community. By discussing these issues with the rabbi, the transition committee can then appropriately answer questions from congregants.

   If your new rabbi has a spouse or partner, the transition committee will want to help integrate that person into the congregational family, just as you would if the new rabbi had an opposite-gender husband or wife. Invitations to the rabbi should always include that partner by name and should never say "and guest." Things to think about might include finding out what terms the rabbi and his or her partner use to describe each other and their relationship.
   - Do they prefer "spouse," "partner," "husband," "wife"?
   - Did they have a wedding or commitment ceremony?
   - How would they like their names to appear in print and in correspondence from the congregation?
   - Are the rabbi and his/her partner comfortable talking about their relationship?

3. **If the rabbi has a partner/spouse, discuss with them what role the partner/spouse might want to play in the synagogue.** This might provide an opportune time for the congregation to think about the role of the rabbi's spouse and assumptions about what role that person might play in the life of the congregation. Clearly your rabbi's male partner does not need to be an honorary member of the Sisterhood. But perhaps he would like to be a member of the Brotherhood? What if the rabbi's female partner's interests do not run toward the Sisterhood's activities? Perhaps your rabbi's spouse might want to join a committee. It is helpful to explore expectations in advance about the role that the rabbi's spouse may take in the congregation.

   Another area where the transition committee might be helpful is in exploring possible reactions to physical affection between the rabbi and his or her partner. Do the other clergy or past clergy of the congregation ever hold hands with or kiss their spouses in public, perhaps after Shabbat services? If this is the case for straight clergy, the committee can help establish this same expectation for GLBT clergy.

In my experience, making your new rabbi who happens to be lesbian or gay feel welcome in your congregation is not difficult. You might even be surprised by how supportive some of your congregants can be. When my partner and I arrived at my first pulpit in 1999, we received our warmest reception by older congregants. We were invited to an afternoon tea where everyone was over the age of seventy! These congregants, many brought up in the classical Reform tradition and deeply committed to social action, could not have been more proud of their new gay rabbi. My partner became a regular at Friday night services and became well-known in the congregation for his baking skills that were enjoyed at the *Oneg Shabbat*.

When we announced that we were adopting a child, the congregation was thrilled. It turned out that our son was the first child of a rabbi or cantor of the congregation to be born while the rabbi or cantor was serving the congregation. They insisted that our son's *b'rit milah* be held at the congregation, and the board hosted a reception following the ceremony.

At my second pulpit, which I joined in 2003, every member of the youth group wanted to be the babysitter for our son, and my partner became an active member of the social action committee.

This can be a very exciting time for your congregation to explore new ideas and learn new things. Planning and dialogue are key ingredients. A transition committee, no matter how prepared your congregation may be, is essential. This committee can anticipate concerns that congregants may have and help the rabbi and his or her family feel comfortable in their new congregation. Open and honest conversations will help both you and your new rabbi get to know each other and gain trust in each other. With some thoughtful discussion and planning, your new rabbi and you can quickly develop a wonderful relationship. You should be proud of both your congregation and your rabbi. *Mazal tov*!

The Role of URJ Regional Offices in Promoting Inclusion of GLBT Jews

Rabbi Richard F. Address, D.Min., and Rabbi Geoffrey Mitelman

Introduction

In order to better include GLBT Jews in congregations, the URJ regional offices truly need to do only one thing: direct their general mission toward the specific goal of GLBT inclusion. With the URJ regional offices acting as a "network center" for congregations in the same geographic area, the regional offices make it easier for local congregations to pool resources, create broad coalitions, bounce ideas off of each other, develop programming, and join together in common causes. These are precisely the actions that need to be done to promote GLBT inclusion.

As such, this article outlines seven tasks that all regional offices can take in order to better promote GLBT inclusion in their congregations. These steps involve only a minimal amount of time and effort, and yet these small actions can have a dramatic effect on creating a community inclusive to GLBT congregants.

1. Create a Regional Committee on GLBT Inclusion

By creating a regional committee consisting of members from various congregations, the regional office does two things.

First, it ensures that specific, local concerns are addressed. A wide variety of issues face GLBT Jews, but with different laws, different cultural norms, and different struggles arising in different states, the tasks for congregations to create "an inclusive community" clearly depend on geography. After all, the struggles for GLBT Jews in the Northeast Council will be very different from those in the Southwest Council. By creating a regional committee, the regional office can make certain that the *specific* concerns for local GLBT Jews are the ones on the agenda.

Second, a regional committee allows congregations to pool resources and ideas. Simply bringing members of different congregations together allows people to explore what has and has not worked in terms of GLBT inclusion. In addition, a regional committee can begin to plan some of the events and programs described below.

The Canadian Council for Reform Judaism and the Greater New York Council have both created excellent regional committees, and to speak with those offices directly, contact:
Canadian Council for Reform Judaism: (800) 560-8242; ccrj@urj.org
Greater New York Council of Reform Synagogues: (888) 634-8242; gnycrs@urj.org

2. Run a Program at a Regional Biennial

If GLBT congregants can share their own experiences of inclusion and exclusion at a Regional Biennial, this issue immediately receives a human face, which is the single most effective way to create an inclusive community. By having the regional committee run a program at a Regional Biennial, congregants will be able to see that GLBT inclusion is important to local synagogues, and then they can learn about programs and ideas to create a more welcoming community for their own congregation.

3. Run a Program with the Department of Outreach and Synagogue Community

The URJ's Department of Outreach and Synagogue Community has years of experience in creating welcoming and inclusive communities. Draw on their experience to find ways of engaging local GLBT Jews and ensuring that they feel welcomed in your synagogue. Contact the Department of Outreach and Synagogue Community at (212) 650-4230; outreach@urj.org.

4. Run a Program with the Department of Synagogue Management

Many congregations define their membership by "families," but the synagogue's definition of "family" may or may not include GLBT couples. By running a program with the URJ Department of Synagogue Management, potential constitutional issues can be avoided, and synagogue membership can be more inclusive of GLBT congregants. Contact the Department of Synagogue Management at (212) 650-4040; synagoguemgmt@urj.org.

5. Establish Local and Regional GLBT Resources

For Reform Jews, the issue of legal rights for GLBT Jews is simply a matter of social justice. However, issues that GLBT Jews often face—such as AIDS, housing problems, marriage, prejudice, and discrimination—are not just *Jewish* problems, but are community-wide concerns, and the synagogue has a responsibility to be engaged and involved in them. By establishing relationships with local and regional GLBT resources, such as PFLAG (Parents, Families and Friends of Lesbians and Gays) or Lambda Legal, it will be easier and more effective for congregations to help address these issues of justice.

6. Create a Liaison to the Regional Youth Group

For many GLBT people, issues of sexual orientation and gender identity begin even before adolescence. Regional offices can run programs and conclaves regarding gender issues, sexual orientation, and prejudice reduction in order to help young people feel more comfortable in their own identity. Most of all, with education on sexual values becoming more and more critical, this can be an opportunity to emphasize early on that no matter what a person's sexual orientation may be, Reform Judaism emphasizes that the ideal relationship is a loving, permanent, monogamous one.

7. Establish a Working Relationship with NFTB and WRJ

With affiliates in the congregations, both the North American Federation of Temple Brotherhoods (NFTB) and the Women of Reform Judaism (WRJ) can be quite valuable for education and raising consciousness of GLBT issues.

Conclusion

Here is one example of what one URJ regional office was able to do to promote GLBT inclusion, from Dr. John Hirsch, chair of the URJ-GNYCRS Gay and Lesbian Resource Committee:

> The Greater New York Council of Reform Synagogues developed a Regional Committee on GLBT Inclusion in 1990. For its entire history, it has had a Speakers Bureau that sends people to congregations for special programming, Friday night sermons, and board retreats. It maintains a presence in organizing the marching in the annual Gay Pride March in New York City with the regional banner, supervising the organization of various synagogues who wish to march with the regional contingent. And for a number of years now, Central Synagogue in Manhattan has hosted a pre-Pride brunch, a tradition that began at Stephen Wise Free Synagogue.

All of this came about through networking among local synagogues—a primary purpose of the URJ regional offices.

Through the seven steps outlined above, the URJ regional offices can act as a "central hub" in helping congregations address GLBT issues. These actions are all small and easily done, and require minimal cost, time, or effort, and yet they can significantly improve the ways congregations can open their doors to the GLBT community.

Angling for Alliances

Rabbi Burt Schuman

During my final year at the Hebrew Union College–Jewish Institute of Religion in New York, my distinguished mentor, Rabbi Lawrence Kushner, taught us about the rabbinic placement process: "God," he said, "is going to put you where God wants you—whether you want it or not."

Indeed, when it came to my "match"—Temple Beth Israel in Altoona, Pennsylvania—God seemed to have demonstrated a perverse and ironic sense of humor. Very funny, God! I, Burt Schuman, whose politics had been compared to a "WPA mural that talks"; whose militant style had been likened to that of my long-deceased Great Aunt Hudya, a ILGWU organizer; and whose belief that "God is a Menshevik"—I was being sent to the "Buckle of Pennsylvania's Bible Belt"! Oy!

Yet, much to my surprise, living and working in the rock-ribbed Republican stronghold of Blair County has been among the richest, most satisfying, and instructive experiences of my life. My neat and pious "progressive" political assumptions have been "tested," and I have come away with a host of insights into why big city liberals like me have such a hard time understanding and communicating with political conservatives in the "Red Zones" of Middle America.

When I arrived at Temple Beth Israel nearly ten years ago, my view of much of Middle America was basically a collage of scenes from the *Beverly Hillbillies, Fernwood Tonight,* and *Mary Hartman, Mary Hartman.* In Altoona, folks' manners were formal, and their affect strangely muted—they seemed to smile incessantly, regardless of the circumstances. Having grown up in New York City, this was foreign terrain. And I knew, erroneously it turned out, just what they needed—a good dose of New York sarcasm.

I also experienced culture shock in adjusting to the region's social fabric. Life here did not revolve around intellectual, arty discussions in cafes but around football (local high schools, Penn State, and the Pittsburgh Steelers); marching band and cheerleader competitions; deer, turkey, and trout season; and county fairs. The local cuisine—with its strong Pennsylvania German influence—was foreign, as was the community's taste for hunting. Church-related activities anchored people's lives, and service and fraternal organizations—such as the Lion's, Rotary and Kiwanis Clubs, the Knights of Columbus, Masons, Shriners, and Elks—seemed omnipresent.

I had to admit, though, that lots of goodness resided in Blair County. In "Red Zone" America, community voluntarism is all-pervasive, from children's tutorial and adult literacy

---

Burt Schuman, "Angling for Alliances," *Reform Judaism* 34, no. 2 (Winter 2005): 60–64.

programs to food banks and charity walks. Moreover, many of the locals shared my passion for choral singing, classical music, ballet, folk music and dance, jazz, "cutting edge" theater, painting, and photography—all interests I had naively believed were by and large the exclusive province of city dwellers. From the first time I attended the Blair County African-American Festival to my first agonizing moments trying to keep up with my fellow second tenors during rehearsals of the Blair Concert Chorale, I could no longer pretend I was the cosmopolite I had imagined myself to be.

Over time—and this was even harder to admit—I began to realize that perhaps it was *I* who was provincial. Perhaps my "New York attitude" was not so clever after all—just my way of masking acute feelings of dislocation and disorientation.

From this new awareness, I began to conduct a *cheshbon ha nefesh* (accounting of the soul), focusing on my attitudes and assumptions. The more I did so, the more I wanted to understand my neighbors' cultural cues and adjust to their social rhythms.

As I changed, my neighbors changed too. The more I showed an interest in them, the more they wanted to understand me. "What was it like to grow up in New York City?" they asked. "Are all New Yorkers like the characters on 'Seinfeld'?" "How do you negotiate life in such a racially, ethnically, religiously, and culturally diverse metropolis?" "What school do you recommend for my daughter who wants to study acting in New York City?"

They asked even more questions about Jewish beliefs and practices. "Do Jews believe in heaven and hell?" "Do Jews take the Bible literally?" "Do Jews have confession?" "What role, if any, does Jesus play in Judaism?" They asked cultural questions, too. The local high school invited me to serve as a consultant on their production of *Fiddler on the Roof* and the Blair Concert Chorale turned to me for suggestions on Jewish music. Later, when I began to give benefit music recitals in Yiddish, Hebrew, and Ladino, the warm and appreciative audiences contributed generously to the concerts' nonprofit beneficiaries.

The community's curiosity frequently extended to Jewish perspectives on social justice, capital punishment, abortion, same-gender marriage, women's rights, war and peace, and the Israeli-Palestinian conflict. When I addressed racism and ethnic prejudice, I pointed to the confluence of Reform Jewish values and Middle American values such as fair play, personal responsibility, and caring about one's neighbors. In discussing the problems of the working poor in our community, I cited the Holiness Code in Leviticus and the writings of the Prophet Amos, and struck a responsive chord among my Christian, Muslim, and Baha'i audiences. Talmudic discussions relating to employer-employee relations, zoning, and the environment became a source of fascination.

By entering into the faith arena, I was not dismissed as a secular humanist espousing "politically correct" doctrines. Even if people did not fully accept my positions, I was heard.

Strategies That Build Alliances

Here's what I learned from my experience in a "Red Zone" community:

Toss Out Tribalism

Too often, we "Progressives" fail to acknowledge our own tendency to be tribal, rejecting others on the basis of appearance and accent.

We can overcome such prejudices by listening actively to our neighbors, taking in their concerns and responding without condescension.

Learn, Then Lead

When we present ourselves as learners and seekers of knowledge, people will often respond with kindness because they feel needed and empowered. My neighbors schooled me in deer, bear, and turkey hunting; the rituals of various fraternal and civic organizations; the flora and fauna of the Southern Alleghenies; the history of the Pennsylvania Railroad; and some of the finer points of successful dairy farming in Blair County. Elected officials of both major parties gave me a positive reception when I sought out their views on strategies for reviving our downtown; building coalitions to fight hate; and securing funding to help children, the elderly, and the developmentally disabled. Because of our good rapport, when I later solicited their assistance regarding pending cuts to family and youth service programs, as well as the possible closure of a successful facility for the severely developmentally disabled, they were approachable and helpful.

Volunteers Are Valued

It is important to be regarded as "doers" who honor our commitments and promises. In a predominantly rural community such as Blair County, people are going to judge you not by what you possess or profess, but by what you do for others.

This is not a foreign concept to us, as Judaism is rooted in "doing." By engaging in righteous conduct, we have an opportunity to model Jewish behavior. Involvement in community projects, such as "walks" to raise money for cancer research, also builds relationships, trust, and credibility. And it is in these activities that we are most likely to encounter kindred spirits who, regardless of their politics, share many of our concerns.

Network In Concentric Circles

If our goal is to build coalitions, an excellent strategy is to network in concentric circles of common interest and concern. This approach was particularly effective when we formed the YWCA Multicultural Panel, a group that conducts training on issues relating to identity and prejudice through the art of "telling our stories" in educational and professional settings. We recruited panelists from socially progressive groups such as Blair County Social Services, the Blair County NAACP, and the Home Nursing Agency's AIDS Intervention Project; and we simultaneously made connections with such religious groups as the Ecumenical Conference of Greater Altoona, the local Baha'i community, and the Sixth Ward Ministry. In another productive concentric-networking experience, my involvement with the Blair Concert Chorale and the County Arts Foundation led to my participation in the local African-American Cultural Foundation—and that led to our temple co-sponsoring a series of interfaith events, including a Martin Luther King, Jr. freedom seder, a women's spirituality service, an AIDS memorial service, an anti-Klan rally, and an "Interfaith Call To Conscience and Compassion" rally in downtown Altoona.

Faith Is Fundamental

Take advantage of the natural credibility that comes from approaching economic and social issues as people of faith. We Jews need to reclaim the language of faith, family, and tradition. Too often, we respond to the blandishments of rightwing Christian fundamentalists by sounding like liberals who just happen to go to temple. Why hide the fact that we are heirs to a 4,000-year-old tradition that lies at the root of Western religion, especially when there is a deep desire on the part of many Christians to examine the Jewish roots of their faith? Discussing the "Old Testament" with them affords us an enormous opportunity to affirm the ethical values of Reform Judaism.

Avoid These Faux Pas:

- Do not portray yourself as the perennial victim whenever you take an unpopular stand that prompts a negative reaction. It's easy to fall into the "poor me" trap and wear one's "victim" status as a badge of pride trumpeting our moral superiority over those poor benighted folks who have the audacity to disagree with us. The more we wallow in our "victimhood," the less we take responsibility for our failure to convey our message. Success, on the other hand, requires networking, long-range planning, reevaluating our language and approach, active listening, and finding common ground.
- Resist righteousness. Recognize that your perspectives—and those of folks in "Red Zone" America—are not one dimensional. They are deeply felt beliefs. Be open to hearing others, and don't be preachy. Doing so is ineffective and alienates the very people we are trying to reach.
- Reject jargon. *Pirkei Avot* teaches: "Do not say something obscure in the hope that it will be understood." Those who are unfamiliar with "liberal language" will only be confused, antagonized, and convinced that you're trying to project an air of intellectual superiority—and while you might imagine yourself to be arrayed in the verbal equivalent of royal robes, your listeners will look at you and think, "You're naked!"
- Steer clear of confrontation. In a place like New York City, being "in your face" is common practice; in Blair County such tactics are perceived as self-indulgent. During my early years in Altoona, whenever I initiated a war of words, the typical response was, "This is all about you, isn't it?" What I construed as a powerful political statement was perceived by others as adolescent acting out.

Yes, we "city folk" do have fundamental differences with "Red Zone" America. But we have much in common, too. Isn't it time that we took advantage of our commonalities and worked together in harmony to make the world a better place?

Creating Welcoming Classrooms and Inclusive Lesson Plans

Ten Dos and Don'ts

David Shneer, Ph.D.

1. ***Do not* assume that talking about inclusion and GLBT issues means talking about sex.** GLBT issues come up naturally when talking about such issues as family, love, text, Creation, justice, and others. Talking about the sexual aspect of what makes GLBT people or relationships different from heterosexual people and relationships *is* appropriate for students emotionally mature enough to talk about sex and for teachers emotionally equipped to handle such open conversations. For most students, we recommend starting discussions of sexuality sometime around bar/bat mitzvah age, and always with the support and inclusion of your students' parents (either by sending letters and lesson plans home for parents to review or, preferably, through family education programs).
2. ***Do not* make assumptions about your students' family structures or backgrounds.** Don't assume that all of your students were born Jewish or that their parents were born Jewish. Don't assume that all of your students have two parents (let alone just a mother and a father). Don't assume that all of your students are Ashkenazi. Let the students tell you their family narratives. You'll be surprised just how diverse the Jewish community and your classrooms have become.
3. ***Do avoid* "opposites," especially in teaching Hebrew.** Focusing on opposites, such as Hebrew learning games emphasizing *abba* and *ima* or using flashcards that show a picture of a mother and then one of a father, encourage students to think in binaries rather than in inclusive spectra. Binaries are almost always *exclusive* rather than *inclusive* and make presumptions about language and society that do not generally work in pluralistic classrooms. If you do use an *abba-ima* game, you as the teacher should be the one to break the binary by offering an example involving an *abba-abba*.
4. ***Do avoid* prepackaged projects on issues of family, love, sex, or identity.** Precreated family trees, identity questionnaires, or other classroom materials almost always *make presumptions* about our students. Family trees usually presume a single mother and single father, each of whom had a single mother and a single father. Identity questionnaires

about Jewishness generally presume a heterosexual family structure and/or a Jew-at-birth life narrative. Be sure to break down these assumptions built into many existing curricular materials. If necessary, make your own project templates that allow for more flexibility and student creativity.

5. ***Do teach* both of the Creation stories from Genesis:** the first where man and woman are created simultaneously and perhaps even in the same body (Genesis 1:27), and then the more well-known story of Eve emerging from Adam's rib (Genesis 2:7-24). Teaching both stories, and the rabbinic commentary surrounding them, serves several functions: (1) it shows that the Torah encourages interpretation rather than regulation (i.e., people, not texts, regulate), (2) it shows a more gender-inclusive vision of Creation, and (3) it offers the potential of the first human being as neither male nor female, breaking down the binaries of gender.

6. ***Do encourage* the uncomfortable laughter that can come from posing examples involving same-sex issues or gender crossing.** But it is *very important* that the teacher be the one to offer up the uncomfortable example, not the shy student with same-sex parents, or the child who is silently questioning her or his sexuality. Examples: For a Purim play, a male teacher can offer to play the role of Esther. If students respond with statements like "But boys can't play Esther," the teacher should acknowledge and address the discomfort of the students and ask them what it is that makes them feel uncomfortable. The students are then forced to examine inclusion and consider a range of alternatives.

7. ***Do include* alternative interpretations for stories like Sodom and Gomorrah and the Leviticus ban on same-sex male sex.** Jewish Mosaic[1] can provide you with entire lesson plans focused on rereading the texts that form the halachic basis for traditional Jewish understandings of homosexuality. *Do not avoid these texts. Confront them directly and openly!*

8. ***Do explore* the same-gender relationships found in Jewish texts.** For example, teach the David character as one who had many loves, including love for his fallen friend Jonathan. Although David is a classic character in "heroes" curricula, his deep love for Jonathan, sexual or not, is rarely discussed. We also recommend including Ruth and Naomi in your list of heroes and discussing the possibility of their relationship as an intimate one.

9. ***Do respond* to seemingly homophobic or hetero-normative comments** *at all times*, not just when a particular kid is targeted or when the example is particularly egregious. This means inviting a discussion about disparaging comments that hurt people (talking about *derech eretz* is a good way to frame it), *not* simply shutting down discussion by saying "that's not allowed."

10. ***Do include* visual representations of GLBT people or families and diverse Jewish people and families** in general when doing units on family, communities, or history.

11. ***Do include* GLBT issues in your Israel curriculum, because it is easy to do so!** For example, examine the role of gay and lesbian people in the military in Israel, or compare and contrast the legal rights same-sex couples have in Israel, versus the rights that same-sex couples have in the United States.

---

1. Jewish Mosaic: The National Jewish Center for Sexual and Gender Diversity, partners with Jewish organizations, communities, and individuals of every denomination to create a world where all Jews are fully included in communal life, regardless of sexual orientation or gender identity. See http://www.jewishmosaic.org.

12. ***Do utilize* holidays as wonderful opportunities to include GLBT issues in your curriculum.** For example, Chanukah can be about different kinds of family celebrations; Purim about gender roles; Shavuot about everyone being at Sinai.

OK, so our list of ten dos and don'ts became twelve, which is appropriate, since being inclusive and welcoming is about avoiding assumptions, breaking down binaries, and including all visions of what it means to be and do Jewish.

Out at School

David Shneer, Ph.D.

Standing at the front of her fifth grade classroom, Jennifer Levinson, a long-time teacher at Congregation Sha'ar Zahav's Kadimah religious school, introduced a lesson on family history. "Today we are going to be making family trees," said Jennifer to her class of energetic, bright Jewish children. She had examined the materials that were part of a curriculum used for Jewish family history projects. The trees she was to hand out to her children had prepackaged spaces for them to fill in: two slots labeled "mother" and "father," and above that, grandparents, and so on. Before class began, Jennifer went through her class list and realized that only one of her eight children would be able to fill in the slots as presented on the curricular materials. In the end, this creative teacher did not hand out the trees. Instead, she asked her students to create their own models of their families, and what resulted was revolutionary. They produced bushes, multibranched trees with vines growing in various places. One student produced a spider web–like image with intersecting lines and round forms encircling the student whose name was at the middle of her "family web." What we were witnessing was the queering of Jewish education, and the queering of Jewish families.

In just 15 years, policies of the Reform Jewish movement have undergone a radical transformation toward the inclusion of queer Jews in their structures. In 1990, the Union of American Hebrew Congregations began ordaining openly gay and lesbian rabbis; in 2000, the Central Conference of American Rabbis agreed to support Reform rabbis who officiated at same-sex weddings. In 2001, the head of Reform Judaism called on Reform synagogues to halt all interactions with the Boy Scouts of America due to the latter's anti-homosexual policies. But progressive Jewish education has not undergone such a transformation. The family structures presented to Jewish children in their school settings are still heteronormative, stressing the traditional Jewish ideal of one mother and one father.

The first steps toward change began in the late 1980s and early 1990s. In the groundbreaking book, *Twice Blessed,* Rabbi Denise Eger and Lesley Silverstone's essay on education lamented that discussion of homosexuality very rarely makes it into any classroom, let alone a Jewish one. They suggested using a text-centered approach and personal speakers to create a more tolerant environment in which to discuss difficult issues of sexuality. Their goal was to "show how the Jewish educator can be more sensitive to the issue of homosexuality," and was visionary for its time in prescribing change within Jewish education. In

---

David Shneer, "Out at School: A Queer Jewish Education," in *Queer Jews*, ed. David Shneer and Caryn Aviv (New York: Routledge, 2002), pp. 135–47.

the early 1990s, some Jewish schools began including units on "tolerance" and "diversity." These units used traditional Jewish values such as being kind to and welcoming of strangers and accepting all people who are made in "God's image," some of the concepts that Eger and Silverstone had proposed in their article. In 1994, Rabbi Camille Shira Angel and Shifra Teitelbaum published "Intimate Connections: Integrating Human Love with God's Love," a curriculum that uses "Jewish values to sensitize students of all ages to the lesbian/gay experience." The curriculum "takes the perspective that challenging anti-lesbian and gay biases, and embracing lesbian and gay members of our community are ways to offer our students a fuller understanding and appreciation of the breadth of human love." (p. ii) The material and structure Angel and Teitelbaum present picked up where Silverstone and Eger left off. They provided Jewish educators of high school students a methodology and resources for educating about sexual diversity and about making a more inclusive community. Other progressive high school programs have incorporated single units about sexual diversity into their curricula. The nondenominational high school program Midrasha located in the San Francisco Bay Area has a unit in its 1996 ninth grade identity curriculum on homosexuality, homophobia, and tolerance called "Do Not Disdain Any Person."

What do both of these pathbreaking curricula have in common? First, that issues of sexual diversity and Jewish values have been reserved for high school–aged children; and second, that both have structured discussions around the question of tolerance, inclusiveness, and combating homophobia. These were the first steps in Jewish education to introduce students to issues of homosexuality in the classroom.

Even with these efforts at educating diversity and tolerance in Judaism's most progressive institutions, there is much more work to be done. The Gay, Lesbian, and Straight Education Network (GLSEN) recently completed a national survey of queer students and found that:

- More than 90 percent reported that they sometimes or frequently hear homophobic remarks in their school.
- More than one-third reported hearing homophobic remarks from faculty or school staff.
- Nearly 40 percent reported that no one ever intervened in these circumstances.

Within Jewish contexts, homophobia and queer invisibility are still the norm. Despite the great strides the Reform and Reconstructionist movements have made in ordaining queer clergy and officiating at same-sex ceremonies, there is still a glass ceiling for queer rabbis. And keep in mind that none of this essay's discussion about change has mentioned the more traditional forms of Conservative Judaism and Orthodoxy. There are limits to tolerance, even in the increasingly open rabbinical schools. Jewish schools have even further to go. But given GLSEN's statistics and the persisting homophobia in the Jewish establishment, tolerance education needs to be a significant aspect of any educational system, and training teachers to be more aware of or proactive on issues of homosexuality must be the first step of such an education.

Although appropriate for many school settings, the tolerance model does not address the changes that have altered American and Jewish society. In 1990, you could count the number of out rabbis on your fingers, and nearly all of them worked in gay Jewish synagogues, where being openly queer was part of the job description. In the past ten years, two social movements have changed the face of the Jewish community. On the one hand, the movement to establish queer Jewish institutions has expanded into new geographic areas and new social arenas. There are queer synagogues all over the country including Seattle, Fort Lauderdale, Louisville, Philadelphia, Chicago, and other cities. There is a gay and lesbian Jewish family camp in Northern California, and gay and lesbian Jewish youth groups on college campuses across the country. And as queer Jews have made Jewish spaces for themselves, progressive non-queer Jewish institutions are responding with a new, unprecedented inclusiveness. There are openly queer rabbis on the *bimah* in mainstream Reform synagogues, gay and lesbian *chavurot*, gay-straight alliances, and other forms of institutional change that point to a new openness in defining and creating the liberal Jewish community.

Despite all of these changes in institutions aimed at adult Jews, no such reform has happened in Jewish education. Education is the place where the Jewish community has, in theory, the most invested in the questions of Jewish continuity, community, and the future of Judaism in America, questions that still, unfortunately, shape Jewish policy-making in the United States.

Jewish education does not reflect the changing diversity of the adult Jewish communities. For example, not a single Jewish children's book explores sexual diversity. Congregation Sha'ar Zahav's children's library includes the ever-popular, but not explicitly Jewish, *Heather Has Two Mommies* and *Daddy's Roommate*, which virtually monopolize the market of children's books that address queer family issues. This suggests either that publishers feel there is no market for Jewish children's books that address sexual diversity, or that the subject is still too politically taboo for a publishing house to address. As individual consumers, queer Jewish families are demanding representation of themselves in children's books, but unfortunately, individual families do not generate the Jewish children's book market—Jewish educational institutions do. Among Jewish schools, there is still only a tiny market for queer Jewish children's books. Hebrew language education still works in the bi-polar world of *aba* (father) and *ima* (mother), even when such concepts do not ring with meaning for children of same-sex families. As queer Jews have more children, the demand for a queer-identified Jewish education will only become stronger, and Jewish educational institutions and publishers need to respond to this emerging demand.

Working at the Other End of the Spectrum

As the former director of the first (and for a long time only) Jewish school at a GLBT synagogue, I have seen how difficult it has been to effect institutional change in Jewish education. The appearance of Congregation Sha'ar Zahav's religious school, Kadimah, in 1988, was a result of the new demographics of the GLBT community—Jewish lesbians, and later gay men, began to have children, and they wanted their children to learn in their synagogue. At the time, the parents saw a queer Jewish school at their queer synagogue as a safe haven from the homophobic world. It mirrored the purpose of the synagogue as a whole—a place where their children would not feel isolated for their different family structures. Parents got together and formed a cooperative school as part of the synagogue—the birth of the first queer Jewish school.

The school was officially founded by several families, the then-rabbi of Congregation Sha'ar Zahav, Yoel Kahn, and long-time Jewish educator Phyllis Mintzer. With just a handful of students, Kadimah felt like a one-room schoolhouse. The curriculum reflected the content of other progressive Jewish educational establishments with special attention paid to finding ways of representing diverse family structures. According to Mintzer, the guiding objectives of the curriculum were "to develop literate, functional Jews, who identified as Jews in their own terms and were members of a diverse community with diverse families." The school was to be a safe space for all of the children to talk about their diverse families and the consequences they faced for being children of diverse families. It is important to note that the founding school had three straight families, showing that from its inception, a "queer" curriculum included all forms of diversity. The content of the curriculum was similar to that of other synagogues: holidays, lifecycles, Torah, ethics/values, and later, included more history and text. Kahn and Mintzer aimed for a rigorous Jewish education with the diversity of the community as the guiding philosophy.

As time has evolved, so has the school. Kadimah now has more than 40 children enrolled, and more than 150 children involved in various children's and family activities, from GLBT families and mixed-gender families as well. And just as Kadimah's student and parent population becomes more diverse, the notion of a queer Jewish school has arrived at other institutions. Queer synagogues from New York, Los Angeles, and in other large metropolitan areas are finally experiencing what Sha'ar Zahav experienced 15 years ago: the emergence of the queer Jewish family constituency as shaping the queer Jewish synagogue. In many ways, Kadimah is the face of the future of queer Jewish institutions' educational systems, and perhaps, for Jewish institutions in general.

The demographics of Kadimah have expanded, as more mixed-gender couples join the synagogue and enroll their children in the school. Simultaneously, other progressive synagogues in Northern California have more GLBT families. Demographically speaking, then, in the most progressive areas of the country, the queer Jewish synagogue movement and the most progressive non-queer synagogues are moving *toward* each other. As part of this milieu on the forefront of change in American Judaism, the school has been forced to define what it means to offer a "queer Jewish education."

Queering the Curriculum

To conceive of a Jewish education at a queer synagogue, the school needed to examine the ways that the synagogue as a whole differentiated itself from other communities, aside from the demographic makeup of the congregation. Were there particular practices or liturgy that defined a queer synagogue? Sha'ar Zahav's Friday Night Siddur includes a special reading as part of the Kaddish that reads, "We remember our gay brothers and sisters who were martyred in years past . . ." and everyone, queer or not, stands and reads this moving and powerful statement together, a collective Kaddish that defines the congregation as queer, regardless of the sexual identity of the person reading it. The Sha'ar Zahav Yahrzeit list includes friends and companions as well as spouses, parents, and children, since for many gays and lesbians, friends were their chosen family. The synagogue board was, until last year, made up entirely of queer-identified people. Adult education classes often have a queer focus to them, such as "Queer Talmud" or "Gay and Lesbian Parenting and Judaism." Was there a way to mirror these signifiers of queer community in children's education?

Given that what identifies queer people as such is, at root, complex sexual identities, dealing with queer issues is especially challenging for children for several reasons. First, talking about issues around sex and sexuality with children makes adults uncomfortable.

In public schools, official discussion of sex and sexual identity (if they even cover the second) does not begin until middle or high school, when students themselves are developing and are reflecting on their own sexuality. Second, for those children who might not be consciously thinking about their sexuality, adults are often afraid of raising the subject of sexual identity, fearing that talking about the ideas will plant them in their moldable minds. Eger and Silverstone felt obliged to mention in their 1989 article that "no one can teach another person to be gay or lesbian." With such fears and stereotypes to deal with, approaching queer issues with prepubescent children can be even more challenging. How do these questions play out in a queer context?

To affirm their queer family structures and the identity of their parents while not sexualizing the educational experience is a tricky path to walk down. For the 1998 San Francisco Israel Fair, Kadimah's sixth grade class did a series of poetry readings of contemporary queer Israeli poets, most of which dealt with the theme of love, and some of which bordered on the erotic. While most parents were very excited to see our creative fusion of queer issues and Israeli culture and politics, some were concerned that the poetry reading sexualized our youth. This event was one of the most contentious in the school's history. It highlighted the challenges implicit in creating an affirming educational experience and one that openly discussed issues of love and sexuality, what I call a "queer-identified" educational experience, while providing the children a context in which to deal with the sexual nature of that which identifies the community as queer. For these sixth graders, same-sex love poetry struck a great balance between textuality, history, Jewish culture, and the identity issues that are part of our curriculum and part of their lives.

Kadimah only educates children up to age 13 (through their Bar/Bat Mitzvah), so the very discussion of sex and sexuality was framed by questions of age appropriateness. At an education board retreat, the board and I outlined the key values that were to guide our curriculum development process. Among such Jewish values or content skills as "provides quality Hebrew education" and "gives children synagogue skills" was included the statement, "creates a sex-positive environment"—not something Mintzer mentioned as one of the original guiding goals of Kadimah. As the education director, I struggled with the idea of a sex-positive children's education. Did that mean talking about sex with eight year olds? Did it mean not shielding children from Biblical innuendos of sex? Did it mean broaching the subject of sexual identity with the older children in the school? To some extent, the school found a balance between creating an environment where talking about sex and sexuality are not taboo, while not bringing up sex in ways that children cannot developmentally understand.

I had a discussion with the seventh grade class about the Biblical injunction against homosexuality from Leviticus. The kids were ready and willing to tackle the text in a direct manner. We talked about the difference between sex acts and sexuality, the injunction against male acts but not female acts, and the historical context in which these injunctions occurred. All the gloves were off, and the children were completely engaged. As parents started arriving, one poked her head into the room, and the kids in chorus screamed out, "No adults. We're having a serious conversation." They understood that we were talking about topics that are traditionally taboo, but also recognized that they were ready and interested in talking about sex and sexuality seriously. In essence, the children determined the boundaries of their "sex-positive" education and, as Jennifer Levinson discovered in her family tree project, the children help us shape a queer Jewish education.

The story also raises the subject of the teacher's role in this process, and her/his own sexuality. There seem to be two variables in exploring the intersections of a teacher's role and discussions of sexuality: the teaching environment and the sexual identity of the teacher. In my discussion with the seventh graders, I, a gay man, was teaching at the queer synagogue. Did it matter that these students knew that I identify as queer? Did they ask me questions they might not ask a teacher whom they knew identified as straight? What if they did not know the sexual identity of the teacher? Would I have been allowed to or felt comfortable enough to have this discussion in a non-queer environment? Could a teacher who identified as straight have had the same experience in that classroom that I had? I'm not sure.

The sexual identities of Kadimah's teaching staff reflect the diversity of the community. There are straight-identified, queer-identified, lesbian, gay, and transgendered teachers. As director, I did not ask prospective teachers their sexual orientation. It is in fact illegal to do so, although there are ways to ascertain that kind of information without asking point blank. All of them were able to bring the values of diversity and community to their teaching and all agreed that quality teaching and experience with diversity were the most important parts about teaching at Kadimah. That said, board members, parents, and teachers always asked me if a new teacher was "gay or straight." Always. And there was a right answer. There are two reasons I see for this persistent question. First, parents wanted their children to see queer people represented in positions of authority. Second, and this is what I see as a teacher and director, when a teacher identifies as queer, it changes the interactions s/he has with the students. The students can ask questions that use the second person, "Do you feel oppressed by the Leviticus text, David?" and perhaps are more able to articulate for themselves their own "I" statements. In a queer context, most agree that it changes the dynamics for the better.

In a non-queer context, some think that it changes them for the worse. Straight teachers who discuss sexuality in non-queer environments have more latitude for sensitive discussions about sexuality and queer issues, because the conversations tend to be *less* "I" centered and more abstract. In other words, they can be more distanced from questions of identity. Queer teachers are often afraid to broach the subject of sexuality in non-queer contexts for the very fears that others have—the fear of "teaching queer" or planting ideas in impressionable children about diverse sexualities.

In 1995, I taught in the Bay Area Midrasha program that I mentioned above. The students and teachers were all on a weekend retreat, and the topic of the weekend's curriculum was "identity." Each of the approximately 15 teachers was asked to teach a lesson about identity. I brought in the Leviticus ban on homosexuality and the David and Jonathon story to talk about polyvocality and sexuality in the Torah with the 16 and 17 year olds. Of the 150 students on the retreat, 50 of them attended my session, and the discussion, scheduled for one hour, lasted more than two hours. Students were interested, angry, excited, and impressed that a teacher would talk this "openly" with them. To drive home the point about identity, I wore a queer-identified shirt about safe sex to the study session. Two students asked if they could borrow my shirt. The session was a huge success.

That is, until the director of the program began getting calls from parents about a teacher who wore some "gay shirt" and talked about homosexuality. The director adamantly defended the program and the class to the parents, but felt obliged to respond to the parents' concerns. The director called me to have a "frank" discussion about "how far" we can go in this program. He was straight-identified, but very supportive of the study session, and asked that I not wear such "sexually explicit" clothing to the camp. I had hit the boundaries. Sexuality in text was one thing; in real life, it was another. Letting students, rather than their parents, determine the boundaries of their education was clearly the direction I favored, and was the direction the parents seemed to fear. They feared that their students might start using "I" statements. In contrast, at Kadimah, after telling the parents about the Leviticus discussion I had with the seventh graders, I received a hearty congratulations from straight and queer parents alike, and was encouraged to keep up the good work. (No, I did not wear the safe sex T-shirt to the seventh grade class. Should I have? Were they too young to see a teacher wearing such a T-shirt? Would the parents have reacted differently to my lesson? This is where the debates of a queer education lie.)

For older kids, queering the curriculum can actually involve discussions about that which makes their parents, and possibly themselves, queer—their particular form of love and their sexuality. As we move down the curriculum, "queering" is about breaking normative models of Jewish values, heroes, and history and emphasizing different aspects of Jewish culture and tradition. In this, queering has much in common with feminist efforts to change curricula in order to remake what it is to be Jewish. Kadimah's fourth grade class studies Jewish history through heroes and heroines. They study some of the old favorites like Solomon, Abraham, and Sarah, but we include the David and Jonathon story and explore the varieties of love that the Torah exposes. They learn about the medieval Hebrew poets, Yehuda Ha-Levi and Solomon Ibn Ezra, who wrote same-sex love poetry, and use that as a jumping off point for discussing Sephardic culture. They also study contemporary Jewish history by learning about Magnus Hirschfeld, the Jewish founder of the Institute of Sexology in Berlin, an institution destroyed when the Nazis came to power, and Bella Abzug, one of the earliest female U.S. senators. In other words, the curriculum "queers" Jewish history by exposing the children to exemplars rarely, if ever, included in canonical Jewish histories.

The Bnei Mitzvah class studies life cycles and learns the Sha'ar Zahav kaddish. In addition, the children watch a video of a same-sex Jewish wedding officiated by a cantor and explore the meaning of a Jewish wedding. For the youngest children, the concept of queering the curriculum is much more abstract, and involves affirming family diversity and exposing the children to queer relationships through example, which were the guiding principles behind the original Kadimah curriculum. Kadimah's children participate in *aufrufs* of queer couples. They watch two men sneak a kiss in the corner of the oneg room; they watch the synagogue's rabbi interact with her same sex partner, as rabbi and rebbetzin.

Is "Queer" Only a Sexual Identity?

A second problem about "queering the curriculum" is the tendency many queer Jews have of projecting the congregation's "identity" onto all of its members, including its children. As members of a queer synagogue, Kadimah's students are all exposed to images of queer couples showing affection for each other in Jewish spaces, seeing non-traditional families as normative, not exceptional, and embracing the philosophy of openness and *tikkun olam* that form the foundation of the congregation's Jewish values. However, most of our children have not explored their own sexual identity, and are part of our congregation by association with queer Jews—notably their parents, adult friends, and relatives. So are these children of gays and lesbians "queer" in any way?

Most definitely. The very fact of having queer parents defines these children as "other" because of issues around sexual identity and family relationships. These children face multiple differences in their schools—as Jews and as children of queer people. As their haven, the school's job is to empower them to embrace their difference, both in their religion and in the sexual identity of their family and congregation. The school also gives them the pride and knowledge they need to brave a world that sees them as different, because of their families. Social homophobia oppresses these children by association, and therefore, society "queers" them. Some of our children are teased on playgrounds for having two mothers; they do not see themselves represented in classroom textbooks or in the media. Many of our children have invented their own defense mechanisms to mask their identity to their peers, in the same way that queer people do in various places in their lives. Most of our Bnei Mitzvah kids have "stories" to explain who that second woman is who picks them up from school on occasion: "It's my aunt." "It's my mom's friend." Queerness, for children of gays and lesbians, is an ascribed identity; no one knows the sexual identity these children will have when they are old enough to articulate such ideas for themselves. But homophobia brings oppression into their lives in a similar way that anti-semitism makes many people "Jewish" who do not think of themselves that way. I'm thinking in particular about how Nazi definitions of Jewishness defined people raised Christian as Jews if they had Jewish grandparents. Or the way Orthodox Judaism defines anyone born of a Jewish mother as Jewish despite personal practice or identity. Ascribed identities may not be self-defined, but they are real. In this way, Kadimah's children of gays and lesbians are queer.

Now, what if I told you that, as a result of the demographic changes of the 1990s, nearly half of Kadimah's children were not children of gays and lesbians. Are they being queered by their association with queer families and a queer congregation, like the children of queer parents are queered by their associations with their parents? The congregation does not know the sexual identity of all of its members, but it does know the family arrangements of the children in the religious school. To date, about forty to fifty percent of Kadimah families are "mixed gender," or in heteronormative parlance, "straight." When asked why a "straight" family joins the "gay shul," most respond that it has to do with two things: the values and the strong sense of community. These families seek a place with progressive values that embrace diversity—diversity of religious background, race, learning styles, and sexual orientation. We have a high number of interracial and interfaith families. We have a high percentage of students with learning disabilities. These families sought out the "gay shul" for its loving openness and strong sense of grassroots community organizing, and often because they were close friends with other queer people who were members of the synagogue. Are these "straight" families queered by being part of this community? How about their children?

Here, we reach both the limit of and the endless opportunities presented by a queered curriculum. These straight folk are still straight, and when asked "are you queer," by and large, only those who have had experience with queer sexuality, not just queer community, answer in the affirmative. Their kids, in ten years, will probably have the same answers. For some queer members of the synagogue, this is a source of sadness. Ten years ago, the synagogue had a queer-centric model that made "queer" normative as a counterbalance to the heteronormativity of the rest of the world and especially the rest of the Jewish establishment. The curriculum of the school, however, always rested on the principles of non-normativity, or a least making diversity normative. It shows diversity of family structures including same-gender, interracial, and other diversities, and does so in order to make sure that all of the childrens' families (including the straight ones) are represented. The mission statement of the synagogue now includes heterosexuals as a key constituent of the congregation, and the school's constituents were largely responsible for the shift. The kaddish for gay martyrs is still part of the Siddur, but ten years from now, I predict that the wording will be changed to reflect all martyrs of oppression, not just those oppressed because of their sexual orientation.

The school and its curriculum are at the heart of this shift in demographics. It is true that the growing presence of straight-identified families who come to this synagogue precisely for its queer curriculum and community values threatens the queerness of the institution, if we define "queer" as queer normativity. But this aspect only looks at the limits of a queer curriculum and a queer synagogue. The opportunities presented by a queer curriculum are, in fact, endless.

The basic values that inform a queer curriculum—multiple family arrangements, progressive politics, sex-positive environment, all underpinning a rigorous Jewish education—must form the basis *of all* Jewish education's curricula as we move into the twenty-first century. All children should be exposed to queer couples kissing in the oneg room, to discussions about the Leviticus's ban on homosexuality. All children should be exposed to the many interpretations of David and Jonathon's love (at Sha'ar Zahav, we used to push the homosexual reading, and now we argue for multiple readings of their relationship). All children should be part of a community that embraces interfaith and interracial couples looking for a spiritual place that supports them. Once they are written and published, all school libraries should have books that reflect queer families in a Jewish context. At the roots of a queer curriculum are the Jewish values of *tikkun olam*, love, the idea that each person is created *be-tselem elohim* (in the image of God), and a space where the lives of children of gays and lesbians are as normative as every other child's life. Some may argue that these are simply quality, progressive educational values. I agree. But only a queer curriculum at the gay synagogue could push Jewish institutions from the "tolerance" model of progressive Jewish education's approach to sexual orientation (which is still a heteronormative approach) and dismantle the very idea of normativity within Jewish education and Jewish institutions.

Know the Heart of the Stranger

A Curriculum on Combating Assumptions and Stereotypes

Rabbi Geoffrey Mitelman and Joel L. Kushner, Psy.D.

Introductory Note to the Facilitator

It is easy when one is in a position of privilege not to be conscious of how stereotyped images of "the other" pervade our media, our discourse, our behavior, and our worldview. When stereotypes are widely shared by the majority group, they often justify discriminatory behavior, exclusion, and humiliation of those in the minority. Moreover, those groups who are treated as "other" often internalize these stereotypes, resulting in self-hating and self-destructive behavior.

A useful metaphor for this kind of treatment is the treatment of the "stranger"—someone who is perceived to be "different" from us and about whom we are ignorant, and thus often inspires fear and hatred.

Judaism has made several statements about how we are to treat "the stranger" and how we are to include people who may be different from us. What follows are activities that can help both Jewish youth and adults confront their own stereotypes and the reality of prejudice facing their GLBT family, friends, colleagues, neighbors, and members of the community.

Target Age Group: Grade 9 through adults

Total Time: 120 minutes

Enduring Understanding

As Jews, we have a responsibility to "know the heart of the stranger" (Exodus 23:9).

Essential Questions and Key Themes

1. How effectively can we empathize with people who are different from us? How can we improve our skills in this regard?

2. What are some issues for GLBT people that non-GLBT people might have trouble recognizing and understanding? How can we facilitate that understanding?

3. How can we move from viewing people who are GLBT as "strangers" to viewing them as part of the community? How do we recognize all people as being treated *b'tzelem Elohim*, "in the image of God" (Genesis 1:27)?

Evidence of Understanding

After this program, participants should be able to do the following:

1. Identify some of their own assumptions, stereotypes, and biases toward people who are GLBT.

2. Empathize with and be able to explain some of the emotional issues that their GLBT peers may experience.

3. Explain why feeling like "a stranger" may keep people from being fully productive in a community.

4. Interpret and apply Jewish tradition to support GLBT inclusion

Curriculum Overview

This curriculum is composed of five activities for a total time of 120 minutes.

- Activity 1 is called **Defining Our Terms.** It is designed to help the participants explore the general associations that the word "stranger" has in our society. It begins to explore what might lead someone to feel like a stranger and what Judaism teaches about our responsibilities to the stranger. It is approximately 25 minutes long.

- Activity 2 is called **Being the Stranger.** It allows the participants to explore their own experiences of when they felt like a "stranger." It is intended to help them recognize that the emotions of rejection and exclusion are universal—the primary difference is what prompts them. It is approximately 35 minutes long.

- Activity 3 is called **"Let Me Ask You This . . . ."** It starkly illustrates many of the stereotypes and assumptions that some people make about GLBT people. It is approximately 25 minutes long.

- Activity 4 is called **Through the Looking Glass, or "Toto, I have a feeling we're not in Kansas anymore!"** It asks participants to discuss scenarios where the societal assumptions about sexual orientation and gender identity are the reverse of our current societal norms. It is approximately 25 minutes long.

- Activity 5 is called **Lessons from the Text.** It brings together the learnings from the previous activities and connects back to biblical texts on how we treat the stranger, so that we remain rooted in Jewish textual tradition. It is approximately 10 minutes long.

Note to Facilitator

We have included set pieces because we have found that many facilitators like to use them. If you are comfortable with the material, you should feel free to add your own thoughts about it.

Activity 1: Defining Our Terms

Total Time: 25 minutes

Materials Needed

- Whiteboard with marker or chalkboard with chalk

Activity Plan

1. Write the words "stranger" and "neighbor" on the board, and ask the participants what connotations each of these words has. Write the participants' responses under each word.
   Ask the following guiding questions:
   - What makes someone a "stranger," and what makes someone a "neighbor"?
   - How do we treat strangers, and how do we think strangers treat us?
   - How do we treat neighbors, and how do we think neighbors treat us? Potential responses may include: *"neighbors" live nearby, "strangers" live far away; "neighbors" are people we can trust, "strangers" are people to fear; "neighbors" are part of our community, "strangers" are not.*

2. Ask the participants if they can name the three "people" that the Torah commands us to love. (Note to facilitator: the reason for the quotation marks is that one of the "people" is God.) When the participants correctly identify one of the three answers below, write it on the board. If after approximately one minute, they have not correctly identified all three, write the answers on the board yourself.
   The answers are as follows:
   - God—Deuteronomy 6:5
   - Our neighbor—Leviticus 19:18
   - The stranger—Leviticus 19:34

3. Explain to participants that given how we tend to view strangers, it would certainly seem challenging to "love" the stranger. Ask the following questions to determine what the phrase "loving the stranger" really means:
   - Does loving the stranger imply an emotion, or does it imply certain kinds of actions?

- If it is the latter, what actions would those be?

Write the participants' responses on the board. Potential responses may include: *kind treatment, nonderogatory remarks, offering a helping hand.*

4. Read the following paragraph to the participants:

   To help us understand how to "love" the stranger and why we would or should want to do this, there is another commandment that may help us. Exodus 23:9 says, "You shall not oppress a stranger, for you know the heart of the stranger, having yourselves been strangers in the land of Egypt."

   Then, ask the participants the following questions, and write the participants' responses on the board:

   - What are some ways that the Jews have been treated as strangers throughout history?

   Potential responses may include: *being made slaves; being called names; being falsely accused of things (such as carrying plague and sacrificing children); being forced to live in certain places; being restricted from certain jobs, professions, and educational opportunities.*

   - What are some ways that GLBT people have been treated as strangers throughout history?

   Potential responses may include: *not being allowed to practice certain professions; being fired because of who they love; being put in prison for who they are; being shunned or disowned by family; being forbidden to worship in their chosen community; being called names such as "degenerate"; being falsely accused of seducing children.*

5. To conclude this part of the activity, read the following to the participants:

   The purpose of this exercise has been to begin exploring what it might feel like to be a "stranger" in particular settings so that we can "know the heart of the stranger," which is the first step to the more challenging task of "loving the stranger."

   In the following exercises, we will be looking at more assumptions and stereotypes of GLBT people in various situations. Our purpose will be to attempt to better understand these factors in ourselves and society and to put ourselves in the shoes of a GLBT person so that we can move from seeing them as "strangers" to seeing them as "neighbors."

Activity 2: Being the Stranger

Total Time: 35 minutes

Materials Needed

- Copies of appendix A, Our Own Experience (page 103)
- A pen or a pencil for each participant

Activity Plan

1. Give each of the students a copy of the question in appendix A (also found below) and a pen or pencil. Tell them to read the handout and write down their response to the questions. You may want to read through the text out loud as a class and then give them time to answer the questions. Let them know that they will be asked to share this answer with a partner but that they can choose what parts of their answer they want to share. The question from appendix A is as follows:

   > Think of a situation you have experienced in your life when you were treated like a "stranger." This can be a time when you were excluded, a time when you were made fun of, or a time when someone made an incorrect assumption about you. As you write, think about:
   >
   > - What was the context of the situation? How did it arise?
   > - Who was there? Were these people you liked or people you didn't like? Did you care about the opinion of these people?
   > - What were you hoping to have happen? What actually happened?
   > - What emotions did you feel in that situation?

   Give the participants approximately five minutes to write down their responses.

2. Pair the students up, and tell them that they are going to do an activity entitled "think-pair-share." In each pair, one person will be "Person A," and the other will be "Person B." They will be sharing their stories in pairs, but they will do it in a particular way.

3. First, for two minutes, *only Person A may talk*. He or she should share his or her story, but may also add more details, emphasize certain pieces, etc. While Person A is talking, Person B *cannot* ask questions or make comments—Person B should simply *listen*.

4. For the next two minutes, only Person B may talk. Again, he or she should share his or her story, but may also add more details, emphasize certain pieces, etc. While Person B is talking, Person A *cannot* ask questions or make comments—Person A should now be the one *listening*.

5. Finally, for the last two minutes, *both people may talk*. They can ask questions for clarification, make comments, share ideas, etc.

6. Bring the participants together as a whole group. Ask the participants, "Based on what you learned in your pairs, what are some common themes that occur when someone is treated like a 'stranger'?"

7. Next, ask the participants, "What might have helped you *not* feel like a 'stranger'?"
   Potential responses may include: *gaining more self-confidence/assertiveness; having a support system; talking with close friends; ignoring the opinions of the people who excluded you.*

8. Looking back on the previous activity where we explored ways that GLBT people have been excluded from society, ask the participants: "Compare some of the *emotions* you *yourselves* felt when you were excluded with the emotions your GLBT colleagues might have felt when they were excluded."
   Potential responses may include: *anger; helplessness; a desire to take action; fear; sadness.*

9. Finally, ask the participants what our responsibilities are to ensure that we do not treat people in general and GLBT people in particular like "strangers."

    Potential responses may include: *identifying and challenging intolerance; not making derogatory remarks about people; not standing by when someone else makes jokes or derogatory comments, and saying that such statements are offensive and not funny; not making assumptions about someone else's identity; correcting people's faulty assumptions when you hear them; showcasing diversity materials; creating opportunities to speak with GLBT people; modeling appropriate behavior for others.*

10. Conclude by reading the following to the participants:

    Even if we do not understand *why* someone may be struggling or hurting, we can see *that* someone is struggling or hurting. While experiences may differ, emotions are universal. Everyone wants to be respected and valued for who they are, and no one wants to feel rejected or excluded.

    For centuries, Jews have often been rejected from society. Similarly, people who are GLBT have also experienced a similar sense of exclusion from society. The goal of this exercise was to explore the question, "What does it feel like to be a 'stranger'?" in order to address the question, "How do we make sure that *no one* in our community feels like a 'stranger'?"

Activity 3: "Let Me Ask You This..."

Total Time: 25 minutes

Materials Needed

- Copies of the questionnaire from appendix B, Test Yourself (pages 104–106)
- A pen or pencil for each student

Activity Plan

1. Copy the questionnaire in appendix B, and distribute it to the participants.

2. Ask the participants to read and answer the questions. Tell them that they *do not need to share their answers*. Give them seven minutes to read and answer the questions.

3. After the participants have completed the questionnaire, ask them, "Regardless of how you might have responded to any of the questions, how many times have you *heard* similar statements using GLBT language?" We can safely assume that all the participants have at least *heard* one of these statements, if not more.

4. Ask the participants, "If we have heard similar-sounding statements about GLBT people, what assumptions underlie those statements?"

5. Brainstorm what the underlying assumptions are when we use similar statements regarding GLBT people. List their responses on the board. Potential responses may include: *homosexuality is a "deviation"; homosexuality is a "choice"; homosexuals are "immoral"; homosexuals are "sex-crazed."*

6. Conclude the discussion by reading the following to the participants:

> Most likely, we have many assumptions about the nature, behaviors, and actions of GLBT people—most of them false. The purpose of this exercise was to highlight how absurd some of these assumptions are. Now, having brought some of these faulty assumptions to the surface, the next exercise will explore another way to try to "step into someone else's shoes" in order to understand some of the emotional struggles facing people who are GLBT.

Activity 4: Through the Looking Glass, or "Toto, I have a feeling we're not in Kansas anymore!"

Total Time: 25 minutes

Materials Needed

- Copies of appendix C, Scenarios (page 107)

Introductory Note to the Facilitator

The scenarios in this activity are presented from a heterosexual perspective. We do *not* assume that every participant in the activity is heterosexual. In fact, depending on the size of the group, it is statistically likely that at least one or more participants *will* be GLBT, and these participants may or may not be out as GLBT. Thus, in discussing the scenarios where each participant "plays a role" that may or may not coincide with how they see themselves, it may be uncomfortable for some, and yet it may also be an opportunity for others to share their experiences under the guise of the assumed identity.

Facilitators can share this understanding that there are likely both straight and GLBT people in the group. This is not meant to force people to come out nor to be an opportunity to speculate on the sexual orientation or gender of others. Rather, it is sharing an understanding and exposing people to a reality that many remain unaware of.

Also, this may be a difficult activity for participants to understand. Facilitators should be prepared that the participants may show a variety of reactions to these scenarios. They may exhibit nervous laughter, eye-rolling, or even silence. Be on the lookout for these responses. You can acknowledge them and explain that these reactions come from a level of discomfort with this activity. Participants should not be shamed for their reactions, but inappropriate behavior also needs to be addressed.

Regarding scenario C, while most participants will have had at least some experience with someone who is gay or lesbian (whether in real life or in the media), it is less likely that they will have come across someone transgender. Some people may have seen the Brandon Teena story in the movie *Girls Don't Cry* with Hilary Swank, or they may have seen *Transamerica* with Felicity Huffman. If people do not know what these terms mean, you may need to start by offering definitions of the word. As this is a complex topic, try not to get stuck with questions about the definition. It is okay to hold more detailed questions for after the program to be able to focus on the exercise.

To support scenario D, we have also included a definition of the word "bisexuality."

Definitions

Transgender

Transgender people are individuals whose gender identity and/or gender expression (i.e., appearance) differs from the physical sex they were born as or assigned at birth. The definition becomes complex, as the word "transgender" is used as an umbrella term to describe a wide range of identities and experiences, including female-to-male transsexuals (FTMs), male-to-female transsexuals (MTFs), cross-dressers, drag queens, drag kings, gender queers, and others. Each of these individuals is likely to have a very different experience from the other of their actual identity, despite all being lumped into one category. It is also important to explain that gender identity and sexual orientation are very different. Transgender people can be gay, lesbian, straight, queer, bisexual, or none of the above. See the glossary for more information.

Bisexuality

Bisexuality is the capacity for emotional, romantic, and/or physical attraction to more than one gender/sex. A person who self-identifies as bisexual affirms this complexity and acknowledges a reality beyond the either/or dualities of assuming everyone is either heterosexual or homosexual.

Activity Plan

1. Read the following to the participants:

   > The scenarios in this activity are presented from a heterosexual perspective. We do *not* assume that every participant in this room is heterosexual. In fact, depending on the size of the group, it is statistically likely that at least one or more participants may be GLBT. This is not a moment to speculate about your peers. Rather, we are sharing a statistical reality that contrasts with heterosexist assumptions that we are all the same, that is, straight. Thus, in discussing the scenarios, we *each* get to "play a role" that may or may not coincide with how we see ourselves. In sharing our views on these scenarios, try to allow for a safe environment where people can freely share their views without fear of being judged by their peers for the comments they make.

2. Divide the participants into groups of four or five, with a facilitator assigned to each group. Hand each group one of the four scenarios from appendix C. It is all right if more than one group has the same scenario. If there are fewer than four groups, you may pick which of the four scenarios are used. In the small groups, discuss the following questions from appendix C:

   - What are your reactions as the person in the scenario?
   - What reasons might lead you to want to fit in with this group, even if you feel uncomfortable?
   - What would happen if you did not conform to the standards of the group in the scenario?

- If you wanted to correct other people's assumptions, what qualities would it take to do so?
- What kind of responses from the rest of the group would make it easier or more difficult to feel included?

The scenarios from appendix C are as follows:

a. You were dragged along to your congregation's singles group by a couple of friends. You believe you are the only heterosexual in the group. Everyone else is talking about their "ideal mate" and describing someone of the same gender. You are looking for a mate of the opposite gender, but you have never told anyone this fact about yourself. Thus in order to fit in with the group, you have to change your pronouns regarding past relationships as well as the names of people that you have dated in the past.

b. You are a heterosexual person visiting a congregation for the first time. During the *oneg*, a rather nosy, aggressive congregant saunters up to you, says how attractive you are, and wonders why such a nice person like you is still single. This congregant then tries to fix you up with his nephew or niece of the same gender as you.

c. You are a non-transgender man who uses male pronouns (i.e., "he" and "him"). You arrive at a Shabbat dinner, and everyone there perceives you as female and consistently uses female pronouns for you, saying things like: "Will you ask her to pass the salt?" You correct the other guests and explain that you see yourself as male, hence male pronouns are more appropriate for you. These corrections are met with a range of responses: some people giggle and continue to call you "she," others apologize but still make mistakes, some people get angry that you would suggest using a different pronoun than the one that they feel is "right" for you, and still others are able to transition into using male pronouns for you.

d. You are a monosexual person (either attracted only to men or only to women) and have been asked to discuss your life experience with a confirmation class studying sexual ethics as part of their diversity module. The assumption is that none of the students share your sexual orientation (i.e., they are all bisexual), though you know that, in fact, some may be monosexual.

   The first few questions ask whether monosexuality is really a cover for fear of sex, fear of intimacy, fear of men or women (depending on your gender attraction), or dislike of human beings in general. The next several questions are variations on whether all monosexual people have an abnormally low sex drive. No matter how many times you say that you're a normal person with a normal sex drive, just attracted to only one gender, the questions continue to assume some form of pathology. The teacher closes by saying, "Though many monosexual people have a fear of intimacy or low sex drive, we see that there are exceptions."

3. Come back together as a large group. Ask the participants, "What do these scenarios teach us about some of the challenges GLBT people may face when they are treated like a 'stranger'?" Share some of the learnings from the small groups.

Activity 5: Lessons from the Text

Total Time: 10 minutes

Materials Needed

- Copies of the text from appendix D, Text Study (page 108)

Activity Plan

1. Post these three verses from the Torah (also found in appendix D) on the board or wall in a larger format, or distribute them to each participant as a handout.

וְגֵר לֹא תִלְחָץ וְאַתֶּם יְדַעְתֶּם אֶת־נֶפֶשׁ הַגֵּר כִּי־גֵרִים הֱיִיתֶם בְּאֶרֶץ מִצְרָיִם׃

You shall not oppress a stranger, for you know the heart of the stranger, having yourselves been strangers in the land of Egypt. (Exodus 23:9)

כְּאֶזְרָח מִכֶּם יִהְיֶה לָכֶם הַגֵּר הַגָּר אִתְּכֶם וְאָהַבְתָּ לוֹ כָּמוֹךָ כִּי־גֵרִים הֱיִיתֶם בְּאֶרֶץ מִצְרָיִם אֲנִי יְהֹוָה אֱלֹהֵיכֶם׃

The strangers who reside with you shall be to you as your citizens; you shall love each one as yourself, for you were strangers in the land of Egypt: I the Eternal am your God. (Leviticus 19:34)

וְאָהַבְתָּ לְרֵעֲךָ כָּמוֹךָ אֲנִי יְהֹוָה׃

Love your fellow [neighbor] as yourself: I am the Eternal. (Leviticus 19:18)

2. Interpret the verses, answering the following questions:

    - How do the verses connect to each other?
    - What do they mean for our everyday lives?
    - What are our moral responsibilities to treat all people as being created *b'tzelem Elohim*, "in the image of God"?

Appendix A: Our Own Experience
(For Activity 2: Being the Stranger)

Think of a situation you have experienced in your life when you were treated like a "stranger." This can be a time when you were excluded, a time when you were made fun of, or a time when someone made an incorrect assumption about you. As you write, think about:

- What was the context of the situation? How did it arise?
- Who was there? Were these people you liked or people you didn't like? Did you care about the opinion of these people?
- What were you hoping to have happen? What actually happened?
- What emotions did you feel in that situation?

_____

_____

_____

_____

_____

_____

_____

_____

_____

_____

_____

_____

_____

_____

_____

_____

Appendix B: Test Yourself
(For Activity 3: "Let Me Ask You This . . .")*

All of the questions below raise issues about heterosexual behavior. For each question:

1. Circle your answer.
2. Circle "yes" or "no" to the last part of each question.

   a. At what age did you realize that you were heterosexual?

   Infancy–age 4
   Age 5–9
   Age 10–12
   Age 13–18
   Age 18 or older
   What do you mean? I was always this way!

   - Have you ever asked or wanted to ask a similar-sounding question of someone who is *not* heterosexual?

         YES   NO

   b. Is it possible that your heterosexuality is just a phase you may grow out of?*

   This is who I am—it isn't a phase.
   Yes, possibly.

   - Have you ever asked or wanted to ask a similar-sounding question of someone who is *not* heterosexual?

         YES   NO

   c. Do your parents know that you are straight?*

   Yes, of course they do—I've already come out to them.
   Yes, of course they do—they automatically assumed it.
   No, I fear what they may say and do if they know. It's so unacceptable in my family, I fear that I'll be ostracized.
   This is a stupid question!

   - Have you ever asked or wanted to ask a similar-sounding question of someone who is *not* heterosexual?

         YES   NO

   d. Why do you insist on flaunting your heterosexuality? Can't you just be who you are and keep it quiet?*

   I'm not flaunting it. It's just who I am. And sometimes I like to be spontaneous.

---

*Please note that those questions marked with an asterisk are from the "Test Yourself" section of "The Heterosexual Questionnaire" by Martin Rochlin, in Michael S. Kimmel and Michael A. Messner, *Men's Lives* (Boston: Allyn & Bacon, 1998). The multiple-choice options and those questions that are not marked by an asterisk were designed by Lori Yetman for The Heterosexism Inquirer, www.mun.ca/the/themain.html.

I try not to be obvious about the love I feel for my partner—but sometimes we do get caught showing affection—I'm sorry.

- Have you ever asked or wanted to ask a similar-sounding question of someone who is *not* heterosexual?

    YES   NO

e. Why do heterosexuals feel compelled to seduce others into their lifestyle?*

It's necessary! We have to ensure the propagation of the species.
It isn't a lifestyle. It's an identity. And you either have it or you don't. Our society, however, does present heterosexuality as the only possible identity—and that discourages many people from recognizing or acknowledging their own identities.

- Have you ever asked or wanted to ask a similar-sounding question of someone who is *not* heterosexual?

    YES   NO

f. A disproportionate majority of child molesters are heterosexual. Do you consider it safe to expose children to heterosexual teachers?[1]

This isn't true. The fact is, most child molesters are homosexuals.
Most of the time I feel safe. Child molesters make up a small segment of the population, and we, as a society, are beginning to take better care of children by putting mechanisms in place for children to recognize inappropriate behavior and to report it.
Most of the time I do feel unsafe, but just about teachers. Historically, our society hasn't had a good track record in terms of recognizing or preventing child sexual abuse.

- Have you ever asked or wanted to ask a similar-sounding question of someone who is *not* heterosexual?

    YES   NO

g. With all the societal support marriage receives, the divorce rate is spiraling. Why are there so few stable relationships among heterosexuals?*

Wow! This is true, but I can't state one cause—there are multiple reasons.
Well, the divorce rate may be high, but we're more stable than homosexuals!

- Have you ever asked or wanted to ask a similar-sounding question of someone who is *not* heterosexual?

    YES   NO

h. Could you trust a heterosexual therapist to be objective? Don't you feel she/he might be inclined to influence you in the direction of her/his own leanings?*

---

1. There is sometimes confusion regarding question f. It is in fact true that the significant majority of child molesters are heterosexual and only a small minority are homosexual.

I don't believe that people of any sexuality seek recruits—sexuality isn't a social club.

Because there are so few of them, only homosexuals seek recruits.

- Have you ever asked or wanted to ask a similar-sounding question of someone who is *not* heterosexual?

YES   NO

i. There seem to be very few happy heterosexuals. Techniques have been developed that might enable you to change if you really want to. Have you considered trying aversion therapy?*

Giving me electric shocks after viewing naked pictures of the sex to whom I'm attracted is not going to change me. My sexuality is part of who I am and is not open to change, like all sexualities.

Heterosexuality is natural; homosexuality is not. Heterosexuality cannot be changed by aversion therapy, whereas homosexuality can.

- Have you ever asked or wanted to ask a similar-sounding question of someone who is *not* heterosexual?

YES   NO

j. Do you feel that heterosexuality is acceptable but only if heterosexuals refrain from public displays of affection?

Yes, it's OK if they refrain from showing affection in public.

No, it's never OK.

It depends on what kind of affection.

It's acceptable whether or not affection is displayed publicly.

- Have you ever asked or wanted to ask a similar-sounding question of someone who is *not* heterosexual?

YES   NO

Appendix C: Scenarios
(For Activity 4: Through the Looking Glass)

- What are your reactions as the person in the scenario?
- What reasons might lead you to want to fit in with this group, even if you feel uncomfortable?
- What would happen if you did not conform to the standards of the group in the scenario?
- If you wanted to correct other people's assumptions, what qualities would it take to do so?
- What kind of responses from the rest of the group would make it easier or more difficult to feel included?

A. You were dragged along to your congregation's singles group by a couple of friends. You believe you are the only heterosexual in the group. Everyone else is talking about their "ideal mate" and describing someone of the same gender. You are looking for a mate of the opposite gender, but you have never told anyone this fact about yourself. Thus in order to fit in with the group, you have to change your pronouns regarding past relationships as well as the names of people that you have dated in the past.

B. You are a heterosexual person visiting a congregation for the first time. During the *oneg*, a rather nosy, aggressive congregant saunters up to you, says how attractive you are, and wonders why such a nice person like you is still single. This congregant then tries to fix you up with his nephew or niece of the same gender as you.

C. You are a non-transgender man who uses male pronouns (i.e., "he" and "him"). You arrive at a Shabbat dinner and everyone there perceives you as female and consistently uses female pronouns for you, saying things like: "Will you ask her to pass the salt?" You correct the other guests and explain that you see yourself as male, hence male pronouns are more appropriate for you. These corrections are met with a range of responses: some people giggle and continue to call you "she," others apologize but still make mistakes, some people get angry that you would suggest using a different pronoun than the one that they feel is "right" for you and still others are able to transition into using male pronouns for you.

D. You are a monosexual person (either attracted only to men or only to women) and have been asked to discuss your life experience with a confirmation class studying sexual ethics as part of their diversity module. The assumption is that none of the students share your sexual orientation (i.e., they are all bisexual), though you know that, in fact, some may be monosexual.

  The first few questions ask whether monosexuality is really a cover for fear of sex, fear of intimacy, fear of men or women (depending on your gender attraction), or dislike of human beings in general. The next several questions are variations on whether all monosexual people have an abnormally low sex drive. No matter how many times you say that you're a normal person with a normal sex drive, just attracted to only one gender, the questions continue to assume some form of pathology. The teacher closes by saying, "Though many monosexual people have a fear of intimacy or low sex drive, we see that there are exceptions."

Appendix D: Text Study
(For Activity 5: Lessons from the Text)

וְגֵר לֹא תִלְחָץ וְאַתֶּם יְדַעְתֶּם אֶת־נֶפֶשׁ הַגֵּר כִּי־גֵרִים הֱיִיתֶם בְּאֶרֶץ מִצְרָיִם:

You shall not oppress a stranger, for you know the heart of the stranger, having yourselves been strangers in the land of Egypt. (Exodus 23:9)

כְּאֶזְרָח מִכֶּם יִהְיֶה לָכֶם הַגֵּר | הַגָּר אִתְּכֶם וְאָהַבְתָּ לוֹ כָּמוֹךָ כִּי־גֵרִים הֱיִיתֶם בְּאֶרֶץ מִצְרָיִם אֲנִי יְהֹוָה אֱלֹהֵיכֶם:

The strangers who reside with you shall be to you as your citizens; you shall love each one as yourself, for you were strangers in the land of Egypt: I the Eternal am your God. (Leviticus 19:34)

וְאָהַבְתָּ לְרֵעֲךָ כָּמוֹךָ אֲנִי יְהֹוָה:

Love your fellow [neighbor] as yourself: I am the Eternal. (Leviticus 19:18)

What Does Biphobia Look Like?

Lani Ka'ahumanu and Rob Yeager

What Is Bisexuality?

Bisexuality is the capacity for emotional, romantic, and/or physical attraction to more than one gender/sex. A person who self-identifies as bisexual affirms this complexity and acknowledges a reality beyond the either/or dualities of heterosexism.

What Is Bisexual Identity?

A bisexual identity speaks to the potential, not the requirement, for involvement with more than one gender/sex. This involvement may mean sexually, emotionally, in reality, or in fantasy. Monogamy and non-monogamy are relationship choices made independently of sexual identity. Some bisexuals are monogamous, some may have concurrent partners, others may relate to different genders/sexes during different times of their lives. Most bisexuals do not have to be involved with more than one person at a time in order to feel fulfilled.

Identity has nothing to do with sexual behavior or experience. Bisexuals, despite the sexually insatiable stereotype, may or may not be sexually active, may or may not have been sexual with more than one person, or may never have been sexual at all. As with all sexual identities, whom one is or is not having sex with, or whether one is being sexual or not, has nothing to do with the validity of a self-professed identity (i.e., a lesbian is still a lesbian, a gay man is still a gay man, and a heterosexual remains a heterosexual whether they are being or have ever been sexual or not).

What Is Heterosexism?

The institution of heterosexism is based on a mutually exclusive heterosexual/homosexual framework. This heterosexist paradigm posits two sexual orientations on either side of

---

Lani Ka'ahumanu and Rob Yeager, "What Does Biphobia Look Like?" (pamphlet, Bisexual Resource Center of Boston, Massachusetts). Based on conversations with Gerard Palmeri, Danielle Raymond, Loraine Hutchins, and Cianna Stewart Portions; adapted from material by the Rape Crisis Center of West Contra Costa County, CA, the Boston Lesbian Task Force, and Building Bridges.

a "fence" that draws the line where privilege begins and ends. Heterosexuals are on the "normal/good" side and homosexuals are on the "abnormal/evil" side. The line separates and protects "us" from "them," while it assures members of each side of what they are not. This line also effectively marginalizes lesbians and gay men as "other" and is the core of homophobia.

Furthermore, lesbian, gay, and heterosexual people are invested and find a sense of security in being the "other" to each other and unite in the fact that they are only attracted to either the "same" or the "opposite" gender/sex. This sets up another "us" versus "them" dynamic that effectively marginalizes bisexual people as "other." Integral to this dynamic is the automatic assumption that people can be defined by the gender/sex of their current or potential romantic interest. For example: two women are assumed to be lesbians in a "lesbian" relationship; two men are assumed to be gay in a "gay" relationship; and a man and woman are assumed to be heterosexual in a "heterosexual" relationship. However, any or all of these people could be bisexual. And depending upon monogamy and non-monogamy agreements and choices, any or all of these folks could have sexual behavior with more than one gender/sex whether they identify as bisexual or not.

What Is Biphobia?

Bisexual women and men cannot be defined by their partner or potential partner, so are rendered invisible within the either/or heterosexist framework. This invisibility (biphobia) is one of the most challenging aspects of a bisexual identity. Living in a society that is based and thrives on opposition, on the reassurances and "balanced" polarities of dichotomy, affects how we see the world and how we negotiate our own and other people's lives to fit "reality."

Most people are unaware of their homosexual or heterosexual assumptions until a bisexual speaks up/comes out and challenges the assumption. Very often bisexuals are then dismissed and told they are "confused" and "simply have to make up their mind and choose." For bisexually identified people to maintain their integrity in a homo-hating heterosexist society, they must have a strong sense of self and the courage and conviction to live their lives in defiance of what passes for "normal."

What Does Biphobia Look Like?

- Assuming that everyone you meet is either heterosexual or homosexual.
- Supporting and understanding a bisexual identity for young people because you identified "that way" before you came to your "real" lesbian/gay/heterosexual identity.
- Expecting a bisexual to identify as heterosexual when coupled with the "opposite" gender/sex.
- Believing bisexual men spread AIDS/HIV and other STDs to heterosexuals.
- Thinking bisexual people haven't made up their minds.
- Assuming a bisexual person would want to fulfill your sexual fantasies or curiosities.
- Assuming bisexuals would be willing to "pass" as anything other than bisexual.
- Feeling that bisexual people are too outspoken and pushy about their visibility and rights.

- Automatically assuming that romantic couplings of two women are lesbian, or two men are gay, or a man and a woman are heterosexual.
- Expecting bisexual people to get services, information, and education from heterosexual service agencies for their "heterosexual side [*sic*]" and then go to gay and/or lesbian service agencies for their "homosexual side [*sic*]."
- Feeling bisexuals just want to have their cake and eat it too.
- Believing that bisexual women spread AIDS/HIV and other STDs to lesbians.
- Using the terms "phase," "stage," "confused," "fence-sitter," "bisexual," "AC/DC," or "switch-hitter," as slurs or in an accusatory way.
- Thinking bisexuals only have committed relationships with "opposite" sex/gender partners.
- Looking at a bisexual person and automatically thinking of their sexuality rather than seeing them as a whole, complete person.
- Believing bisexuals are confused about their sexuality.
- Assuming that bisexuals, if given the choice, would prefer to be within an "opposite" gender/sex coupling to reap the social benefits of a "heterosexual" pairing.
- Not confronting a biphobic remark or joke for fear of being identified as bisexual.
- Assuming bisexual means "available."
- Thinking that bisexual people will have their rights when lesbian and gay people win theirs.
- Being gay or lesbian and asking your bisexual friend about their lover only when that lover is the same sex/gender.
- Feeling that you can't trust a bisexual because they aren't really gay or lesbian or aren't really heterosexual.
- Thinking that people identify as bisexual because it's "trendy."
- Expecting a bisexual to identify as gay or lesbian when coupled with the "same" sex/gender.
- Expecting bisexual activists and organizers to minimize bisexual issues (e.g., HIV/AIDS, violence, basic civil rights, fighting the Right, military, same-sex marriage, child custody, adoption) and to prioritize the visibility of "lesbian and/or gay" issues.
- Avoid mentioning to friends that you are involved with a bisexual or working with a bisexual group because you are afraid they will think you are a bisexual.

Understanding Your Bisexual Congregants (Colleagues, Friends, Family Members...)

Rabbi Jane Rachel Litman

Bisexuality Is a Continuum: Sheep and Goats

In 1948, the pioneering sex researcher Dr. Alfred Kinsey wrote in his book *Sexual Behavior in the Human Male*, "The world is not divided into sheep and goats.... The living world is a continuum in each and every one of its aspects."[1] So Kinsey developed a seven-point scale (zero is exclusively heterosexual; six exclusively homosexual) to represent the "continuum" of sexual identity. Although most people can find a way to roughly fit into one of two available sexual identity labels (homosexual and heterosexual), some people cannot fit, and for many people there is a more complex story. Seven gives more possibilities than two and implies by its structure that sexuality is a spectrum rather than an on/off switch. Of course, zero to six is an arbitrary gradation; it could as easily be a scale of one hundred or one thousand points.

People who do not fit into the binary heterosexual/homosexual categories are called bisexual. Bisexual people can be equally attracted to men and women (a Kinsey three); attracted more to one gender, but still significantly attracted to the other gender (Kinsey one, two, four, and five); or indifferent to gender, more attracted to other qualities or each person as an individual. Bisexual people may have actual sexual experience with women and men or may have erotic feelings, but not experience, in regard to both men and women.

Some bisexual people perceive themselves as "born" bisexual, while for others, bisexual feelings emerge over a lifetime. Bisexual identity is an inner understanding of self. A single person without a partner can still identify as bisexual (just as a single hetero- or homosexual person retains sexual identity even without a partner). Similarly, a bisexual person in an exclusive relationship (with either a woman or a man) can still identify as bisexual in terms of self-understanding. This means that people who outwardly "appear" to be homo- or heterosexual because they are in relationships may, in fact, identify as bisexual.

The category of bisexual is also a bit of a catchall. Human sexuality is complex, not only reliant on gender. For some people, other qualities such as intelligence, sociability, warmth,

---

1. Alfred Kinsey, Wardell Pomeroy, and Clyde Martin, *Sexual Behavior in the Human Male* (Philadelphia: W. B. Saunders, 1948), p. 639.

or body type are more primary than gender. In the current sexual identity model, these people fall into the category of "bisexual" though there is nothing binary about their sexuality. I might also argue that in our society, women in general are socialized to be erotically attracted to emotion-based romance. It is my experience that women (in our culture—I'm not making a biological argument) tend to be a little more flexible about gender in the presence of a strong emotion-based romance. Similarly, men deprived of women as a sexual "outlet," that is, men in all-male schools or other institutions, may turn to other men for sex. Though they might not identify as bisexual (or gay), the sexual urge in and of itself is stronger than gender preference and societal restrictions.

Even gender itself is complex. The existence of transgender and intersex people shows that the binary system of gender may not describe factual reality. Over time, a more nuanced and flexible descriptive system may emerge. If gender itself is not binary, then a sexual identity system based on binary gender attraction will also need more complexity. A time may arrive when the terms "hetero-," "homo-," and "bisexual," and even the seven-point Kinsey continuum, will seem too limited to describe human sexual identity.

Bisexuality Isn't a Stereotype: Blondes and Redheads

As with any minority group, there are persistent negative stereotypes about bisexual people. One common stereotype is that a bisexual person needs both a man and a woman partner at all times in order to be sexually fulfilled. However, in current usage, bisexuality is primarily a description of identity. It is a global characterization of feelings over a lifetime rather than a snapshot of any one moment. Rabbi Debra Orenstein once rhetorically asked me, "In your entire lifetime have you ever been a attracted to a redhead? To a blonde? Yes? Do you then always need one of each in order to be sexually fulfilled?" Though this is not a perfect parallel, it makes the point. Over the course of a lifetime, a person can be (will be) attracted to more than one kind of person and yet not "need" more than one person in order to be fulfilled. For many bisexual people, the gender of the partner is not the primary salient quality of attraction.

During the normal life stage of dating and experimentation, bisexual people are particularly targeted by negative "myths." It is assumed that both homosexual and heterosexual people will date for awhile and then eventually settle down to a committed relationship (or not). In my (extensive) experience of bisexual people, this is true as well, yet there is a persistent belief that bisexual people cannot make an interpersonal commitment. Sometimes non-bisexual dating partners feel threatened and insecure due to the difference in sexual identity. Though in general people mostly date people of the same sexual identity, that is, heterosexual people mostly date heterosexual people and homosexual people mostly date homosexual people, this is not the case for bisexual people. The difference in sexual orientation/identity pairings can cause problems. Some monosexual (non-bisexual) people have trouble believing that a bisexual person won't leave them for someone of the other gender. This myth about bisexuality can ultimately undermine a successful trust relationship.

There are other negative stereotypes that bisexual people fear intimacy and that bisexual people have an abnormal sexual desire/drive. These are hateful "myths," similar to the myths that gay men are predators, that lesbians hate men, or that Jews are stingy with money. These myths are a combination of ignorance and xenophobia. Education and actual experience show the falseness of these stereotypes to people of goodwill.

Some Bisexual People Are Jewish: Ruths and Davids

What is the significance of bisexuality in Jewish terms? For liberal Judaism, bisexuality mostly fits the same paradigm as homosexuality. It is a reality of life. It is a minority sexual identity. There is nothing overtly sinful or harmful about it. Just like homosexual people, bisexual people are members of Jewish congregations, communities, friendship circles, and families. Supporting people in being authentically themselves is a form of *tikkun olam*. Jewish tradition teaches that all people are made in the image of God, *b'tzelem Elohim*, and that Jews have a special charge to look after the welfare of strangers, for Jews were strangers in the land of *Mitzrayim*, Egypt (Exodus 23:9; Leviticus 19:34).

Jewish role models such as Ruth, Naomi, David, and Jonathan give us insight into same-gender bonding and love, both platonic and otherwise. Ruth and Naomi manage to create a thriving, loving extended family across cultural boundaries that heals a grievous past filled with loss. David and Jonathan forge a bond of trust that cuts across politics and power. Historical parts of the Jewish tradition that are homophobic need to be reinterpreted or discarded as based on ignorance and cultural limitations, just like many other obsolete prescriptions such as exiling Shabbat breakers or stoning rebellious children to death. In the last thirty years, Reform and Reconstructionist Judaism have made tremendous progress in including gay and lesbian Jews in their movements. Current efforts to expand that inclusivity to bisexual and transgender Jews are simply the logical next step.

However, in terms of the system of halachah (Jewish law), bisexuality raises questions and issues that trouble or threaten some gay rights advocates who are not part of the liberal Jewish world. This has the very unfortunate result of hostility toward bisexuality in some Conservative/Orthodox gay rights circles. These gay rights advocates base their analysis of the subject on the belief that all people are born with a static sexual identity that cannot be changed or chosen. Historical Jewish law stipulates that people need not fulfill certain mitzvot if by circumstances of birth they are unable to fulfill such mitzvot. These categories usually apply to people with what we might term physical disabilities, and is intended compassionately. For example, a person with no hands does not need to fulfill the mitvah of wrapping *t'fillin* around the hands. Arguing by analogy, halachic gay rights advocates say that a person born without an ability to engage sexually with the opposite sex does not need to do so. However, though many bisexual people experience themselves as bisexual from birth, others develop their sexual identities over their lifetimes and do not view themselves as part of a static system. They therefore "muddy" the black-and-white nature of this halachic argument. In addition, these halachically based gay rights advocates almost always say that it is better to be heterosexual, but that homosexuals are born with a form of physical (and halachic) deficiency. By definition, bisexuality is a rejection of this idea.

As a religious Jew, I find these specific gay rights arguments particularly sad. Isn't it better just to affirm everyone's human worth and not discriminate at all? I believe that acceptance of GLBT people is a form of human liberation, a way that all human beings can experience their most true selves. I don't think that people need to justify their sexual identities or rank them in order or feel bad for having a minority sexual identity. I think that people can change over time if they wish but can also maintain a constant identity if they wish. This is true for all people, whatever their sexual experiences and feelings. The concept that people can change their sexual self-perceptions is not a justification to force people into "retraining" programs or unhealthy relationships, but a way of allowing people to find what is best for them after having enough experience to understand themselves.

Understanding Bisexual People: Pat Parker and Martin Buber

In explaining how to be supportive of minority people, the African-American lesbian poet Pat Parker wrote, "You must forget that I am Black; you must always remember that I am Black." The most important thing to know about any person is that he/she is a human being. As human beings, we share a deep and profound humanity, a set of universal core values and experiences. But each of us also has a particular context, a set of values and experiences emerging out of our culture(s), and an individual context that is our own unique heritage. As Martin Buber, the Jewish German philosopher, said, "Every person born into this world represents something new, something that never existed before, something original and unique. It is the duty of every person in Israel to know and consider that he [or she] is unique in the world in his [or her] particular character and that there has never been anyone like him in the world, for if there had been someone like him [or her], there would have been no need for him [or her] to be in the world. Every single man [or woman] is a new thing in the world, and is called upon to fulfill his [or her] particularity in the world."[2]

In each interpersonal encounter, there is a balance of shared humanity and the discovery of difference. It is possible to make generalizations about all the members of a group, but it is always important to realize the limitations inherent in such generalizations. That said, bisexual people, as a group, tend to have certain kinds of problems in our society. Aside from being the target of nasty stereotypes and the discrimination accorded all GLBT people, the most common particular issue facing bisexual people is invisibility, which can lead to inner insecurity.

In our society it is assumed that everyone is heterosexual. Over the past forty or so years, courageous individuals with a strong sense of same-sex gender attraction have pioneered gay/lesbian identity. But many bisexual people feel that they don't exist in either camp. They know they're not heterosexual, which can be confusing, but they also don't have a strong defining exclusive attraction to the same sex. Young bisexual people often feel pressured to "choose" either a hetero- or homosexual identity. Sometimes they capitulate to that pressure, and sometimes they just feel more confused. It is difficult to constantly assert a misunderstood minority sexual identity—sometimes for bisexual people it is just easier to let heterosexual culture assume one is heterosexual and to let gay culture assume one is gay. This beating down of one's authentic self is a form of internalized oppression. Most people prefer not to "pass" as something other than they are. Passing is a response to overt discrimination and a more subtle lack of emotional safety.

Bisexual people with partners become even more invisible. A bisexual person with an opposite-gender partner is assumed to be heterosexual. A bisexual person with a same-gender partner is assumed to be homosexual. Despite a person's past life experience, inner feelings, or self-identification, she/he is often placed in the wrong box. Once this occurs, past experience (no matter how profound and life altering), inner feelings, and self-identification all become invisible. American Jews also experience this kind of invisibility and can empathize by recalling their experience during the Christmas season when they are continually greeted by "Merry Christmas." It just feels better to be met with openness rather than assumptions.

---

2. Martin Buber, *The Way of Man: According to the Teaching of Hasidism* (New York: Kensington, 1994), p. 16. Brackets not in the original.

On Beyond Zebra

I deeply appreciate that this essay is part of a book entitled *Kulanu*—"all of us." For Jews, becoming truly *kulanu*, an inclusive, unified Jewish community, is larger than an essay about understanding bisexuality or even the complexity of human sexuality. *Kulanu* does not only apply to bisexual people, the subject of this essay, and to lesbian and gay people and transgender and intersex people, who are also the topic of this book. The idea of becoming *kulanu* applies to all Jews—the disenfranchised and/or marginalized—to intermarried Jews, racially mixed Jews, immigrant Jews, poor Jews, Jews-by-choice, Jews raised not knowing they were Jews—as well as to Jews who do not experience marginality or misunderstanding. The process of becoming truly *kulanu* is a slow one. It begins by telling and listening—our own stories and those of others. It is furthered by actions, by mitzvot of inclusion rather than exclusion, by creating communities of inclusion rather than exclusion. Our tradition teaches, *Lo alecha ham'lachah ligmor*—"it is not up to you to complete the task"—*v'lo atah ven chorin l'hibateil mimenah*—"but neither are you free to ignore your piece of it" (*Pirkei Avot* 2:16).

Beyond Stick Figures: Why Congregations Should be Concerned with Transgender Inclusion

Rabbi Elliot Kukla

You're in a mall, a restaurant, a movie theater, or a synagogue. You look up and see a sign with two stick figures, one in pants and one in a triangular skirt. What does it mean? To many people, this is the most familiar and unquestioned symbol we could possibly encounter: a bathroom. But for some, standing underneath this sign and trying to choose between these two options can be the scariest moment in the day.

Jacob plans his entire schedule carefully in order to not need a public restroom and face these two possibilities and the exclusion and humiliation that can lie behind each door. Jacob is a transgender man; he was assigned female gender at birth and raised as a girl, but transitioned into living as a man as an adult. In crossing the threshold into the segregated space of a public restroom, Jacob is crossing one of the most fiercely defended borders in modern society.

Reform Judaism has always tried to reach out to those who are marginalized. Jewish tradition teaches us to put mezuzot on our doorways to make the entryway into our homes and synagogues places of welcome and holiness. We have led the way in opening the doors of our synagogues to invite the full participation of women, Jews-by-choice, and interfaith families. We are learning how to include gay men and lesbians into our communities, but we have barely begun to find ways to include those who break down gender lines.

Unfortunately, the social stigma that transgender and intersex individuals face in wider society sometimes makes its way into our synagogues, despite our goal to create caring, holy communities open to all people. Many of the gender-nonconforming individuals who come to me for support have already been turned down for spiritual care by other liberal Jewish leaders. They have been embarrassed in our synagogues, consistently being called by the wrong name and/or pronoun and denied the right to ritually celebrate life-cycle events such as conversion, marriage, or name changes. They have even been harassed in synagogue bathrooms.

What's at Stake?

Many people assume that there are only two possible answers to the bathroom dilemma and we *must* fit under one sign or the other, either the stick legs or the pyramid skirt. We refuse to see how many of us can't or don't want to fit into the confines of these two-dimensional symbols. There are countless people in our communities who are excluded in varying degrees and ways because of society's rigid definitions of gender: the eight-year-old boy who was suspended from school for wearing his ballet tutu to class in upstate New York, the flight attendant in Atlanta who is currently suing her employer for firing her because of her refusal to wear makeup, and the transgender man who was shouted at and harassed in a women's restroom in a synagogue in Los Angeles.

Transgender and gender-nonconforming individuals, who can't or won't conform to the behaviors and roles that "match" the gender they were assigned at birth, experience day-to-day challenges because of this worldview. Children who do not gender-conform are often met with physical, verbal, and sexual cruelty and are sometimes forced to drop out of school. Some are even disowned by their families and lose familial economic support systems. Transgender adults face rampant employment discrimination, often have difficulty accessing health care and other services, and are frequently humiliated by doctors and government officials. Today, gender-variant communities live in relative poverty, habitually alienated from social services, spiritual care, or support.[1]

Transphobia, the fear of gender variance, also leads to violence and even murder. In the past year alone, more than thirty transgender and gender-nonconforming people worldwide have been killed in hate crimes.[2] Gender-based violence begins early in life. On January 28, 2005, in Tampa, Florida, Ronnie Paris Jr., a three-year-old, died from swelling on both sides of the brain caused by his father, Ronnie Paris Sr. The toddler had been slapped against the head numerous times, until the child went into a coma. The father claimed that he was provoked because the toddler had not acted masculine enough, and he did not want to raise a "sissy."

We are even willing to harm infants in order to enforce our strict definitions of sex and gender. Approximately 1 in 2,000 babies born in the United States is intersex, which means that they are born with physical traits that cannot be clearly labeled "male" or "female."[3] Think about what this number means. Each of us has met far more than 2,000 people in our lifetime, and intersex people are born in every region and within every socioeconomic group. This means that the odds are that we *all* know someone who is intersex, yet many of us may never realize this. Intersex people are invisible in our society, as their gender is usually "normalized" during infancy, childhood, or adolescence with invasive medical procedures. These interventions frequently result in loss of sexual sensation, infertility, psychological scars, and even occasional deaths.

Andie, an intersex teenager says, "I have not suffered because of my birthright, which is really how I now feel about having an intersex condition. I have suffered because of well-intentioned intervention along the way that was meant to shape me into a person that someone else wanted me to be, that someone else believed I should be, that someone else

---

1. For more information on the manifestations of transphobia, see the Sylvia Riviera Law Project, www.srlp.org.
2. For more information on gender-related crimes and the Transgender Day of Remembrance, see www.gender.org.
3. For more information on intersexuality, see The Intersex Society of North America, www.isna.org.

thought was best for me. I was prodded and poked, photographed, examined, and cut. I was six years old."

Opening the Doors

Gender rigidity impacts all of us, even if we are not transgender or intersex. There are many ways that we can create a congregation that welcomes all people, including those who are transgender, gender nonconforming, and intersex. This can be started by making small, but significant changes. Some areas to consider include our synagogue's language, facilities, political and social action, rituals, and educational programming. These are discussed more fully elsewhere in *Kulanu*.

Jewish tradition and texts also offer us resources for creating an atmosphere that is spiritually vital and welcoming to all genders. The midrash, in *B'reishit Rabbah*, posits that Adam, the first human being, was actually an *androgynos*, an intersex person. In the Babylonian Talmud (*Y'vamot* 64a), the radical claim is made that the first Jews, Abraham and Sarah, were actually *tumtumim*, intersex individuals, who later transitioned genders to become male and female. Exploring Jewish texts can be done through the exercises in the Gender Diversity in Judaism curriculum included in this book (pages 129–144).

Taking steps to create a transgender-friendly congregation will help to create a diverse and growing community where everyone, regardless of sexuality or gender identity, is more able to express their fabulously unique individuality. In her book *Sex Changes: The Politics of Transgenderism,* author and activist Pat Califia asks: "Who would you be if you had never been punished for gender inappropriate behavior? What would it be like to walk down the street, go to work or attend a party and take it for granted that the gender of the people you met would not be the first thing you ascertained about them? What if we all helped each other to manifest our most beautiful, sexy, intelligent, creative, and adventurous inner selves, instead of cooperating to suppress them?"[4]

Two stick figures, one in pants and the other in a triangular skirt. These images are too flat to express any of our realities. Let us build joyful and expansive congregations where each of us is free to express the fullness of our multidimensional humanity.

---

4. Pat Califia, *Sex Changes: The Politics of Transgenderism* (San Francisco: Cleis Press, 1997).

Making Your Community More Transgender Friendly:

Guidelines for Individuals and Congregations

Reuben Zellman

In recent years transgender people have begun to take a more visible place in the GLBT and wider communities. Many non-transgender people want to be respectful of transgender community members and want their community to be transgender friendly and welcoming, but they don't necessarily know how to do that or where to begin. This chapter is intended to answer some common questions and to provide some basic ways to make your synagogue more transgender friendly.

Just like other Jews, transgender Jews want to participate in community as their whole, true selves. Every shul could have transgender members. It is up to each community to decide how welcoming it will be and whether transgender people will find there a safe and affirming place to study, grow, celebrate, and contribute.

What Every Person Can Do

When interacting with transgender people in any setting, the most important thing to remember is to respect each person and their identity and experience. The important thing is how they feel inside, not how they look outside—just as we all hope that people will treat us according to who we are and not how we appear.

Asking Questions

Transgender people understand that gender can be complicated and confusing and that most people do not know very much about these issues. The important thing is that peo-

---

Adapted from the Web site of Congregation Beth Simchat Torah, New York, NY: http://cbst.org/transinterlinks.shtml (first published in 2005).

ple be respectful, and it is generally appreciated when people want to learn. There are ways to ask questions that are respectful and other ways that are not.

The first question to ask about someone else's gender is: **"Do I really need to know?"** There are many situations in which it is really not important what a person's gender status or situation is. For example, if someone walks into Shabbat services and their gender is unclear, there is almost certainly no reason to ask or comment in any way. The person is there to pray and to be among community. They can be welcomed without knowing what their gender identity is.

There may be times in which you decide that you do need to know or understand something about someone else's gender. Most people are welcoming of respectful and appropriate questions. This is often better than making assumptions that may not be true. If the person doesn't want to answer, then they will choose not to.

What Is a Respectful Question?

The most important guideline is a version of Hillel's rule: If you yourself would not wish to be asked a given question, it is probably not respectful to ask it of someone else.

- **Instead of asking, "What are you?" or "Are you a man or a woman?" try:** "What is the respectful pronoun to use for you?" or "I'm interested in hearing about your gender identity if you are comfortable telling me" or "Is there anything I/we/the community can do to make this a more comfortable place?"
- **Don't ask about anyone's body, genitals, medical procedures, or medical history.** If they want to share that information, they will. If you are concerned about someone's health, it is fine to ask, "How is your health?" as you would for any other community member.

Other Dos and Don'ts

- **Don't unnecessarily refer to a person's previous gender status or a previous name.** If this information is not known publicly, revealing it could put the person at risk of harm. Regardless of how open a person is about being transgender, referring to their previous status usually makes that person uncomfortable. This can be analogized to the situation of a person who has converted to Judaism. They may choose to refer to their previous religion or identity, but others do not bring it up.
- **Don't insist that someone must be either a man or a woman.** Some people identify themselves as neither gender, as both genders, or as a third gender. This may seem confusing, but this is a legitimate choice. Some people are in a process of discovering their identity or deciding how they wish to live. People may be in various stages of a gender transition. If you need clarification on which pronoun to use, ask.
- **Don't say things like:** "But you look like a woman!" or "But I've always known you as a man" or "But you made such a good/attractive woman." Comments like these are disrespectful and make people feel bad.
- **Don't be afraid to say,** "I don't understand, but I want to be respectful of you." Being a good ally to transgender people does not mean that you never get confused or make mistakes. It means that you are doing everything in your power to learn and to act in a respectful way, always—even when you don't understand.

- **Do take other people's identities seriously, even though it may not conform to your own ideas about gender or sex.** Remember to treat other people's identities and choices with the respect that you would want for yourself.
- **Do respect a person's choice of name/gender/pronoun.** If a person expresses that they prefer a certain name or pronoun, take care to use only the name/gender/pronoun that they prefer, and strongly encourage others in the community to do the same. This can take time to get used to, and most people do make mistakes—don't worry. The person is almost certainly used to mistakes. The important thing is that that person knows that you respect their preference and are trying.
- **Do remember that not all transgender people are the same.** Like everyone else, different transgender people have different identities, experiences, needs, and interests.
- **Do act as an ally with others in the congregation.** If you notice noninclusive language, suggest to the appropriate person that it be corrected. If you know that someone prefers a certain pronoun, it is appropriate to gently inform or remind someone else who is not using that correct pronoun.
- **Do remember that you may be interacting with a transgender person and not know it.**
- **Do seek out information on your own.** Transgender community members will be very appreciative of your efforts to learn about the experience of transgender people.

What the Synagogue Can Do

Synagogues and other Jewish organizations are beginning to make changes and develop programming ideas to make their community more transgender friendly and to help educate members about transgender experiences. The following are examples of some steps that synagogues have taken to become more educated and welcoming.

Language

Language is very important. People pick up on small cues. The following changes may seem minor, but they are among the most important ways to indicate that a community is making an effort to be transgender friendly. It often makes the difference in whether a transgender person will approach a community and whether they will choose to stay.

- On flyers, in newsletters, event announcements, etc.: Instead of writing "men and women welcome" or "for both men and women," try "all genders welcome" or "for all genders."
- In articles, sermons, essays, etc.: Rather than "both genders" or "men and women," refer to "all genders" or "people of any gender."
- If events, groups, or programs (event, social group, *chavurah*, etc.) are advertised or indicated as "gay and lesbian," consider whether it really is only for gay and lesbian people or whether a transgender (or bisexual person, for that matter) would be welcomed. If the latter is true, change the language.

Facilities

If possible, it is very important to have a non-gender-specific restroom. Again, this may seem like a minor matter. But for many people who have a "nontraditional" gender presentation, using public restrooms can be a particularly frightening and unpleasant experience. They are often much more inclined to go to places that have a non-gender-specific facility. (Often these are single-person restrooms.)

- Consider whether all of your facility's restrooms must be gender-specific or whether one could be made available to everyone. This need not be complicated; covering the "men" or "women" sign with "all-gender restroom" is sufficient. Remember to do this for temporary, shared, or rental facilities also.

Ritual

Ritual has the potential to be powerfully affirming. It also has the potential to be marginalizing or humiliating at important life moments.

- Consider how comfortable a transgender person might be marking a wedding, bar or bat mitzvah, conversion, loss, or other life-cycle event in your congregation. How open could they be about their identity during the process? What about from the bimah?
- Specific rituals: Transgender people often experience particular life-cycle events such as a gender change or a name change. Some wish to mark these events in a Jewish way, either publicly or privately. Consider how open your community is to developing new rituals or adapting existing ones.
- It is important to be especially sensitive around vulnerable experiences such as the *mikveh* or illness. The best approach is to listen carefully to the needs that the transgender person expresses and to accommodate those to the greatest possible extent—even if it's not the way things are "usually" done.
- Rethinking liturgy: Consider how your synagogue's liturgy appears to a transgender person. Are there nongendered options for human beings and for God? Are there readings or prayers that speak to major life transitions? Could an option be included that specifically reflects a transgender experience?
- If Gay/Lesbian/Bisexual/Transgender Pride Month is observed in your congregation, make sure that the "transgender" part is included in a substantial way. If you do not currently acknowledge the GLBT community specifically in the ritual life of your congregation, consider making that change.
- Consider observing the national Transgender Day of Remembrance in your congregation. Commemorations are held annually on November 20. Observing this at services on the preceding Shabbat is an excellent opportunity to reach out to transgender people and to educate and involve the whole congregation in a meaningful way. For more information: www.gender.org/remember.

Education

- Invite the whole community to a panel discussion, workshop, or other event that will open up dialogue. This gives willing transgender members or guests an opportunity to talk about their experience and gives others an opportunity to ask questions and generate ideas in a safe and understanding environment.
- Offer an adult education class about transgender issues in general or about transgender and intersex issues in Jewish text or Jewish community.
- If another organization is putting on a transgender-related program, offer to host it, cosponsor it, or advertise it.

- Include transgender community concerns in a sermon.
- Consider what messages are conveyed in your religious school or children's programs about gender and gender roles. What do the words and images you use—in books, posters, music—teach about how different genders are "supposed to be"? How are children taught about Jewish ways of respecting and welcoming many different kinds of human beings? Could transgender people be included?
- Put a column or information about transgender issues in your newsletter or other publication.

Political and Social Action

- Include transgender and gender diversity issues as part of your community's social action work. There are many transgender community services and advocacy organizations that are in great need of our support.

Outreach

- Make sure to publicize changes that your congregation is making, as well as programs that you are planning. This will help to let transgender people know that your community cares about being an affirming place for them.
- Consider an outreach plan. The world at large is not very welcoming to transgender people. Therefore, transgender people often must assume that they are not welcome or included—unless it is stated otherwise.

More and more resources are being developed to help congregations and other Jewish organizations become more transgender-friendly. Transgender people have been made invisible in Jewish communities for a long time; today many people are working to change that, and every congregation can choose to be a part of this change and to become models for others. Contact one of the organizations listed in this edition of *Kulanu*, or reach out to your local gay/lesbian/bisexual/transgender community center. Support and resources are there to help. If you want to become more welcoming to transgender Jews, you can.

Transgender 101

A Curriculum on Gender Diversity in Judaism

Rabbi Elliot Kukla and Reuben Zellman

Introductory Note to Facilitator

Although there are a number of more specific terms that people use to self-identify, "transgender" can be understood as a broad category that encompasses many different types of gender diversity. There are a number of understandings about gender diversity that facilitators need to have in order to be fully prepared to lead this workshop. These include the following:

- Understanding and being able to explain the difference between "sex" (physiological characteristics) and "gender" (social roles and behaviors). These two categories are separate, but interrelated for most people. *Both* sex and gender can be complex for transgender and intersex individuals.
- Understanding that everyone's gender is complicated, including people who are not transgender or intersex.
- Understanding that there are many types of transgender experience: some people choose to modify their physical appearance with surgeries and/or hormone therapies, others may want to take these steps but cannot or cannot yet afford them, while still others have chosen not to take these steps at all. These decisions are personal and should not affect how much we respect someone else's gender, choice of name, pronoun, or identification.
- Understanding the terms and being able to give equal weight to the experiences of MTF (male-to-female), FTM (female-to-male), and gender-queer people (individuals who identify as both male and female, neither male nor female, or claim an alternate gender identity). For more information, see appendix A, Matching Game—People and Labels (pages 138–139).
- Understanding that intersex experiences raise unique issues that may not be fully covered in this workshop.

Many thanks to S. C. K. Spingarn for contributing sources, activities, and ideas to this workshop.

As noted, if you are unfamiliar with transgender issues, it is important to learn about and achieve some level of fluency and comfort with them before thinking about leading the workshop. As this information may be new for you and is complex, if you are not comfortable leading the workshop yourself, consider seeing if there is a transgender member of your congregation or in the wider community who can co-lead the sessions with you as a subject matter expert. Since a congregant may not be comfortable in that role, most major urban centers have a GLBT community center. If you call them, they might be able to find someone who can help you. In more rural areas, you may still be able to find a transgender co-leader through a larger geographical Internet search.

If you feel that you need a trained facilitator to run this workshop, e-mail the authors at transtorah@gmail.com, and they will try to help find someone in your area.

Target Age Group: Grade 10 through adults

Total Time: 3.5 hours

Enduring Understanding

Gender rigidity impacts everyone. Historically and in the present, Judaism recognizes that gender is complex and provides us with the tools to build a community that celebrates gender diversity.

Evidence of Understanding

After this program, participants should be able to do the following:

1. Recognize that gender is complicated for everyone whether or not you are transgender or intersex.

2. Understand some of the vocabulary that is used by individuals within the transgender, gender-nonconforming, and intersex communities to self-identify.

3. Understand texts from classical Judaism that refer to gender diversity.

4. Know how to find more information on gender diversity.

5. Take action steps to build a congregation that is welcoming to transgender, gender-nonconforming, and intersex individuals.

Curriculum Overview

This curriculum is composed of four activities for a total time of 3.5 hours.

- Activity 1 is called **Introduction to the Issue.** It is designed to introduce participants to the complicated factors that create gender identity. It is approximately 45 minutes long.

- Activity 2 is called **People and Labels.** It is designed to teach people some of the language that is used by individuals both within and without the transgender community to describe their experience, as well as some of the limits of that language. It is approximately 60 minutes long.

- Activity 3 is called **Discussion with a Transgender Person.** It is designed to create a personal connection with this issue and to give the participants an opportunity to ask any questions they may have. It is approximately 45 minutes long.

- Activity 4 is called **Moving Forward.** It is designed to give the participants a sense of closure to the program and create concrete action steps. It is approximately 60 minutes long.

Note to Facilitator

We have included set pieces because we have found that many facilitators like to use them. If you are comfortable with the material, you should feel free to add your own thoughts about it.

Facilitators should also be prepared that the participants may show a variety of reactions to these scenarios. They may exhibit nervous laughter, eye rolling, or silence. Be on the lookout for these responses. You can acknowledge them and explain that these reactions come from a level of discomfort with this activity. Participants should not be shamed for their reactions, but inappropriate behavior also needs to be addressed. Throughout this activity, the facilitator should do the following:

- Validate that this may be an uncomfortable topic for some people.

- Mention that if people find the workshop particularly difficult, they should seek out and discuss this with the facilitator in private.

At the beginning of the workshop, say to the participants:

> We do *not* assume that there are no people in this room who are transgender or intersex. Even we may not know who identifies in this way. This is also not a moment to speculate about your peers. Rather, we are asking you to be careful and considerate in your comments with the understanding that this topic may impact all of us in different ways.

Activity 1: Introduction to the Issue

Total Time: 45 minutes

Essential Questions and Key Themes

1. What causes us to see someone as "male" or "female"?

2. What factors might complicate our definitions?

Materials Needed:

- Chalkboard with chalk or whiteboard with marker
- Large pieces of paper with the words "AGREE" and "DISAGREE" written on them

Part I: Set Induction

The point of this induction is to get participants up and moving and thinking about their own gender. It visually illustrates, in a light-handed way, that everyone has a complex gender identity that does not fit simply into one of two categories.

Time: 15 minutes

Activity Plan

1. On one side of the room, post the word "AGREE" in large letters on a large piece of paper. On the other side of the room, post the word "DISAGREE" in large letters on a large piece of paper.

2. Say the following to the participants:

   Imagine a line going along the room from the "AGREE" poster to the "DISAGREE" poster. I am going to read several statements, and I want you to think about how strongly you agree or disagree with the statement. The poles indicate complete agreement or disagreement, with the area in between as shades of agreement. After each statement, stand in the place that represents how strongly you agree or disagree with it.

3. Read the following statements:

   - I would like to (or currently do) make parenting a primary part of my life.
   - I can fix things.
   - I like to cook.
   - I have been told not to cry.
   - I have worried that I am not strong enough.
   - I have exercised to make myself look buffer.
   - I have worried that I am not attractive enough.
   - I have felt afraid walking home alone at night.
   - I am or would like to be a financial supporter of other family members.
   - I sometimes prevent myself from expressing affection.
   - I have pretended to be less intelligent than I am to protect someone else's ego.
   - I have dieted.
   - I carry a purse.
   - I have at one point in my life had long hair.
   - I play sports.
   - I like to take care of other people.

4. Tell the participants:

   These statements are related to socialization and Western concepts of masculinity and femininity. However, if you noticed, for quite a few statements, while the *statement* might have implied something about being "male" or "female," in the *reality of our agreement-disagreement continuum*, it was not so clear. We will now be exploring how cues lead us to determine if someone is a male or a female and how those cues are complicated for everyone regardless of whether or not we are transgender or intersex.

Part II: Gender "Cues" Activity

The goal of this activity is to begin to see how quickly we judge other people's genders, how many of these "cues" are culturally determined, and how often traditionally "male" cues are possessed by "women" and vice versa.

Time: 30 minutes

Activity Plan:

1. Write the words "MAN" and "WOMAN" on the board.

2. Ask the group what "cues" they use to decide whether the people they meet are either male or female. Write their responses in the appropriate list. Potential responses may include the following:

    a. **Man**
    - Strong
    - Loud voice
    - Can fix things
    - Facial hair

    b. **Woman**
    - Soft voice
    - Gentler
    - Crosses legs

3. Next, write the words "JEWISH MAN" and "JEWISH WOMAN" on the board.

4. As in step 2, brainstorm two lists of gender cues for "Jewish man" and "Jewish woman." Potential responses may include the following:

    a. **Jewish man**
    - Studious
    - Nerdy
    - *Can't* fix things

    b. **Jewish woman**
    - Loud voice
    - Powerful
    - Controlling

5. Point out how different these lists are from the original brainstorm that highlights the cultural role of gender. Many of these gender stereotypes are equally rigid and harmful, but Jewish gender stereotypes are different from modern Western ones; in fact sometimes they appear to be inverted. This highlights how culturally determined gender "cues" are and how what makes someone read as a "man" or a "woman" can and does change over time and between cultures.

6. After this group activity, ask participants to turn to a partner and discuss these questions about gender "cues." Questions to address include the following:

    - How do you react to these lists? Thoughts? Feelings?

- Do they fit who you are, or do you feel confined by them?
- What is your reaction if you discover that your first assumption about someone's gender, based on some of these "cues," is wrong?
- How do you feel if someone makes an incorrect assumption about your own gender or the gender of someone close to you?

7. Come back together as a large group, and have the participants share some of what they learned in their pairs.

Activity 2: People and Labels

Total Time: 60 minutes

Essential Questions and Key Themes

1. What language do people in the contemporary transgender community use to describe their identities?
2. What role do labels play in "boxing people in" and preventing them from showing their own identity?
3. How do classical Jewish texts show a variety of gender representations?

Materials Needed

- Copies of appendix A, Matching Game—People and Labels (pages 138–139), and appendix B, Classical Jewish Texts on Gender (page 140)
- Chalkboard with chalk or whiteboard with marker

Part I: Matching

Time: 15 minutes

Activity Plan

1. Copy the worksheet in appendix A (pages 138–139) and distribute it to the participants. This worksheet is designed to help each participant think critically about familiar language, as well as to discover language that is new to them.

2. Tell the participants:

    The format of this worksheet is a simple matching activity. Try to match each description with the term that denotes it. Much of this language has been developed by people who use it to self-identify and to be better understood in order to have their basic health-care, educational, and employment needs met. However, vocabulary is constantly changing and expanding to meet the shifting realities of people's lives. The best way to find out more about someone's identity is to ask.

3. After the participants have completed the worksheet, give the answers:
    1, C; 2, F; 3, B; 4, H; 5, A; 6, K; 7, D; 8, I; 9, G; 10, E; 11, J

4. Ask the participants if they have any questions about the vocabulary or need any clarification about a person or label.

Part II: Text Study

Time: 45 minutes

Activity Plan

1. Read the following to the participants:

   Not all language for gender diversity is new. The Mishnah and the Talmud (the earliest forms of Jewish law and folklore, which were compiled between the first and the seventh centuries) extensively explore the role of exceptionally gendered individuals in Jewish society. In addition to *ish* and *ishah*, "man" and "woman," our Sages identify four other genders.

   Share the following terms for gender diversity in Jewish texts:

   - A person with *both* male *and* female sexual characteristics (called *androgynos*)
   - A person with *neither* fully developed male *nor* female genitals (called *tumtum*)
   - A person who was assigned female gender at birth, but developed male characteristics during maturation (called *ay'lonit*)
   - A person who is assigned male gender at birth but lacks male genitals, either since birth or due to a medical intervention (called *saris*)

2. Tell the participants:

   Interestingly, a midrashic text (specifically, *B'reishit Rabbah*) posits that Adam, the first human being, was actually an *androgynos*, while in the Babylonian Talmud (*Y'vamot* 64a) the radical claim is made that Abraham and Sarah were *tumtumim*, people with exceptional gender.

3. Next, divide the group into *chevrutot* (study partners). Hand out copies of appendix B (page 140), a section from the Mishnah exploring legal issues surrounding gender. Give the participants approximately 20 minutes to read through the texts and begin to answer the study questions. Circulate among the groups offering assistance as needed.

4. After 20 minutes, bring the participants back together as a whole group, and have them share some of what they learned in *chevruta*, focusing especially on the final question, "What does it mean to you to be 'a created being of its own'? Do you experience yourself as a uniquely and divinely created being? In what ways might the world be different if we treated everyone as beings uniquely created by God?"

Activity 3: Discussion with a Transgender Person

Time: 45 minutes

Activity Plan

1. Invite a transgender person to come and speak to the participants. The point of this exercise is for participants to connect abstract ideas to real people's stories. However, it

is important to create an atmosphere that is as safe and comfortable as possible for both the participants (who might be new to this topic and need an opportunity to work through their feelings) and the transgender speaker (who probably deals with people's discomfort with this topic on a daily basis and is personally impacted by these issues).

2. **If workshop length or time availability is an issue, this activity can also be done at a later date as one of the action steps that are created in the next section.**

3. To prepare for the discussion, ask the transgender speaker to address questions like the following:

    - What pronouns do you prefer (i.e., male pronouns "he" and "him"; female pronouns "she" and "her"; or gender-neutral pronouns "zie" [zee] and "hir")?
    - How did you grow up?
    - What challenges have you faced and do you face on a day-to-day basis?
    - What strengths helped you become who you are today?
    - Where did you learn/discover/develop those strengths?
    - What is the role of faith/spirituality/religion in your life?
    - What could a congregation do to help you feel welcome and safe in their community?

4. Encourage the participants to write out their own questions in advance to have ready for the discussion period.

Activity 4: Moving Forward

Total Time: 60 minutes

Essential Question and Key Themes

What are some concrete action steps we can take to include transgender people in our congregation?

Materials Needed

- Chalkboard with chalk or whiteboard with marker
- Copies of appendix C, Resource List (pages 141–144)

Part I: Action Steps

Time: 30 minutes

Activity Plan

1. Write the following on the board:

    Based on this learning designed to make your congregation more welcoming for transgender and intersex people:

    - What is one thing you have done in the *past* that you would like to change?
    - What is one thing you are currently doing in the *present* that you would like to continue doing?
    - What is one thing you can commit to doing in the *future*?

2. Have the participants turn to a study partner with whom they have not yet talked and discuss the questions above. You can also suggest that they think in terms of key areas of synagogue life, such as language, facilities, political and social action, ritual, and education.

3. Come back together as a group and share some of the suggestions that were made for future commitments and write them on the board. Depending on how many were shared, brainstorm for additional ones if you need to.[1]

4. Try to agree to at least one action that you will undertake as a community in the coming year. Some possibilities may include the following:
   - Change the language used in your publicity for upcoming events to say "all genders welcome" as opposed to "open to both men and women."
   - Create a gender-neutral bathroom in your synagogue.
   - Include a special prayer or reading before Mourner's *Kaddish* as a part of Shabbat services in honor of Transgender Day of Remembrance on November 20, which honors the victims of gender-based murders.
   - Publicly celebrate a life-cycle event of a transgender member of your community.[2]

5. Distribute to the participants appendix C (pages 141–144), a reading list that will help them to get educated about this issue and fulfill these commitments!

Part II: Checkout

Time: 15–30 minutes (depends on the number of participants in the group)

Activity Plan

1. Reconvene the group into a circle where everyone can see one another. Go around the circle and invite participants to share how they are feeling in the moment.

2. Go around the circle a second time, asking participants to offer one word that describes their self-image of their own gender (possible responses: *fluid, sexy, soft, strong, shifting, tomboy, tough, sissy*).

3. Conclude by reading the following statement:

   This workshop was designed to help each of us think about our own gender, as well as to learn about some of the challenges that transgender people face on a daily basis. Hopefully, it has helped us to think about how we can make this community a more welcoming space where all of us can express the fullness of our unique and diverse identities.

---

1. For detailed suggestions and guidance with this discussion, see "Making Your Community More Transgender Friendly: Guidelines for Individuals and Congregations" (pages 123–127).
2. For an example of a ritual that celebrates transgender milestones, see "A Blessing for Transitioning Genders" by Rabbi Elliot Kukla (pages 233–234).

Appendix A: Matching Game—People and Labels
(For Activity 2: People and Labels, Part I)

Some of these labels have been coined by people who do not have the traits or experience that the labels purport to describe. Some of the labels have been coined or chosen by those who do have the traits or experience that the labels are intended to describe. These labels may or may not capture, distort, disparage, or honor the person that they are meant to describe. The only way to know how any individual truly identifies is to ask that individual.

In every time and place, some labels mean different things to different people and are used differently by different people. Since the mid-1990s, a great deal of language has emerged to discuss gender-queer experience; and the language continues to change and expand quickly. You may find other sources that "define" these "terms" somewhat differently.

Read through the "Labels" and the "People" lists below. Place the letter that corresponds to each label next to the person associated with that description.

Labels

A. FTM ("female-to-male"; also transgender man, transman)
B. Gender expression
C. Sexual orientation (homosexual, heterosexual, bisexual, queer)
D. Intersex
E. Transgender (can include transsexual)
F. Gender identity (female, gender queer, transgender, two-spirit, male, femme, butch)
G. Queer
H. Biological sex (male, female, many different ways of being intersex)
I. Gender nonconforming
J. Gender queer
K. MTF ("male-to-female"; also transgender woman, transwoman)

People

_____ The aspect of a person that describes the relationship between the gender they consider themselves to be and the gender of the people to whom they are attracted.

_____ A person's inner understanding of what gender(s) they belong to or identify with. This is each person's unique knowing or feeling and is separate from a person's physical body or appearance (although often related).

_____ Outward behaviors and appearances (e.g., hair, clothing, voice, body language) by which people manifest their gender identity or gender choices.

_____ The set of physical traits (chromosomes, hormones, gonads, internal and external sexual and reproductive organs) which are, in Western society, culturally and medically associated with a particular gender or combination of genders. It is commonly believed that there are only two "packages" of these traits—one called "male," and the other called "female."

"People and Labels" was first prepared by Rabbi Margaret Moers Wenig and Reuben Zellman in April 2005 for a workshop at Congregation Beth Simchat Torah in New York. That longer version is available on request from transtorah@gmail.com. This version was edited and revised by Rabbi Elliot Kukla for this edition of *Kulanu*.

____ A person who, at birth, appeared or was assigned to be female and was raised as a girl, but knows himself to be male and wishes to or does live as a male part or all of the time.

____ A person who, at birth, appeared or was assigned to be male and was raised as a boy, but knows herself to be female and wishes to or does live as a female part or all of the time.

____ A physical status consisting of a combination of "male" and "female" sexual traits (chromosomes, anatomy, hormones)—for example, a person with XX chromosomes and a penis.

____ An umbrella term that can include anyone whose gender identity, expression, or behavior is outside of social norms of women who are "feminine" and men who are "masculine."

____ A broad political and cultural identity that includes many (but not all) lesbian, gay, bisexual, and transgender people, as well as others who see their sexuality as falling outside of mainstream heterosexual norms.

____ Anyone who does not identify with the gender that he or she was assigned at birth. This can include people who take medical steps to modify their appearance and those who do not.

____ Anyone who sees their gender as falling outside of mainstream understandings of "male" and "female." This can include transgender men and women, and people who identify as neither male nor female, both male and female, or who claim an alternate gender identity.

Appendix B: Classical Jewish Texts on Gender—Text Study on *Mishnah Bikurim* 4: 1–5 (abridged text)
(For Activity 2: People and Labels, Part II)

An *androgynos* is in some respects legally equivalent to men, and in some respects legally equivalent to women, in some respects legally equivalent to men and women, and in some respects legally equivalent to neither men nor women. (*Mishnah Bikurim* 4:1)

How is the *androgynos* legally equivalent to men? The *androgynos* conveys impurity with white [penile discharge] like men, dresses like men, marries but is not taken in marriage like men . . . is not financially supported like the daughters . . . and is responsible for all the commandments uttered in the Torah like men. (*Mishnah Bikurim* 4:2)

How is the *androgynos* legally equivalent to women? The *androgynos* conveys impurity with red [menstrual blood] like women, cannot be left alone with men like women . . . does not inherit with the sons like women, does not eat of the really Holy Holy Things [of the Temple], and is not fit to give testimony like women. . . . (*Mishnah Bikurim* 4:3)

How is the *androgynos* legally equivalent to men and women? One is liable for hitting and cursing the *androgynos* as it is with men and women. The one who kills the *androgynos* by accident is exiled, and the one who [kills] intentionally is executed as it is with men and women. . . . (*Mishnah Bikurim* 4:4)

How is the *androgynos* legally equivalent to neither men nor women? Unlike men and women, the *androgynos* is not sold as a Hebrew slave, because unlike men and women, the *androgynos* cannot be valued. . . . . Rabbi Yosei says: an *androgynos* is a created being of its own. (*Mishnah Bikurim* 4:5)

Questions on *Mishnah Bikurim* 4:1–5

1. In what ways is the *androgynos* legally equivalent to a man? In what ways is the *androgynos* legally equivalent to a woman? Equivalent to neither men nor women? Equivalent to both men and women? Try to make a list. How do these lists compare to the opening brainstorm on gender "cues"?

2. Can you use this text to think about the way you read gender "cues" in a contemporary context?

3. Are you surprised by this text? Does it change your image of "traditional" Jewish gender?

4. What does it mean to you to be "a created being of its own"? Do you experience yourself as a uniquely and divinely created being? In what ways might the world be different if we treated everyone as beings uniquely created by God?

Translations and text study questions created by Rabbi Elliot Kukla, 2006. For more information: transtorah@gmail.com.

Appendix C: Resource List

Transgender 101

Alexander, Jonathan, and Karen Yescavage, eds. *Bisexuality and Transgenderism: InterSEXions of the Others*. Binghamton, NY: Harrington Park Press, 2004.
This is a thoughtful anthology of articles that contemplate gender and sexual identities that have too often been marginalized and pushed to the side. This book places them front and center as a topic for deep introspection through essays, interviews, poems, and research.

Bornstein, Kate, and Diana DiMassa, eds. *My Gender Workbook: How to Become a Real Man, a Real Woman, the Real You, or Something Else Entirely*. New York: Routledge, 1997.
A guide to living with or without a gender, or at least defining the one you do have. The workbook includes quizzes and exercises that determine how much of a man or woman you are and gives you the tools to reach whatever point you desire on the gender continuum.

Califia, Pat. *Sex Changes: The Politics of Transgenderism*. San Francisco: Cleis Press, 1997.
Springing from the author's "own profound discomfort with gender," this honest, meticulously researched analysis on the contemporary history of transsexuality features in-depth interviews with gender transgressors. Writing about both male-to-female and female-to-male transsexuals, Califia examines the lives of Christine Jorgenson, Jan Morris, Kate Bornstein, and others.

Feinberg, Leslie. *Stone Butch Blues*. Los Angeles: Alyson Books, 1993.
A novel about lesbian Jess Goldberg, who, coming to age in the 1950s–60s pre-Stonewall, attempts to come to grips with her identity as a butch lesbian, undergoing transformations, including hormone treatments, along the way. Leslie Feinberg is also the author of *Trans Liberation: Beyond Pink or Blue* and *TransGender Warriors*, and is a noted activist and speaker on transgender issues.

_____. *Transgender Warriors: Making History from Joan of Arc to Dennis Rodman*. Boston: Beacon Press; 1997.
Leslie Feinberg uncovers persuasive evidence that there have always been people who crossed the cultural boundaries of gender. *Transgender Warriors* explores the history of gender expression and is a powerful testament to the rebellious spirit.

Jacobs, Sue-Ellen, Wesley Thomas, and Sabine Lang, eds. *Two Spirit People: Native American Gender Identity, Sexuality and Spirituality*. Urbana, IL: University of Illinois, 1997.
According to the publisher, "this landmark book combines the voices of Native Americans and non-Indians, anthropologists and others, in an exploration of gender and sexuality issues as they relate to lesbian, gay, trans-gendered, and other 'marked'

Native Americans. Focusing on the concept of two-spirit people—individuals not necessarily gay or lesbian, transvestite or bisexual, but whose behaviors or beliefs may sometimes be interpreted by others as uncharacteristic of their sex—this book is the first to provide an intimate look at how many two-spirit people feel about themselves, how other Native Americans treat them, and how anthropologists and other scholars interpret them and their cultures."

Nestle, Joan, Riki Wilchins, and Claire Howell, eds. *GenderQueer: Voices from Beyond the Sexual Binary*. New York: Alyson Books, 2002.
This anthology includes thirty first-person accounts from writers and activists on gender construction, exploration, and questioning and provide a groundwork for cultural discussion, political action, and even greater possibilities of autonomous gender choices.

Scholinski, Daphne, and Jane M. Adams. *The Last Time I Wore a Dress: A Memoir*. New York: Riverhead Trade, 1998.
With a depressed mother and a father traumatized by service in Vietnam, Scholinski had an adolescence marked by physical and emotional abuse at home, teasing by schoolmates about her tomboyish appearance, and sexual molestation by strangers and others in positions of authority. This perspective from the patient's viewpoint of life in a psychiatric hospital in the 1980s explores the gender identity disorder diagnosis that Scholinski was given.

Wilchins, Riki Anne. *Read My Lips: Sexual Subversion and the End of Gender*. Ithaca, NY: Firebrand Books, 1997.
In the United States, the gay and lesbian movement has entered the public domain and has been extensively researched and discussed. However, the transsexual movement is not well-known, even in the GLBT community. This book begins to fill that gap and challenges the way society constructs and defines gender and sexuality.

Intersex 101

Dreger, Alice Domurat. *Hermaphrodites and the Medical Invention of Sex*. Cambridge, MA: Harvard University Press, 1998.
This book explores the history of sex, sexuality, gender, and medicine in the nineteenth and twentieth centuries in France and Britain through the condition of hermaphroditism. The book includes case histories of people with intersexual conditions and their encounters with science and medicine of those periods. The author also includes an epilogue on current treatment of intersexual conditions.

Kessler, Susanne. *Lessons from the Intersexed*. New Brunswick, NJ: Rutgers University Press, 1998.
This book is an attempt to better inform health professionals, parents, and the general public about intersexed children and the need for a fresh perspective apart from the two sexes society generally accepts.

Preves, Sharon E. *Intersex and Identity: The Contested Self.* New Brunswick, NJ: Rutgers University Press, 2003.
According to the publisher, "statistics point out that one in every two thousand infants born in the United States each year is sexually ambiguous in such a way that doctors cannot immediately determine the child's sex. Some children's chromosomal sexuality contradicts their sexual characteristics. Others have the physical traits of both sexes, or of neither. Drawing upon life history interviews with adults who were treated for intersexuality as children, Sharon E. Preves explores how such individuals experience and cope with being labeled sexual deviants in a society that demands sexual conformity."

Gender Theory

Fausto-Sterling, Anne. *Sexing the Body: Gender Politics and the Construction of Sexuality.* New York: Basic Books, 2000.
This book examines the history of what we would call "scientific ideas" about hormones, the "gay brain," and intersexuality. The author points out "even the most fundamental knowledge about sex is shaped by the culture in which scientific knowledge is produced."

Laquer, Thomas. *Making Sex: Body and Gender from the Greeks to Freud.* Cambridge, MA: Harvard University Press, 1992.
This book explores the social and political context of various scientific explanations of gender difference and sex throughout history. Through her research, the author has identified two interweaving views that women are imperfect men and that they are completely opposite.

Providing Services

Israel, Gianna E., and Donald E. Tarver II, M.D. *Transgender Care: Recommended Guidelines, Practical Information and Personal Accounts.* Philadelphia: Temple University Press, 1998.
This is a helpful book for mental health care providers and people who are contemplating, going through, or have been through a sex reassignment surgery/transition (as well as their friends and family). It is full of practical information and firsthand accounts of what it's like to deal with gender dysphoria.

Web Sites

Transgender

Gender Education and Advocacy (GEA) is a national organization focused on the needs, issues, and concerns of gender variant people in human society. It seeks to educate and advocate, not only for ourselves and others like us, but for all human beings who suffer from gender-based oppression in all of its many forms. This Web site includes educational training materials as well as information to help your community mark the Transgender Day of Remembrance: www.gender.org.

The National Center for Transgender Equality (NCTE) is a social justice organization dedicated to advancing the equality of transgender people through advocacy, collaboration, and empowerment. This Web site includes fifty-two things you can do for transgender equality for use in your community group: www.nctequality.org.

The Sylvia Riviera Law Project (SRLP) works to guarantee that all people are free to self-determine gender identity and expression, regardless of income or race, and without facing harassment, discrimination, or violence. This Web site includes educational and training materials as well as good information on the social and legal impacts of transphobia: www.srlp.org.

Intersex

Bodies Like Ours provides peer support and advocacy for Intersex individuals: www.bodieslikeours.org.

The Intersex Society of North America (ISNA) is devoted to systemic change to end shame, secrecy, and unwanted genital surgeries for people born with an anatomy that someone decided is not standard for male or female: www.isna.org.

Youth

Advocates for Youth is an organization dedicated to helping youth make informed decisions about their sexual health and gender identity. They publish a pamphlet for youth, "I Think I Might Be Transgender, Now What Do I Do?" which can be downloaded and distributed in your community: http://www.advocatesforyouth.org/youth/health/pamphlets/transgender.htm.

Marriage Matters

In North American society, few issues are as controversial and as emotionally charged as same-gender marriage. Both sides of this argument feel strongly that they are in the right, and each side claims their position as "defending moral values." It is often difficult for either side to engage in discussion or even to hear *why* the other side feels the way they do.

Since 1977, the Reform Movement has said that civil rights for same-gender couples are a matter of equality and nondiscrimination and, therefore, a matter of justice. Yet, there are still challenges to overcome. Even thirty years after the Reform Movement's initial statement on civil rights for same-gender couples, the battle for marriage equality is still being waged across the United States. Also, while Reform Jewish resolutions support civil rights for same-gender couples, the religious aspects of marriage remain controversial. In 2000, the CCAR resolved to support the decision of each individual rabbi to choose to perform or not perform same-gender unions.

This section explores these difficult issues. Among other topics, it includes the following:

- A curriculum on Reform Jewish views on same-gender marriage, helping people develop an opinion on this topic that is consistent with Reform Jewish values
- Two articles for rabbis, cantors, and same-gender couples on using legal tools to support and protect same-gender unions and on ways to deepen a relationship through premarital counseling
- A scholarly article showing how and why Judaism demands that monogamous homosexual relationships be sanctified, which includes addressing the controversial texts from Leviticus and placing them in historical context
- The story of how three Canadian congregations and their rabbis worked together to come to a conclusion on same-gender officiation

For further information, and especially blessings and texts used in same-gender marriages see Blessings and Texts, pages 205–237.

A Curriculum on Reform Jewish Views on Same-Gender Marriage

Rabbi Geoffrey Mitelman and Joel L. Kushner, Psy.D.

Introductory Note to the Facilitator

A marriage is many things: it is a spiritual moment, a life-cycle event, a Jewish legal contract, a civil legal contract, and a public proclamation by two people to show their love for each other. When we as Reform Jews look at the issue of same-gender marriage, we are in fact trying to come to terms with these different aspects of "marriage," and we are exploring the possibility of changing some of these facets —at times, radically changing them. To inform our decisions, we look to traditional Jewish sources, contemporary Jewish thought, Reform Movement resolutions, as well as civil legal rulings, but these sources do not always point us in the same direction. Thus the goal of this curriculum is to begin to understand Jewish law, Jewish tradition, and Jewish values in order for the participants to create their own perspective on same-gender marriage that is consistent with the values of Reform Judaism.

This curriculum is intended for just over three class hours total. It can be used as a one-day seminar, such as an adult education retreat, or as several sessions in a larger course, such as confirmation or a high school program. However, there is also some flexibility in the curriculum based on time and resources. Activity 1 sets the context for the curriculum and is essential. Depending on the particular interests of the participants, time constraints, or issues of resources, either or both of activities 2 and 3 can be used. **However, we highly recommend using all three activities.**

Target Age Group: Grade 10 through adults

Total Time: Approximately 3 hours, depending on how many activities are done

Enduring Understanding

As Reform Jews, we strive to balance the historical values and perspectives of our tradition with the evolving realities of contemporary life. Same-gender marriage is a prime example of striving to create that balance.

Evidence of Understanding

After this program, participants should be able to do the following:

1. Identify the purposes, benefits, and elements of a Reform Jewish marriage (regardless of whether it is heterosexual or same-gender).

2. Interpret part of the legal marriage formula—*k'dat Moshe v'Yisrael*, "according to the laws of Moses and Israel"—from a liberal perspective, especially with respect to a same-gender ceremony.

3. Explain what some of the challenges would be for a same-gender couple looking to get married, and begin to consider ways they could personally address some of these challenges.

4. Offer an opinion on same-gender marriage consistent with Reform Jewish values.

Curriculum Overview

This curriculum is composed of three exercises for a total time of just over 3 hours.

- Activity 1 is called **What Is a "Jewish Marriage"? What Is a "Same-Gender Jewish Marriage"**? It explores the various facets of marriage and begins to explore the similarities and differences between a heterosexual marriage and a same-gender marriage. It is approximately 75 minutes long but can be divided over two class periods as need be.

- Activity 2 is called **Discussion with the Rabbi**. It allows the participants to explore what their own rabbi's position is on same-gender marriage and how their rabbi reached it. It is approximately 45 minutes long.

- Activity 3 is called **Reform Jewish Texts on Same-Gender Marriage**. It is designed to help the participants create their *own* position on same-gender marriage based on Reform Jewish values. It is approximately 60 minutes long.

Note to Facilitator

We have included set pieces because we have found that many facilitators like to use them. If you are comfortable with the material, you should feel free to add your own thoughts about it.

Activity 1: What Is a "Jewish Marriage"? What Is a "Same-Gender Jewish Marriage"?

Total Time: 75 minutes

Essential Questions and Key Themes

1. What are some of the similarities and differences between a traditional heterosexual marriage and a same-gender marriage in terms of the following?

    - The purposes

- The elements
- The benefits

2. What does the phrase *k'dat Moshe v'Yisrael*—"according to the laws of Moses and Israel"—mean in a traditional Jewish wedding ceremony? How do we interpret this phrase as nonhalachic Jews?

Materials Needed

- Chalkboard with chalk or whiteboard with marker
- Copies of the wedding ceremony from the CCAR *Rabbi's Manual: Maaglei Zedek*, found on pp. 50–59
  Note to Facilitator: You may need to ask the rabbi for copies of this document.
- Copies of appendix A, Automatic Legal Benefits to State-Sanctioned Married Couples (page 157)
- Copies of the "Union Ceremonies for Same-Gender Couples" (pages 211–226)

Part I: Defining "Marriage"

Time: 30 minutes

Activity Plan

Post the lists that are generated from this exercise around the room so that they can be a reference for the rest of the curriculum.

1. Write the word "Marriage" in the top center of the board, with three lines coming down from it, as follows:

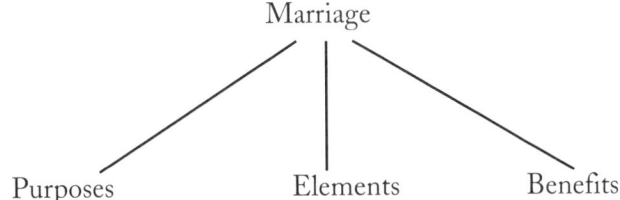

2. Explain to the participants that "marriage" may seem like a simple concept, but it has many facets to it.

3. Write the word "Purposes" under the first line, and begin by asking the participants to generate a list of *reasons why* two people would want to get married. Write these responses under the word "Purposes." Potential responses may include: *sharing a life together, public proclamation of love, sex, getting wedding gifts, etc.*

4. Next, write the word "Elements" under the second line, and ask the participants to generate a list of *what happens during a Jewish ceremony* where two people get married. Write these responses under the word "Elements." Potential responses may include: *breaking of the glass, a ketubah, exchanging rings, dancing, the Sheva B'rachot, etc.*

5. Finally, write the word "Benefits" under the third line, and ask the participants to generate a list of *benefits that happen after* two people get married. Write these responses under the word "Benefits." Potential responses may include: *joint bank accounts, raising children together, someone to come home to at the end of the day, tax benefits, etc.*

6. Ask the participants, "Does every couple receive all of these benefits?" Depending on the responses, you may say, "Correct [or not correct], not every couple automatically receives all of these benefits. There are some benefits that a same-gender couple does *not* automatically receive."

7. Then, looking at the list of benefits that they had created, ask the participants to guess which of these benefits a same-gender couple would automatically receive, and circle any of their guesses, regardless of whether or not they are correct.

8. Hand out copies of appendix A (page 157), which explains the various legal benefits automatically obtained in state-sanctioned marriages. Ask the participants, "How many of the benefits from appendix A did we identify correctly? Which ones did we get wrong?"

9. Highlight the benefits that same-gender couples do not automatically receive, such as visitation (in hospital and with children), adoption, property, taxes, Social Security, and inheritance. Then explain that while these full rights of marriage are not yet available to same-gender couples, there are other legal ways to ensure some protection in these areas through the use of the following:

- Domestic Partnerships
- Wills
- Cohabitation Agreements
- Co-Parent Agreements
- Advanced Directives

For further discussion of these methods, see the article entitled, "What Rabbis Should Do to Help Protect Legal Rights in Same-Sex Couples," on pages 167–175.

Part II: Heterosexual and Same-Gender Jewish Marriages

Time: 45 minutes

Activity Plan

1. Hand out copies of the wedding service from the CCAR *Rabbi's Manual: Maaglei Zedek* (pp. 50–59). Have the participants compare the list on the board of the "elements" of a Jewish marriage with the wedding ceremony in front of them. What did they identify correctly? What did they miss?

2. Going back to the "Elements" list on the board, ask the participants:

- Would a same-gender ceremony and a heterosexual ceremony be the same or different? Have a brief discussion.
- Assuming that there might be some differences, which elements of a heterosexual ceremony would likely *remain the same* for a same-gender ceremony? Potential responses may include: *blessings and readings,* Sheva B'rachot, *exchange of rings, reading of a* ketubah, *etc.*
- Which elements of a heterosexual ceremony might likely *differ* for a same-gender ceremony? Potential responses might include: *different pronouns, alternative translations of the* Sheva B'rachot, *no* k'dat Moshe v'Yisrael, *etc.*

A Curriculum on Reform Jewish Views on Same-Gender Marriage 151

You may wish to quote Rabbi Janet Marder, who, when asked about how to officiate at gay and lesbian ceremonies explained, "First, our relationships are no less valid or worthy than heterosexual ones and we therefore deserve no less. Second, we are not exactly the same and therefore we do not need to do everything exactly the same" (from "Why Union Ceremonies for Lesbian and Gay Jews," Rabbi Yoel Kahn, Ph.D., 1989).

3. Divide the participants into groups of four to five students. Hand out copies of the "Union Ceremonies for Same-Gender Couples" (pages 211–226). (Note to Facilitator: There are two services in the "Union Ceremonies for Same-Gender Couples." One is called "*Kiddushin* Service," and one is called "Affirmation Service." Two different services were created so that both rabbis and GLBT couples would be able to have a choice for what they each felt was the most appropriate ceremony. For this exercise, use the "*Kiddushin* Service," pages 211–219.) Have each small group compare the same-gender ceremony to the heterosexual ceremony. Discuss questions like the following:

    - How accurately did the participants predict the similarities and differences between a same-gender ceremony and a heterosexual ceremony?
    - What other similarities or differences did the participants notice that surprised them?

4. Tell the participants: "Possibly the most controversial aspect for a same-gender ceremony is the phrase *k'dat Moshe v'Yisrael*, 'according to the laws of Moses and Israel,' which is on page 54 in the heterosexual ceremony. According to halachah, this is the formula that allows two people to get married. By saying these words and exchanging an object of value in front of two witnesses, no matter what else may or may not happen, two people are married."

    Then, based on the translation in the heterosexual ceremony, ask the participants what they think the phrase "leading a life according to the laws of Moses and Israel" could mean for the couple's life after marriage. Try to elicit as wide a range of potential responses as possible, such as the following:

    - Lighting Shabbat candles
    - Raising children
    - Participating in social justice causes
    - Keeping kosher
    - Following all 613 mitzvot
    - Going to synagogue
    - Hosting a seder
    - Going to High Holy Day services

5. Given this list of what *k'dat Moshe v'Yisrael* could mean for a couple's life after marriage, give each participant three minutes to write:

    - A halachic definition of *k'dat Moshe v'Yisrael*.
    - A Reform definition of *k'dat Moshe v'Yisrael*.
      Share these definitions as a whole group.

6. Finally, ask the participants:

    - Why do you think the same-gender *Kiddushin* ceremony does *not* say, *k'dat Moshe v'Yisrael*?
    - Should a same-gender ceremony use the phrase *k'dat Moshe v'Yirael*? Why or why not?

7. Read the following paragraph to the participants: "Reform Jewish views on same-gender marriage are reflective of the way Reform Jews have always interpreted and reinterpreted Jewish tradition for contemporary life. As Reform Jews, we have *never* simply taken tradition at face value—we change (a.k.a. "re-form") it based on study of our ancient and modern Jewish texts, new scientific information, issues of social justice, and our own sense of personal autonomy.

    When looking at the issue of marriage as a whole, Reform Judaism has made many modifications based on changing social realities, such as having *both* partners exchange rings, and creating more egalitarian *ketubot*. Clearly, we have also used the phrase *k'dat Moshe v'Yisrael* for couples who do not necessarily live up to that standard halachically, and as such, we are reinterpreting that phrase in a more liberal way. Similarly, *same-gender marriage* can be seen as another step in the evolution of the way Reform Judaism interprets Jewish tradition.

Activity 2: Discussion with the Rabbi

Total Time: 45 minutes

Essential Questions and Key Themes

1. What role does a rabbi play in preparing a couple for marriage?
2. How do Reform rabbis decide whether or not to perform a same-gender wedding ceremony?
3. What are some of the challenges facing Reform rabbis regarding same-gender marriages?

Materials Needed:

- Chalkboard with chalk or whiteboard with marker
- Copies of appendix B, text 1, the 2000 CCAR Resolution on Same-Gender Officiation (pages 158–159)
- A rabbi who can speak with the participants for approximately 30 minutes

You should speak with the rabbi **beforehand** to know what his or her position is on same-gender marriage. Show the rabbi this exercise and the questions that he or she will be asked so that he or she can prepare for the discussion. You may also wish to read "Working Together: Rabbis, Congregations, and Same-Gender Marriage" on pages 183–190, which describes three congregations' journeys toward a decision on this issue.

Part I: Preparation for the Discussion

Time: 15 minutes

Activity Plan

1. Ask the participants what roles the rabbi plays in any kind of wedding, and write their responses on the board. Guide the participants toward ideas like the following:

    - Helping the couple lead a Jewish life after marriage

- Ensuring the integrity of Jewish tradition
- Exploring potentially emotionally difficult issues

2. Next, ask the participants what factors might lead a rabbi to choose to perform or not to perform a same-gender ceremony. Write the words "Reasons for Yes" and "Reasons for No" on the board, and place the participants' responses on the board under the appropriate heading.

    a. Potential responses under "Reasons for Yes" may include: *wanting to be inclusive, feeling a moral obligation, reinterpreting Jewish tradition.*
    b. Potential responses under "Reasons for No" may include: *not wanting to change Jewish tradition, discomfort, state marriage laws.*

3. Hand out the CCAR Resolution on Same Gender Officiation (appendix B, text 1, pages 158–159). Point out these three phrases:

    - FURTHER RESOLVED, that we recognize the diversity of opinions within our ranks on this issue. We support the decision of those who choose to officiate at rituals of union for same-gender couples, and we support the decision of those who do not, and
    - FURTHER RESOLVED, that we call upon the CCAR to support all colleagues in their choices in this matter, and
    - FURTHER RESOLVED, that we also call upon the CCAR to develop both educational and liturgical resources in this area.

    Ask the participants, "What do these sections imply for rabbis performing same-gender officiation?"

4. Tell the participants that they will now be discussing with the rabbi what his or her position is on same-gender officiation and how the rabbi came to this conclusion.

Part II: The Discussion Itself

If the congregational rabbi does not officiate at same-gender unions, the program can still be done as an exploration of that choice, but it should then be modified to be done as a panel or as two meetings where there is also a rabbi who does same-gender officiation.

Time: 30 minutes

Activity Plan

1. When the rabbi comes to speak with the participants, assign different participants to ask the following questions:

    - What does the rabbi do to prepare any given couple for marriage?
    - What is the rabbi's position on same-gender officiation?
    - How did the rabbi come to that position?
    - What process did the rabbi go through to reach that decision?
    - Did the rabbi engage the congregation in the discussion? If so, how?
    - What challenges does the rabbi see in terms of same-gender marriages?
    - If the rabbi has done a same-gender officiation, can he or she share what it was like and how it was memorable?

Make sure to allow additional time for the participants to ask any questions they might have that are not listed above.

2. Read the following paragraph to the participants:

   > Personal autonomy is just as important for rabbis as it is for laypeople. Each rabbi makes an individual choice about whether and how to perform a same-gender union, and the process each rabbi goes through is an individual one based on Jewish tradition, contemporary realities, and his or her own feelings. Notice how comparable that process is to any decision that any Reform Jew makes—we make *our* Jewish choices based on those criteria, as well, so how we form our opinion on same-gender marriage should be consistent with how we form our opinion on *any* aspect of Jewish tradition.

Activity 3: Reform Jewish Texts on Same-Gender Marriage

Total Time: 60 minutes

Essential Questions and Key Themes

1. What is Reform Judaism's position on same-gender officiation?
2. What are some of the values that guide Reform Jews in forming an opinion on same-gender officiation?
3. What are some of the conflicts that arose within Reform Judaism when trying to formulate a position on same-gender marriage?

Materials Needed

- Chalkboard with chalk or whiteboard with marker
- Copies of the following texts from appendix B:
    1. CCAR Resolution on Same Gender Officiation, from 2000 (pages 158–159)
    2. Laura Wolfson, "Exiled," from 2004 (pages 160–161)
    3. CCAR Responsum on Homosexual Marriage, from 1996 (pages 162–163)
    4. Rabbi Bradley Shavit Artson, "Enfranchising the Monogamous Homosexual" from 1993 (page 164)
    5. URJ Resolution on Civil Marriage for Gay and Lesbian Jewish Couples, from 1997 (pages 165–166)

Activity Plan

Tell the participants:

> Your synagogue has asked you to present a position on same-gender marriage that is consistent with Reform Jewish values. Before you create your position, you will need to see what these values *are*, so you are going to be divided into smaller groups to study this material. First, you will be divided into "Subject Matter Expert Groups" and learn to become experts on one aspect of Reform Jewish views on same-gender marriage. Then, you will be divided into "Committee Groups," learning what the

other groups have learned and finally working together to form a position on same-gender marriage to be presented to your synagogue.

Part I: Subject Matter Expert Groups

Time: 25 minutes

Activity Plan

1. Divide the participants into four groups. These groups will become Subject Matter Experts (SME). Each SME Group will be given one text that explains one aspect of Reform Judaism's views on same-gender marriage. In their groups, participants will read and study together, share the important information, and determine a means of presenting this information to the rest of the participants.

2. Give each group copies of the appropriate text:
   - Expert Group 1 receives copies of the CCAR Resolution on Same Gender Officiation, from 2000 and "Exiled" by Laura Wolfson, from 2004, (appendix B, text 1 and text 2—pages 158–161)
   - Expert Group 2 receives copies of the CCAR Responsum on Homosexual Marriage, from 1996 (appendix B, text 3—pages 162–163)
   - Expert Group 3 receives copies of "Enfranchising the Monogamous Homosexual" by Rabbi Bradley Shavit Artson, from 1993 (appendix B, text 4—page 164)
   - Expert Group 4 receives copies of the URJ Resolution on Civil Marriage for Gay and Lesbian Jewish Couples, from 1997 (appendix B, text 5—pages 165–166)

3. Give the participants 15 minutes in their SME Groups time to read their text and address these questions:
   - What is the position of the author(s) on same-gender marriage?
   - What values guided the author(s) to the position described?
   - How can you best explain your answers to other people?

   After the 15 minutes, tell the participants, "We will now be moving into our Committee Groups and will be sharing what we have learned in our Expert Groups with other participants."

4. While the participants are still in their SME Groups, have them create three new groups by counting off "A, B, C, A, B, C, A . . . ." These will be their Committee Groups.

5. Based on the letter groups they now have, the participants should form Committee Group A, Committee Group B, and Committee Group C. In the end, each Committee Group should be composed of participants from all the different SME Groups.

Part II: Committee Groups

Time: 25 minutes

Activity Plan

1. In each Committee Group, have the participants share what they had learned in their Subject Matter Expert Groups. They should discuss:

- What was the position of their author(s) on same-gender marriage or officiation?
- What values guided their author(s) to the position described?

2. Based on what they have learned, have each Committee Group write a position on same-gender marriage for the presentations to the synagogue. Tell them that their positions will be presented to the whole group.

Part III: Conclusion

Time: 10 minutes

Activity Plan

1. Tell the participants, "It is now time for you to present your position to the synagogue. Each Committee Group will present their position and their thought processes."

2. Have each Committee Group present their position. If they do not share the process, ask them to address the following questions:

   - How did they come to their conclusion?
   - What were some of the debates?

3. Conclude by reading the following to the participants:

   Clearly, Reform Judaism has tried to balance a variety of factors when creating a position on same-gender marriage. Jewish tradition, social justice, societal realities, and personal autonomy sometimes point to very different conclusions on this issue. You have now created your own position on this topic. Indeed, the goal of this curriculum was to help *you* to create *your own* position on same-gender marriage consistent with Reform Jewish values. There may be many different conclusions to this issue, but the critical piece to remember is that as Reform Jews, we strive to balance the historical values and perspectives of our tradition with the evolving realities of contemporary life. Same-gender marriage is a prime example of striving to create that balance.

Appendix A: Automatic Legal Benefits to State-Sanctioned Married Couples[1]

According to a 2004 report from the U.S. General Accounting Office, there are at least 1,138 tangible benefits, protections, rights, and responsibilities that marriage brings to couples and their children—and that is just at the federal level. Add in state and local law, and the policies of businesses, employers, universities, and other institutions, and it is clear that the denial of marriage to couples and their kids makes a substantial impact on every area of life, from raising kids, building a life together, and caring for one another, to retirement, death, and inheritance. Most of these cannot be secured by private agreement or through lawyers.

Here are just some of the ways in which government's denying the freedom to marry punishes couples and families by depriving them of critical tangible as well as intangible protections and responsibilities in virtually every area of life:

- **Taxes:** Unmarried couples cannot file joint tax returns and are excluded from tax benefits and claims specific to marriage. In addition, they are denied the right to transfer property to one another and pool the family's resources without adverse tax consequences.
- **Parenting:** Unmarried couples are denied the automatic right to joint parenting, joint adoption, joint foster care, and visitation for non-biological parents. In addition, the children of unmarried couples are denied the guarantee of child support and an automatic legal relationship to both parents, and are sometimes sent a wrongheaded but very real negative message about their own status and family.
- **Health:** Unlike spouses, unmarried partners are usually not considered next of kin for the purposes of hospital visitation and emergency medical decisions. In addition, they can't cover their families on their health plans without paying taxes on the coverage, nor are they eligible for Medicare and Medicaid coverage.
- **Death:** If a couple is not married and one partner dies, the other partner is not entitled to bereavement leave from work, to file wrongful death claims, to draw the Social Security of the deceased partner, or to automatically inherit a shared home, assets, or personal items in the absence of a will.
- **Housing:** Denied marriage, couples of lesser means are not recognized and thus can be denied or disfavored in their applications for public housing.
- **Inheritance:** Unmarried surviving partners do not automatically inherit property should their loved one die without a will, nor do they get legal protection for inheritance rights such as elective share or bypassing the hassles and expenses of probate court.

---

1. Evan Wolfson, *Why Marriage Matters: America, Equality, and Gay People's Right to Marry* (New York: Simon and Schuster, 2004), p. 194.

Appendix B: Text 1

Questions to Address

- What is the position of the author(s) on same-gender marriage?
- What values guided the author(s) to the position described?
- How can you best explain your answers to other people?

Resolution Adopted by the Central Conference of American Rabbis 111th Annual Convention, 2000: Same Gender Officiation[2]

Background

Over the years, the Central Conference of American Rabbis has adopted a number of positions on the rights of homosexuals, on homosexuality in the rabbinate, and advocating changes in civil law pertaining to same-gender relationships

In 1977, the CCAR adopted a resolution calling for legislation decriminalizing homosexual acts between consenting adults, and calling for an end to discrimination against gays and lesbians. The resolution called on Reform Jewish organizations to develop programs to implement this stand.

In 1990, the CCAR endorsed the report of the Ad Hoc Committee on Homosexuality and the Rabbinate. This position paper urged that "all rabbis, regardless of sexual orientation, be accorded the opportunity to fulfill the sacred vocation that they have chosen." The committee endorsed the view that "all Jews are religiously equal regardless of their sexual orientation." The committee expressed its agreement with changes in the admissions policies of the Hebrew Union College–Jewish Institute of Religion, which stated that the "sexual orientation of an applicant [be considered] only within the context of a candidate's overall suitability for the rabbinate," and reaffirmed that all rabbinic graduates of the HUC-JIR would be admitted into CCAR membership upon application. The report described differing views within the committee as to the nature of *kiddushin*, and deferred the matter of rabbinic officiation.

A 1996 resolution resolved that the CCAR "support the right of gay and lesbian couples to share fully and equally in the rights of civil marriage," and voiced opposition to governmental efforts to ban gay and lesbian marriages.

In addition to these resolutions, two CCAR committees have addressed the question of same-gender officiation. The CCAR Committee on Responsa addressed the question of whether homosexual relationships can qualify as *kiddushin* (which it defined as "Jewish marriage"). By a committee majority of 7 to 2, the committee concluded that "homosex-

---

2. Central Conference of American Rabbis 111th Annual Convention, "Resolution Adopted on Same Gender Officiation" (2000), http://www.ccarnet.org.

ual relationships, however exclusive and committed they may be, do not fit within this legal category; they cannot be called *kiddushin*. We do not understand Jewish marriage apart from the concept of *kiddushin*." The committee acknowledged its lack of consensus on this question.

The Ad Hoc Committee on Human Sexuality issued a report in 1998 which included its conclusion, by a committee majority of 11 with 1 abstention, that "kedushah may be present in committed same-gender relationships between two Jews and that these relationships can serve as the foundation of stable Jewish families, thus adding strength to the Jewish community." The report called upon the CCAR to support all colleagues in their choices in this matter, and to develop educational programs.

Resolution

WHEREAS justice and human dignity are cherished Jewish values, and

WHEREAS, in March of 1999 the Women's Rabbinic Network passed a resolution urging the Central Conference of American Rabbis to bring the issue of honoring ceremonies between two Jews of the same-gender to the floor of the convention plenum, and

WHEREAS, the institutions of Reform Judaism have a long history of support for civil and equal rights for gays and lesbians, and

WHEREAS, North American organizations of the Reform Movement have passed resolutions in support of civil marriage for gays and lesbians, therefore

WE DO HEREBY RESOLVE, that the relationship of a Jewish, same-gender couple is worthy of affirmation through appropriate Jewish ritual, and

FURTHER RESOLVED, that we recognize the diversity of opinions within our ranks on this issue. We support the decision of those who choose to officiate at rituals of union for same-gender couples, and we support the decision of those who do not, and

FURTHER RESOLVED, that we call upon the CCAR to support all colleagues in their choices in this matter, and

FURTHER RESOLVED, that we also call upon the CCAR to develop both educational and liturgical resources in this area.

Appendix B: Text 2

Questions to Address

- What is the position of the author(s) on same-gender marriage?
- What values guided the author(s) to the position described?
- How can you best explain your answers to other people?

Exiled[3]

Laura Wolfson

In December 2003, after nine years of living in a committed, loving relationship with my Jewish partner, I was finally able to be married in a synagogue with both Jewish and Canadian legal sanction. Tish and I were among the ranks of thousands of Canadian gay and lesbian couples who have walked down the aisle following the landmark 2003 court rulings instructing municipal licensing offices in the provinces of British Columbia and Ontario to issue marriage licenses to same-sex couples—but with one significant difference: few of these weddings have taken place in synagogues. Ours was only the third to be celebrated in a synagogue—but, sadly, not in our own.

Let me explain. My partner and I had discussed marriage with our rabbi some years ago, but he was unwilling to officiate. Accustomed to waiting for others to become more comfortable with us, we decided to wait until he was ready. After much study and reflection, he said yes, but our congregation's lay leadership said no. Exiled, we sanctified our marriage in the presence of our family, friends, community, and our rabbi at a Reform synagogue in another city that is more than an hour's drive from our home.

While my partner and I are accustomed to waiting for others to become comfortable *with* us, waiting for acceptance is not comfortable *for* us. We are active contributors to the Jewish community, and I am a respected community leader. When others sit in judgment, debate the legitimacy of our "lifestyle," and determine whether the Jewish community should recognize it, we feel something akin to the indignation, fear, and rage that public expressions of anti-semitism evoke in us and in all Jews worldwide—only it's more personal.

Like most Jewish parents, we want our two-year-old daughter, Hannah, to feel connected to the Jewish people. If she someday learns that our synagogue refused to affirm the sacred union that binds her parents together and forms the basis for her family, will Hannah still feel that she belongs? And will she find it incongruous—even hypocritical— that our synagogue has accepted an openly lesbian Jew as a congregational leader, accepted our money, and was willing to celebrate her *Brit bat* by welcoming both her mothers to the *bimah*—all the while refusing to embrace us fully as a family?

---

3. Laura Wolfson, "Exiled," *Reform Judaism* 33, no. 1 (Fall 2004): 88.

Being a religious Reform Jew is at the very core of my identity; it informs each decision I make and everything I do. Being rejected hurts, but as an adult I understand that change takes time. My preschool daughter, though, has no such patience or understanding. It would break my heart if someday she were to abandon the Jewish community because the congregation in which she grew up had not fully accepted her family.

Can the Jewish people risk losing even one Jew? As a Jewish educator who has dedicated her life to strengthening our community by helping children and families improve their ability to live Jewishly, I say no. We cannot afford to lose even one Jew. And as a mother, I weep at the thought that my own daughter could be that Jew.

Appendix B: Text 3

Questions to Address

- What is the position of the author(s) on same-gender marriage?
- What values guided the author(s) to the position described?
- How can you best explain your answers to other people?

CCAR Responsum on Homosexual Marriage (1996)[4]

[**Editors' note:** This responsum was one of the most controversial in the history of the CCAR. It is over twenty-five pages long, and explores this issue from multiple perspectives. Both majority and minority opinions were written, and the majority opinion is the more conservative one, claiming that same-gender unions cannot be considered as "marriage." Interestingly, the *minority* opinion—the opinion that same-sex ceremonies *can* be considered as "marriage"—is the one that most (though not all) Reform rabbis hold today. It is also important to remember that in the CCAR, responsa are not binding on their members—no rabbi is obligated to abide by them. Thus this reponsum is not an "official position," but rather an attempt to create guidelines for rabbis based on balancing Jewish tradition and liberal values. It is likely that if a new responsum were written today, a different conclusion would be reached.

We have chosen an excerpt from the majority opinion, the more conservative side, in order to show a different perspective on this issue, as well as to show how the Reform Movement has changed since 1996.]

... This Committee has held that "however we may understand homosexuality ... we cannot accommodate the relationship of two homosexuals as a 'marriage' within the context of Judaism," for none of the elements of *kiddushin*, of traditional Jewish marriage, can be invoked for that relationship. And such was the position of the CCAR's Ad Hoc Committee on Homosexuality and the Rabbinate, whose majority stated in 1990:

> In Jewish tradition heterosexual, monogamous, procreative marriage is the ideal human relationship for the propagation of the species, covenantal fulfillment, and the preservation of the Jewish people. While acknowledging that there are other human relationships which possess ethical and spiritual value and that there are some people for whom heterosexual, monogamous, procreative marriage is not a viable option or possibility, the majority of the committee reaffirms unequivocally the centrality of this ideal and its special status as *kiddushin*. [*CCAR Yearbook* 100 (1990), 110]

---

4. Excerpted from CCAR Responsa Committee, Central Conference of American Rabbis, "Responsum on Homosexual Marriage" (1996), http://www.ccarnet.org.

. . . We begin by suggesting that, in this argument, the burden of proof does not rest with us. This is no mere debaters' quibble. Frequently, in discussions of this sort in liberal circles such as ours, one hears the question as "why not?" That is to say, "why *shouldn't* we, as liberals who are open to new ideas, adopt this change?" To frame the issue in this way is to declare that, at least on this subject, the cumulative weight of millenia of Jewish tradition hardly counts. . . . As members of the Responsa Committee, we take tradition seriously and consider it prayerfully. Even on this subject, so often (and, to some of us, falsely) presented as a stark contrast between the values of the present versus those of an outdated past, tradition serves as our interpretive starting point. Those who advocate a revolutionary transformation of Jewish marriage law and practice rightly shoulder the burden of proving that theirs is the better position. . . .

C.C.A.R. Responsa Committee
Mark Washofsky, *Chair*
Joan S. Friedman
David Lilienthal
Bernard Mehlman
W. Gunther Plaut
Richard S. Rheins
Jeffrey K. Salkin
Daniel Schiff
Faedra L. Weiss

Joan S. Friedman and Bernard Mehlman side with the minority position as expressed in this responsum.

Moshe Zemer agrees with the conclusion and the decision of the majority of the Committee that same-sex unions do not qualify as *kiddushin* and that Reform rabbis should not officiate at wedding or commitment ceremonies for gay or lesbian couples. He will append a separate responsum.

Appendix B: Text 4

Questions to Address

- What is the position of the author(s) on same-gender marriage?
- What values guided the author(s) to the position described?
- How can you best explain your answers to other people?

Enfranchising the Monogamous Homosexual: A Legal Possibility, a Moral Imperative[5]

Rabbi Bradley Shavit Artson

... By developing a public ceremony to mark the beginning and termination of an exclusive, committed homosexual relationship, the traditional Jewish standards would be clear and enforceable. In fact, by extending those standards to include responsible gay and lesbian love, we would simultaneously strengthen our resolve to place sexual expression within the confines of commitment and fidelity for heterosexuals as well—applying one clear and moral standard to all.

By insisting on a public ceremony, *b'rit ahavah* [a covenant of love], we assert that our commitment to stable homes in which responsible adults live their lives in accordance with the *mitzvot* and values of traditional Judaism is absolute and uncompromising. ...

There is no reason to presume that two Jewish homosexuals, having sought rabbinic recognition of their commitment to each other and to establishing a Jewish home, should be any less a source of strength and vitality to the Jewish community and to Judaism as a religion than any other similar heterosexual couple. ... Encouraging a commitment ceremony for monogamous Jewish homosexuals serves only to strengthen Judaism. ...

Now, as always, we must remember the fundamental goal of Jewish law: "Clearly justice is the ultimate value to which God's will must conform; any dichotomy between them is unthinkable. The demand of ethics and the command of God are one" [Robert Gordis, *The Dynamics of Jewish Law* (Bloomington: Indiana University Press, 1990), p. 68)].

In our day, the command of God is to enfranchise the monogamous homosexual.

---

5. Excerpted from Bradley Shavit Artson, "Enfranchising the Monogamous Homosexual: A Legal Possibility, a Moral Imperative," *S'vara: A Journal of Philosophy, Law, and Judaism* 3, no. 1 (1993).

Appendix B: Text 5

Questions to Address

- What is the position of the author(s) on same-gender marriage?
- What values guided the author(s) to the position described?
- How can you best explain your answers to other people?

Resolution Adopted by the 64th General Assembly of the Union of American Hebrew Congregations Biennial, 1997: Civil Marriage for Gay and Lesbian Jewish Couples[6]

Background

In 1987, the Union of American Hebrew Congregations (UAHC) reaffirmed its commitment to welcoming gay and lesbian Jews into its congregations and encouraging their participation in all aspects of synagogue and communal life. In 1993, Rabbi Alexander M. Schindler, President of the UAHC, called upon the Reform Movement to support the right of gay and lesbian couples to adopt children, to file joint income-tax returns, and to share in health and death benefits provided to heterosexual couples by federal, state, and local governments and by both large and small corporations. Following Rabbi Schindler's call, the UAHC, in 1993, resolved that full equality under the law for gay men and lesbians requires legal recognition of monogamous domestic gay and lesbian relationships.

In 1990, the Central Conference of American Rabbis (CCAR) adopted a position paper encouraging rabbis and congregations to treat with respect and to integrate fully all Jews into the life of the community regardless of sexual orientation and acknowledging the need for continuing discussion regarding the religious status of monogamous domestic relationships between gay men or lesbians and the creation of special ceremonies. In April 1996, the CCAR adopted a resolution supporting the right of gay and lesbian couples to share fully and equally in the benefits of civil marriage....

In the years since first the UAHC and subsequently the CCAR gave their support for full equality for gay men and lesbians in congregational life, gay men and lesbians have increasingly come forward to participate in the life of Reform Judaism on national, regional, and local levels. No less than heterosexual couples, gay men or lesbians living in monogamous domestic relationships have demonstrated, like their counterparts, love for one another, compassion for the sick, and grief for the dead.

The UAHC has for decades provided moral leadership to the Jewish community and to our nation, recognizing our differences and diversity, but acknowledging that we are but one family, equal before God. In this spirit, the UAHC must now move more forcefully to support the monogamous domestic relationships of gay men and lesbians . . .

---

6. Union of American Hebrew Congregations 64th General Assembly, "Resolution Adopted on Civil Marriage for Gay and Lesbian Jewish Couples" (Dallas, 1997), http://www.urj.org.

THEREFORE, the Union of American Hebrew Congregations resolves to:
1. Support secular efforts to promote legislation which would provide through civil marriage equal opportunity for gay men and lesbians;
2. Encourage its constituent congregations to honor monogamous domestic relationships formed by gay men or lesbians; and
3. Support the efforts of the CCAR in its ongoing work as it studies the appropriateness of religious ceremonies for use in a celebration of commitment recognizing a monogamous domestic relationship between two Jewish gay men or two Jewish lesbians.

What Rabbis Should Do to Help Protect Legal Rights in Same-Sex Couples

Rabbi Arthur Gross-Schaefer and Robert Dixon

> In a place where there are no human beings, try to be one.
> —Hillel, Pirkei Avot 2:5

Introduction

In a period of thirty days in early 2004, San Francisco City Hall issued over four thousand same-sex marriage licenses, and city officials performed more than thirty-four hundred marriages.[1] The presiding officials in San Francisco were then ordered to prove why they had not "exceeded their authority" by performing the marriages, and in August of that year, the marriages were declared null and void by the California State Supreme Court. Clearly, there is no guarantee for even small victories for same-sex couples looking to receive legal sanction for their marriage. Thus for the rabbi who performs same-sex unions in the absence of the legal protections of civil marriage, there are several potential legal issues that need to be discussed in order to protect the legal and financial rights of the couple.

We do not want rabbis to become lawyers or give legal advice. We do, however, want rabbis to become familiar with the potential for legal abuses in the absence of the official protections that automatically follow a legally recognized marriage and to learn how those abuses can potentially be avoided with the execution of wills, advanced directives, and several property and parenting agreements.

When a rabbi is counseling a gay or lesbian couple about the various issues involved in strengthening their spiritual connection and the creation of their particular marriage or commitment ceremony, there are responsibilities for the spiritual leader. Those responsibilities include being aware of and actively discussing the legal issues surrounding property rights, medical decisions, adoption potentials, funeral considerations, and inheritance. Although a rabbi is not to give legal advice or act like the couple's attorney, as a spiritual leader the rabbi can be an important source for appropriate referrals. In requiring that certain minimal documents be drafted and signed

---

1. CNN.com, March 12, 2004, "California Court Halts Same-Sex Marriages."

prior to commencement of the ceremony, the rabbi is not practicing law but is rather acting as a responsible spiritual counselor who is helping to protect that couple's future in terms of legal, emotional, and financial security.

It is important to remember that when a rabbi is working with *any* couple in preparation for a union, the rabbi is helping them prepare for their new life together, both spiritually and emotionally. However, for same-sex unions, there is an additional complicating factor. In *heterosexual* unions, legal rights tend not to be discussed, because heterosexual unions are recognized by the state. Since the legal landscape for *same-sex* unions is still unclear in most of the country, when preparing for a same-sex union, the rabbi also has a responsibility to discuss legal documents that will protect that couple's future in terms of legal, emotional, and financial security.

Through creative use of existing legal agreements, rabbis can greatly reduce situations of financial and emotional hardship that occur in some same-sex relationships. As such, this is a practical guide both for rabbis and for same-sex couples. It outlines some of the avenues currently available to alleviate some of the legal nightmares that may arise in same-sex relationships that do not have the automatic protections that come with civil heterosexual unions.

There are two critical factors that a rabbi needs to address to protect the legal rights of same-gender couples.

- **Advise each couple to retain competent counsel to draft legal documents.** First and foremost, rabbis who choose to perform same-sex unions should strongly advise same-sex couples to retain competent counsel(s) to draft legal documents that will afford each couple certain legal rights in case of separation, death, or incapacity. Marriage/commitment ceremonies allow for important ritual, religious, and spiritual moments; however, in the absence of legal substance, such a relationship can lead to problematic, confusing, and even appalling consequences.
- **Each rabbi needs to be familiar with the rules in his or her state.** It cannot be emphasized enough that each state, and in some cases each jurisdiction, has its own rules, and thus it is imperative that each rabbi become familiar with the rules in his or her area and find appropriate legal advisers so that he or she can be kept aware of the constantly changing legal landscape.

Four Potential Problem Areas

There are, at a minimum, four basic areas that same-sex couples need to consider in order to avoid potential problems down the road (in more complex situations, additional areas of legal concern may exist). Again, each couple needs to find their own legal adviser or advisers who will assist them as to their particular needs.

The four main problem areas are as follows:

1. Adoption
2. Single-income households
3. Property distribution in case of dissolution or death
4. Medical decisions

Below, we illustrate potential problems or worst-case scenarios in these areas if the appropriate forms are not filled out.

Adoption

In some states, adoption by gay and lesbian couples is limited to only one legal parent, and so the nonadoptive gay or lesbian partner would lose all legal rights should the couple separate. Since current laws state that only the legal adoptive parent has parental rights, the nonadoptive partner has no right to visit or to co-parent. With only one parent as the legal guardian, the parent who has legally adopted or birthed the child may restrict his or her former partner from seeing the child. In addition, from the perspective of the child's welfare, there are other issues, such as the nonadoptive parent's ability to make medical decisions for the child. If the adoptive parent dies, the nonadoptive parent has no legal rights to custody or financial support for the child from the estate of the deceased.

Currently, joint adoptions or second-parent adoptions have been granted to lesbian and gay couples in a minority of states, which include California, Connecticut, Massachusetts, New York, New Jersey, Pennsylvania, and Vermont, as well as the District of Columbia.[2]

Single-Income Households

Without the solutions discussed below, if only one partner is the major breadwinner, upon the dissolution of the relationship the major wage earner will be able to claim all assets, thus leaving the former partner disenfranchised. Without various protections in place, the other partner could have no legal claim to the bank accounts, stock interests, car, or other assets. Moreover, if any of these assets appreciated during the relationship, the "major breadwinner" would be able to claim most if not all of the appreciated value, leaving the other partner little if any equity.

Property Distribution

If the property is under one partner's name and the couple were to separate, the other partner might not be entitled to any ownership rights. Accordingly, that partner could be forced out of the home and would not have shared in any of the equity appreciation should the residence have increased in value during their relationship. If the property-owning partner were to die suddenly, the surviving partner would have no legal right of inheritance. In the absence of a legal agreement, the assets acquired during the term of the relationship do not automatically pass to the surviving partner.

Medical Decisions

Gay and lesbian couples do not have legal rights in most jurisdictions to make medical or funeral decisions for their partner. If a couple gets into a major auto accident, the uninjured partner would have no right to direct or be legally involved in the partner's medical care or even be allowed in the emergency room. The partner would be completely excluded from making decisions regarding extraordinary lifesaving measures such as life support. Moreover, in the event of death, the surviving partner would have no legal right to direct or be involved in funeral arrangements.

---

2. Human Rights Campaign Foundation, http://www.hrc.org/Content/NavigationMenu/Family/Get_Informed1/Parenting/Adoption/Second-Parent_Adoption/Second_Parent.htm.

Potential Solutions

Many of the issues described above for same-sex couples can be circumvented through the use of legal documents. The five most helpful are as follows:

1. Domestic partnerships
2. Wills
3. Cohabitation agreements
4. Co-parent agreements
5. Advanced directives

In their counseling sessions with a prospective couple who want a marriage or commitment ceremony, rabbis should raise these issues and suggest these documents. These five simple legal documents will entitle same-sex couples to many of the same rights heterosexual married couples obtain automatically when they are married.[3] These documents are by no means an equitable substitute for legally recognized marriages, but they do provide benefits that current law would otherwise fail to grant them.

In order to minimize the risk of being left out of an emergency room when a loved one is in dire straights, of losing custody rights of a child, or of being left homeless and penniless due to separation, gay and lesbian couples should not rely on or wait for the state or federal government to produce a remedy. Instead, gay and lesbian couples should use existing legal agreements, and simultaneously, both they and their rabbis need to advocate for better legal protections. In summary, when entering into a committed relationship, gay and lesbian couples can effectively gain some of the benefits of marriage by filing these five documents. The purposes and benefits of each document are outlined below.

Domestic Partnership

Creating a domestic partnership prior to a marriage ceremony is a step in the right legal direction, because it recognizes the union between a same-sex couple in a legal manner. Domestic partners are unmarried couples who live together and seek monetary and other benefits that are granted to their married counterparts. Domestic partner registry in general requires that both partners be present at the time of registry, are at least eighteen years of age, reside together and are sharing the common necessities of life, are not married or registered to any other person, are not related by blood, and intend on remaining each other's sole partner and providing for the common welfare indefinitely.

By meeting these requirements and registering as domestic partners, a same-sex couple can become eligible in many states for what are known as "domestic partner benefits." This is the term for employment benefits that are allocated to the same-sex partner of an employee, and death benefits, health insurance, and sick leave are just a few of the benefits that registered domestic partners can receive.[4] In California, registered domestic partners receive rights with regard to family crisis, children, family work benefits,[5] and inheritance rights[6] (one can obtain a California Domestic Partnership form from www.ss.ca.gov).

---

3. Hayden Curry, Denis Clifford, Robin Leonard, and Frederick Hertz, *A Legal Guide for Lesbian and Gay Couples* (Berkeley, CA: Nolo Press, 1999), p. 1/5.
4. Ibid.
5. www.ss.ca.gov.
6. Kevin Moss, "Legitimizing Same-Sex Marriages," *Peace Review: A Journal of Social Justice* (2002): p. 103.

The complete list of institutions that offer domestic partnership benefits is widespread from state governments to private employers, but the benefits they offer are not universal.[7] In some cases, the only benefit for domestic partners is sick leave. Since there is no uniform benefit law, benefits vary from state to state, or even from city to city. Thus, even if you live in a state with a Domestic Partnership Law or work for an employer who offers certain benefits, one should still take legal preventive measures.

Will

A will is one's last testament. Because there is no right of inheritance for a surviving partner in same-sex relationships, the absence of a will allows property to be distributed based solely on state intestacy law, which will deny that partner the right to any property or inheritance. Intestacy laws normally pass the property first to the surviving parents and then to the siblings (personal property passes based on the state laws of where the descendant was domiciled, and the real property passes based on the laws of the state in which the property is located).[8] To ensure that the surviving partner and/or the nonadopted child inherit, a will is required. A traditional will is a formal agreement requiring witnesses and follows the format required in each state. Unlike many other types of agreements, it is imperative that a will follow the exact rules of that jurisdiction and should be drafted by an attorney. Since legal rules regarding wills differ, a new will may be required when one moves to another location. Wills not only deal with issues of property passing after one's death, but also have major tax effects and long-term implications, so consulting a financial planner and/or accountant is also an important part of this process. No matter how young or old an individual may be, death is never predictable, and both partners should have a will.

Scenario

Mark and Jesse have been together for over twenty-five years. They have had a strong relationship, and both have been in excellent health. Jesse notes at their anniversary dinner that they need to draft wills, as he wants to make sure that Mark inherits his estate should anything happen. However, before Jesse can contact a lawyer, Jesse is hit by a car while walking his dog and dies of his injuries. Since there is no will, all of Jesse's assets pass intestate (without a will) and will probably go to his parents, if they are living. If Jesse had a will, he could have left all his assets to Mark.

Cohabitation Agreement

One contract that protects both parties in case of a separation is the cohabitation agreement. This agreement is made between two individuals who are living together and who are not married. This type of agreement can eliminate a variety of disputes (especially property and financial) and can protect both individuals from unnecessary cost and litigation. This agreement allows a same-sex couple to specify assets and predetermine what will happen to assets that have been purchased jointly in the event of separation.

---

7. Hayden Curry, Denis Clifford, Robin Leonard, and Frederick Hertz, *A Legal Guide for Lesbian and Gay Couples* (Berkeley, CA: Nolo Press, 1999) p. 1/8.
8. Ibid.

When a couple begins to set up a household together, it may become apparent that certain expectations regarding financial obligations may be different for each party. For instance, one partner may believe that he or she will retain his or her own separate property, while the other partner may have the opposite expectation. Should the relationship dissolve, these conflicting expectations can lead to a tremendous amount of pain and anguish. In order to avoid this, couples should discuss specific expectations regarding financial and property matters beforehand. This will ensure that each person is aware of his or her partner's expectations and thus be able to create a mutual understanding about each individual's responsibility to the union. The cohabitation agreement can be applied to mitigate a number of these issues.

After discussing their mutual expectations, needs, and concerns, the couple's next step in establishing legal cohabitation would be to retain separate attorneys, who would then be able to negotiate and draft an agreement that would be enforceable in their jurisdiction. Even though two attorneys will be expensive, it would be beneficial in the end, as claims of unfairness or duress, which may arise if only one attorney is used, could be avoided. Furthermore, one attorney may cast doubt on the enforceability of the agreement.[9] An attorney is more likely to add provisions within mutual agreement to ensure that problems do not arise in the future.

An entire host of provisions can be outlined in the cohabitation agreement, including a living expense provision that indicates how much both parties will contribute to the household each year, and what percentage each month.[10] It would specify how property or assets obtained after the execution of this agreement would be viewed (e.g., as joint title).

Scenario

Sarah and Jill have been together for seven years. Five years ago they had a commitment ceremony, where their friends and family witnessed them profess their love for one another. Sarah owns and operates her own telecommunications business, while Jill is a stay-at-home mom. In the last few years, Sarah has been seeing her secretary romantically, unbeknownst to Jill. One day Sarah informs Jill that she has fallen out of love with Jill and that she has sold her company as well as the house and is moving to Hawaii with her secretary. Jill's world has been turned upside down, and unfortunately, when Jill and Sarah expressed their love for one another years ago, they never drafted a cohabitation agreement. If Sarah and Jill had a cohabitation agreement, the situation could have been drastically different.

For instance, in the cohabitation agreement, Jill and Sarah could have specified a separation agreement stating that upon disillusionment of the relationship, alimony would be paid to either party. This agreement could have been set up similar to a prenuptial agreement that indicates the specific monetary amount to which each party is entitled. With regard to the house, Sarah and Jill would have benefited from a cohabitation agreement that specified that both individuals were joint owners. In addition, stipulations could have been included requiring both parties to place the house on the market, so that one individual would not be able to sell the house unbeknownst to her partner.

---

9. Ibid.
10. Ibid.

Co-Parent Agreement

Usually, the most challenging issues in divorce cases tend to arise around the children. Questions raised include: Who is entitled to primary care? Who gets what time with the child? These questions and many more plague courtrooms. Therefore, having a written agreement for same-sex couples that outlines both parents' legal roles with regard to the child is crucial to avoid a great deal of extra hardship should a breakup ever occur. One way same-sex couples can avoid this unpleasant issue is to have a co-parent agreement.

If the issue of children comes up when the rabbi prepares a same-sex couple for their wedding, the rabbi should know that there are several ways gay and lesbian couples can have children, such as through adoption, surrogacy, artificial insemination, or from previous relationships. Looking specifically at issues around adoption, when one adopts a child, one then becomes the child's legal parent,[11] and the biological parents' rights are terminated,[12] except if one is adopting his or her partner's child. Certain states allow gay couples to jointly adopt a child, but in many other states, gays and lesbians are allowed to adopt only as a single parent.[13] The only state that specifically prohibits lesbian and gays from adopting is Florida.[14]

In the case of a single-parent adoption, a co-parent agreement would outline that *both* partners are parents of the child. This document should state that both individuals have the same rights and responsibilities that come with parenting, and the contract should indicate that in the case of a breakup, all disputes should be dealt with through mediation or arbitration. With or without a written agreement, the nonadoptive parent cannot seek custody of the child but may be able to request visitation.[15] A written contract that specifically explains each partner's role in the child's life can only bolster the case of visitation.

If a breakup occurs and there has been joint adoption or second-parent adoption, any child-related disputes would be dealt with just as if it were a divorce.[16] The judge has the power to make all the decisions and is supposed to make them with the child's best interests in mind.[17] In most situations, both individuals will retain legal custody of the child, which allows both parents to have equal input over the central decisions in the child's life and the responsibility of taking care of the child financially.[18]

The co-parent agreement protects not only the parents, but the child as well. Regardless of the circumstances of a breakup, an innocent child is in the middle. This contract virtually ensures that both parents will raise this child even if they are not living together, and it may be useful in case of the untimely death of the legally adoptive parent and absence of a will in proving intent of the other parent to parent or adopt.

Scenario

Laura and Miriam want to raise a child together. In their particular state, only one of them can legally be the adoptive parent. They decide that Laura will be the "official" par-

---

11. Ibid.
12. Ibid.
13. Ibid.
14. Ibid.
15. Ibid.
16. Ibid.
17. Ibid.
18. Ibid.

ent, and they adopt Richard, a three-year-old little boy. Unfortunately, they decide to separate six years later, when Richard is nine. Both Laura and Miriam have jointly raised Richard for the past six years and both love him very much. However, by law, Laura may be entitled to exclude Miriam from any future relationship with Richard. Had Miriam and Laura entered into a co-parenting agreement, the court might have been more willing to award Miriam certain privileges, including visitation rights.

Advance Directives

One of the scariest things in the world is to hear that a loved one is seriously ill and is in the hospital. Possibly the most frustrating thing to hear is that one has no input over the type of care given to this person because one is not legally part of the family. This is the grim reality that many gay and lesbian couples face because their local and federal governments refuse to recognize them as a legally bonded couple. To avoid this outcome, gay and lesbian couples should enter into a durable power of attorney for finances as well as for medical care.

In the durable power of attorney for finances, one can name the individual who will handle his or her financial tasks. This person is called one's attorney-in-fact.[19] The power of the attorney-in-fact can also be regulated through stipulations in the contract. For example, a person may want the sale of only certain items to help pay for hospital bills. Another may want his or her cars and other luxury items to be sold to help defer the cost of the hospital stay. However, a third person may want to ensure that the home is not sold at any cost. This document will benefit the couple in case of a medical crisis where one is unable to manage one's own finances. It also allows the partner to take care of daily tasks such as paying bills, making deposits, and watching investments.[20]

In a traditional marriage, the spouse would be granted decision-making authority with regard to the administration of medicine, withholding of treatment or surgery, or similar decisions. This responsibility is not granted to a gay or lesbian partner. However, the durable power of attorney for health care can be used to empower the partner to make the decisions typically granted to a spouse. In this capacity, a partner may make decisions regarding certain medical treatment or whether to pursue painful and complex procedures. Similar to a durable power of attorney for financial matters, the appointed person's power can be specific. One can authorize the attorney-in-fact to be able to hire and fire medical personnel and allow visitation even when other visiting is restricted.[21] The most important factor to consider when choosing an attorney-in-fact is to appoint a person who truly understands your wishes and is trustworthy.[22]

Scenario

Milton and Sam have been together for over thirty years. Sam suffers a heart attack and is placed on life support. Sam's brother, the only living relative, was never that close to Sam but now appears and insists that he make the decision about whether or not Sam should

---

19. Ibid.
20. Ibid.
21. Ibid.
22. Ibid.

be taken off life support. In addition, Sam's brother has made it clear that he does not want Milton to visit Sam in the ICU and does not plan to involve Milton in any of the medical decisions. Had Sam executed an advanced directive and entered into a durable power of attorney for health care with Milton, Milton would be able to visit Sam in the ICU and make medical decisions.

Conclusion

It is recommended that rabbis who perform marriage and commitment ceremonies for gay and lesbian couples incorporate these legal documents into the counseling process prior to the ceremony. Without the execution of the aforementioned documents, the ceremony will have important religious significance but will be bereft of any legal weight [within the U.S.]—except in Massachusetts. By incorporating the documents into the practice, rabbis will give the ceremony some of the essential added protections that are automatic with a heterosexual civil ceremony.

It is noted that the recommendations of these documents to file are merely general guidelines and are by no means exhaustive. The type of documents to be filed will vary from state to state based upon the laws of the local governing body, be it state or local. Therefore, it is further recommended that both the rabbi and the couple check the local law to determine which documents should be filed. Additionally, seeking professional legal advice to guide a couple through this process will be beneficial to the rabbi involved as well as the couple. Gays and lesbians need to take preemptive steps toward protecting their assets to be able to ensure their quality of life. Until the government allows the same legal rights for the union of same-sex couples as they do for a heterosexual marriage, it is the job of the rabbi who provides or performs marriage and commitment ceremonies to ensure that these ceremonies have weight in both the spiritual *and* the legal world.

Further Online National Resources

National Center for Lesbian Rights: 415-392-6257, www.nclrights.org, info@nclrights.org

Lambda Legal: 212-809-8585 (national headquarters), www.lambdalegal.org

ACLU Lesbian, Gay Bisexual, Transgender and AIDS Rights Project: 212-549-2627, www.aclu.org/LesbianGayRights/LesbianGayRightsmain.cfm

National Lesbian and Gay Law Association: 202-637-6384, www.nlgla.org, info@nlgla.org (a bar association with state affiliates)

Gay & Lesbian Advocates & Defenders: www.glad.org

Premarital Counseling for Same-Sex Couples: Highlights for Rabbis and Cantors

Rabbi Nancy H. Wiener, D.Min.

In 1991, my life partner and I asked our dear friend, a rabbi, to help us prepare for our wedding. She met with us to discuss our feelings for each other, our desire to get married, and details about our ceremony. During our meetings it became clear that we were teaching her more about some of the unique aspects of our lives, as lesbian Jews preparing for a wedding, than any of us had imagined. Our wedding was wonderful. But we wondered how it might have been different if she had been able to anticipate some of our specific needs.

In 1994, I completed my doctoral work by creating and implementing a premarital counseling model for same-sex couples. I wanted to find a way to help rabbis and cantors prepare themselves to provide meaningful premarital counseling for same-sex couples. Little did I know at the time that I would come to use the model with *all* couples. What follows are some highlights of the model.

Before the First Meeting: Preparing Ourselves for the Counseling

Assessing the Limits of Our Own Experience and Knowledge

Before engaging in pastoral counseling, we should always consider the preconceived notions we have about the people we will counsel, the fears and anxieties they evoke in us, and the expectations we have for our interactions with them.

When it comes to working with same-sex couples, we must recognize that we are all products of a Jewish world that, for millennia, said: Jewish weddings are for men and women only. We are products of a Jewish world that could not even conceive of a same-sex Jewish wedding. Only in recent decades have some of our communities begun to learn,

---

Adapted from Nancy Wiener, "Pre-Marital Counseling for Same-Sex Couples: Highlights for Rabbis and Cantors," The Shalom Center, http://www.shalomctr.org/node/316 (accessed October 24, 2006).

and perhaps teach others, that people of all sexual orientations can have loving, committed, and enduring relationships. Only in recent decades have some of our communities seriously challenged their assumptions about the nature of Jewish marriage and pondered the very real possibility that it is the content of a relationship, rather than its form (sexual orientation of its members) that we gather as a community to celebrate and sanctify.

Setting Goals

Every time a couple asks us to meet with them prior to their wedding, we receive an invitation to participate in a potentially transformative process. Couples generally arrive prepared to plan their weddings: intellectually, emotionally, and pragmatically. As *m'sadrei kiddushin* (people empowered to develop ritual and conduct life-cycle events), we can facilitate much more than the ceremony. We can guide a holy process that leads to a wedding filled with emotional, interpersonal, spiritual, and religious meaning.

Our responsibilities as *m'sadrei kiddushin* are as follows:

1. To create a safe space for couples to explore their strengths and weaknesses.
2. To hear and respect varied personal histories.
3. To validate personal experiences.
4. To encourage couples to express concerns and issues they may have about each other, their families, their futures, and so on.
5. To teach couples about Jewish wedding options and assist them in creating a personally and religiously meaningful ceremony.
6. To help couples acknowledge the changes inherent in their new status: from single to married; from member of one family to member of a newly formed family.
7. To provide appropriate referrals for further counseling, when necessary.

Working with the Couple

There are five premarital counseling goals that can be established for all couples. Given the legal and social realities of our world, I include one additional goal that is specific for same-sex couples.

Goal 1: Reviewing the Relationship

A wedding is not an end point, but a high point in a relationship that has both a history and a future. Many couples, swept up in the premarriage whirl, lose sight of this truth. The relationship time line is designed to help a couple move beyond simple recitation of "their story," by contextualizing their relationship on a continuum with prior relationships and future expectations. As our study of midrash has taught us, in the telling and retelling of our stories we develop a changing understanding of ourselves.

As couples narrate their relationship history, I literally map it out on paper, indicating who is speaking (by keeping parallel lines) and when the event mentioned took place. The oral recitation and the graphic depiction often jog long-forgotten milestones, large and small, that have dropped out of the "official story."

Ask the couple to work backwards, providing information about past relationships. If they have had other significant relationships, this process can help them gain insights into the distinctiveness of this one and their desire to build a future with this particular person.

If this is a first serious relationship, they can reflect on how they have reached this point in their lives.

Finally, ask couples to share their future expectations. This projective piece can reveal important information about the compatibility of their short- and long-term expectations, serving as a catalyst to address any discrepancies that exist.

The time line of same-sex couples may include data that does not come up regularly with heterosexual couples. Gay men and lesbians tend to be more open about and accepting of previous periods of promiscuity and experimentation than their heterosexual counterparts. They may share information about periods of heterosexual dating or marriage, or even periods of dating members of both sexes, while they struggled to determine their sexual orientation. They may have had previous relationships that they hid from family, friends, or coworkers. It is the sharing of this type of information that challenges us to remember our responsibility to maintain a safe space and validate personal experiences.

Goal 2: Understanding the Relationship in a Jewish Framework
Goal 3: Fostering a Sense of Belonging to the Jewish Community

Couples come to us believing that their relationship is special and different from all others they have had. However, they usually do not arrive able to express this idea in uniquely Jewish language. Therefore, don't be surprised that couples generally respond with a sense of profound recognition to the notion of *k'dushah*. They can readily identify ways in which they have set each other apart and treated each other in ways that they treat no others. They then can understand their Jewish wedding, their *kiddushin*, as a ritual celebrating the ever-increasing *k'dushah* of their relationship.

As the couple reviews their relationship, highlighting moments that contributed to its *k'dushah*, create another time line. Ask the couple to discuss how their families, friends, and coworkers have responded to and supported the growing *k'dushah* of their relationship. This is often an opening to explore potentially difficult or painful relationships, such as with their future in-laws. Helping the members of a couple hear each other's experiences and perceptions and encouraging them to acknowledge the ways they have offered and received support from each other can contribute greatly to their understanding of themselves as individuals and as a couple.

As they reflect on the *k'dushah* of their relationship, same-sex couples may mention moments not commonly part of the experiences of heterosexual couples, including going out together in public for the first time; showing physical affection in front of friends or family or in public; establishing joint bank accounts; "going public" about their relationship in the context of daily life or in anticipation of their wedding—speaking with caterers, florists, and bands; arranging for wills, powers of attorney, health care proxies, and so on.

Same-sex couples often need extra time to explore the ways in which others have responded to their relationship's *k'dushah*. Often long-buried wounds inflicted during early stages of "coming-out" surface when they encounter hostility, rejection, or incredulity as they plan for their wedding. It is important to remember that sources of tension and resistance are not always external. Members of same-sex couples are often not "out" to the same extent or have not found similar degrees of acceptance in their individual family and social circles. The disparities that exist affect their wedding plans: whom they inform, whom they invite, and perhaps even how they plan their ceremony and reception. We can help the couple acknowledge and process tensions that may arise.

Every couple anticipates their wedding differently. For same-sex couples, this truth is heightened. The absence of religious ritual was a reality with which same-sex couples lived until very recently. As a result, most members of same-sex couples over the age of thirty-five or forty never anticipated getting married to the person they loved. These couples will need time to marvel at the changes that have occurred and to process them. Members of same-sex couples under the age of thirty-five have often had radically different life experiences. This is all the more profound as civil acceptance of gay and lesbian marriage has become a reality in parts of our own country, Canada, and some European countries. In contrast, we will also work with couples whose members came out to themselves and others in their teens; they came of age in a world saturated with media coverage of same-sex couples, weddings, and adoptions, and many have even fantasized about and mentally planned their same-sex ceremonies. We need to be open to every couple's experiences and help each one continue the journeys they have lived.

Finally, same-sex couples come to us personally motivated to sanctify their relationship in a Jewish context; they rarely come because of external pressures imposed by family. When we welcome them, acknowledge the *k'dushah* in their relationships, and affirm it in a ceremony, we can counter some of their negative preconceptions of or personal experiences with the established Jewish community.

Goal 4: Creating a Ceremony That Is Personally and Religiously Meaningful
Goal 5: Affirming Their Change of Status

Prior to any discussion about their ceremony, ask couples three questions: What do you know about Jewish weddings? Why do you want a "Jewish wedding"? What will make the wedding Jewish for you? Recommend books for them to read so that you can have an informed discussion about their ritual and liturgical options.

As a rule, we spend time discussing details of the ceremony. Most heterosexual couples are helped through the process of planning a wedding and reception by family and friends, and we make it clear that this is not our bailiwick. With same-sex couples, we may find that we cannot distance ourselves from discussions about wedding and reception plans as we might tend to do with heterosexual couples. Many same-sex couples come to us with little or no knowledge about weddings and without family or experienced friends lending support and advice as they plan. We can be of particular help by recommending books on same-sex weddings, offering a list of "gay friendly" caterers and photographers, and putting them in contact with other couples who have already celebrated their same-sex ceremonies.

When working with same-sex couples, language has a heightened importance. Same-sex couples often use the word "wedding" to establish parity, validation, and clear understanding of the meaning this event has for them. Others intentionally avoid "wedding" and "marriage," because of their heterosexual connotations. We should be ready to hear and consider the couple's preferred language and to explore the meaning it holds for them. In our own conversations about the ceremonies we do, we must remember that the language we use, both English and Hebrew, conveys powerful messages for the couple and for the larger community.

In addition, we must discuss the language of the ceremony itself: the words used in the exchange of rings, the blessings offered at the time of the *Sheva B'rachot*, the type of pronouncement we make at the end of the ceremony. Many of us already consider these issues in our discussions with heterosexual couples. It is essential for us to do so with same-sex couples—particularly if we find ourselves considering a change that does not imply or assume parity.

The *ketubah* holds special significance for same-sex couples. To date, in most U.S. municipalities, it is the only documentation that validates their change of status. They want its wording and artwork to be aesthetically pleasing, personally expressive, and religiously meaningful. We should respect its heightened importance for the couple and discuss at length its particulars.

For same-sex couples, the ceremony's choreography and their own attire often become very significant. Until recent decades, certain aspects of Jewish weddings (e.g., arriving first at the chuppah, breaking the glass) had been rigidly gender-bound. Many couples need time to articulate and deal with their fears that guests might incorrectly make gender and role assumptions about their relationship based on the choreographic and sartorial decisions they make for their ceremony. There is no single solution. Each couple must resolve these issues for themselves.

All couples deserve a ritual that establishes them as a new family and facilitates the reorganization of family and friendship structures. The rituals we help create need to clearly convey the message that their new family is holy and valid in the eyes of God and the community. Families, both accepting and rejecting, remain tremendously significant players in the lives of same-sex couples. Ritual and aesthetic decisions are often made with them in mind. Their absence needs to be mourned, their support and rejoicing celebrated. Flexibility in allocating counseling time to process these issues is important.

Goal 6 (Unique to Same-Sex Couples): Creating Legal Protections

When a heterosexual couple marries, the government extends to them 1,049 rights and privileges, as next of kin, that are effective until death or legal divorce severs the relationship. These include inheritance, pension benefits, power of attorney, joint ownership, ability to file joint tax returns, options for family-plan insurance, and joint adoption rights. A heterosexual couple married for one minute enjoys all of these rights; in all but a few municipalities, a same-sex couple together for twenty-five years enjoys none (in the absence of a civilly recognized marriage).

We must clearly articulate this reality to each same-sex couple that we counsel. While we and those in attendance will respect and honor their relationship, most civil authorities will not. Their union will have no official legal and civil status. Particularly as laws are evolving, we, as rabbis and cantors, have an obligation to become familiar with our state and local legal definitions of marriage and civil union and guide couples to experienced lawyers. The laws are different in each state, city, and municipality; the couple should contact their local office of Lambda Legal Defense and Education Fund, a national gay and lesbian legal advocacy group, to get appropriate information.

A Final Word

The success of the counseling we do depends upon our own supportive and positive attitudes. We must be open, empathic, and available. We, *m'sadrei kiddushin*, teach, guide, and officiate. Our counseling and ceremonies contribute to *tikkun olam*.

Working Together: Rabbis, Congregations, and Same-Gender Marriage

Rabbi Sharon L. Sobel

Different rabbis have different positions on officiating at same-gender marriages, and when a rabbi and a congregation formulate their policy on the "how," "where," and "why" of same-gender officiation, there can be any number of outcomes. Some rabbis will not perform same-gender marriages, and therefore topics like whether or not to allow such ceremonies in their sanctuaries is not an issue for their congregations. Other Reform rabbis have chosen to perform same-gender marriages, regardless of whether or not the congregation will allow them to be performed in their sanctuaries (that is, the rabbi will perform the ceremony elsewhere). Still other rabbis have chosen to enter into a "partnership" with their congregations, arriving at a mutual decision about what the practice is to be. Other congregations have decided that the decision to perform same-gender marriages is strictly a rabbinic decision and that the congregation will agree with whatever the rabbi chooses to do.

This article explores how three Canadian Reform rabbis made their decision regarding same-gender officiation, as well as the way they engaged their respective congregations in the discussion. Although the legal landscape on this issue is different in Canada than in the United States, the course of action from both the rabbi and the congregation can be instructive for those attempting to address the topic of same-gender marriage.

Background: The Landscape of Canada

Currently, in Canada, the federal government is responsible for defining what constitutes a marriage. Provincial governments are responsible for the administration and procedural requirements of the marriage ceremony and for issuing marriage licenses.

In December 2004, the Canadian Supreme Court issued a historic opinion to permit same-gender couples to marry throughout the country. The Canadian Parliament passed the law in June 2005, and the operative sections of the Proposed Marriage Act read:

1. Marriage, for civil purposes, is the lawful union of two persons to the exclusion of all others.
2. Nothing in this Act affects the freedom of officials of religious groups to refuse to perform marriages that are not in accordance with their religious beliefs.

(It should be noted that section 1 of the Proposed Act deals only with civil marriage, not religious marriage.)

In fact, same-gender marriage has been legal in:
- The province of Ontario since June 10, 2003
- The province of British Columbia since July 8, 2003
- The province of Quebec since March 19, 2004
- The Yukon territory since July 14, 2004
- The province of Manitoba since September 16, 2004
- The province of Nova Scotia since September 24, 2004
- The province of Saskatchewan since November 5, 2004
- The province of Newfoundland and Labrador since December 21, 2004

In each of these jurisdictions, same-gender marriage was legalized as a result of court cases in which provincial or territorial justices ruled that existing bans on same-gender marriage were unconstitutional.

The Canadian Council of Reform Judaism

At a meeting on October 22, 2003, the Canadian Council for Reform Judaism voted unanimously to endorse the following resolution, which was then distributed to all CCRJ congregations:

> Be it resolved that the Canadian Council for Reform Judaism approves and supports Canadian legislation that will permit and recognize same-sex unions, thus ensuring those unions are fully recognized for all legal benefits and rights within Canada that married couples have.
>
> *Furthermore the Canadian Council for Reform Judaism affirms rabbinic autonomy regarding the decision to officiate at any type of marriage.*

In 2005, in response to Parliament's passing the law to legalize same-gender marriage, the CCRJ issued a press release saying:

> The Canadian Council for Reform Judaism applauds the House of Commons for voting to extend Canadian legislation that permits and recognizes same-sex unions, thus ensuring those unions are fully recognized for all legal benefits and rights within Canada that married couples have.
>
> This vote is a victory for all who have worked hard to ensure the equal rights and protections under the law of all individuals who are in healthy and loving relationships.
>
> Canada has shown remarkable leadership as the third country in the world to legalize same-sex marriage. This decision gives Canadians many more reasons to be proud of our country and its accomplishments.
>
> We understand that this law will in no way infringe upon the role that religious communities have in determining for themselves whether or not they choose to sanction such marriages. Furthermore, the Canadian Council for Reform Judaism, based on a resolution dated October 22, 2003, affirms rabbinic autonomy in the decision to officiate at any type of marriage.

We pray that this decision will serve as an example for the rest of the world and we will work toward the day when all peoples will be guaranteed civil rights, liberties and protections of every type in the countries in which they live.

With this context in mind, we now turn to the journeys of three Canadian congregations.

Three Congregations' Journeys

As you read these stories, consider how the following factors allowed for a productive discussion on the topic of same-gender marriage:

1. **Use of Jewish texts and Jewish values**: Each of these three rabbis made sure that a deep analysis of Jewish texts was part of the process. With education as a critical factor in creating a more inclusive community, the rabbis felt it was important that all participants be educated *Jewishly* on this issue as well. Indeed, when working in a synagogue, any controversial or difficult decision needs to be based on Jewish values and Jewish language—after all, the synagogue is a Jewish religious institution. Thus all three rabbis made sure that Jewish texts and Jewish values were integral to the discussion.
2. **Involvement of stakeholders**: Almost every congregant feels a sense of ownership over their congregation and would not want "the congregation" to make a decision without providing them an opportunity to express their own viewpoints. All three of these congregations allowed any congregant who wished to share concerns, support, or even simply emotional responses a chance to do just that. The decision did not come down from "up on high," but rather all concerned parties had an opportunity to share their position.
3. **Careful Planning and Long-Range Goals**: By allowing congregants an opportunity to share their perspectives, the congregations understood that there would be no quick answer on this topic. They all allowed several months, and sometimes a year or more, before coming to a conclusion. In addition, each congregation and rabbi had a clear plan in terms of how to move from one stage of the discussion to the next. While always allowing people an opportunity to share their voice, the congregation began with a small committee or task force, *then* ran educational programs, *then* brought the issue to the whole congregation, and *then* made a decision. Each step had a clear purpose, goal, and plan, and each step led into the next one.
4. **Use of personal stories**: Each of these congregations made personal stories a part of their process. Sometimes it was gays and lesbians sharing their own journeys, sometimes it was panel discussions exploring the different sides to this issue, and sometimes it was discussions between congregants and outside lecturers, but the congregations ensured that part of the educational process was people sharing their own stories. The congregations made sure that this was not an abstract discussion, but rather a human issue with human faces.

Temple Sinai, Toronto, Ontario: Senior Rabbi, Michael Dolgin

Temple Sinai is the second-largest Reform synagogue in Canada, with a membership of close to eighteen hundred families. Rabbi Michael Dolgin has been there for his entire rabbinic career, first as the assistant rabbi beginning in 1992, and then eventually becoming senior rabbi in 1997.

Prior to the Ontario Court's decision in 2003, people had been asking Rabbi Dolgin whether or not he would perform same-gender ceremonies. He was undecided at the time. The decision by the Ontario Court in June 2003 permitting same-gender marriage in the province spurred his congregants to action. They were afraid that the court decision would not be a long-lasting one and that this "window of opportunity" would be short-lived. They therefore began requesting a decision from Rabbi Dolgin with more urgency.

Rabbi Dolgin viewed this as a "growth opportunity for the congregation and himself." He decided that he would engage the congregation in an educational process and what he learned from his congregation would be part of his decision as to whether or not he would perform same-gender marriages.

This was the process that led Rabbi Dolgin and Temple Sinai to their decision:

Step 1: The issue of same-gender marriage went to the Temple Sinai Ritual Committee for discussion and study. They examined the following question: "On what basis do we make such a decision?"

Step 2: The issue went to the Executive Committee of the congregation and the senior staff. Their roles were to plan for how the congregation was going to address the issue. The Temple Sinai board agreed that this decision should be a rabbinic decision. They said that it would not be right for them to say, "You are the rabbi, but it is our bimah." There was total agreement that whatever Rabbi Dolgin's decision would be, the board would support him 100 percent.

Step 3: Rabbi Dolgin held a special night of education and discussion for the board and past presidents in the synagogue chapel. He felt that by holding this session in the chapel (and not the boardroom), it set a different tone and people approached the whole topic with a greater sense of mutual respect, understanding, and *k'dushah*, "holiness." It was also agreed that the formal process would begin *after* the High Holy Days (that is, there would be no sermon on the High Holy Days about same-gender marriage). They didn't want to start the year off with any sense of contention or bitterness.

Step 4: The synagogue president wrote a letter in the bulletin explaining that Rabbi Dolgin had been asked to perform a same-gender wedding by congregants. The president then asked people to make their feelings known about this issue, and they set up a special e-mail address for the rabbi just for this response.

Step 5: Rabbi Dolgin wrote a discussion paper and taught a four-session class in the autumn on "The Evolution of Jewish Marriage." He addressed questions like: Is it a mitzvah to marry? Is gender a basic element of marriage? Do same-gender and heterosexual couples have more in common or more that differentiates one from the other? Under what circumstances should a rabbi refuse to perform a marriage? How is the Jewish consideration of this issue unique? Does marriage take place when two Jews of the same gender have a ceremony?

Step 6: The Temple Sinai board received copies of all the study materials. At the January 2004 board meeting, Rabbi Dolgin presented a position paper with his decision to perform same-gender marriages. A shorter version of his position paper was printed in the Temple Sinai bulletin.

There was very little backlash to this decision, because the nature of the discussion was intentionally very inclusive, and the rabbi and the board created opportunity for dialogue and response.

Today, Rabbi Dolgin performs same-gender marriage and does so in the sanctuary of the synagogue.

Solel Congregation, Mississauga, Ontario: Rabbi Lawrence Englander

Rabbi Englander was student rabbi at Solel Congregation in Mississauga, Ontario, for two years and became its first full-time rabbi upon his ordination in 1975. The synagogue is a 345-family congregation located just west of Toronto.

Rabbi Englander decided that he wanted his board to make the decision about whether or not to allow same-gender weddings to take place inside the sanctuary, as he already performed them outside the building. He opted to make this a congregational decision because he wanted to make it part of a communal process and wanted them to "own the decision." Like Temple Sinai, the June 2003 Ontario Court decision permitting same-gender marriage was a catalyst for Solel Congregation to spur them into making a decision.

This was the process that led Rabbi Englander and Solel Congregation to their decision:

Step 1: The Executive Committee assigned the Religious Committee the task of making a recommendation to the board regarding the decision of whether or not to allow same-gender weddings in the synagogue. For nine months, the Religious Committee studied texts with Rabbi Englander at each meeting. Among the texts they studied were:
   a. "CCAR Responsum on Homosexual Marriage," 1996 (see pages 301–325).
   b. Joan Friedman's minority response to "CCAR Responsum on Homosexual Marriage."
   c. Articles by Rabbi Bradley Shavit Artson and Rabbi Joel Roth in *S'vara: A Journal of Philosophy, Law, and Judaism* (Rabbi Artson's article is on pages 191–203).
   d. Report of the CCAR Ad Hoc Committee on Sexuality, June 1998 (see pages 259–264).
   e. "Homosexuality," *Keeping Posted* 32, no. 2 (November 1986).

Step 2: During the middle part of this study period, Laura Wolfson, director of education at Temple Anshe Sholom, Hamilton, Ontario, spoke at Solel Congregation. Laura is a lesbian married to her partner. They have a daughter together, and the congregation is extremely supportive of their family. However, since Anshe Sholom was between rabbis, the congregation had not made any decisions regarding the issue of whether or not they would permit same-gender weddings to take place in their sanctuary. The board did not feel that they could make such a decision until they had a permanent rabbi in place. Laura and her partner, Tish, wanted to get married at Anshe Sholom, their spiritual home (and Laura's professional home), and were not totally comfortable with the position their congregation had taken. She spoke about her professional versus personal dilemma in a most moving way. A condensed version of her talk was published in *Reform Judaism* a short time later (see "Exiled," pages 11–12).

Step 3: After about seven months, the Religious Committee decided to take a vote. The vote was nearly unanimous in favor of allowing same-gender marriages in the sanctuary. They felt that their study process changed their minds profoundly.

Step 4: The decision went to the board. The board had two study sessions on the topic with the rabbi, and there was an open discussion to which the entire congregation was invited. The board voted unanimously in favor of allowing same-gender marriages to take place in their sanctuary.

Step 5: The decision had to go to the annual general meeting of the congregation. There were three speakers at the meeting: one who spoke in favor of the board's decision, one who spoke against the board's decision, and finally, Rabbi Englander. Rabbi Englander led a text study on "The Deaf and the Evolution of Jewish Law." He chose this text to show a paradigm for how Jewish law can change when we receive new information about a topic—Jewish law changed with regard to how we treat the deaf, and therefore it can change with regard to how we treat those who are homosexual. The motion passed overwhelmingly.

Today, Rabbi Englander performs same-gender ceremonies and does so in the sanctuary of the synagogue.

First Narayever Congregation, Toronto, Ontario: Rabbi Ed Elkin

Rabbi Ed Elkin is a Reform rabbi serving an unaffiliated, "traditional egalitarian" congregation in downtown Toronto. The congregation is composed of urban, professional Jews, many of whom view themselves as being "countercultural." He has been with them since 2000.

Because of the "downtown, counterculture" nature of First Narayever, the issue of same-gender marriage became an issue in their community prior to the Ontario Court decision of June 2003. The issue first arose when a lesbian couple wanted to join the congregation as a family in the 1990s. The controversy was resolved by the congregation abolishing the notion of "family memberships" altogether. Now, one can join First Narayever only as an individual member.

In the fall of 2000, a lesbian couple approached Rabbi Elkin to perform their wedding. Since he had been there for only three months, and since he was a Reform rabbi in a "traditional" synagogue, he did not feel that he could decide on his own whether or not to officiate at such a ceremony. He said that he was personally prepared to do it, but he also felt that this needed to be a congregational decision.

Rabbi Elkin discussed the issue with his president, who then brought it to the board. The majority of the board felt comfortable with Rabbi Elkin making his own decision and performing same-gender ceremonies. However, an extremely vocal minority was adamantly opposed. Therefore, both Rabbi Elkin and the board decided that it would be in the best interest of the congregation to make this an issue for the entire congregation to study and address.

This was the process that led Rabbi Elkin and First Narayever Congregation to their decision:

Step 1: In 2001–2, a committee was formed and asked to examine two issues:
   a. Whether or not the rabbi could perform same-gender marriage ceremonies in their building.
   b. Whether or not it would be acceptable to publicly acknowledge same-gender relationships on the bimah (e.g., having the same-gender parents of a bar or bat mitzvah student stand on the bimah together, acknowledging the death of a same-gender partner, or congratulating someone on becoming engaged), as well as determining what to acknowledge in the bulletin regarding same-gender relationships, which had been a hot topic in the congregation.

Step 2: The committee met monthly for one year and sponsored three public educational programs for the congregations with outside speakers:
   a. A discussion between Rabbi Irwin Zeplowitz, former rabbi of Temple Anshe Sholom, Hamilton, Ontario, who does perform same-gender marriages, and Rabbi Benjamin Hecht, a liberal Orthodox rabbi, who says that because he is Orthodox he cannot perform same-gender marriages, but sees no reason why the other denominations of Judaism cannot.
   b. A discussion between Rabbi Dow Marmur, rabbi emeritus of Holy Blossom Temple, who does *not* perform same-gender marriages, and then HUC rabbinic student (now a rabbi) and First Narayever member Lisa Grushcow, who is a lesbian.
   c. A panel with gay and lesbian members from within the congregation, who spoke about their own experiences.

Step 3: The committee and Rabbi Elkin put together a "sourcebook" of readings to study on the topic. The committee studied these sources for a year and then came together to vote on the issue. The committee voted unanimously on acknowledging same-gender relationships on the bimah and in the bulletin; they were, nevertheless, divided on whether rabbis could perform same-gender marriages. Thus their discussion continued.

Step 4: The committee prepared a "Report of the Committee on Inclusion," which included history, study materials, and recommendations and was made available to the whole congregation in March 2003.

Step 5: On December 1, 2003, Rabbi Elkin wrote a letter to the entire congregation sharing his position on same-gender marriage, elucidating some text sources, background information, and why his decision would be that he would indeed perform them. The board was to vote on the same-gender marriage issue at its January 2004 board meeting. The board agreed with the committee's decision that this should go to a full-congregational vote. Since the First Narayever's constitution states that "all major religious changes need to be brought to the membership for a vote," they decided that this was a "major religious change" and decided to bring it to the membership.

Step 6: In June 2004, the issue of whether to allow marriage for same-gender couples on the bimah and in the sanctuary was brought to a congregational vote. The vote came out 71 percent in favor of the motion. However, First Narayever's constitution requires that all religious changes receive 80 percent of votes in favor at a congregational meeting. Thus the motion failed but showed that a strong percentage of their congregation supports allowing same-gender marriage on their bimah.

Today, Rabbi Elkin and First Narayever are reviewing their constitution and will be recommending a constitutional amendment lowering the percentage needed to effect a major religious change. As of this writing, the issue of same-gender marriage at First Narayever is still ongoing.

Conclusion

As civil rights for gays and lesbians are being guaranteed by the Canadian Charter of Rights and Freedoms, liberal Jews are being inspired to examine Jewish traditions and attitudes with regard to same-gender marriage. More and more frequently, Reform rabbis and congregations are finding validation from within Jewish tradition and from our view of how Judaism evolves to broaden our own definition of what constitutes "marriage" from a Jewish perspective. This is an ongoing process, and divergent views still exist among our clergy, laypeople, and congregations regarding the issue of same-gender marriage from a Jewish perspective. But the commitment to education, dialogue, and discussion remains strong, and as one can see from the above stories, the process *leading to* the decision is just as important as the final decision itself.

Enfranchising the Monogamous Homosexual: A Legal Possibility, a Moral Imperative

Rabbi Bradley Shavit Artson

Traditional Jewish standards for sexuality are in almost complete disarray. Widely ignored, if not regarded with explicit skepticism, are rabbinic prohibitions against masturbation, the use of condoms (even within marriage), and premarital sex. In no other area of human society is the gap between traditional Jewish law and modernity so stark. There looms a chasm between rabbinic sex ethics and contemporary ideas of right and wrong, even among those who profess loyalty to the rabbinic tradition. More striking than the gap between sex ethics and modernity is the background question of gender roles and distinctions. The essence of what it means to be male and female, the role of men and women in society and in religion, and issues raised by gay men and lesbian women (not to mention the claim of the bisexual) threaten to reduce Jewish law to irrelevancy.

Without a willingness to work within the framework of rabbinic tradition and of Torah law, without integrating the latest insights of the social sciences back into the structure of Judaism, the gap between what appears self-evident to moderns and what is commanded in the Torah moves beyond the possibility of unification. In this context, an unwillingness to interpret the Torah in the light of contemporary social science and historical knowledge constitutes an act of unwitting hostility to the Torah as a living tradition and the embodiment of God's imperatives for the Jewish people. It takes one more step toward sealing the Torah between the covers of a book and placing it, closed and unread, on a shelf.

Accordingly, in loyalty to the Torah and the Jewish community, this article raises the question of homosexuality in Jewish law.[1] Drawing from traditional modes of Jewish legal method and authoritative extralegal sources, I lay out an authentic jurisprudential basis in favor of enfranchisement.[2]

Bradley Shavit Artson, "Enfranchising the Monogamous Homosexual: A Legal Possibility, a Moral Imperative," *S'vara: A Journal of Philosophy, Law, and Judaism* 3, no. 1 (1993).

1. My previous writings on the subject include "Judaism and Homosexuality," *Tikkun, 3(2)*, pp. 52-54, 92-93; "Gays and Lesbian Jews: An Innovative Jewish Legal Position," *Jewish Spectator*, Winter 1990–1991, fr–14; and "Homosexuality and Judaism: Synthesis or Impasse," *New Menorah*, Spring 1991.
2. The alert reader will notice that the sources cited from antiquity (Jewish and non-Jewish) pertain directly to male homosexuals. There is almost no testimony to the nature of female homosexual expression before the modern

The Issue

In examining the Torah and rabbinic tradition's assessment of homosexuality, I seek to support two central assertions: (1) that committed, permanent, exclusive homosexual relationships between equals were unknown until the modern era and therefore could not have been explicitly prohibited by earlier Jewish law, and (2) that our current construal of homosexuality has so radically shifted from what was practiced in the past that the traditional prohibition of male-male sex does not (and should not) expand to include this novel form of homosexuality. If it is true that neither the Torah nor Jewish law explicitly prohibits committed exclusive gay or lesbian relationships, and contemporary science indicates that sexual orientation is fixed irrevocably, then it follows that a contemporary decision-maker may legitimately choose to sanction such relationships as are otherwise consistent with Jewish law.[3] I then argue that simple justice, compassion, and a commitment to strengthening Jewish life make it imperative to do so.

These claims require, consequently, establishing the nature of homosexual acts in antiquity and the current understanding of homosexuality as an orientation. These facts engage traditional categories of Jewish law to arrive at a finding at once compassionate, sophisticated, moral, and halakhic. Throughout, I insist on the authority of the Torah (and subsequent rabbinic traditions) as the preeminent vehicle for establishing the Jewish understanding of divine will.[4]

Within that religious framework, we must first confront the passages in the Torah, and second consider rabbinic writings that address the issue of homosexuality and seek to understand them in the context of their own age and practice. Only after taking that preliminary step can we examine contemporary homosexuality and inquire whether or not it is even the same phenomenon. I analyze some of this data in a more detailed fashion, but for now I dwell on two theoretical questions: does shifting non-legal data have significance for legal decision-making, and to what extent is sexual practice a product of social construal?

Halakhah generally utilizes a method of reading the Torah and rabbinic sources as a way of developing applications of old rulings to new circumstances, or to generate new rulings

---

period. Certainly in the Mesopotamian, Greek, Roman, and Jewish cultures, the perspectives of the male writers focused on their own gender. While my moral stance toward contemporary lesbianism is the same as is my stance toward gay men, the silence about the practices of women with women precludes historical comment here. That should not be construed as indifference. However, that silence is immaterial to my argument.

3. Thereby precluding gay incest, pederasty, or intermarriage, even if loving or monogamous.

4. Of course, were it impossible to utilize interpretation to reach a moral conclusion, a decision-maker could still argue, within traditional forms of Jewish legal method, that the issue of enfranchising monogamous gays and lesbians is a moral mandate of such urgency that contemporary law should override the Torah on this one point. This would be an example of *la'aqor davar min haTorah*, a procedure by which the rabbis removed a verse from the Torah when its legal retention threatened the survival of the broader Torah tradition or of the Jewish community. *See* Rashi, *Berakhot* 54a, s.v. *v"omer*, *Yomah* 69a, *Temurah* 14b, *Yevamot* 79a, *Menahot* 99a, and *Nazir* 43b, s.v. *d chaff*. *See* Eliezer Berkovits, *Not In Heaven: The Nature and Function of Halakha* (New York: Ktav, 1983) [hereinafter Berkovits], pp. 57–64. An alternative would be the enactment of *a takkanah*. *See*, for example, *Berakhot* 26b, *Bava Kamma* 80b-81b, *Sanhedrin* 46a, *Sifra*, *Acharei Mot* 10:22, *Yevamot* 21a. According to Elliot N. Dorff and Arthur Rosett: "*Takkanot* are used either to fill a lacuna in the law that cannot be treated through interpretation or precedent, or to amend an existing law." In *A Living Tree: The Roots and Growth of Jewish Law* (Albany: State University of New York Press, 1988) [hereinafter Dorff], p. 403. My primary commitment, however, is to solve the problem by the method of interpretation rather than amendment. *See* Sanford Levinson, "On the Notion of Amendment," *S'vara, 1(1)*, 1990, 25–31.

when no established precedent exists. This process of legal development relies frequently on the evolution of knowledge, technology, and moral standards. A long tradition within the Halakhah reflects the impact of non-textual data on legal consequences.[5] Particularly in areas of medical science and technology, new knowledge can lead, without any other change, to new legal rulings.[6] Citing the legal principle referred to as *shinnui ha'ittim*, the Tosafot argue that new knowledge leads to a new ruling because "the times have now changed."[7] Several medieval and modern authorities affirm that the present reality is different than it was in talmudic times, stating explicitly that this should lead to different legal conclusions.[8]

Less objective, but no less forceful are perceptions of sociological shifts. Yet here, too, changes in social practice do lead to changes in legal rulings. The shift from *yibbum* [the obligation of levirate marriage] to *chalitzah* [negation of the obligation] is a classic example of a new social norm impelling a new halakhic ruling.[9] Even ethical and psychological data have the power to affect the law, as new insights and heightened sensitivities lead to abrogation of previous legal standards and understanding.[10] The history of halakhah on *mamzerut*, on capital punishment, on inheritance by women, and on funeral practices for suicides all attest to the power of an ethical imperative (often never articulated) to shift legal rulings in the direction of greater equity and compassion for individual suffering. In the words of Rabbi Elliot Dorff: "[T]he law can be changed on moral grounds.... The rabbis of the Talmud did precisely the same thing."[11] The problem in our inquiry, of course, is whether changes in the practice and the perception of homosexuality should have a bearing on Halakhah.

The thesis is worth repeating: Committed, permanent, exclusive homosexual relationships between equals were unknown until the modern era, and therefore could not have been explicitly prohibited by earlier Jewish law. When speaking of "committed, exclusive homosexual relationships," I refer to relationships that parallel the contemporary heterosexual marital ideal, except that the gender of the two adults is the same. Admittedly, in ages gone by, there is ample attestation to passionate love between males. Irrefutable evidence exists of jealousy, passion, and long-term relationships. However, there is a clear distinction between homosexual relationships of the past and the admittedly limited number of committed gay couples under discussion in this article.

When speaking of the relationship that meets the religious ideal, we speak of the partners in a couple who are exclusive in their legal, sexual, and emotional commitment to each other. Their primary emotional nurturance is from and toward each other, and each

---

5. Exhaustive documentation is provided in Joel Roth, *The Halakhic Process: A Systemic Analysis* (New York: The Jewish Theological Seminary, 1986), Chapter 9. Much of the subsequent discussion is based on his compilation of sources.
6. *See,* for example, *Bekhorot* 4:4 and *Sanhedrin* 33a.
7. *Avodah Zarah* 24b, s.v. *parah*. See also *Hullin* 47a, s.v. *kol*.
8. Rama, *Shulkhan Arukh, Even ha'Ezer,* 156:4, *Magen Avraham* at EH, 156:4, paragraph 1, *Tiferet Israel* to M. *Shabbat* 19:2.
9. *Yevamot* 39b and 6:9. *See also Avodah Zarah* 31a, *Sanhedrin* 25b, *Kiddushin* 41a, *Tosafot Kiddushin* 12b, *Tosafot Beitzah* 30a, s.v. *tenon,* and *Hullin* 93b for other examples of new social practice leading to changing the law.
10. Often based on *hayashar v'hatov,* Deuteronomy 6:18. On the power of ethics to drive the Halakhah, *see* Berkovits, pp. 19–47, and the trail-blazing work of Robert Gordis, most recently in *The Dynamics of Jewish Law* (Bloomington: Indiana University Press, 1990) [hereinafter Gordis].
11. Dorff, p. 254. Saul Berman, in Menachem Eton, *Principles of Jewish Law* (Jerusalem: Keter, 1974), p. 157, writes: "[T]he morality of one generation frequently became the law of the next."

intends (and creates) legal obligations toward the other—commitments such as providing housing, clothing, joint ownership of assets, and inheritance. These bonds differ from the recorded homosexual relationships of the past. The historical evidence is limited to sexual ties between generations (men and boys), relations of unequal status that could be abruptly terminated by one partner only (master and slave), and homosexual love that coexists with an already established heterosexual marriage.

Homosexuality in Antiquity and Today

Surprisingly, given the force of many contemporary Jewish responses to homosexuality, there are remarkably few verses in the Torah that even deal with it at all. One solitary verse in Deuteronomy (23:18) was, until recently, understood to refer to cult prostitution, both male and female.[12] However, more recent scholarship has challenged that presumption[13] by interpreting *qadesh* as a cult officiant in an idolatrous rite. That reading renders Deuteronomy 23:18 irrelevant in this discussion, leaving only the two prohibitions found in the Book of Leviticus (18:22 and 20:13).

Those two passages explicitly prohibit *mishkav zakhar* [to lie with a man] as a *to'evah* [abhorrence]. Both of these prohibitions are part of a long list of sexual offenses that constitute Leviticus 18. As a normal jurisprudential (and literary) procedure, clarifying the Torah's intention would require searching the Torah, the Tanakh, and contemporary non-Israelite practice for use of the same term or examples of the same practice that might reflect back on the terse language of the Torah itself. Here that logical step gains added force by the insistence of the Torah that these offenses are prohibited specifically because "[I]t is by such that the nations that I am casting out before you defiled themselves" (Leviticus 18:24).

In its summation of the prohibitions, the Torah repeats: "[Y]ou must not do any of those abhorrent things, neither the citizen nor the stranger who resides among you; for all those abhorrent things were done by the people who were in the land before you, and the land became defiled" (Leviticus 18:26–27).[14] Thus the Torah explicitly identifies these prohibited practices, these abominations, with the accepted practices of the non-Israelites of the period. The logic of the Torah mandates a reading of *mishkav zakhar* as one limited to the practice of the period and, accordingly, one that permits reflection on the distinctive practice of twentieth-century homosexuality. Only when we familiarize ourselves with sex as it was practiced in antiquity can we know what the Torah and subsequent Jewish tradition were addressing and recoiling against.[15]

---

12. *See*, for example, the translation used as recently as 1985 in *Tanakh: The Holy Scriptures* (Philadelphia: Jewish Publication Society, 1985), p. 31, where *qadesh* is translated as cult prostitute.

13. Jacob Milgrom, in *The JPS Torah Commentary: Numbers* (Philadelphia: Jewish Publication Society, 1990), p. 479, says that the term connotes "officiants or devotees of an idolatrous cult. . . . There is no evidence of . . . being a prostitute." He bases his claim on the now-canonical articles of M.I. Gruber, "The Kadesh in the Book of Kings and in Other Sources," *Tarbiz 52,* 1982/1983, 167–176 and "Hebrew Qedushah and her Canaanite and Akkadian Cognates," *Ugarit-Forschungen, 18,* 1986, 133–148.

14. A similar summation occurs at the end of Chapter 20 of Leviticus (20:2–26), again making explicit that the Torah is prohibiting specifically the kind of *mishkav zakhar* practiced by the surrounding peoples.

15. This hermeneutical guide, provided by the Torah itself, will be the basis for the *diyyuq* [distinction] that will allow the halakhic ruling of this article. For a discussion of this traditional legal procedure, consult Ephraim E. Urbach, *The Halakhah: Its Sources and Development* (Jerusalem: Yad La-Talmud, 1986), 109–110.

Before reviewing homosexual practices in the ancient world, a word of distinction about the other sexual practices in the list of Leviticus 18 and 20 is in order. After all, if the argument is made that one form of expression of homosexuality today is significantly different from the *mishkav zakhar* of the biblical and talmudic periods, could not the same argument be made about any of the other sexual practices found in that same list? Would not this argument end up permitting loving adultery, bestiality, or incest?

Fortunately for our research, the ancients were in no way reticent to share the details of their sexuality.[16] Scholars of antiquity have found ample attestation to the practice of all the other prohibited sexual practices listed in Leviticus, many in the Tanakh itself. Adultery and sex with children or parents or animals were familiar to the ancients. These practices were considered pathological and socially destructive as they are today. None of these practices has changed much over the years, nor do the findings of psychology, anthropology, or sociology suggest that their context or construal is much different today. None of them has gained as a sexual orientation in their own right, hormonally or genetically predetermined, or beyond the reach of psychotherapy. Each of them is a warning sign of psychological illness, abuse, or involves the exploitation of some third party. Their status, therefore needs no review and their identity remains the same.

Not so homosexuality. Alone of all the sexual prohibitions listed in Leviticus, homosexuality has been radically reinterpreted by the social sciences in reliance on a wealth of empirical data. In modern times, homosexuality (and heterosexuality) has come to describe sexual orientations—a blend of eroticism, fantasy, and emotional satisfaction, which in most cases is irrevocably set by the end of childhood. The terms *homosexual* and *heterosexual* now are understood to apply to persons, not actions. Although there is still disagreement about the specific etiology of sexual identity—whether genetic, hormonal, social, or psychological—there is no significant debate within the mental health sciences about whether or not a homosexual orientation can be replaced by a heterosexual one[17]:

> There is no published evidence to support the efficacy of reparative therapy as a specific treatment for homosexuality.... Reparative therapy is not described in the scientific literature, and is not mentioned in the APA's comprehensive new task force report, "Treatments of Psychiatric Disorders." There are a few reports in the literature of efforts to use psychotherapeutic and counseling techniques to treat persons troubled by homosexuality who want to become heterosexual; however, results have not been conclusive, nor have they been replicated.[18]

---

16. Here I rely primarily on the magisterial and exacting work by David F. Greenberg, *The Construction of Homosexuality* (Chicago: University of Chicago Press, 1988) [hereinafter D. Greenberg]. Other primary sources are cited in John Boswell, *Christianity, Social Tolerance, and Homosexuality* (Chicago: University of Chicago Press, 1980) [hereinafter Boswell]. Boswell's work—however valuable—must, however, be read with great care and skepticism due to his rather idiosyncratic interpretations of primary texts and his assertion of claims without supporting evidence.
17. In his unpublished paper "Homosexuality," Rabbi Joel Roth asserts that there is, indeed, such debate among mental health professionals. Yet he cites as support of this claim studies conducted by a few individuals in the 1970s, as opposed to the consensus of the three major mental health associations in the 1990s. It needs to be stated that those studies in the 1970s were methodologically flawed, have not been replicated, and no longer reflect a real option among mental health practitioners, as the quotations on this page attest.
18. Press release of the American Psychiatric Association, January 26, 1990.

We don't know the cause of homosexuality, although genetic factors are clearly involved. What we do know is that homosexuality *per se is* not a mental illness.... We found that a significant portion of gay and lesbian people are clearly satisfied with their sexual orientation and show no signs of psychopathology. They are able to function effectively in society, and those who see psychiatrists for treatment most often do so for reasons other than their homosexuality. For a mental condition to be considered a psychiatric disorder, it should either regularly cause emotional distress or regularly be associated with generalized impairment of social function. Homosexuality does not meet these criteria.[19]

The research on homosexuality is very clear. Homosexuality is neither mental illness nor moral depravity. It is simply the way a minority of our population expresses human love and sexuality. Study after study documents the mental health of gay men and lesbians. Nor is homosexuality a matter of individual choice. Research suggests that the homosexual orientation is in place very early on in the life cycle, possibly even before birth. Indeed, these research findings suggest that efforts to "repair" homosexuals are nothing more than social prejudice garbed in psychological accoutrements.[20]

In addition to this new knowledge that homosexuality is not sickness, not choice, and is irrevocable, modern socio-economic structures have created the possibility—for the first time in recorded history—of exclusive homosexual love within the context of a committed relationship. This is precisely the new kind of data that the halakhic categories of *shinnui ha'ittim* and *davar chadash* describe. Our new understanding of homosexuality as the unprecedented possibility of (and desire for) monogamous and responsible love—of sexual expression firmly within the context of commitment—goes a long way toward fulfilling the halakhic requirements for considering monogamous and committed homosexual relationships as beyond the prohibitions of Leviticus. That conclusion becomes inescapable if we recall that the Torah specifically limits what it intends by *mishkav zakhar* to what was actually practiced in the period of the Torah and subsequent rabbinic Judaism. It is to that contemporary practice that we must, therefore, turn.

In antiquity, there was no categorical distinction of humanity into heterosexual and homosexual as sexual orientations.[21] Instead, all people were divided into two groups: pleasure-takers and pleasure-givers.[22] Free adult males were considered takers of sexual pleasure. Women, slaves (male and female), prisoners, and children were all considered legitimate sources or givers of sexual pleasure. The more numerous his chosen objects of pleasure, the greater the virility of the man taking the pleasure.

---

19. Melvin Sabshin, MD, American Psychiatric Association Medical Director, January 26, 1990.
20. Bryant L. Welch, JD, PhD, Executive Director for Professional Practice, American Psychological Association, 1990.
21. Thus Greenberg writes: "Greeks of the classical age had no word for a homosexual (or heterosexual) person. With few exceptions, the Greeks assumed that ordinarily sexual choices were not mutually exclusive, but rather that people were generally capable of responding erotically to beauty in both sexes. Often they could and did" (D. Greenberg, pp. 143–144). Similarly, Boswell points out that "there was no word in Latin for 'homosexual'"(Boswell, pp. 79–89).
22. For this argument and supporting evidence, *see* Paul Veyne, "Homosexuality in Ancient Rome," in Philippe Aries and Andre Bejin (eds.), *Western Sexuality: Practice and Precept in Past and Present Times* (Oxford: Basil Blackwell, 1985), pp. 26–35.

The relevant civilizations of the period of the Tanakh are those in Mesopotamia and Egypt. None of the Ancient Near Eastern codes of law refers to homosexual practice.[23] However, the Hittite laws of the second millennium B.C.E. do make father-son incest (along with father-daughter and mother-son incest) a capital crime.[24] But the issue seems to be incest, not homosexuality *per se*. The Middle Assyrian Laws of the second millennium B.C.E. stipulate that a person who falsely accuses a man of taking the passive role in a homosexual act will be whipped (fifty lashes).[25] Similarly, one who falsely accuses someone's wife of taking many lovers receives forty lashes. Arguably, it was the receptive sexual role that was considered the insult punishable by law, whether for men or for women. These same laws also mandate that a man who rapes another man will be subjected in turn to anal penetration and then castrated. The crime, it seems, was not the homosexual act, but the rape.[26]

Two Mesopotamian kings had male sexual partners: Zimri-lin of Maria and Hammurabi of Babylon. Zimri-lin's wife, the Queen, refers to those lovers in her correspondence.[27] In these instances, as in the legal codes, "what matters are the roles and statuses of the parties.... To prefer the receptive role, perhaps exclusively, appears to have been negatively regarded except in a cultic context."[28] In each case, male sex was "properly" the demonstration of virility—the gender of the object of lust was considered immaterial.

Lacking any legal texts from Egypt, there is even less evidence of attitudes toward homosexuality in Egyptian society than there was in Mesopotamia. However, a few examples bear out that "the Egyptians stigmatized the receptive role in anal intercourse between men just as the Mesopotamians did."[29] Summarizing the scanty evidence, Greenberg notes that "homosexuality *per se* was not a category in Egyptian thought. There was no word for a homosexual person, only composite terms suggesting that gender was the critical category. Involvement with homosexuality was not assumed to be exclusive.... The negative confessions and temple inscriptions refer to acts, not inclinations or states of being."[30]

The varied civilizations of Greece and Rome express in greater abundance the same understanding and practice of homosexual intercourse as did the documents of Mesopotamia and Egypt. Thus, Martial brags of his sexual desire for women and boys when he writes:

And when your lust is hot, surely
If a maid or a pageboy's handy, to attack Instanter, you won't choose to grin and bear it?
I won't! I like a cheap and easy love.[31]

---

23. Included in this claim are the Laws of Urukagina (2375 B.C.E.), of Eshnunna (1750 B.C.E.), and the Laws of Hammurabi (1726 B.C.E.).
24. *See* Pritchard, *Ancient Near Eastern Texts Relating to the Old Testament* (Princeton: Princeton University Press, 1969), p. 196.
25. *Ibid.*, p. 181.
26. *Ibid.*, para. 20.
27. *See* W. L. Moran, "New Evidence from Mari on the History of Prophecy," *Biblica.* 50, pp. 15–56.
28. D. Greenberg, p. 127.
29. D. Greenberg, p. 130.
30. *Ibid.*, p. 135.
31. Martial, *Satires* 1.2.116.

Other writers in antiquity provide more than ample evidence that the relevant concern was not the gender of the object of lust, boys and women were equally acceptable recipients of adult male desire;[32] it was written of Alcibiades "that in his adolescence he drew away the husbands from their wives, and as a young man the wives from their husbands."[33] Xenophon remarks that prisoners of war were released as ordered "except where some smuggler, prompted by desire for a good-looking boy or woman, managed to make off with his prize."[34] Plato records his praise of the athlete Ikkos of Taras, who "never had any connexion with a woman or a youth during the whole time of his training."[35] Even the great Socrates, whose liaisons with Athenian youths are a matter of public record,[36] also sought out the services of female prostitutes,[37] and all that activity while married! Meleander (around 100 B.C.E.) writes:

> Aphrodite, female, ignites the fire that makes one mad for a woman, but Eros himself holds the reins of male desire. "Which way am I to incline? To the boys or to his mother? I declare that even Aphrodite herself will say, 'The bold lad is the winner!'"[38]

No social stigma attached to a man because of his sexual pursuits, so long as he was the one getting, rather than giving, satisfaction. A boy, because of his inferior social standing, could be the object of male lust. But upon reaching adulthood, this role was considered a disgrace. Thus, Plutarch writes: "[W]e class those who enjoy the passive part as belonging to the lowest depths of vice and allow them not the least degree of confidence or respect or friendship."[39]

As a result of this way of categorizing sexual acts (rather than orientations), antiquity knew of no exclusive, committed homosexual relationships between equals. David Greenberg summarizes the abundant evidence by noting that "preoccupation with status pervaded sexual culture to the point where the Greeks could not easily conceive of a relationship based on equality. Sex always involved superiority."[40] He goes on to observe that "the idealized homosexual relationship thus involved an adult lover, usually between the ages of twenty and thirty (the *erastes*) and a prepubescent adolescent (*eromenos* or *paidika*), whose beard had not begun to grow. The relationship was ordinarily temporary."[41] Instead, masters took their slaves (often designating a slave—known as *concubines*—as a

---

32. A count of Greenberg's cited references includes 70 pre-Christian authors on the subject of homosexuality (D. Greenberg). This in addition to his extensive anthropological citations and his references in medieval and modern times.
33. Diogenes Laertius, *Lives and Opinions of Eminent Philosophers* (London: George Bell and Sons, 1891, trans. C.E. Yonge), p. 172. This sounds strikingly similar to the reason given by *Bar Kapparah* (*Nedarim* 51a) for why *mishkav zakhar* is a *to'evah*. Later Jewish sources understand him to infer that lust for males will draw them away from their wives. See *Lirsho' Miyyuchas* and *Ba'alei IfaTosafot 'al haTorah* at the end of *Parshat Acharei*.
34. Anabasis, 4.1.14.
35. Laws 840A.
36. *See* Plato's *Charmides*, 154c, 155c–e, *Phaedrus* 241d.
37. Xenophon, *Memorabilia* 3.11.
38. Cited in Kenneth J. Dover, *Greek Homosexuality* (Cambridge: Harvard University Press, 1978) [hereinafter Dover], p. 63.
39. Plutarch, *Moralia*, 768E.
40. D. Greenberg, p. 147.
41. *Ibid.*

sexual object), and men took boys (who had to serve the "passive" sexual role until freed by the onset of puberty). The use of children was not infrequent, without distinction made to the gender of the child. Most often, the men who were involved in this homosexual sex were, simultaneously, married and often had mistresses at the same time.[42]

The conclusion is therefore inescapable that the loving, committed, and exclusive homosexuality of contemporary society is an innovation of modernity. It never existed in the past. Indeed, the noted scholar, Shaye J. D. Cohen confirms as much when he writes:

> The sort of homosexual relationships which we are encountering more and more frequently in our society and about which you are speaking, that is, stable, monogamous, loving relationships between adults of equal status—relationships of this kind were unknown in antiquity.... Consequently, we may assume that the rabbis of antiquity did not know, and therefore were not addressing, this type of homosexual relationship.[43]

That same caveat appears to be equally true for the Torah and the Hebrew Scripture. Only two narratives in the entire Tanakh exist that offer instances of *mishkav zakhar*.[44] Both of these narratives tell of a hostile group of villagers who demand that a host release male guests to be raped by the householders of the town. These locals were not "homosexual" in the sense of deriving their primary erotic, emotional, and fantasy nurturance from other men. Rather, they were married men, respected leaders, who were attempting to humiliate visitors to their towns through a well-attested ancient form of humiliation. In fact, there exists a remarkably similar story from Roman antiquity: Ammianus Marcillinus records that the consul Tertullus offered his own children to an angry crowd in an attempt to spare himself.[45]

The fact that females (children at that) are offered indicates that exclusive homosexuality is not the source of moral repugnance here. Later biblical passages which speak of the sin of Sodom do not even object to the threatened homosexual rape, but focus instead on the violation of hospitality to strangers,[46] a finding confirmed by Robert Gordis and Louis Epstein.[47]

All we know then, from the sparse testimony of the Tanakh, is that homosexual rape by typical townsmen—married and generally practicing heterosexual intercourse—is prohibited. In fact, in only a handful of rabbinic passages is the possibility of a contractual relationship between men even raised. These apparent challenges to the evidence adduced above dissolve when examined in the light of their own testimony. In *Genesis Rabbah* 26:5, *Sanhedrin* 58a, *Hullin* 92a–b, and *Sifra*, *Aharei Mot* 9:6–8, the rabbis expound on the biblical insistence *"uv'chuqqoteihem lo telekhu"* [nor shall you follow their laws] (Leviticus 18:3). It has already been observed that this verse and the concluding paragraph of this

---

42. As, e.g., Harmodius and Aristogiton of sixth-century Athens *(see* Dover, p. 1), or Hadrian and the youth Antinous (Spartianus, 1.7.23), which reports on Hadrian's wife and his male sexual partners.
43. Private correspondence, November 15, 1991.
44. Genesis 19:5 and Judges 19:22.
45. Ammianus Marcillinus, *The Later Roman Empire*, 19:10.
46. Deuteronomy 29:23; Lamentations 4:6; Ezekiel 16:46–56; Amos 4:11; and Zephaniah 2:9.
47. Robert Gordis, "Homosexuality and Traditional Religion," *Judaism 32(4),* 1983, p. 390, and Louis Epstein, *Sex, Laws and Customs in Judaism* (New York: Ktav, 1967), p. 136.

chapter form an *inclusio*, clarifying that to which the specific prohibitions listed between introduction and summation pertain. Understanding what "their laws" were becomes essential according to the Torah's own understanding as well as that of the rabbis.

These talmudic verses speak of non-Israelite men issuing (or refraining from issuing) marriage contracts to other men. In the case of *Hullin*, the Talmud praises the children of Noah for their restraint—they do not issue these *ketubbot*. In *Sifra*, the Gentiles are condemned for lacking that restraint. In each case, however, appreciating the contextual background of the rabbinic comment prevents the unwitting intrusion of twenty-first-century reality, with the consequent distortion of the rabbis' meaning to accord with our own.

There are two cases of men issuing the equivalent of a *ketubbah* in antiquity. The first is the Roman Emperor Nero, who issued marriage contracts to two men: Suetonius records that Nero "tried to turn the boy Sporus into a girl by castration, he went through a wedding ceremony with him—dowry, bridal veil and all."[48] At the same time as he issued this "*ketubbah*," Suetonius also reports that Nero took on a mistress who was the spitting image of his mother, so great was his lust for her, committed repeated incest with his mother while in public, and had himself "released from a cage dressed in the skins of wild animals" and attacked the private parts of men and women who stood bound to stakes. After working up sufficient excitement by this means, he was dispatched—shall we say—by his freedman Doryphorus. Doryphorus now married him—just as he himself had married Sporus.[49] All the while he was married to the Empress Octavia![50]

A similar "marriage" is recorded about the Emperor Elagabalus to Zoticus.[51] Yet Elagabalus's reputation for depravity exceeded even that of Nero. He was known to have dispatched emissaries throughout the Empire to seek out men "hung like mules."[52] He also forced open private bath-houses to inspect the men who frequented them and frequented the docks of Rome at night. In both cases, his goal was men with large genitalia.[53] For all that, the evidence of his issuing a wedding contract is rather thin: the "*ketubbah*" given by Elagabalus is reported only by Lampridius. According to Boswell, "the authority for the marriage of Elagabalus might be impugned"[54] and Greenberg fails even to mention it.

Even taken as factual, these "*ketubbot*" hardly correspond to the *ketubbot* of rabbinic society, where they were intended to signify a legal commitment to the welfare, care, and support of the receiving party. Monogamy, while not legally mandated, was the norm in rabbinic society, and appears to have been so even in biblical Israel.[55] That the two known instances of issuing "*ketubbot*" for males are at the hands of the most depraved of Rome's emperors, for whom these documents were simply evidence of their frenzied lust and their callous mockery of accepted piety and custom, is a serious abomination indeed. What they are charged with by the rabbis is cloaking their depravity under the cover of sanctity. Hypocrisy is here the proper subject of condemnation.

---

48. Suetonius, *The Twelve Caesars*, 6, para. 28.
49. *Ibid.*, para. 29. Nero's publicized "*ketubbah*" *is* confirmed by the testimony of Tacitus (15.37), Dio Cassius (61.28, 62.12), and others.
50. *Ibid.*, para 7.
51. Lampridius 10–11
52. Juvenal on Naevolus, in Boswell, p. 80.
53. Lampridius, 5, 8.
54. Boswell, p. 82–102.
55. Moshe David Herr, "Monogamy," *Encyclopedia Judaica* (Jerusalem: Keter, 1971), Vol. 12, pp. 258–260. *See also* Isaiah Gafni, "The Institution of Marriage in Rabbinic Times," in David Kraemer (ed.), *The Jewish Family: Metaphor and Memory* (Oxford University Press, 1989), p. 22.

The temptation of any age is to impose its social constructs on the past. What appears to be "common sense" actually mirrors the practices and perceptions of our age. Yet these rabbinic passages, as challenging as they may have first appeared, do not address our context. They address their own. The examples of men issuing *ketubbot* to men, as recorded in the sources, are indeed abominations. They are between sovereign and slave, without legal intent or enforcement. They did not convey a promise to maintain or to provide for the recipient of the *ketubbah*, nor did they imply a promise that sexual expression was restricted to the "marital" relationship.

Context bears on our perception of an act as prohibited, permissible, or commanded. Plunging a dagger into someone's back can be murder (prohibited), self-defense (permitted), or a *mitzvah* (the act of a Jewish soldier during a commanded war). Closer to home, a man and a woman engaging in sex either can be performing a meritorious act (and a *mitzvah* too!) or can be violating the Ten Commandments. Context should also bear on our perception and understanding of homosexuality. Whether or not homosexual acts take place in the context practiced in antiquity—outside of a larger obligation to the sexual partner—similarly ought to have legal consequences.

In every way, the examples of antiquity—as correctly condemned by these rabbinic sources—fail to address the nature of homosexual relationships made possible by modernity. It is to that new possibility that we now turn.

Gay and Lesbian Commitment: A Moral Imperative, a Legal Possibility

The great revolution of the Torah in the realm of sexuality is to insist that sexual expression is legitimate only within the confines of a commitment to the sexual partner as a complete person. Sexuality outside of these bounds necessarily devolves into a form of objectification, in which a human being—a reflection of the image of God—is reduced to a useful (even if voluntary) object for sexual release. The Torah and subsequent rabbinic tradition, in defiance of the devaluation of the human being so prevalent in the world, insist that sexuality ought to further human dignity by embracing the entire person, not take advantage of their willingness or their utility. From the perspective of the Jewish tradition, sexual intercourse is an expression and an outcome of commitment and responsibility toward another human being.

That standard still has not persuaded the rest of the world. The vast majority of human beings act in violation of this lofty ideal, exulting in their passions and explaining their disregard for the full human being as the consequence of simple human nature or the exigency of circumstance. Thus, for Judaism, the vast majority of heterosexual expression is prohibited. Only a narrow range of heterosexual intercourse is permitted, that which occurs within a permanent, exclusive, and public commitment.

The time has come to provide that same guidance and stability for homosexuals as well. Indifference has now become complicit in illness. In the age of the AIDS epidemic, the failure to encourage stability furthers, for many, a tortured and early death. We have seen that the prohibition in Leviticus and the rabbinic tradition knows nothing about the possibility of homosexuality as an orientation and does not address the question of an exclusive, public commitment between two Jewish men or two Jewish women. There is no legal impediment to recognizing—and indeed encouraging—stable and faithful homosexual relationships now that such relationships do exist.

To condemn monogamous homosexual commitment with the same legal opprobrium properly addressed to promiscuous sexuality, anonymous sex, coercive sex, or sex with children, is to discourage the former and to encourage the latter. It is consistent with the sexual revolution initiated in the Torah to seek to strengthen the possibility of stable relationships and loving commitment among homosexuals no less than among their heterosexual brothers and sisters.

By developing a public ceremony to mark the beginning and termination of an exclusive, committed homosexual relationship, the traditional Jewish standards would be clear and enforceable. In fact, by extending those standards to include responsible gay and lesbian love, we would simultaneously strengthen our resolve to place sexual expression within the confines of commitment and fidelity for heterosexuals as well—applying one clear and moral standard to all.

By insisting on a public ceremony, *b'rit ahavah*, we assert that our commitment to stable homes in which responsible adults live their lives in accordance with the *mitzvot* and values of traditional Judaism is absolute and uncompromising. To posit a norm without providing a means for all people to attain that norm is an act of shortsighted cruelty: it engenders unnecessary suffering and subverts the norm itself by forcing people to live outside of its parameter. The institution of a ceremony prevents the "slippery slope." Note that as with heterosexual practice, the vast preponderance of homosexual intercourse is prohibited. All the approach articulated here authorizes is monogamous, committed homosexuality. All else remains, as the Torah labels it, a *to'evah*.

There is no reason to presume that two Jewish homosexuals, having sought rabbinic recognition of their commitment to each other and to establishing a Jewish home, should be any less a source of strength and vitality to the Jewish community and to Judaism as a religion than any other similar heterosexual couple. As opposed to intermarriage, which undermines the Jewish people, encouraging a commitment ceremony for monogamous Jewish homosexuals serves only to strengthen Judaism.

Living in commitment and love, monogamous gay and lesbian Jews are, regrettably, the butt of endless hostility, beatings, and discrimination in employment, housing, insurance, and tax benefits. Much as some would like to deny it, a significant catalyst of this continuing injustice is the reading of the biblical tradition that construes their sexual orientation as itself an abomination. There is simply no way to maintain that homosexuality is abominable and not to reinforce the pervasive oppression and suffering of gay and lesbian people.[56]

The choice before us is to enfranchise monogamous gay and lesbian Jews, or to sever their connection to Judaism entirely. We can extend the traditional condemnation of abusive homosexuality as an abomination to include monogamous homosexuals. By doing so, however, we should admit that we intentionally close off Judaism to a large segment of the Jewish population seeking spiritual growth, belonging, and wisdom. Not only homosexual Jews, but their parents, siblings, relatives, and friends are all distanced from their tradi-

---

56. See Joel Roth, "Homosexuality" (unpublished paper of the Rabbinical Assembly Committee on Jewish Law and Standards), Section Five, for a sincere attempt to straddle this impossible contradiction. If all homosexuality is abominable and threatens the social order, then there should, indeed, be civil disabilities. The revulsion of decent people would then be the appropriate response (as it is for murderers and child-molesters). The fact that reasonable people recoil from this level of bigotry and abuse for gays and lesbians is evidence that most people do not really hold that monogamous homosexuality is an abomination.

tion and their God by this way of construing our tradition, which, despite intentions that are often decent, proves to be harsh and cruel. All Jews who cherish the attribute of *rachamim* [mercy] will feel alienated by this rigid and harsh jurisprudence.

Simple justice cries out for decriminalization of homosexuality in Jewish law. Homosexuality is no illness, nor is it necessarily unethical. As with heterosexuality, it can be expressed in ways that are degrading to human dignity or in ways that are nurturing and ethical. Encouraging sexual responsibility and stability among homosexuals can only strengthen family values and traditional communities. Lacking any compelling reason for stigmatizing monogamous gays and lesbians, the clear moral imperative is to take a bold stand with these innocent and seeking Jews rather than with those who would oppress them. We must find a way to draw these people into the fabric of Jewish community, with the goal of bringing them to a life of Torah and *mitzvoth*.

Now, as always, we must remember the fundamental goal of Jewish law: "Clearly justice is the ultimate value to which God's will must conform; any dichotomy between them is unthinkable. The demand of ethics and the command of God are one."[57]

In our day, the command of God is to enfranchise the monogamous homosexual.

---

57. Gordis, p. 68.

Blessings and Texts

Congregational inclusion cannot be addressed without going to the heart of our Jewish practice—our rituals and our liturgy. GLBT liturgy is a relatively new but fast-growing area. Owing a debt of gratitude to the Jewish feminists starting in the 1970s who began to write new liturgies and evolve the old, gay, lesbian, bisexual, and transgender Jews are now engaging in the same process. In fact, the Institute for Judaism and Sexual Orientation, which compiled the resource bibliography for *Kulanu*, is now collecting and publishing these new liturgical resources on the Jeff Herman Virtual Resource Center (http://www.huc.edu/IJSO/jhvrc.).

We have included a few of these new liturgies and rituals, but there are many more. Rabbi Richard Levy, the author of *A Vision of Holiness: The Future of Reform Judaism*, was gracious enough to consent to review these new liturgies and rituals and share his reflections on them.

Reflections on Liturgy, Ritual Texts, and Innovations by the GLBT Community

Rabbi Richard N. Levy

> Taking him outside, [God] said, "Turn your gaze toward the heavens and count the stars, if you can count them!" And [God] promised him: "So shall your seed be!" And he put his trust in the Eternal, who reckoned that as loyalty in him, saying to him: "I am the Eternal who brought you out of Ur of the Chaldeans, to give you this land as an inheritance." He then said, "Eternal God, how can I know that I shall take possession of it?"
> [God] answered, "Bring Me a three-year-old calf, a three-year-old kid, a three-year-old ram, and a young turtledove." So he took all these and split them—all but the bird—in the middle, placing each half opposite the other."
> —Genesis 15:5–10

> When David finished speaking to Saul, Jonathan's being became connected to the being of David, and Jonathan loved him like himself. . . . Jonathan and David cut a covenant because he loved him like himself: Jonathan removed the cloak from his body and gave it to David along with his tunic, down to his sword and his bow and his belt.
> —I Samuel 18:1–4

In the Genesis passage above, God makes a promise to Abraham of land and progeny, but the words of the promise were not sufficient. Perhaps because Abraham is unsure whether God means the promise ("How can I know?"), God wants Abraham to engage in what we might call a "virtual" experience of its fulfillment: creating a drama enabling the patriarch to visualize the bond between them, which the Bible calls a covenant (*b'rit* in Hebrew). While words have great power (God creates the world through them), these two passages demonstrate that ritual, a formal acting out of the innermost meaning of a relationship, can sometimes be more powerful.

Part of the power of ritual is its ambiguity. What is suggested by Abraham cutting up animals in two pieces? What is suggested by Jonathan giving his clothes—particularly his armor—to David? We all know the "official" meanings of breaking a glass or exchanging rings at weddings, but we are less clear what drinking *Kiddush* wine connotes, or removing the foreskin at a bris.

Many of the rituals in Jewish life seem to be ways to make palpable the ineffable. Like Abraham, we ask, "How will I know?"—what is the tangible evidence that we have passed from a single into a married state? What is the visible evidence that we have passed from ordinary time into Shabbat—short of looking at the clock, where there is no qualitative difference between one number and another? Perhaps Jonathan is saying, "By giving you some of the clothes that identify who I am, that have touched my body, I am sharing myself, and my love, with you." By drinking deeply of the wine in a *Kiddush* cup, perhaps we are saying, "This is the taste of the *k'dushah*, the holiness, that constitutes Shabbat; this is how my body knows that Shabbat has arrived."

But if ritual is often the dramatization of a relationship, it is classically the dramatization of an unequal relationship—Abraham with God; David the common shepherd with Jonathan the son of the king; the bride with the husband who is acquiring her; ordinary Jews with the majestic holiness of Shabbat. In addition to the struggle of a physical being to comprehend an invisible/spiritual entity, ritual also seems to assist us to bridge the gap between unequals. If Abraham can walk between the cut-up pieces of animals and birds, so can he be a partner in a covenant, a pact, with the creator of animals, birds, and human beings. (It is not insignificant that the covenantal rite of *b'rit milah* also includes cutting.) If David the shepherd can wear the princely clothes of Jonathan, he can perhaps experience Jonathan's love for someone just like himself.

But if one of the purposes of a ritual between unequals is to bridge the gap, we have learned over the ages that sometimes we have to alter the ritual. If only one partner gives a ring, one partner is always the acquirer and the other is the acquired. So over the past fifty years a double-ring ceremony has developed, suggesting either that each partner acquires the other or that the ring is no longer a sign of marriage as acquisition but marriage as an exchange between equals.

The ritual of love between Jonathan and David suggests something else as well. Before Saul invited him in, David was an outsider, excluded by his rural mien from the court precincts. In our time, in the United States, gays and lesbians are excluded from the community of civil marriage (with the exception of Massachusetts) and are sometimes legally barred from adopting children, two areas rich in the rituals of marking a new identity. That Jewish gays and lesbians have sought not only to formalize their partnerships through the name and the legal rites of marriage, but through Jewish rites as well, indicates that part of the power of the Jewish marriage ritual is its removal of the "outsider" status. In a sense, David donning Jonathan's clothes is analogous to the gay or lesbian Jew donning the straight world's ring: the qualities of marriage from which you have so long felt excluded now encircle you as well, as Jonathan's armor envelops David (both ring and armor, interestingly, have the protective power of metal).

Another ritual in this compendium borrowed from traditional Jewish rites is a Document of Separation, written by Rabbi Denise Eger, when two partners have decided to dissolve their relationship. It seems to be inspired by the *Seder Preidah*, the Ritual of Release in the *Rabbi's Manual* published by the Central Conference of American Rabbis (CCAR) in 1988, which represented an attempt to fill the void created by the CCAR's decision one hundred years before to relegate divorce to the civil realm, abolishing the traditional ritual of delivering and receiving a *get*. It appears that the *Seder Preidah* has been used only sporadically, which makes Rabbi Eger's rite all the more remarkable. Here, rather than creating a ceremony that would include gays and lesbians in a ritual from which they had been excluded, Rabbi Eger's text parallels the CCAR's attempt to fill a void—but an even more poignant one. Without even a legal acknowledgment of their relationship, a gay or lesbian partnership is faced with a similar dilemma to the Jew wondering how to know that Shabbat has come: what evidence is there of our new status? If the commencement of new status is to be marked by a Jewish marriage ceremony, the knowledge that there is also a ceremony for its ending can be crucial to two partners yearning for some public, visible evidence that the unseen bond between them is real—in a sense, this is what Rabbi Yoel Kahn calls "witnessing." Rabbi Eger speaks of the *Shechinah* (often seen as one of God's feminine manifestations) having withdrawn from the relationship and resting instead with each of the two individuals—a powerful reminder that a Jewish marriage brings God's spiritual presence to rest with two physical individuals.

But Rabbi Eger's text reminds us of something else as well: that though words by themselves may not be sufficient to demonstrate the transformations discussed above, they make the transformations explicit. *Kiddush* wine could taste the same on Friday night as it does on Wednesday, but it is the text of the *Kiddush* that enables the individual to understand the significance of the taste. Do the words of *Kiddush* create or alter the taste of the wine itself, or only create a deeper understanding of its meaning for us? We can believe that the words have this transformative power, though we cannot prove ("know") it—we can allow the words to transform our experience of tasting the wine. To use the words with which God created the world to announce that the *Shechinah*, one of God's manifestations, has departed from a human partnership helps us experience the breakup in a profound form and reminds us of what the reality of partnered life felt like, as opposed to single life.

Another ritual included in this collection that relies almost solely on words is Rabbi Elliot Kukla's blessing for stages in the process of transitioning into what one experiences as one's true gender. A blessing is a means of consciously acknowledging the presence of God in an aspect of nature or of human life—the profusion of blessings in a marriage ceremony contrasted with the absence of blessings in the separation rite is telling. Reflecting current Israeli usage of the word *maavar* (from the verb *avar*, "to cross over"), meaning "sex change," Rabbi Kukla uses the phrase *HaMaavir l'ovrim* to describe God as the agent of the change, in keeping with God's original creation of a single human being who was both masculine and feminine. This usage reminds the person undergoing this change that he or she is not alone in the difficult process and that indeed it was God who created the possibility for such change at the beginning of Creation. Rabbi Kukla leaves it up to the individual to offer the blessing at whatever stage in the process seems to call for it. It is significant that this rite does not invoke the *Shehecheyanu*, which technically should be reserved for events or times that will recur (like reading Torah for the first time or affixing a mezuzah), but which in our time has come to accompany any joyous occasion. But stages in transitioning may not be perceived as totally joyous (though that may be true upon entering any new stage of life), but more significantly, because the rite understands transitioning as a process with many stages, to say the *Shehecheyanu* might suggest that the process were completed.

A transitioning rite can also encourage the person to reflect on the meaning of moving from one gender to another, or to embracing both genders, on the nature of physical and sexual (and intellectual) ambiguity, as well as the possibility and difficulty of joining a new gender community. In this case, the covenant ritual of David and Jonathan may offer some suggestions, as a person who has lived life in one gender now takes on the clothes typically worn by another. Friends might each offer the transitioner an article of clothing that suggests an aspect of the new (or old) gender to which the transitioner can relate.

We have seen in the past ten years an example of the power of ritual to affect people's attitudes. In 1998, the polarized nature of the Reform rabbinate persuaded the leadership of the CCAR to postpone a vote on whether to authorize rabbis to conduct same-gender ceremonies. Instead, we asked colleagues in the Gay and Lesbian Task Force of the CCAR to send couples who had had such ceremonies to speak at the regional conventions of the CCAR and discuss their *ketubot* (marriage contracts) and their experiences. For many rabbis, this was their first encounter with Jews who had engaged in these rituals, and it was very moving. I am convinced that these meetings had much to do with the near-unanimous decision two years later to authorize rabbis to conduct or not to conduct such ceremonies as they saw fit.

As often happens when an excluded group begins to articulate its life with greater visibility and power, they need both new and old rituals. In turn, these rituals developing in the GLBT community throw new light on the meaning of the ancient rites that inspired the new ones. When gays and lesbians who have been barred from civil marriage rites embrace the opportunity to express their relationships through Jewish rites, it reminds all Jews that these rituals have profound meaning, that they cannot be taken for granted, and that sometimes we must struggle for the right to carry them out. When God, the Creator of us all, in all our physical and spiritual diversity, is invoked so often and so passionately in these new rituals that celebrate the spiritual significance of one's body, one's life, one's relationships, and one's commitment to the Jewish people, it is hard not to imagine the Holy One rejoicing.

Union Ceremonies for Same-Gender Couples

Kiddushin Service for Same-Gender Couples
Affirmation Service for Same-Gender Couples

Working Group on Same-Gender Officiation
Central Conference of American Rabbis

Peter Knobel, Chair
Denise Eger
Arthur Gross-Schaefer
Nancy Weiner
Yoel Kahn

Kiddushin Service for Same-Gender Couples

This ceremony is a model *kiddushin* rite for same-gender couples. It is modeled on the ceremonies found in *Ma'aglei Tzedek*. It is one of two ceremonies created by the CCAR's ad hoc Working Group on Same-Gender Officiation.

The ceremony should be modified appropriately to reflect: 1) the length of the couple's existing relationship; 2) the presence and/or absence of family of origin; 3) the legal status of the relationship and the ceremony. Suggested variations are included in the ceremony.

The *Sheva Berakhot* are presented in two Hebrew versions, a traditional text and a shorter version based on the *Rabbi's Manual*. In both versions, the Hebrew text has been modified for this ceremony. Modern and creative translations of the Hebrew text of the blessings are included.

© 2004 Central Conference of American Rabbis.

This ceremony was created by Rabbis Denise Eger and Yoel Kahn and edited for publication by Yoel Kahn. The creative translation of the *Sheva Berakhot* was written by Denise Eger.

Opening

Ceremony takes place beneath the chuppah.
Each member of the couple may be escorted down the aisle by family, parents, friends, or they may choose to walk down the aisle together.

Circles

Couples may circle as the verses below are read, chanted, or sung.

Suggestion: *One person walks around the other three times, stops; the second partner walks around three times, and then the two take hands and turn in a circle together once for a total of seven circles.*

פִּתְחוּ־לִי שַׁעֲרֵי־צֶדֶק אָבֹא־בָם אוֹדֶה יָהּ:

Open for me the gates of righteousness, I will enter and give thanks to God! (Psalm 118:19).

אֶבֶן מָאֲסוּ הַבּוֹנִים הָיְתָה לְרֹאשׁ פִּנָּה:

The stone the builders rejected has become the chief cornerstone (Psalm 118:22).

מֵאֵת יְיָ הָיְתָה זֹּאת הִיא נִפְלָאת בְּעֵינֵינוּ:

From the Eternal does this come; it is wondrous in our eyes (Psalm 118:23).

זֶה־הַיּוֹם עָשָׂה יְיָ נָגִילָה וְנִשְׂמְחָה בוֹ:

This is the day God has made, let us rejoice and be happy in it! (Psalm 118:24).

Welcome

May you be blessed beneath the wings of *Shechinah*.
Welcome into the loving embrace of God's Presence.

בְּרוּכִים הַבָּאִים בְּשֵׁם יְיָ

If in the synagogue:

בֵּרַכְנוּכֶם מִבֵּית יְיָ

We bless you in the House of God.

מִי אַדִּיר עַל הַכֹּל, מִי בָּרוּךְ עַל הַכֹּל,
מִי גָּדוֹל עַל הַכֹּל, הוּא יְבָרֵךְ אֶת ....
— רֵעִים הָאֲהוּבִים
— רֵעוֹת הָאֲהוּבוֹת
וְנֹאמַר אָמֵן

May the Source of power, blessing, and glory bless these loving companions, _____ & _____, and let us say: Amen.

Reading

One of the following selections may be read:

1.
שִׂימֵנִי כַחוֹתָם עַל־לִבֶּךָ כַּחוֹתָם עַל־זְרוֹעֶךָ
כִּי־עַזָּה כַמָּוֶת אַהֲבָה קָשָׁה כִשְׁאוֹל קִנְאָה
רְשָׁפֶיהָ רִשְׁפֵּי אֵשׁ שַׁלְהֶבֶתְיָה:
מַיִם רַבִּים לֹא יוּכְלוּ לְכַבּוֹת אֶת־הָאַהֲבָה
וּנְהָרוֹת לֹא יִשְׁטְפוּהָ

Let me be a seal upon your heart, like the seal upon your hand.
For love is fierce as death, passion is mighty as Sheol;
Its darts are darts of fire, a blazing flame.
Vast floods cannot quench love, nor rivers drown it (Songs of Songs 8:6–7).

2.
צַר־לִי עָלֶיךָ אָחִי יְהוֹנָתָן
נָעַמְתָּ לִּי מְאֹד
נִפְלְאַתָה אַהֲבָתְךָ לִי מֵאַהֲבַת נָשִׁים

My brother Jonathan; very pleasant have you been unto me;
wonderful was your love to me, passing the love of women (II Samuel 1:26).

3.
וַתֹּאמֶר רוּת
אַל־תִּפְגְּעִי־בִי לְעָזְבֵךְ לָשׁוּב מֵאַחֲרָיִךְ
כִּי אֶל־אֲשֶׁר תֵּלְכִי אֵלֵךְ וּבַאֲשֶׁר תָּלִינִי אָלִין
עַמֵּךְ עַמִּי וֵאלֹהַיִךְ אֱלֹהָי:
בַּאֲשֶׁר תָּמוּתִי אָמוּת וְשָׁם אֶקָּבֵר
כֹּה יַעֲשֶׂה יְיָ לִי וְכֹה יֹסִיף כִּי הַמָּוֶת יַפְרִיד בֵּינִי וּבֵינֵךְ:

And Ruth said: "Entreat me not to leave you, and to return from following after you; for wherever you go, I will go; wherever you lodge, I will lodge; your people shall be my people, and your God my God; wherever you die I will die, and there I will be buried. The Eternal do so to me, and more also, if anything but death part you and me" (Ruth 1:16-17).

Shehecheyanu

We celebrate this joyous occasion with words that link us to our people's rejoicing throughout the generations. We give thanks for this opportunity to affirm the recognition of this family and household as we join together in our prayer of gratitude.

בָּרוּךְ אַתָּה יְיָ, אֱלֹהֵינוּ מֶלֶךְ הָעוֹלָם, שֶׁהֶחֱיָנוּ וְקִיְּמָנוּ וְהִגִּיעָנוּ לַזְּמַן הַזֶּה:

Praised are You, Adonai our God, Source of the Universe, who has given us life, sustained us, and brought us to this joyous occasion.

Wine and *Birkat Eirusin*

This is a time for rejoicing. Family and friends have come together to celebrate with _____ and _____ as they affirm their love and devotion to one another. Through this sacred rite we affirm the desire of _____ and _____ to become beloved partners and life-companions, and together to create *bayit u'mishpachah*, household and family. Let us celebrate this moment and sanctify the recognition of their household and family together with these ancient words of blessing:

Couple holds the Kiddush *cup.*

בָּרוּךְ אַתָּה יְיָ, אֱלֹהֵינוּ מֶלֶךְ הָעוֹלָם, בּוֹרֵא פְּרִי הַגָּפֶן׃

Praised are You, Adonai our God, Source of the Universe, who creates the fruit of the vine.

בָּרוּךְ אַתָּה יְיָ, מְקַדֵּשׁ עַמּוֹ יִשְׂרָאֵל עַל יְדֵי חֻפָּה וְקִדּוּשִׁין׃

Praised are You, Adonai, who sanctifies the people Israel at this ceremony of *kiddushin* beneath the chuppah.

Rabbi's Remarks

Reading

One of the readings from above (starting with "Let me be a seal upon your heart . . .") or one of the following:

1. Adrienne Rich [1929–]
   excerpt from "Phantasia for Elvira Shatayev" [*The Dream of a Common Language* (New York: W. W. Norton: 1978)]

   Now we are ready
   and each of us knows it   I have never loved
   like this   I have never seen
   my own forces so taken up and shared
   and given back
   After the long training   the early sieges
   we are moving almost effortlessly in our love
   . . . .
   What does love mean
   . . . .
   A cable of blue fire ropes our bodies
   burning together in the snow   We will not live to settle for less   We have dreamed
      of this
   all of our lives

2. Walt Whitman [1819–1892]
   "When I Heard at the Close of the Day" [*Leaves of Grass*]

   When I heard at the close of the day how my name had been received with plaudits in
      the capitol, still it was not a happy night for me that followed,
   And else, when I caroused, or when my plans were accomplished, still I was not happy,
   But the day when I rose at dawn from the bed of perfect health, refreshed, singing,
      inhaling the ripe breath of autumn,
   When I saw the full moon in the west grow pale and disappear in the morning light,
   When I wandered alone over the beach, and, undressing, bathed, laughing with the
      cool waters, and saw the sun rise,

And when I thought how my dear friend, my lover, was on his way coming, O then I
  was happy,
O then each breath tasted sweeter—and all that day my food nourished me more—
  and the beautiful day passed well,
And the next came with equal joy—and with the next, at evening, came my friend,
And that night, while all was still, I heard the waters roll slowly continually up the shores,
I heard the hissing rustle of the liquid and sands, as directed to me, whispering, to con-
  gratulate me,
For the one I love most lay sleeping by me under the same cover in the cool night,
In the stillness, in the autumn moonbeams, his face was inclined toward me,
And his arm lay lightly around my breast—and that night I was happy.

Vows

Couple turn to one another and exchange vows. The couple may read their own vows, ask the officiant to read them, or respond to the vows below:

Do you, _____, take _____, to be your companion in life, to love, honor, and cherish?

Do you, _____, take _____, to be your companion in life, to love, honor, and cherish?

Rings—Version I

As a token of these vows of commitment you have made, you each give and receive a ring. I ask you, _____, to take this ring and place it on your beloved's finger and say these traditional words of commitment:

הֲרֵי אַתָּה מְקֻדָּשׁ לִי בְּטַבַּעַת זוֹ
לִפְנֵי אֱלֹהִים וְאָדָם . . .
בְּרוּחַ עַמֵּינוּ . . .

הֲרֵי אַתְּ מְקֻדֶּשֶׁת לִי בְּטַבַּעַת זוֹ
לִפְנֵי אֱלֹהִים וְאָדָם . . .
בְּרוּחַ עַמֵּינוּ.

By this ring are you consecrated unto me
before God and these witnesses
in the spirit of our people.

Rings—Version II

As a token of these vows of commitment you have made, you each give and receive a ring. I ask you, _____, to take this ring and place it on your beloved's finger and say these words:

זֹאת דּוֹדָתִי וְזֹאת רַעְיָתִי

זֶה דּוֹדִי וְזֶה רֵעִי

This is my beloved and this is my friend.

Officiant:

וְאֵרַשְׂתִּיךְ לִי לְעוֹלָם
וְאֵרַשְׂתִּיךְ לִי בְּצֶדֶק וּבְמִשְׁפָּט וּבְחֶסֶד וּבְרַחֲמִים:
וְאֵרַשְׂתִּיךְ לִי בֶּאֱמוּנָה וְיָדַעַתְּ אֶת־יְיָ:

I betroth you to me forever
I betroth you to me in righteousness and justice.
In love and compassion;
I betroth you to me in everlasting faithfulness.

Reading of the *Ketubah*

A sample text:

On the first day of the week on the _____ day of the month of _____ in the year _____ since the creation of the world as we reckon here in _____

The beloved _____
  Daughter of (son of) _____
  And
The beloved _____
  Daughter of (son of) _____

Say to one another:

We affirm our commitment to one another in love and devotion and promise to be open to one another. We commit this day to becoming one in spirit as a family. We will cherish our unique visions of the world and challenge one another to continue our growth as individuals. We promise to work towards reaching our dreams and goals. Through mutual love, support, respect and honor, we will help each other through times of difficulty and times of joy and celebration.

We also affirm the sanctity of our Jewish home. We commit our family life to be one filled with the celebrations of the Jewish year. We promise to be active in the life of our Jewish community and we promise to fill our home with Jewish learning, *tzedakah*, and a commitment to the care and well being of all humanity through the practice of *tikkun olam*.

וְהַכֹּל שָׁרִיר וְקַיָּם.

All is valid and binding.

Rabbi's Remarks [if not previously]

Seven Blessings

Couple may hold the cup together.

Officiant or seven other invited guests:

1. בָּרוּךְ אַתָּה יְיָ אֱלֹהֵינוּ מֶלֶךְ הָעוֹלָם, בּוֹרֵא פְּרִי הַגָּפֶן.

2. בָּרוּךְ אַתָּה יְיָ אֱלֹהֵינוּ מֶלֶךְ הָעוֹלָם, שֶׁהַכֹּל בָּרָא לִכְבוֹדוֹ.

3. בָּרוּךְ אַתָּה יְיָ אֱלֹהֵינוּ מֶלֶךְ הָעוֹלָם, יוֹצֵר הָאָדָם.

Union Ceremonies for Same-Gender Couples

4. בָּרוּךְ אַתָּה יְיָ אֱלֹהֵינוּ מֶלֶךְ הָעוֹלָם, אֲשֶׁר יָצַר אֶת הָאָדָם בְּצַלְמוֹ,
בְּצֶלֶם דְּמוּת תַּבְנִיתוֹ, וְהִתְקִין לוֹ מִמֶּנּוּ בִּנְיַן עֲדֵי עַד.
בָּרוּךְ אַתָּה יְיָ, יוֹצֵר הָאָדָם.

5. שׂוֹשׂ תָּשִׂישׂ וְתָגֵל הָעֲקָרָה, בְּקִבּוּץ בָּנֶיהָ לְתוֹכָהּ בְּשִׂמְחָה.
בָּרוּךְ אַתָּה יְיָ, מְשַׂמֵּחַ צִיּוֹן בְּבָנֶיהָ.

6. שַׂמֵּחַ תְּשַׂמַּח רֵעִים הָאֲהוּבִים, כְּשַׂמֵּחֲךָ יְצִירְךָ בְּגַן עֵדֶן מִקֶּדֶם.
בָּרוּךְ אַתָּה יְיָ, מְשַׂמֵּחַ רֵעִים הָאֲהוּבִים/רֵעוֹת הָאֲהוּבוֹת.

7. בָּרוּךְ אַתָּה יְיָ אֱלֹהֵינוּ מֶלֶךְ הָעוֹלָם, אֲשֶׁר בָּרָא שָׂשׂוֹן
וְשִׂמְחָה, רֵעֶה וְרֵעוֹ/רֵעָה וְרֵעָה גִּילָה רִנָּה דִּיצָה וְחֶדְוָה, אַהֲבָה וְאַחֲוָה, שָׁלוֹם וְרֵעוּת.
מְהֵרָה, יְיָ אֱלֹהֵינוּ יִשָּׁמַע בְּעָרֵי יְהוּדָה וּבְחוּצוֹת יְרוּשָׁלָיִם, קוֹל שָׂשׂוֹן וְקוֹל שִׂמְחָה,
קוֹל אַהֲבָה וְקוֹל אַחֲוָה, [קוֹל מִצְהֲלוֹת חֲתָנִים מֵחֻפָּתָם וּנְעָרִים מִמִּשְׁתֵּה נְגִינָתָם].
בָּרוּךְ אַתָּה יְיָ, מְשַׂמֵּחַ רֵעִים הָאֲהוּבִים/רֵעוֹת הָאֲהוּבוֹת.

Seven Blessings—Translation

1. We praise the Eternal, Source of Creation, Creator of the fruit of the vine.

2. We praise the Eternal, Source of Creation, Creator of all things.

3. We praise the Eternal, Source of Creation, who has fashioned humankind.

4. We praise the Eternal, Source of Creation, Creator of humankind in the divine image. Praised are You, O God, Creator of humanity.

5. Surely the solitary one rejoices and is jubilant, being made part of a household. We praise You, O God, who gives joy to Zion in the beloveds she harbors.

6. May these two, lovers and companions to one another, rejoice as did God's first creations in the Garden of Eden. We praise You, O God, who gladdens those bound together by their love.

7. We praise the Eternal, Source of Creation, who creates people bound together in love, along with joy and gladness, mirth and merriment, song, joy and delight, happiness, love and devotion, peace and companionship. Soon may be heard in the streets of Jerusalem and the hills of Judah, yea, in every city and in the streets of every town, the sound of joy and the sound of gladness, the sounds of those who are bound together by their love. We praise You, O God, who rejoices with these lovers.

Seven Blessings—Alternative Translation

We look to our ancestors for guidance and ask God's blessing:

1. Praised are You Adonai, Ruler of the Universe, who creates the fruit of the vine.

2. Just as Sarah brought new life into this world with laughter, so may God bless you with the ability to create a new life together—a life full of joy and laughter and happiness.

3. Just as Rebekah at the well satisfied the thirst of Eliezer and the camels, so may God bless you with the flow of generosity and lovingkindness in your home.

4. Rachel and Leah were sisters; they were the same and yet were different. May God bless you with the gift of respecting each other's capabilities and may you help each other to grow in strength.

5. Just as Miriam led her people to freedom, may God bless you with the power to inspire others to sing and dance freely.

6. Just as Deborah was a prophet and a judge, may God bless you with eyes that see the good and bad in this world so that you may be partners with God in healing the world, *tikkun olam*.

7. Like Ruth who in love and devotion declared, "For wherever you go I will go, wherever you lodge I will lodge; your people shall be my people and your God, shall be my God," may you both be strengthened in your commitment to one another as you journey from year to year.

Declaration and Priestly Benediction

Choose the passage(s) below appropriate for the circumstances of this ceremony. Usually, a statement of civil status will be followed by a declaration of religious and communal recognition.

Civil Status

—Acknowledge absence of civil recognition
While we recognize that this ceremony does not yet enjoy civil recognition in this jurisdiction . . .

—Civil union/domestic partnership
Your *union/domestic partnership* has been duly registered by the civil authorities of _____ and . . .

—Marriage license
By the power vested in me by the State of _____ and . . .

Religious and Communal Recognition

—Version I
. . . We who are gathered affirm as a community today that _____ and _____ have said the words and performed the rites that unite their lives.

—Version II
. . . We declare now that in the sight of our Jewish community and before God, _____ and _____ are united in *kiddushin*, the sacred bond of commitment, and we recognize their relationship as *bayit u'mishpachah b'Yisrael*—a household and family amongst the people of Israel.

Let us now bless you with an ancient blessing in the hopes that God will look kindly upon your home and lives together and grant you a strong bond of love and protection:

Priestly Benediction

יְבָרֶכְךָ יְיָ וְיִשְׁמְרֶךָ:
יָאֵר יְיָ פָּנָיו אֵלֶיךָ וִיחֻנֶּךָּ:
יִשָּׂא יְיָ פָּנָיו אֵלֶיךָ וְיָשֵׂם לְךָ שָׁלוֹם:

May God bless you and keep you.
May the *Shechinah* shine upon you and be gracious to you.
May the Holy One of Blessing grant you *shalom*, peace.

Breaking of the Glass

There are many explanations for the custom of breaking a glass at this Jewish rite. One interpretation is that this practice reminds you, _____ and _____, along with all who are present, that the Jewish people have a partnership with God in the task of *tikkun olam*, the healing and repair of the world. Anywhere there is oppression and pain, the Jew is asked to respond.

Because so many gays and lesbians sadly still know the oppression and pain of hiding, because so many gays and lesbians still lack equality of civil rights in our world, we break a glass/glasses on this day of celebration to remind us that even in this hour of great joy, our world is still incomplete and in need of healing. May the time be soon, speedily and in our day, when all who are in hiding shall be free and all who are in exile shall come home.

May the shattering of these glasses by _____ and _____ remind them and us to work towards this time of wholeness, this *tikkun*, for ourselves and our world. Amen.

Affirmation Service for Same-Gender Couples

This ceremony of affirmation was created as an alternative to the historical *kiddushin* rite. It is based on the *Brit Ahuvim* of Rachel Adler.[1]

The ceremony is specifically intended for couples who have already been together for a significant period of time but who now choose—or newly have the opportunity—to sanctify their relationship. It is one of two ceremonies created by the CCAR's ad hoc Working Group on Same-Gender Officiation.

The ceremony should be modified appropriately to reflect: 1) the length of the couple's existing relationship; 2) the presence and/or absence of family of origin; 3) the legal status of the relationship and the ceremony. Suggested variations are included in the ceremony.

---

1. Rachel Adler, *Engendering Judaism: An Inclusive Theology and Ethics* (Boston: Beacon Press, 1998), chap. 5.

The *Sheva Berakhot* are presented in two Hebrew versions, a traditional text and a shorter version based on the *Rabbi's Manual*. In both versions, the Hebrew text has been modified for this ceremony. Modern and creative translations of the Hebrew text of the blessings are included.

This ceremony was created by Rabbis Denise Eger and Yoel Kahn and edited for publication by Yoel Kahn. The second translation of the *Sheva Berakhot* is based on a translation by Rabbi Margaret Holub as taught by Rabbi Nancy Flam; the alternative version is by Rabbi Denise Eger.

Opening

Ceremony takes place beneath the chuppah.

Each member of the couple may be escorted down the aisle by family, parents, friends, or they may choose to walk down the aisle together.

Upon arrival under the chuppah:

בְּרוּכִים הַבָּאִים בְּשֵׁם יְיָ

Blessed are those who come in God's name.

If in the synagogue:

בֵּרַכְנוּכֶם מִבֵּית יְיָ

We bless you in the House of God.

You stand now beneath this chuppah—the symbol of the home you make with one another. All who have gathered on this special day pray that your home be a place of safety and sanctity. God, bless _____ and _____ who seek Your presence in their home and relationship. Help them sustain their love; deepen their faith in You; and throughout their years together, may they open their hearts and souls and minds to one another and to Your mitzvot.

Circles

As _____ and _____ circle one another at this time, let them know the encircling of Your *Shechinah*, Your Divine Presence and protection, throughout their days together.

Couples circle as the verses below are read, chanted, or sung.

Suggestion: *One person walks around the other three times, stops; the second partner walks around three times, and then the two take hands and turn in a circle together once for a total of seven circles.*

פִּתְחוּ־לִי שַׁעֲרֵי־צֶדֶק אָבֹא־בָם אוֹדֶה יָהּ:

Open for me the gates of righteousness, I will enter and give thanks to God! (Psalm 118:19).

Union Ceremonies for Same-Gender Couples

אֶבֶן מָאֲסוּ הַבּוֹנִים הָיְתָה לְרֹאשׁ פִּנָּה:

The stone the builders rejected has become the chief cornerstone (Psalm 118:22).

מֵאֵת יְיָ הָיְתָה זֹּאת הִיא נִפְלָאת בְּעֵינֵינוּ:

From the Eternal does this come; it is wondrous in our eyes (Psalm 118:23).

זֶה־הַיּוֹם עָשָׂה יְיָ נָגִילָה וְנִשְׂמְחָה בוֹ:

This is the day God has made; let us rejoice and be happy in it! (Psalm 118:24).

Sanctification

God, on this day of rejoicing and celebration, we gather to affirm and celebrate the relationship of _____ and _____ in this holy setting. We lift our voices in thanksgiving and praise. [We honor the years they have already celebrated together and now] at this holy moment we unite them in sacred partnership with the blessings of [family and] community.

In these hearts You, Eternal One, have implanted the ability to love. Let their home be filled with love and devotion to one another. Let their home be filled with love and commitment to our Jewish heritage. With this sacred rite beneath the *chuppah*, may _____ and _____ deepen their commitment to share life's joys and life's trials. May companionship and peace abide within their home and their hearts, and may their lives be filled with contentment, happiness, and peace.

As we lift the cup of wine, we sanctify this moment [and all that has come before]:

כּוֹס־יְשׁוּעוֹת אֶשָּׂא וּבְשֵׁם יְיָ אֶקְרָא.

I lift up the cup of salvation and call upon the name of God!

בָּרוּךְ אַתָּה יְיָ אֱלֹהֵינוּ מֶלֶךְ הָעוֹלָם, בּוֹרֵא פְּרִי הַגָּפֶן.

Praised are You, Adonai Our God, Source of the Universe, who creates the fruit of the vine.

The couple drinks from the cup.

Musical interlude or other readings.

B'rit

This sacred gathering [celebrates the shared life you have had together these ___ years and] sanctifies your commitment to bind your lives to one another and to establish your household within the greater house of the People of Israel. Each of you has brought to this ceremony a token of the values and history which will be cherished in your home through the days and years ahead.

[Officiant or celebrants may briefly describe objects and their significance.]

Objects are placed in a bag or basket.

[If desired, rings may be also be placed inside.]

At the beginning of the Torah, God makes a covenant with all creation. The sign of God's covenant with creation is the rainbow. Throughout the generations, Jews have recited a blessing which honors the faithful keeping of a covenant whenever they have seen a rainbow in the sky. In our own generation, the rainbow has come to symbolize our own faith in the goodness of creation, and our hope for the time when the diversity of creation will be recognized and celebrated like the first rainbow God placed in the sky.

We bless your covenantal pledges to each other with these ancient words of blessing:

As they lift the bag or basket, couple says:

בָּרוּךְ אַתָּה יְיָ אֱלֹהֵינוּ מֶלֶךְ הָעוֹלָם,
זוֹכֵר הַבְּרִית וְנֶאֱמָן בִּבְרִיתוֹ וְקַיָּם בְּמַאֲמָרוֹ.

Praised are You, Adonai our God, Source of the universe, who remembers the covenant, is faithful to Your covenant and fulfills Your promise.

Couple may exchange personal words of commitment or vows.

Rings

If couple chooses, rings are exchanged.
Rings can be exchanged serially or simultaneously.

As token of your covenant together, you each give and receive a ring. I ask you, _____, to take _____'s ring and hold it on her/his index finger, which, according to Jewish teaching, is the shortest distance to her/his heart.

[If there is no exchange of rings, begin:]

I ask you to turn to each other, take hands and say after me:

[for women]
אֶל־אֲשֶׁר תֵּלְכִי אֵלֵךְ
וּבַאֲשֶׁר תָּלִינִי אָלִין
בַּאֲשֶׁר תָּמוּתִי אָמוּת וְשָׁם אֶקָּבֵר
כִּי זֹאת דּוֹדָתִי וְזֹאת רַעֲיָתִי

[for men]
אֶל־אֲשֶׁר תֵּלֵךְ אֵלֵךְ
וּבַאֲשֶׁר תָּלִין אָלִין
בַּאֲשֶׁר תָּמוּת אָמוּת וְשָׁם אֶקָּבֵר
כִּי זֶה דוֹדִי וְזֶה רֵעִי

[Ruth 1:16–17; Song of Songs 5:16]

Wherever you go, I will go;
Wherever you lodge I will lodge;
Wherever you die I will die, and there I will be buried . . .
For this is my beloved
And this is my friend.

Union Ceremonies for Same-Gender Couples

In the words of the prophet Hosea:

וְאֵרַשְׂתִּיךְ לִי לְעוֹלָם
וְאֵרַשְׂתִּיךְ לִי בְּצֶדֶק וּבְמִשְׁפָּט וּבְחֶסֶד וּבְרַחֲמִים:
וְאֵרַשְׂתִּיךְ לִי בֶּאֱמוּנָה:

I betroth you to me forever;
I betroth you to me in righteousness and justice, in love and compassion;
I betroth you to me in faithfulness.

Seven Blessings

1. בָּרוּךְ אַתָּה יְיָ, אֱלֹהֵינוּ מֶלֶךְ הָעוֹלָם, בּוֹרֵא פְּרִי הַגָּפֶן.

2. בָּרוּךְ אַתָּה יְיָ, אֱלֹהֵינוּ מֶלֶךְ הָעוֹלָם, שֶׁהַכֹּל בָּרָא לִכְבוֹדוֹ.

3. בָּרוּךְ אַתָּה יְיָ, אֱלֹהֵינוּ מֶלֶךְ הָעוֹלָם, יוֹצֵר הָאָדָם.

4. בָּרוּךְ אַתָּה יְיָ, אֱלֹהֵינוּ מֶלֶךְ הָעוֹלָם, אֲשֶׁר יָצַר אֶת־הָאָדָם בְּצַלְמוֹ,
בְּצֶלֶם דְּמוּת תַּבְנִיתוֹ, וְהִתְקִין לוֹ מִמֶּנּוּ בִּנְיַן עֲדֵי־עַד.
בָּרוּךְ אַתָּה יְיָ, יוֹצֵר הָאָדָם.

5. שׂוֹשׂ תָּשִׂישׂ וְתָגֵל הָעֲקָרָה, בְּקִבּוּץ בָּנֶיהָ לְתוֹכָהּ בְּשִׂמְחָה.
בָּרוּךְ אַתָּה יְיָ, מְשַׂמֵּחַ צִיּוֹן בְּבָנֶיהָ.

6. שַׂמֵּחַ תְּשַׂמַּח רֵעִים הָאֲהוּבִים כְּשַׂמֵּחֲךָ יְצִירְךָ בְּגַן עֵדֶן מִקֶּדֶם.
בָּרוּךְ אַתָּה יְיָ, מְשַׂמֵּחַ רֵעִים הָאֲהוּבִים/רֵעוֹת הָאֲהוּבוֹת.

7. בָּרוּךְ אַתָּה יְיָ, אֱלֹהֵינוּ מֶלֶךְ הָעוֹלָם, אֲשֶׁר בָּרָא שָׂשׂוֹן וְשִׂמְחָה,
רֵעַ וְרֵעוֹ/רֵעָה וְרֵעָה גִּילָה, רִנָּה, דִּיצָה וְחֶדְוָה, אַהֲבָה וְאַחֲוָה, שָׁלוֹם וְרֵעוּת.
מְהֵרָה, יְיָ אֱלֹהֵינוּ יִשָּׁמַע בְּעָרֵי יְהוּדָה וּבְחוּצוֹת יְרוּשָׁלָיִם, קוֹל שָׂשׂוֹן וְקוֹל שִׂמְחָה,
קוֹל אַהֲבָה וְקוֹל אַחֲוָה, [קוֹל מִצְהֲלוֹת חֲתָנִים מֵחֻפָּתָם, וּנְעָרִים מִמִּשְׁתֵּה נְגִינָתָם.]
בָּרוּךְ אַתָּה יְיָ, מְשַׂמֵּחַ רֵעִים הָאֲהוּבִים/רֵעוֹת הָאֲהוּבוֹת.

Seven Blessings—Translation I

1. We praise the Eternal, Source of Creation, Creator of the fruit of the vine.

2. We praise the Eternal, Source of Creation, Creator of all things.

3. We praise the Eternal, Source of Creation, who has fashioned humankind.

4. We praise the Eternal, Source of Creation, Creator of humankind in the divine image. Praised are You, O God, Creator of humanity.

5. Surely the solitary one rejoices and is jubilant, being made part of a household. We praise You, O God, who gives joy to Zion in the beloveds she harbors.

223

6. May these two, lovers and companions to one another, rejoice as did God's first creations in the Garden of Eden. We praise You, O God, who gladdens those bound together by their love.

7. We praise the Eternal, Source of Creation, who creates people bound together in love, along with joy and gladness, mirth and merriment, song, joy and delight, happiness, love and devotion, peace and companionship. Soon may be heard in the streets of Jerusalem and the hills of Judah, yea, in every city and in the streets of every town, the sound of joy and the sound of gladness, the sounds of those who are bound together by their love. We praise You, O God, who rejoices with these loving companions.

Seven Blessings—Translation II

1. Blessed is the sweet Source of all, Creator of the fruit of the vine!

2. Blessed is the Spring of life, who fills creation with glory.

3. Blessed is the Heart of the world, which created human beings.

4. Blessed is the Artisan who created human beings in Her image, after His likeness, and whose creative spirit renews creation and brings forth life. Blessed is the Artisan who created human beings.

5. May she who is alone now rejoice when a community is gathered to her in joy. Blessed is the Mother of all, who fills Zion with the joy of community.

6. May these beloved companions know the joy that filled the hearts of those who dwelt in the garden of Eden. Blessed is the Source of joy, which rejoices the hearts of people in love.

7. Blessed is the One who invited us to joy and gladness, to falling in love, to mirth and exultation, pleasure and delight, love, fellowship, peace and friendship. Soon may there be heard in the cities of Judah and the streets of Jerusalem—yea, in every city and every town—the voice of joy and gladness, the voices of those bound together by their love. Blessed are You who created the love of ***these men/these women/this couple*** for each other

Blessings—Alternative Version

1. בָּרוּךְ אַתָּה יְיָ אֱלֹהֵינוּ מֶלֶךְ הָעוֹלָם, יוֹצֵר הָאָדָם.

2. בָּרוּךְ אַתָּה יְיָ אֱלֹהֵינוּ מֶלֶךְ הָעוֹלָם, אֲשֶׁר יָצַר אֶת הָאָדָם בְּצַלְמוֹ.

3. בָּרוּךְ אַתָּה יְיָ אֱלֹהֵינוּ מֶלֶךְ הָעוֹלָם, אֲשֶׁר בָּרָא שָׂשׂוֹן וְשִׂמְחָה, רֵעָה וְרֵעוֹ/רֵעָה, גִּילָה, רִנָּה, דִּיצָה וְחֶדְוָה, אַהֲבָה וְאַחֲוָה וְשָׁלוֹם וְרֵעוּת מְהֵרָה יְיָ אֱלֹהֵינוּ יִשָּׁמַע בְּעָרֵי יְהוּדָה וּבְחֻצוֹת יְרוּשָׁלַיִם קוֹל שָׂשׂוֹן וְקוֹל שִׂמְחָה, קוֹל אַהֲבָה וְקוֹל אַחֲוָה, [קוֹל מִצְהֲלוֹת חֲתָנִים מֵחֻפָּתָם וּנְעָרִים מִמִּשְׁתֵּה נְגִינָתָם].

4. בָּרוּךְ אַתָּה יְיָ, מְשַׂמֵּחַ רֵעִים הָאֲהוּבִים/רֵעוֹת הָאֲהוּבוֹת.

5. בָּרוּךְ אַתָּה יְיָ אֱלֹהֵינוּ מֶלֶךְ הָעוֹלָם, בּוֹרֵא פְּרִי הַגָּפֶן.

1. Praised are You, O God, Creator of humanity.

2. We praise the Eternal, Source of Creation, Creator of humankind in the divine image.

3. We praise the Eternal, Source of Creation, who creates people bound together in love, along with joy and gladness, mirth and merriment, song, joy and delight, happiness, love and devotion, peace and companionship. Soon may be heard in the streets of Jerusalem and the hills of Judah, yea, in every city and in the streets of every town, the sound of joy and the sound of gladness, the sounds of those who are bound together by their love.

4. We praise You, O God, who rejoices with these loving companions.

5. We praise the Eternal, Source of Creation, Creator of the fruit of the vine.

Priestly Benediction

[You are blessed to have present today loving members of your families of origin who have come to celebrate the sanctification of this family of choice. We invite the family members who are present to rise (and come forward)].

[*To family members:* Your presence today is a token of love and a token of hope, as . . .]

We look forward to a time when all who have been separated are united,
and all who are in exile can come home.

יְבָרֶכְךָ יְיָ וְיִשְׁמְרֶךָ:
יָאֵר יְיָ פָּנָיו אֵלֶיךָ וִיחֻנֶּךָּ:
יִשָּׂא יְיָ פָּנָיו אֵלֶיךָ וְיָשֵׂם לְךָ שָׁלוֹם:

May God bless you and keep you.
May the Divine Countenance shine upon you and be gracious to you.
May God's Presence be lifted before you and may you be blessed with peace.

Pronouncement

_____ and _____, you have declared your commitment and pledges to one another before God and this community.

Civil Union/Domestic Partnership

[Your union/domestic partnership] has been duly registered by the civil authorities of
_____ . . .

Marriage License

By the power vested in me by the State of _____ . . .

I therefore do declare that you are spouses-for-life and *mishpachah*—a family in the household of Israel.

Breaking of Glass

There are many explanations as to the origin of the custom of breaking a glass at a joyous ceremony like this one. One traditional explanation is that even in the midst of our joy we acknowledge the brokenness and incompleteness of the world around us; may your love and commitment to each other be a source of strength in your commitment to engage in the work of *tikkun olam*, of repairing the world. [Another explanation is that anyone who wants to come between you must first put all the pieces of the broken glass back together again!]

The glass is broken.

Document of Separation

Rabbi Denise Eger

On this day of _____ st/th of the month of _____ 57__ corresponding to the ___st/th day of_____, 200_ in the city of _____, _____, we acknowledge the sadness in the separation and dissolution of the relationship of _____ and _____.

They once shared a common love and vision for their lives together. They blessed that relationship beneath the chuppah and invited the *Shechinah* to dwell with them. Sadly, now, as they have decided to separate, so too, the *Shechinah* has withdrawn from their relationship.

May you both find your own way in the world. May you both feel embraced by the *Shechinah* and comforted by her wings.
Today, we, _____ and _____, acknowledge that we, formally, dissolve the bonds of relationship and family with one another.

_____   _____

Adoption/Hebrew Name-Taking Ceremony

Rabbi Yoel Kahn, Ph.D.

Adapted from a speech given by Rabbi Yoel Kahn, Ph.D., entitled "Filling in the Gaps: Creating New Lifecycle Ceremonies," delivered to the Committee on Jewish Family Life at the Convention of the Central Conference of American Rabbis in San Antonio, Texas, April 8, 1992.

While I was the rabbi of Congregation Sha'ar Zahav (San Francisco, California), we created a completely new ceremony, but one grounded in tradition, when a young boy was legally adopted by a gay couple in our congregation who had been his foster parents. His fathers wanted a ceremony that celebrated his becoming Jewish, marked his acceptance into his new and first real family, recognized the extended family that had helped the boy and his parents through the lengthy adoption process, and not least, acknowledged the challenges the boy had overcome in order to survive his difficult early years.

We used the model of the *b'rit* ceremony but expanded it to encompass this family's narrative and the active participation of the young boy himself. The public ceremony, following the *mikveh*, included the following:

1. The congregation rose and made a tunnel for the boy to walk through, while we all sang "Hinei Mah Tov."
2. The axes of the covenant were explained through displays illustrating the boy's understanding of God, Torah, and Israel.
   a. Torah: pictures of biblical scenes that the boy had learned about in religious school and colored in.
   b. *Am Yisrael*: a photo collage of everyone in the boy's extended personal and synagogue family.
   c. God: a beautiful drawing by the boy in the shape of a heart, illustrating how and when he feels God's love.
3. The boy was conferred with his new Hebrew name, Yochanan.
   a. Linking his name to the history of the Jewish people and to his adoptive family helped to emphasize to this child, who spent his first years without an intact family, how connected he now had become.
   b. Talking about historical figures who had overcome adversity, like Yochanan ben Zakkai, was also our opportunity to acknowledge God's presence as a source of inner strength for the boy in his early years.

4. The boy was presented with seven small, symbolic gifts by family friends, each representing one of the blessings of family life. This portion was unique to this ceremony. The gifts ranged from a *kippah*, symbolizing Judaism, to a stone that the boy had found on a hike with an adult friend, now polished and hung on a necklace, symbolizing discovery.

These elements came together in a ceremony that was familiar and readily identifiable as *b'rit* and at the same time original and personal. This ceremony felt authentic because it was grounded in the images and rituals assigned by our tradition and community to such a time, and it honestly and openly accommodated the unique narrative of the boy's life and the *kavanah* his family brought to the occasion.

A Coming-Out Prayer for Lesbian, Gay, Bisexual, and Transgender People and Those Who Love Them

O God of truth and justice, the evasions and deceits we practice upon others and ourselves are many.

We long only to speak out and to hear the truth, yet time and again, from fear of loss or hope of gain, from dull habit or from cruel deliberation, we speak half-truths, we twist facts, we are silent when others lie, and we lie to ourselves.

Whether we are lesbian, gay, bisexual, transgender, or questioning, family or friends, we sometimes feel forced to pretend to be that which we are not, to present ourselves in ways which are not truthful, and sometimes with outright lies.

But as we stand before You, our words and our thoughts speed to One who knows them before we utter them. We do not have to tell untruths to You as we are often forced to do in the world. We know we cannot lie in Your presence.

May our worship help us to practice truth in speech and in thought before You, to ourselves, and before one another; and may we finally complete our liberation so that we no longer feel the need to practice evasions and deceits.

Adapted from the siddur of Congregation Sha'ar Zahav (San Francisco, CA; www.shaarzahav.org), "Prayers, Poems, and Songs."

A Blessing for Transitioning Genders

Rabbi Elliot Kukla

Jewish tradition teaches us that we should be saying a hundred blessings a day to mark all the moments of *k'dushah*, "holiness," that infuse our lives. There are blessings to recite before eating and drinking; performing religious commandments; witnessing rainbows, oceans, thunder, or lightning; seeing old friends; tasting new fruits; and arriving at a new season. And yet many of the most important moments in the lives of transgender, intersex, and gender-queer Jews are not honored within our tradition.

I wrote this blessing for a friend who wanted to mark each time that he received testosterone (hormone therapy), but it could be used for any moment in transitioning such as name or pronoun changes, coming out to loved ones, or moments of medical transitions. Jewish sacred texts such as the Mishnah, the Talmud, midrash, and classical legal codes acknowledge the diversity of gender identities in our communities, despite the way that mainstream Jewish religious tradition has effaced the experiences of transgender, intersex, and gender-queer Jews. This blessing signals the holiness present in the moments of transitioning that transform Jewish lives and affirms the place of these moments within Jewish sacred tradition.

This blessing takes the same form and grammatical structure as classical blessings that mark wondrous occasions. "The Transforming One" as a name for God appears in the traditional blessings of gratitude that are recited each morning. The Hebrew verb root of this word, *avar*, has multiple layers of meaning within Judaism. Most literally it means to physically cross over; however, it also implies spiritual transformation in High Holy Day prayers. It lies at the root of the word *Ivrim*, Hebrew people. We are the *Ivrim*, the crossing-over people, because we physically crossed over the Jordan River to escape from slavery and oppression and we spiritually transformed ourselves. At its core, our ancestral sacred memory holds this moment of painful and yet redemptive physical and spiritual transition. In Modern Hebrew, this same verb root is used to form the word *maavar*, which means to transition genders.

The second blessing is also taken from morning liturgy. It is based on the Book of Genesis, which teaches that male and female bodies were equally created in God's image. The midrash, classical Jewish exegesis, adds that the *adam harishon*, the first human being formed in God's likeness, was an *androgynos*, an intersex person. Hence our tradition teaches that *all* bodies and genders are created in God's image whether we identify as men, women, intersex, or something else. When we take physical or spiritual steps to more honestly manifest our gender identities, we are fulfilling the foundational mitzvah, religious commandment, to be partnered with God in completing the work of Creation.

The final blessing is classically recited each time we reach a new event or season. Saying it at moments of transition celebrates God's nurturing and sustaining presence in allowing us to reach this moment of self-transformation. However, this blessing is in the first person plural and also marks our collective transition as a people as we begin to transform our tradition in order to honor and celebrate the lives of transgender, intersex, and gender-queer Jews.

- This blessing may be recited before any moment in the transitioning process:

בָּרוּךְ אַתָּה יְיָ, אֱלֹהֵינוּ מֶלֶךְ הָעוֹלָם, הַמַּעֲבִיר לְעוֹבְרִים.

Baruch atah Adonai Eloheinu Melech haolam, haMaavir l'ovrim.

Blessed are You, Eternal One our God, Ruler of time and space, the Transforming One to those who transform/transition/cross over.

- Afterwards recite:

בָּרוּךְ אַתָּה יְיָ, אֱלֹהֵינוּ מֶלֶךְ הָעוֹלָם, שֶׁעָשַׂנִי בְּצֶלֶם אֱלֹהִים.

Baruch atah Adonai, Eloheinu Melech haolam, she-asani b'tzelem Elohim.

Blessed are You, Eternal One our God, Ruler of time and space, who has made me in God's image.

- For special events taking place for the first time or for the first time in this season (e.g., a name or pronoun change, beginning hormone therapies or surgeries), add:

בָּרוּךְ אַתָּה יְיָ, אֱלֹהֵינוּ מֶלֶךְ הָעוֹלָם, שֶׁהֶחֱיָנוּ וְקִיְּמָנוּ וְהִגִּיעָנוּ לַזְּמַן הַזֶּה:

Baruch atah Adonai, Eloheinu Melech haolam, shehecheyanu, v'kiy'manu, v'higianu laz'man hazeh.

Blessed are You, Eternal One our God, Ruler of time and space, who has kept us alive and sustained us and helped us to arrive at this moment.

Liturgical Resources

A "Commentary" on Leviticus 19
(Known in Judaism as the Holiness Code)

Rabbi Lisa A. Edwards, Ph.D.

We are your gay, lesbian, bisexual, transgendered children:
"You shall not take vengeance or bear a grudge against members of your people." [Leviticus 19:18]

We are your bi, trans, lesbian, and gay parents:
"You shall each revere your mother and your father. . . ." [Leviticus 19:3]

We are older lesbians, bisexuals, gay men, and transgendered people:
"You shall rise before the aged and show deference to the old. . . ." [Leviticus 19:32]

We are the stranger:
"You must not oppress the stranger." [Based on Leviticus 19:33]
"When strangers reside with you in your land, you shall not wrong them." [Leviticus 19:33]
"The strangers who reside with you shall be to you as your citizens; you shall love each one as yourself, for you were strangers in the land of Egypt. . . ." [Leviticus 19:34]

We are lesbian, gay, trans, and bi Jews:
"Do not deal basely with members of your people. . . ." [Leviticus 19:16]

We are your trans, gay, bi, and lesbian siblings:
"You shall not hate your kinfolk in your heart." [Leviticus 19:17]

We are lesbian, gay, trans, and bi victims of gay bashing and murder:
"Do not profit by the blood of your fellow. . . ." [Leviticus 19:16]

We are your bi, gay, trans, and lesbian neighbors:
"You shall not defraud your fellow." [Leviticus 19:13]
"You shall not render an unfair decision. . . ." [Leviticus 19:15]
"Love your fellow as yourself." [Leviticus 19:18]

Maariv Aravim

Written for Pride Shabbat by Rabbi Lisa A. Edwards, Ph.D.

Blessed are You, Eternal One our God, Spirit of the world, Creator of day and night, of wind and rain, of sun and moon, of stars and seasons.

It was You who spread a rainbow across the sky as an *ot hab'rit*, a sign of the covenant between You and all living things, telling us then and forever that all of us are Your creation, blessed and approved of by You. Loving and enduring God, remember Your rainbow, and remind us that it is a symbol of Your covenant, of Your love, of Your brilliant creativity, and of the endless variety of Your creations.

Blessed are You, Almighty One, who makes the colors of light shine forth—a vision of Your glory.

V'ahavta

Written for Pride Shabbat by Rabbi Lisa A. Edwards, Ph.D.

A little bit shy, God told Moses to tell us:
Love God with all your heart, with every breath you take,
with as much as is in you.
Willing to share the wealth, God also told Moses to tell us:
Love your neighbor as you love yourself.
God's requests tell us some things about love:
They tell us that it's OK to ask for what we want.
They tell us that even God sometimes needs a spokesperson.
They tell us that we can't always know what others want unless they ask.
They tell us that love has no borders—one can love God with all one has, and still have love available for everyone else, and still have love available to love oneself.
If we take God's words to heart, then our struggle is also our reward: unconditional love.
Love without borders.

Modim Supplement

Written for Pride Shabbat by Rabbi Lisa A. Edwards, Ph.D.

In the days before Stonewall, many GLBT Jews were among those who felt the sting of prejudice, who suffered from misunderstanding and rejection by family and Jewish community. But You, Creator of us all, stand firm, reminding us what happened on the sixth day of Creation: *Vayivra Elohim et haadam b'tzalmo, b'tzelem Elohim bara oto, zachar un'keivah bara otam*, "So God created the human beings in [the divine] image, creating [them] in the image of God, creating them male and female" [Genesis 1:27]. Until many came to understand that You do not create in vain, do not create without intent; until many of us came to understand that we too are part of Your design, loved equally by You. And the more we have learned and understood, the more has Pride returned to our spirit and the more our Spirits have turned toward You, Holy One of Blessing. We pray for the day when *kol han'shamah t'haleil Yah*, when all spirits, "every soul that breathes shall praise You" [Psalm 150:6] and admire Your diverse creations.

Sh'ma/V'ahavta

Adapted from Deuteronomy 6:4–9 by Bracha Yael, Congregant of Beth Chayim Chadashim, Los Angeles

Hear O Israel!

Just as God is One, so are We!

Just as you shall love your God with all your heart, with all your soul, and with all your might, so shall you love all people. Teach love, compassion, and understanding to your children when you sit in your home, while you walk on your way, when you retire, and when you arise. Bind these words as a sign upon your arm so that you may fight against prejudice, between your eyes so that you may not be blind to the suffering of others, and write them on the doorposts of your homes and gates so that you remind yourself and others that intolerance will not be tolerated within these walls.

Aleinu

Excerpted from *Mahzor Ubecharta Chaim*, Congregation Sha'ar Zahav, San Francisco

We are called to praise the Ruler of all things, and to magnify the Creator of all beginnings, who has made all people different, and has given us each a special destiny; who has led our souls to worship the one God of all creation, and who has formed our hearts to love in our own unique way. . . .

And so our hope, our Almighty God, is that all peoples abandon their empty worship of human bigotry, and cease the blasphemy of calling on Your Name to justify oppression and hatred. Speedily turn all hearts to You, and soften our human arrogance, and make the lives of all women and men a source of honor to Your glorious Name; for Your rule is meant to make all Your creation a reflection of Your glory, as it is written, "God will reign forever in all things." And it is said, "Adonai will be Ruler over all the earth; for in that day God will be one, and will be called by one Name."

History of the Reform Movement's Positions on GLBT Issues

There have been over forty years worth of documents from the Reform Movement on issues facing gay, lesbian, bisexual, and transgender Jews. This chapter provides nearly every statement on GLBT issues from the Union for Reform Judaism (URJ, formerly the Union of American Hebrew Congregations [UAHC]), the Central Conference of American Rabbis (CCAR), the Commission on Social Action (CSA), the North American Federation of Temple Youth (NFTY), Women of Reform Judaism (WRJ), the American Conference of Cantors (ACC), and the National Association of Temple Educators (NATE).

Documents in this section range from official Reform Movement statements, to excerpts from speeches and articles, to resolutions to responsa. We have also included a tribute to Rabbi Alexander Schindler *(z˝l)* and an excerpt from one of his speeches. As president of the UAHC in the 1980s, he was instrumental in advocating for the inclusion of gay and lesbian people in Jewish communal life, and without him, neither the original *Kulanu* nor this revision would exist.

Another important pair of documents that we have included are the two responsa from the CCAR on homosexual marriage, which are now seen to be more conservative than the current stance of the Reform Movement. We have included the long and detailed 1996 responsum "On Homosexual Marriage" in its entirety, not only because we feel it is a valuable historical document, but because the thought process in the responsum is instructive for how Reform Jews can grapple with difficult issues.

Since one of the central tenets of Reform Judaism is the capacity to adjust and adapt based on new information, a main purpose of this section is to show how the Reform Movement has developed over time with regard GLBT issues. As such, this section allows people to see almost everything that the Reform Movement has said on GLBT issues over the last forty years—all in one place.

Tribute to Rabbi Alexander M. Schindler (1995)

Rabbi Margaret Moers Wenig

To appreciate the magnitude of the support Rabbi Alexander Schindler and the Union of American Hebrew Congregations have offered lesbian and gay Jews, in fact, all gay men and lesbians in America, we have to remember what it was like to be gay in America *before* Rabbi Schindler became president of the UAHC.

In the 1950s and '60s:

- Gay people were banned from civil service jobs.[1]
- Thousands of gay federal employees were fired (800 between 1953 and 1955 alone).[2]
- Tens of thousands were entrapped by undercover police officers or arrested in police raids (made possible by laws prohibiting homosexuals from dancing, even gathering in any state licensed public place).
- Lesbians and gay men were denied state licenses to teach.
- [Lesbian and gay men were] Not admitted to the bar to practice law.
- [Lesbian and gay men were] Denied U.S. citizenship.
- [Lesbian and gay men were] Denied custody of their children.
- The Motion Picture Production Code prohibited films from including gay characters, and from even using the word "homosexual."
- Betty Friedan and the leadership of NOW deemed lesbians a threat to the women's movement.
- Sodomy was a crime in most states. Gay people were demonized in the press as perverts and child molesters or considered psychologically ill. Many voluntarily subjected themselves to electroshock aversion therapy in their attempts to be cured.

Address given by Rabbi Margaret Moers Wenig to honor Rabbi Alexander M. Schindler upon his impending retirement, Religious Action Center of Reform Judaism's Consultation on Conscience—May 2, 1995.

1. The Civil Service Commission did not officially change its policy of discriminating against lesbians and gay men until 1973 when it decreed that "homosexual employees of federal agencies would be judged unsuitable only if their conduct was found to affect job fitness." The euphemism "immoral conduct" was not removed from the list of disqualifications for federal employment until 1975 (Sue Fox, "In the '50's, a Community Emerged," *The Washington Blade,* March 10, 1995, p. 10).
2. "According to Senate documents, between 1953–55 more than 800 federal employees were accused of 'sex perversion' and dismissed from their jobs" (ibid.).

- In synagogues, there was no safe place for lesbian and gay Jews. To come out of the closet, most left Judaism. Psychological tests were used to weed out lesbian and gay applicants to the Hebrew Union College–Jewish Institute of Religion, and those who escaped detection lived in fear of being discovered later on. Some were, and were expelled or fired. Many left the rabbinate.

Imagine the fear of being caught merely reading a gay book. Imagine not being able to walk down the street holding your partner's hand. Imagine having to pretend, at work, that nothing has happened when your lover is ill, or dies, or has a baby.

Following the passage of the 1964 Civil Rights Act, when gay men and lesbians began public demonstrations to repeal sodomy laws and to end legal discrimination, no national Jewish leader walked side-by-side with leaders of the gay community.[3] Only one national Jewish organization called for the decriminalization of sodomy—that was the National Federation of Temple Sisterhoods in 1965![4]

Nineteen-seventy-three, however, the year Rabbi Schindler became President of the UAHC, will go down in gay history and gay Jewish history as a watershed: It was the year the American Psychiatric Association removed homosexuality from its list of psychiatric disorders and it was the year that Metropolitan Community Temple (later Beth Chayim Chadashim), a newly-formed synagogue for lesbian and gay Jews returning to Judaism, applied to the UAHC for membership.

Over the course of Rabbi Schindler's presidency the Reform Movement radically transformed its attitude toward homosexuality:

- Admitting to membership in the UAHC the first gay synagogue in history (over the objection of the CCAR)[5]
- Supporting legislation to decriminalize sodomy and protect gay people from discrimination[6]
- Responding to the AIDS crisis[7]
- Welcoming lesbian and gay Jews to membership in mainstream congregations[8]
- Eliminating the ban against lesbians and gay men in the rabbinate[9]
- Promoting equal employment opportunities within the Reform Movement[10]
- Opposing discrimination against gays in the military[11] and by the Boy Scouts[12]
- Responding to anti-gay rights referenda[13]

---

3. There was no official Jewish presence (though there were thousands of Jews) at the national marches on Washington for lesbian and gay rights in 1979 or 1987.
4. The other arms of the Reform Movement didn't follow suit until twelve years later.
5. Freehof Responsum, 1973.
6. Resolutions of the National Federation of Temple Sisterhoods (1965), the Central Conference of American Rabbis (1977), the UAHC (1977), and the National Federation of Temple Youth (1983).
7. Resolutions of the UAHC (1985, 1986, 1987).
8. Resolutions of the UAHC (1987 and 1989), Women of Reform Judaism (Formerly NFTS) (1991).
9. Report of the CCAR Ad Hoc Committee on Homosexuality (accepted June 1990).
10. Resolutions of the Commission on Social Action (1991), the National Association of Temple Educators (1991), and the American Conference of Cantors (1991).
11. Resolution of the Commission on Social Action (1991).
12. Letter from Rabbi Alexander Schindler to the Boy Scouts (1992–1993), and resolutions of the Executive Boards of the CCAR (1992) and NFTY (1992).
13. Resolutions of the UAHC (1993) and of the CCAR (1993).

- Calling for spousal benefits for gay couples and legal means of acknowledging our relationships.[14]

The struggle is by no means over. The anti-gay backlash currently sweeping the country is every bit as virulent as was Anita Bryant's crusade in 1977. We have not completed the task but we can say with pride that every arm of the Reform Movement has grappled with this issue: in the pages of *Reform Judaism* and *Keeping Posted*; in our youth groups and at our camps; in our seminaries and professional associations; at Political Action Seminars and Consultations; at regional biennials and at every UAHC General Assembly since 1985; on UAHC committees, boards, commissions; and in our congregations. Rabbi Schindler, himself, installed the rabbi of the world's largest lesbian and gay synagogue. Over half a dozen gay synagogues are now members of the UAHC, and over one hundred mainstream Reform congregations say they would admit gay couples to family membership.[15] When asked, many rabbis have agreed to bless our committed relationships, name our babies, celebrate our anniversaries. Several congregations have retained and a few have even hired openly gay rabbis or cantors. The UAHC has openly lesbian and gay staff members.

All this has happened during Rabbi Schindler's tenure as president.

It might not have happened were it not for the perseverance of many of you who wrote and spoke, lobbied and organized, who formed gay synagogues and who served them, who came out to Alex or who told him about your gay siblings or gay children. You who urged and helped the UAHC fashion its positions—all this would not have happened without you. But neither could it have happened without Alex, without his leadership, his public, national, unwavering, uncompromising, bold leadership.

He resisted speculations about etiology.

He did not pity lesbians and gay men on the grounds that we "had no other choice."

He did not ask us to remain celibate.

He did not counsel us to remain invisible.

He did not relegate us to second-class status.

He did not maintain a double standard, exempting our own Reform Movement from extending rights it demanded that governments extend.

He did not keep silent when the actions of the UAHC were less forthright than our resolutions. He called on the UAHC to fulfill the promises it had made and to expand them.[16]

He boldly risked condemnation from the Orthodox and opposition from within the Reform Movement.

He courageously interpreted the written Torah through the lens of the Torah of life.[17]

---

14. Rabbi Schindler's Presidential Address to the 62nd General Assembly of the UAHC, October 21–25, 1993, San Francisco, CA, "Lifelong Learning: The Path to Informed Choices," pp. 16–17 and resolutions of the UAHC (1993) and the Commission on Social Action (1995). The CSA's resolution supports the legalization of lesbian and gay marriage.
15. Of 294 congregations responding to a survey, 170 replied that the issue of family membership for lesbian or gay couples had never been raised. Eleven said the matter was currently under discussion. One hundred four, among them many congregations in which the topic had not been raised, asserted that full membership had been or would be offered under any circumstances. "Gay and Lesbian Couples in Reform Congregations: Member Status. A UAHC Committee on the Jewish Family Special Report," by Rabbi Sanford Seltzer, 1994.
16. "The Covenant of the Generations," Rabbi Alexander M. Schindler's Presidential Address, 60th General Assembly of the UAHC, Nov. 2–6, 1989, New Orleans, LA, p. 11.
17. Address by Rabbi Alexander M. Schindler at a Jewish Community Service in Support of People With AIDS, sponsored by the AIDS Committee of the UAHC–Pacific Southwest Council, at Leo Baeck Temple, in Los Angeles, CA, March 12, 1989, p. 7.

He welcomed us as full and active members of Reform congregations, as singles, as couples, as families with "no limits on our communal or spiritual aspirations."[18]

Rabbi Alexander Schindler listened to those who were calling for change and he understood. And when, finally, he spoke, lives were forever changed!

In March 1989, Los Angeles, at a Jewish community service in support of people with AIDS, Rabbi Schindler confessed:

> AIDS has revealed a deficiency in our Jewish community's own immune system—we are not immune to prejudice. . . .

And then like a prophet, he adjured us:

> We who were beaten in the streets of Berlin, cannot turn away from the plague of gay bashing. We who were Marranos in Madrid, who clung to the closet of assimilation and conversion in order to live without molestation, cannot deny the demand for gay and lesbian visibility. . . .

And then he proclaimed:

> I declare myself a rabbi for all Jews—at every moment of life, not only for heterosexual Jews or for gay Jews only at their funerals. I declare myself a consoler for those who have passed through the valley of the shadow of death accompanying friends and loved ones on their last painful journey. I declare myself the compassionate ally of every heterosexual and homosexual who is wrestling with the shame, the confusion, the fear . . . involved in the inner struggle for sexual identity. It is a struggle that includes but also goes beyond civil liberties. It is, when all is said and done, a struggle for the integrity of selfhood.[19]

Alex, you have been our consoler. You have been our compatriot. You have been our compassionate ally. You have been our rabbi. You have been our hero. Thank you!

---

18. "The Covenant of the Generations," p. 12.
19. Address at a Jewish community service in support of people with AIDS, pp. 4–6.

Including Gay and Lesbian Jews (1989)

Rabbi Alexander M. Schindler

Yes, our resolutions express our resolve to act. There is one realm, however, in which our resolutions have been forthright, but our actions considerably less so. I speak now of the plea of gay and lesbian Jews for fuller acceptance in our midst.

I know that I raise a subject which will make many here feel uncomfortable, but this is precisely why I must raise it. Our discomfort is a measure of our continuing prejudice. I do not exclude myself from this harsh decree, for in thinking about what I would say on this subject, I had to wrestle with demons in the depths of my own being, demons I never acknowledged were there. Let us admit it, then: that in spite of past declarations urging the contrary, the singling out of homosexuality from the whole human constellation as a loathsome affliction remains a widespread sentiment in our midst.

True enough, over fifteen years ago, we admitted the first synagogue with an outreach to gay and lesbian Jews into the UAHC, and we have added three since. Gay men and lesbians by the hundreds who had felt themselves alienated from Judaism have joined these congregations and have added their strength and commitment to our religious community. But in most mainstream congregations, we have not extended our embrace to include gay and lesbian Jews. We have not acknowledged their presence in the midst of our synagogues. We have not dispelled the myth of the "corrupting homosexual" or the counselor or teacher who would fashion children in his or her sexual image. And we have not consciously included gay and lesbian parents as part of the Jewish family circle.

To be sure, many of us feel pity for gays and lesbians, and we agree, intellectually, that it is a grievous wrong to stigmatize them, to ostracize them, to hold them in moral disdain. But something more than a grasp of the mind is required; there is a need for a grasp of the heart. Something different from pity is called for; we need, as a community, to cross those boundaries of Otherness, those fringed boundaries where compassion gives way to identification.

Indeed, we have not affirmed that we *all* are family. We speak of "them" and "us," as though gay men and women were descended from a distant planet. If those who have studied these matters are correct, one-half million of our fellow Jews, no less than one

---

Excerpt from the Presidential Keynote Address presented to the Biennial Assembly of the Union of American Hebrew Congregations, November 4, 1989, New Orleans, LA.

hundred thousand Reform Jews, are gay. They are our fellow congregants, our friends and committee members and yes, our leaders both professional and lay. Whether we know it or not, whether we acknowledge it or not, some of them are our sisters and brothers, our daughters and our sons.

In our denial, in our failure to see one another as one family indeed, as one holy body—we forget Jewish history, we opt for amnesia. We who were beaten in the streets of Berlin cannot turn away from the plague of gay bashing. We who were Marranos in Madrid, who clung to the closet of assimilation and conversion in order to live without molestation, we cannot deny the demand for gay and lesbian visibility!

I know full well what our literal tradition has to say on the subject. Yet built within it is the possibility of change, once advancing knowledge enlarges our understanding. There was a time—so our colleague Gene Mihaly instructed us—when deaf-mutes were considered mentally incompetent and, hence, denied the right to participate in the religious life. But no less an authority than Maimonides was prepared to lift this restriction when deaf-mutes give evidence of a capacity to learn; he codified the flexibility provided by the Talmudic sages themselves. Similarly, the Bible enjoins us to sequester lepers, to isolate them. Like AIDS patients today, they were not only shunned but told that they suffer only because they sinned. Yet few indeed are the *poskim*, the halachic decisors, of today who would enforce the biblical ostracism of lepers. Then why are we and especially we Reform Jews, not willing to set aside the halachic disposals of homosexuality in order to reflect equally our newer knowledge?

In any event, the Torah has many strands; seen singly, they do not reveal the whole; the tapestry must be seen in all its wondrous fullness. There is one text, but there are others, and beyond them, there is their interpretation, which is never fixed but ever in flux. Yes, there is the reproving God who visited His wrath upon the men of Sodom; but there is also the loving God who enjoins us not to "stand idly by while our neighbor perishes." Our Torah has many faces, but the most authentic is the one that reflects its heart.

Our Rabbinic Conference, through its Committee on Homosexuality, which has yet to render a final report—has called on the Union to embark on a "movement-wide program of heightened awareness and study." Very well! I support its summons to do so, hence my comments on the subject. I endorse the notion of dialogue and education in regard to sensitive issues. But education in a vacuum is not enough. Ultimately, there must be a policy enunciated by which the many gay and lesbian Jews of our community can know that they are accepted on terms of visibility, not invisibility. Ultimately, they must know that we place no limits on their communal or spiritual aspirations.

In all of this, I am working to make the Reform Jewish community a home: a place where loneliness and suffering and exile ends; a place that leaves it to God to validate relationships and demands of us only that these relationships be worthy in His eyes; a place where we can search, together, through the written Torah and the Torah of life, to find those affirmations for which we yearn.

Resolution of the Women of Reform Judaism National Federation of Temple Sisterhoods 25th Biennial Assembly, 1965: Homosexuality

The Bible treats homosexuality as an "abomination" (cf. Lev. 18:22, 20:13) and penalties for its practice were severe. Today, however, enlightened men understand that homosexuality may be a symptom of psychiatric disturbance which requires sympathetic understanding and psychiatric evaluation.

We, therefore, deplore the tendency on the part of community authorities to harass homosexuals. We associate ourselves with those religious leaders and legal experts who urge revisions in the criminal code as it relates to homosexuality, especially when it exists between consenting adults. While the young or nonconsenting person must be protected from the advances of disturbed individuals, the aberrations of such individuals must be considered as expressions of possible illness rather than of criminality. We further urge that all available resources of society be brought to bear on the alleviation of this problem.

According to Rabbi Yoel Kahn, in a 1989 article, this resolution was passed, but never implemented, because the UAHC never passed the resolution on which this was based at its own 1965 Biennial convention.

Yoel Kahn, "Judaism and Homosexuality: The Traditionist/Progressive Debate," *Journal of Homosexuality* 18, no. 3/4 (1989).

Resolution Adopted by the 45th General Assembly of the Union of American Hebrew Congregations Biennial, 1977: Human Rights of Homosexuals

WHEREAS the UAHC has consistently supported civil rights and civil liberties for all persons, and

WHEREAS the Constitution guarantees civil rights to all individuals,

BE IT, THEREFORE, RESOLVED THAT homosexual persons are entitled to equal protection under the law. We oppose discriminating against homosexuals in areas of opportunity, including employment and housing. We call upon our society to see that such protection is provided in actuality.

BE IT FURTHER RESOLVED THAT we affirm our belief that private sexual acts between consenting adults are not the proper province of government and law enforcement agencies.

BE IT FURTHER RESOLVED THAT we urge congregations to conduct appropriate educational programming for youth and adults so as to provide a greater understanding of the relation of Jewish values to the range of human sexuality.

Union of American Hebrew Congregations 45th General Assembly, "Resolution Adopted on Human Rights of Homosexuals" (San Francisco, 1977), http://www.urj.org.

Resolution Adopted by the Central Conference of American Rabbis 88th Annual Convention, 1977: Rights of Homosexuals

WHEREAS, the Central Conference of American Rabbis has consistently supported civil rights and civil liberties for all people, especially for those from whom these rights and liberties have been withheld, and

WHEREAS, homosexuals have in our society long endured discrimination,

BE IT THEREFORE RESOLVED, that we encourage legislation which decriminalizes homosexual acts between consenting adults, and prohibits discrimination against them as persons, and

BE IT FURTHER RESOLVED, that our Reform Jewish religious organizations undertake programs in cooperation with the total Jewish community to implement the above stand.

Central Conference of American Rabbis 88th Annual Convention, "Resolution Adopted on Rights of Homosexuals" (1977), http://www.ccarnet.org.

Resolution Adopted by the National Federation of Temple Youth, 1983: Homosexuality

Resolved

That homosexuals are entitled to equal protection under the law, and NFTY, in accordance, opposes discrimination against homosexuals and urges the public to affirm this opposition by providing protection from such discrimination, and

That NFTY urge its member youth groups to study the issue of homosexuality, the Jewish view of homosexuality and to educate the community by designing programming for adults and youth on the topic of homosexuality.

Resolution Adopted by the 59th General Assembly of the Union of American Hebrew Congregations Biennial, 1987: Support for Inclusion of Lesbian and Gay Jews

Background

God calls upon us to love our neighbors as ourselves. The prophet Isaiah charges us further: "Let my house be called a house of prayer, for all people . . ." (Isaiah 56:7). And, armed with the other teachings of our faith, we Jews are asked to create a society based on righteousness, the goal being *tikkun olam*, the perfection of our world. Each of us, created in God's image, has a unique talent which can contribute to that high moral purpose; and to exclude any Jew from the community of Israel lessens our chances of achieving that goal.

In consonance with these teachings, in 1977 the Union of American Hebrew Congregations resolved to support and defend the civil and human rights of homosexuals, and we have welcomed into the UAHC congregations with special outreach to lesbian and gay Jews. But we must do more.

Sexual orientation should not be a criterion for membership or participation in an activity of any synagogue. Thus, all Jews should be welcome, however they may define themselves.

Service of lesbian and gay Jews as rabbis is currently under consideration by the Central Conference of American Rabbis. It has appointed a Committee on Homosexuality in the Rabbinate to consider all aspects of the subject. The committee is directed to present a final report at the 1989 CCAR convention. Representatives of the UAHC and the Hebrew Union College–Jewish Institute of Religion are serving on the committee.

Union of American Hebrew Congregations 59th General Assembly, "Resolution Adopted on Support for Inclusion of Lesbian and Gay Jews" (Chicago, 1987), http://www.urj.org.

THEREFORE, BE IT RESOLVED that the Union of American Hebrew Congregations:

1. Urge its congregations and affiliates to:
    A. Encourage lesbian and gay Jews to share and participate in the worship, leadership, and general congregational life of all synagogues.
    B. Continue to develop educational programs in the synagogue and community which promote understanding and respect for lesbians and gays.
    C. Employ people without regard to sexual orientation.
2. Urge the Commission on Social Action to bring its recommendations to the next General Assembly after considering the report of the CCAR committee and any action of the CCAR pursuant to it.
3. Recommend to the CCAR Committee on Liturgy that it develop language that is liturgically inclusive.

Resolution Adopted by the 60th General Assembly of the Union of American Hebrew Congregations Biennial, 1989: Gay and Lesian Jews

In North America today, it is estimated that 100,000 Reform Jews—and 500,000 members of the larger Jewish community—are gay or lesbian.

Over the last fifteen years, the UAHC has admitted to membership four synagogues with an outreach to gay and lesbian Jews. Hundreds of men and women who once felt themselves alienated from Judaism and unwelcome in mainstream congregations have joined these synagogues, adding their strength and commitment to our religious community.

In 1977, the UAHC General Assembly called for an end to discrimination against homosexuals, and expanded upon this in 1987 by calling for full inclusion of gay and lesbian Jews in all aspects of synagogue life.

While that resolution urged that congregations not discriminate in employment, it did not address rabbinic employment, pending the report of the CCAR ad hoc Committee on Homosexuality and the Rabbinate. The CCAR Committee continues its work, and we eagerly await its report.

Within the larger context of UAHC congregational life, however, we have yet to shed the destructive anti-gay and anti-lesbian prejudices and stereotypes that preclude a genuine embrace of the heart.

Our union of congregations must be a place where loneliness and suffering and exile end, where gay and lesbian Jews can know that they are accepted on terms of visibility, not invisibility; that we place no limits on their communal or spiritual aspirations.

THEREFORE, the Union of American Hebrew Congregations resolves to:
1. Reaffirm its 1987 resolution and call upon all departments of the UAHC and our member congregations to fully implement its provisions.
2. Embark upon a movement-wide program of heightened awareness and education to achieve the fuller acceptance of gay and lesbian Jews in our midst.
3. Urge our member congregations to welcome gay and lesbian Jews to membership, as singles, couples and families.

Union of American Hebrew Congregations 60th General Assembly, "Resolution Adopted on Gay and Lesbian Jews" (New Orleans, 1989), http://www.urj.org.

4. Commend the CCAR for its sensitive and thorough efforts to raise the consciousness of the rabbinate regarding homosexuality. We urge the CCAR to pursue its own mandate with vigor and complete its tasks as soon as possible in order to respond to the communal and spiritual aspirations of gay and lesbian Jews.

Report of the Ad Hoc Committee on Homosexuality and the Rabbinate of the Central Conference of American Rabbis Annual Convention, 1990

Composition of the Committee

Chair: Selig Salkowitz, Norman J. Cohen, A. Stanley Dreyfus (RPC), Joseph B. Glaser (CCAR), Walter Jacob, Yoel H. Kahn, Samuel E. Karff, Peter S. Knobel, Joseph Levine, Jack Stern, Richard S. Sternberger (UAHC), Ronald B. Sobel (RPC), Elliot L. Stevens (CCAR), Harvey M. Tattelbaum, Albert Vorspan (UAHC), Margaret M. Wenig, Gary Zola (HUC-JIR)

Origin of the Committee

The committee was formed in response to a resolution proposed by Margaret Holub (then student rabbi) and Margaret Wenig for the June, 1986, convention of the Central Conference of American Rabbis in Snowmass, Colorado. The proposed resolution dealt with the admissions policies of the Hebrew Union College–Jewish Institute of Religion and of the Central Conference of American Rabbis and with the placement policy of the Rabbinical Placement Commission. The matter was referred for further study.

Given the seriousness of the issues and the broad implications for the Reform rabbinate and for the entire Movement, President Jack Stern appointed a broadly representative ad hoc committee and named Selig Salkowitz as its chair. The committee's first meeting took place in the Fall of 1986. Following that meeting, in order to insure adequate institutional participation, the committee invited the Union of American Hebrew Congregations, the Hebrew Union College–Jewish Institute of Religion and the Rabbinical Placement Commission to appoint official representatives. The committee has met regularly during the past four years. Through extensive study and discussion, the committee has sought to arrive at a unified position on homosexuality and the rabbinate. From the outset, the committee was keenly aware of both the controversial nature and the complexity of the issues. The committee's deliberations have been characterized by vigorous debate carried on in a spirit of warm collegiality. All members found themselves profoundly moved. However, the committee did not achieve consensus on every issue, and recognized that there are legitimate differences of opinion. The committee calls upon members of the Conference to be sensitive to and accepting of those whose positions differ from their own.

The committee undertook a comprehensive investigation of the subject. Its members read studies on the origin and nature of sexual identity, and of homosexuality specifically, and reviewed some of the contemporary legal literature, and studied documents prepared by Christian groups grappling with the status of homosexuals and homosexuality within their own denominations with a specific focus on the question of ordination. Yoel H. Kahn prepared an extensive anthology of articles on Judaism and homosexuality which cut across denominational lines. The committee commissioned Eugene B. Borowitz, Yoel H. Kahn, Robert S. Kirschner and Peter S. Knobel to prepare working papers.[1] Consultations were held with leaders of other Jewish streams. The committee solicited and received anonymous personal testimony from gay and lesbian rabbis and rabbinic students. It reviewed the admissions policies of the College-Institute and the Central Conference of American Rabbis as well as the placement policy of the Rabbinical Placement Commission. It read previous resolutions of the UAHC Biennial Conventions and the CCAR conventions, and related Reform Responsa. The work of previous committees was also reviewed. It convened a late night information session at the Tarpon Springs Convention of 1987; submitted a draft resolution to the CCAR Executive Board in 1988 (which was sent back to the committee for further consideration); sponsored a plenary session at the Centennial Convention in Cincinnati in 1989 at which Leonard S. Kravitz and Yoel H. Kahn presented papers[2] followed by workshops; held consultations at each of the regional CCAR Kallot and with MaRaM; requested that the UAHC sponsor workshops at upcoming regional biennials.

This document is meant to summarize the results of our deliberations, to indicate areas of agreement and disagreement and to encourage further discussion and understanding. It represents four years of struggle and growth. We hope that it will serve as a model for those who take up these matters upon which we have diligently and painstakingly deliberated.

Concern for Gay and Lesbian Colleagues

The committee is acutely aware that the inability of most gay and lesbian rabbis to live openly as homosexuals is deeply painful. Therefore, the committee wishes to avoid any action which will cause greater distress to our colleagues. As a result, the committee has

---

1. *Homosexuality, the Rabbinate, and Liberal Judaism: Papers Prepared for the Ad-Hoc Committee on Homosexuality and the Rabbinate.* Selig Salkowitz, Chair. *Halakhah and Homosexuality: A Reappraisal* by Robert Kirschner. *On Homosexuality and the Rabbinate, a Covenantal Response* by Eugene B. Borowitz. *Judaism and Homosexuality* by Yoel H. Kahn. *Homosexuality: A Liberal Jewish Theological and Ethical Reflection* by Peter S. Knobel. Copies of these were distributed to the entire Central Conference of American Rabbis prior to the June, 1989 convention in Cincinnati. These papers should be consulted for a description of the range of positions considered by the Committee.

2. *Homosexuality and the Rabbinate.* Yoel H. Kahn, *The Kedusha of Homosexual Relationships* and Leonard S. Kravitz, *Address.* The papers were distributed to the members of the Conference through the regional presidents as material for discussion at the regional kallot. They should be consulted for an understanding of the two different approaches to the subject of the religious status of homosexual relationships.

determined that a comprehensive report is in the best interest of our Conference and the Reform Movement as a whole.

Publicly acknowledging one's homosexuality is a personal decision which can have grave professional consequences. Therefore, in the light of the limited ability of the Placement Commission or the Central Conference of American Rabbis to guarantee the tenure of the gay or lesbian rabbis who "come out of the closet," the committee does not want to encourage colleagues to put their careers at risk. Regrettably, a decision to declare oneself publicly can have potentially negative effects on a person's ability to serve a given community effectively. In addition, the committee is anxious to avoid a situation in which pulpit selection committees will request information on the sexual orientation of candidates. The Committee urges that all rabbis, regardless of sexual orientation, be accorded the opportunity to fulfill the sacred vocation which they have chosen.

Civil Rights For Gays and Lesbians

All human beings are created *betselem elohim* ("in the divine image"). Their personhood must therefore be accorded full dignity. Sexual orientation is irrelevant to the human worth of a person. Therefore, the Reform Movement has supported vigorously all efforts to eliminate discrimination in housing and employment.[3] The Committee unequivocally condemns verbal and physical abuse against gay men and lesbian women or those perceived to be gay or lesbian. We reject any implication that AIDS can be understood as God's punishment of homosexuals. We applaud the fine work of the gay and lesbian outreach synagogues, and we, along with the Union of American Hebrew Congregations, call upon rabbis and congregations to treat with respect and to integrate fully all Jews into the life of the community regardless of sexual orientation.

Origin and Nature of Sexual Identity

The committee's task was made particularly difficult because the specific origin of sexual identity and its etiology are still imperfectly understood.

> Scholars are not likely to come to an agreement anytime soon about the causes of sexual orientation, or its nature. Various disciplines look at sexuality in different ways and rarely confront each other's ideas. . . . Short of definitive evidence, which no theory has thus far received, the disagreement is likely to continue. Cognitive and normative pluralism will persist for the indefinite future.[4]

The lack of unanimity in the scientific community and the unanimous condemnation of homosexual behavior by Jewish tradition added to the complexity. It is clear, however, that for many people sexual orientation is not a matter of conscious choice but constitutional and

---

3. CCAR resolution 1977. UAHC resolutions 1975, 1985, 1987, 1989.
4. David Greenberg, *The Construction of Homosexuality* (Chicago, 1988), pp. 480–481.

therefore not subject to change. It is also true that for some, sexual orientation may be a matter of conscious choice. The committee devoted considerable time in its discussion to the significance of conscious choice as a criterion for formulating a position on the religious status of homosexuality. The majority of the committee believes that the issue of choice is crucial. For some on the committee the issue of choice is not significant.

In Jewish tradition heterosexual, monogamous, procreative marriage is the ideal human relationship for the perpetuation of species, covenantal fulfillment and the preservation of the Jewish people. While acknowledging that there are other human relationships which possess ethical and spiritual value and that there are some people for whom heterosexual, monogamous, procreative marriage is not a viable option or possibility,[5] the majority of the committee reaffirms unequivocally the centrality of this ideal and its special status as *kiddushin*. To the extent that sexual orientation is a matter of choice, the majority of the committee affirms that heterosexuality is the only appropriate Jewish choice for fulfilling one's covenental obligations.

A minority of the committee dissents, affirming the equal possibility of covenantal fulfillment in homosexual and heterosexual relationships. The relationship, not the gender, should determine its Jewish value—*kiddushin*.

The committee strongly endorses the view that all Jews are religiously equal regardless of their sexual orientation. We are aware of loving and committed relationships between people of the same sex. Issues such as the religious status of these relationships as well as the creation of special ceremonies are matters of continuing discussion and differences of opinion.

Sexual Morality and the Rabbi

The general subject of sexual morality is important. The committee, in various stages of its deliberations, sought to discuss homosexuality within that larger framework. However, it concluded that while a comprehensive statement on sexuality and sexual morality was a desideratum, it was beyond the mandate of the committee.

Nevertheless, rabbis are both role models and exemplars. Therefore, the Committee calls upon all rabbis—without regard to sexual orientation—to conduct their private lives with discretion and with full regard for the mores and sensibilities of their communities, and in consonance with the preamble to the Central Conference of American Rabbis' *Code of Ethics:*

> As teachers of Judaism, rabbis are expected to abide by the highest moral values of our religion: the virtues of family life, integrity and honorable social relationships. In their personal lives they are called upon to set an example of the ideals they proclaim.

Our Relationship to *Kelal Yisrael* and the Non-Jewish Community

The committee devoted considerable discussion to the effect of any statement on our relationship to *Kelal Yisrael*. The committee expressed deep concern about the reactions of the

---

5. Cf. *Gates of Mitzvah*, p. 11, note at bottom of page.

other Jewish movements and strongly urges that the dialogue continue with them on this issue. Nevertheless, it concluded that our decision should be governed by the principles and practices of Reform Judaism. Similarly the committee considered and discussed with the members of MaRaM the possible effects of a statement on Reform Judaism in Israel. Again, it concluded that while sensitivity was in order, the committee could only address the North American situation. In addition, the committee attempted to assess how various stands would affect our relationship with non-Jewish groups. Again, the committee was concerned but felt that it had to make its decision independent of that consideration.

Congregational Issues

The acceptance by our congregations of gay and lesbian Jews as rabbis was a topic of discussion. We know that the majority of Reform Jews strongly support civil rights for gays and lesbians, but the unique position of the rabbi as spiritual leader and Judaic role model make the acceptance of gay or lesbian rabbis an intensely emotional and potentially divisive issue. While we acknowledge that there are gay and lesbian rabbis who are serving their communities effectively, with dignity, compassion and integrity, we believe that there is a great need for education and dialogue in our congregations.

Admissions Policy of the College-Institute

One of the original issues which brought the committee into existence was a concern about the admissions policy of the College-Institute. President Alfred Gottschalk has recently set forth the admissions policy of HUC-JIR. The written guidelines state that the College-Institute considers sexual orientation of an applicant only within the context of a candidate's overall suitability for the rabbinate, his or her qualifications to serve the Jewish community effectively, and his or her capacity to find personal fulfillment within the rabbinate. The Committee agrees with this admissions policy of our College-Institute.

Membership in the Central Conference of American Rabbis

The Central Conference of American Rabbis has always accepted into membership upon application all rabbinic graduates of the College-Institute.

The committee re-affirms this policy to admit upon application rabbinic graduates of the College-Institute.

Placement

Since its inception, the Rabbinical Placement Commission has provided placement services to all members of the Central Conference of American Rabbis in good standing, in accordance with its rules.

The committee agrees with this policy of the Rabbinical Placement Commission which provides placement services to all members of the Central Conference of American Rabbis in good standing, in accordance with the Commission's established rules.

Respectfully submitted,

Chair: Selig Salkowitz, Norman J. Cohen, A. Stanley Dreyfus (RPC), Joseph B. Glaser (CCAR), Walter Jacob, Yoel H. Kahn, Samuel E. Karff, Peter S. Knobel, Joseph Levine, Jack Stern, Richard S. Sternberger (UAHC), Ronald B. Sobel (RPC), Elliot L. Stevens (CCAR), Harvey M. Tattelbaum, Albert Vorspan (UAHC), Margaret M. Wenig, Gary Zola (HUC-JIR).

Committee Endorsement

The committee expresses its sincere appreciation to the many members of the Central Conference of American Rabbis who communicated with it in writing and orally. We urge all rabbis to study and reflect on these critical issues in order to lead their congregations and other members of the Jewish community toward greater awareness and sensitivity through education and dialogue. The committee unanimously endorses this report as a fair reflection of four years of deliberation and urges its adoption.

Resolution Adopted by the National Federation of Temple Youth, 1991: Homosexuality

RESOLVED:

That NFTY respond to the CCAR resolution [on homosexuality] as follows:

1. NFTY officially commends the CCAR for taking a stance that allows rabbis to be ordained on the basis of their integrity and ability and not on the basis of their sexual orientation.
2. NFTY, as an organization founded upon the ideas that people should be judged solely upon the content of their character, does, however, express concern over the blanket-type statement which states that homosexuals cannot fulfill their covenental obligations, and therefore requests that the CCAR examine the possible implicatons of this phrase to see whether or not a change on the basis of phrasing, ideology, etc. is warranted. That in order to effectively voice this opinion, the following be done:

    1. NFTY undertakes to send a letter to the President and Executive Vice President of the CCAR and the 17 members of the Ad-hoc committee who drafted the resolution commending the CCAR's resolution overall and respectfully voicing concern about the aforementioned statement.
    2. The NFTY Executives undertake to send a letter to the President of the UAHC, the President of HUC, and the National Dean of Admissions of HUC voicing NFTY's opinion on the CCAR Resolution.

Resolution Adopted by the National Association of Temple Educators, 1991

Preamble:

In 1977 the UAHC General Assembly called for an end to discrimination against homosexuals and expanded upon this in 1987 by calling for the full inclusion of gay and lesbian Jews in all aspects of synagogue life. The UAHC urged its congregations and affiliates to "encourage lesbian and gay Jews to share and participate in the worship, general congregational life, employment, and leadership of all synagogues; implement programs supportive of Jewish lesbians and gays; and continue to develop educational programs in the synagogue and the community which promote understanding and respect for lesbians and gays."

THEREFORE BE IT RESOLVED THAT THE NATIONAL ASSOCIATION OF TEMPLE EDUCATORS:

1. Accept all Jewish educators who meet eligibility requirements for membership in NATE regardless of sexual orientation;
2. Welcome openly gay and lesbian educators to serve in positions of leadership in NATE;
3. Afford to all members of NATE regardless of sexual orientation all the benefits of membership including those related to placement and leadership responsibilities within the Jewish community;
4. Support the rights of all individuals within our profession to equal consideration and equal opportunities regardless of sexual orientation;
5. Consider all applicants for positions in our congregational schools, regardless of sexual orientation;
6. Act as educational leaders in the Jewish community by developing curricula and outreach programs to help gay and lesbian Jews become fully integrated members of the Jewish community;
7. Encourage our members to create educational experiences curricula and materials which will promote positive attitudes toward all Jews, regardless of sexual orientation.

Resolution Adopted by the Women of Reform Judaism National Federation of Temple Sisterhoods 38th Biennial Assembly, 1991

Issue

1. To insure civil rights protection for gay men and lesbian women.
2. To encourage full inclusion for gay and lesbian Jews in all areas of synagogue life.

Background

In accordance with the teaching of our faith that all human beings are created *betselem elohim* (in the divine image) the National Federation of Temple Sisterhoods passed the 1977 resolution, "Rights of Individuals," which establishes commitment to a society in which "the civil, legal, social and political rights and guarantees for education, housing, employment, pursuit of self-fulfillment, the expression of cultural and ethnic identity and the absence of coercion or invasion of privacy shall be guaranteed for all persons regardless of color, sex, sexual preference of consenting adults, national origin, religion and political point of view."

During the last fifteen years the Union of American Hebrew Congregations has admitted to membership congregations with a special outreach to gay and lesbian Jews, there are others who wish to be part of mainstream congregational life. In 1987 the Union of American Hebrew Congregations expressed its commitment to full inclusion of gay and lesbian Jews in all areas of synagogue life.

In 1990 the Central Conference of American Rabbis adopted the report which recommended that "all rabbis, regardless of sexual orientation, be accorded the opportunity to fulfill the sacred vocation which they have chosen."

Resolution

Therefore to support gay and lesbian Jews in fulfilling their communal and spiritual aspirations, the National Federation of Temple Sisterhoods calls on member Sisterhoods to:

1. Support legislation and regulations on the state and federal levels which provide full opportunity and civil protection to gay men and lesbian women.
2. Advocate the full integration of gay and lesbian Jews within our congregations and communities.
3. Accept gay and lesbian individuals and families into congregations and affirm their right to affiliate as individuals or as families with all the privileges thereof.
4. Educate their members that commitment to human rights includes that gay and lesbian Jews have the opportunities to fulfill their aspirations to serve as rabbis, cantors and other professionals in any of our synagogues.
5. Urge their religious schools to sensitize our youth to the diversity of families and life styles.

Guide for Advocacy and Action by the Women of Reform Judaism National Federation of Temple Sisterhoods Implementing Resolutions Adopted in 1991 at the NFTS 38th Biennial Assembly: The Rights of Gay Men and Lesbian Women

Supports civil rights protection for gay men and lesbian women and full inclusion of gay and lesbian Jews in all areas of synagogue life.

Sisterhood's interest in including gay and lesbian Jews as individuals and families in all aspects of congregational life is not a social justice issue alone. Many Jewish gay and lesbian families include children and need Jewish community and educational resources.

- Invite gay and lesbian Jews and temple families that include gay and lesbian members to speak.
- Hold focus groups to sensitize congregants to full gay and lesbian family participation in the congregation.
- Speak with the rabbi and religious school director about including curricula on diversity of families and life styles.
- Ask for Sisterhood representation on congregational search committees for professionals and other staff so that Sisterhood can advance selection policies unlimited by sexual orientation.

Statement Adopted by the Convention of the American Conference of Cantors, 1991: Homosexuality in the Cantorate

We, as members of the American Conference of Cantors, acknowledge that there are members of our organization who are gay and lesbian. We respect and value their contributions to the cantorate. We therefore urge that all cantors regardless of sexual orientation be accorded the opportunity to fulfill the sacred vocation which they have chosen.

And in accordance with the Union of American Hebrew Congregations and the Central Conference of American Rabbis, we further urge cantors, rabbis and congregations to treat with respect and integrate fully all Jews into the life of the community regardless of sexual orientation.

Respectfully Submitted,
Social Action Committee
Ad Hoc Committee on
Homosexuality in the Cantorate

This statement on homosexuality in the cantorate was presented for a policy vote to the plenary of the American Conference of Cantors at [its] 1991 Convention, June 30–July 4, at the Concord Hotel in Kiamesha Lake, New York. It was brought to a vote and was passed by the plenary.

Resolution Adopted by the Commission on Social Action of Reform Judaism, 1991: Eliminating Discrimination against Gays and Lesbians in the Military

Whereas preceding an Executive Order in 1948 by President Harry Truman, African-Americans were barred from equal participation in military service as a result of the belief that their service was incompatible with the efficient and harmonious operation of the Armed Forces, and

Whereas today, the same unfounded justifications are used to support discrimination against gay and lesbian military personnel despite the fact that many objective studies, even those commissioned by the Pentagon, have shown that gay men and lesbians can and do serve as well as their heterosexual brothers and sisters, and

Whereas soldiers who are discovered to be gay or lesbian receive discharges and, depending upon the type of discharge, can be denied benefits that come from military service,

Be it therefore resolved:

That the Union of American Hebrew Congregations calls upon the President of the United States to issue an Executive Order and upon Congress to enact appropriate legislation eliminating discrimination against gays and lesbians in the Armed Forces.

Resolution Adopted by the Executive Board of the Central Conference of American Rabbis, 1992: The Boy Scouts of America

WHEREAS, the Boy Scouts of America has taken a position that excludes gay scouts and scout leaders, and

WHEREAS, the Central Conference of American Rabbis passed a resolution in 1990, that expresses the full acceptance of our gay and lesbian colleagues, and

WHEREAS, the Union of American Hebrew Congregations, in more than one resolution, has promoted civil rights for all, regardless of sexual orientation;

THEREFORE BE IT RESOLVED, that the Central Conference of American Rabbis call upon the Boy Scouts of America to open its membership and leadership to all men and boys without regard to their sexual orientation, and that the CCAR begin discussions with the Boy Scouts on this matter.

Resolution Adopted by the Executive Board of the National Federation of Temple Youth, 1992–1993: The Boy Scouts of America

WHEREAS the Boy Scouts of America has taken a position that excludes homosexual scouts and scout leaders, and

WHEREAS NFTY has passed a resolution at Convention 1991 expressing full acceptance of gay and lesbian members, and

WHEREAS the Union of American Hebrew Congregations, in more than one resolution, has promoted civil rights for all, regardless of sexual orientation,

THEREFORE LET IT BE RESOLVED that NFTY call upon the Boy Scouts of America and all other organizations affiliated with the Boy Scouts having the same policy to open their membership and leadership to all men, women, and boys without regard to their sexual orientation, and that NFTY begin discussion with the Boy Scouts of America on this matter through the efforts of the TYG [Temple Youth Group], and

LET IT BE FURTHER RESOLVED that NFTY encourage all of its members to divest from the Boy Scouts of America and all other organizations affiliated with the Boy Scouts having the same policy financially and to withdraw their membership from the Boy Scouts until basic civil rights are extended to include homosexuals.

Resolution Adopted by the 62nd General Assembly of the Union of American Hebrew Congregations Biennial, 1993: Recognition for Lesbian and Gay Partnerships

Background

The Union of American Hebrew Congregations has been in the vanguard of support for the full recognition of equality for lesbians and gays in society. This has been clearly articulated in UAHC resolutions dating back to 1977. But far more remains to be accomplished. Today, committed lesbian and gay couples are denied the benefits routinely accorded to married heterosexual couples: they cannot share in their partner's health programs; they do not have spousal survivor rights; and, as seen in recent court rulings, individual lesbian or gay parents have been adjudged unfit to raise their own children because they are lesbian or gay and/or living with a lesbian or gay partner, even though they meet the "parenting" standards required of heterosexual couples.

It is heartening to note the steps being made toward recognition of the legitimacy of lesbian and gay relationships. Adoption of Domestic Partnership registration in cities such as San Francisco and New York and extension of spousal benefits to partners of lesbian and gay employees by companies such as Levi Strauss, Lotus, Maimonides Hospital in New York City, are models for adoption by other governmental authorities and corporations.

THEREFORE, the Union of American Hebrew Congregations resolves to:
1. call upon our Federal, Provincial, State and local governments to adopt legislation that will:
   a. afford partners in committed lesbian and gay partnerships spousal benefits, that include participation in health care plans and survivor benefits;
   b. ensure that lesbians and gay men are not adjudged unfit to raise children because of their sexual orientation; and

---

Union of American Hebrew Congregations 62nd General Assembly, "Resolution Adopted on Recognition for Lesbian and Gay Partnerships" (San Francisco, 1993), http://www.urj.org.

    c. afford partners in committed lesbian and gay relationships the means of legally acknowledging such relationships; and
2. call upon our congregations, the Central Conference of American Rabbis and the Hebrew Union College–Jewish Institute of Religion to join with us in seeking to extend the same benefits that are extended to the spouse of married staff members and employees to the partners of all staff members and employees living in committed lesbian and gay partnerships.

Resolution Adopted by the 62nd General Assembly of the Union of American Hebrew Congregations Biennial, 1993: Responding to Anti–Gay Rights Referenda

Background

In 1977, the UAHC Biennial Convention strongly affirmed the right of gay men and lesbians to equal protection of the law and to full protection of their civil rights. This resolution was reaffirmed in 1987 and 1989.

Currently, efforts are underway to enact national legislation protecting the civil rights of gay men, lesbians, and bisexuals. Until such legislation passes, it is at the state and local levels that the struggle for equal rights is being fought. Alarmingly, across the country, growing numbers of state and local referenda and statutes are being considered which could deny civil rights protections to gay men, lesbians, and bisexuals.

On November 3, 1992, Colorado voters approved Amendment Two, one of several anti-gay ballot initiatives in the 1992 election. The Amendment to the state constitution strictly prohibits the State of Colorado and any component of state government from taking any action which would prevent or redress discrimination against gay men, lesbians, and bisexuals because of their sexual orientation.

The amendment is part of a burgeoning trend of discrimination and homophobia throughout the country as evidenced by similar 1992 ballot initiatives in Oregon, Portland, Maine and Tampa, Florida. Anti-gay statewide ballot measures are anticipated in six more states and 35 municipalities in the next election cycle. These ballot measures would enact discrimination in its most pernicious form as they seek to create (and in Tampa and Colorado have created) constitutionally "protected discriminatory rights," without limitation, against gay men, lesbians, and bisexuals.

The goal of these initiatives—to deny fundamental human rights—is antithetical to our beliefs. Moreover, even if the initiatives are defeated, the very process of gathering peti-

---

Union of American Hebrew Congregations 62nd General Assembly, "Resolution Adopted on Responding to Anti–Gay Rights Referenda" (San Francisco, 1993), http://www.urj.org.

tions, funds, and momentum for these measures has created an atmosphere of hatred in which there has been an alarming increase in bias-related crime against gay men and lesbians. The spread of the anti-gay agenda has intensified as the Religious Right has found discrimination against homosexuals to be an effective rallying point for the broader agenda; homophobic organizing tools and rhetoric make their way into school board elections, censorship battles, and anti-choice demonstrations.

While civil rights activists continue to try to overturn the Amendment in Colorado and prevent adoption of similar measures in other states and localities, the proponents of these ballot initiatives have already coalesced around an ideology of hate that transcends state and local laws. It is a national movement and we must respond to it as such.

The reprehensible nature of the anti-gay initiatives and the fact that they are spreading throughout the body politic obligate us as a religious body to register a strong protest when such referenda or statutes pass. In certain instances, when the discrimination practiced by states or governments has been particularly blatant, the UAHC has registered its protest by the use of a boycott; the boycott against South Africa and against states which did not pass the ERA are precedents for such action. We call for such a boycott now.

A boycott is both a symbolic and a practical step. It is an emphatic moral statement, but it also serves, as was the case in Colorado, to move an otherwise neutral business community to a position of active opposition to the anti-gay measure.

We call for the boycott to take effect on January 1, 1995, in order to give those states and municipalities which currently have discriminatory legislation on the books an opportunity to reverse their actions, and in order to alert those who now contemplate supporting similar statutes that their action will have certain and serious consequences.

THEREFORE, the Union of American Hebrew Congregations resolves:

1. To actively oppose state and local referenda and statutes restricting the civil rights of gays, lesbians, or bisexuals;
2. To work in coalition with other national and local organizations (including, but not limited to, religious organizations) to mount a national campaign to counter the anti-gay rhetoric of the Religious Right;
3. Not to hold regional or national meetings in any state or municipality which has a law in effect on or after January 1, 1995, denying legal protection to the civil rights of gays, lesbians, or bisexuals. If a regional body cannot comply with this resolution within its own boundaries, it will be exempted;
4. To call upon its affiliates and the Central Conference of American Rabbis to adopt a similar position;
5. To call upon the Commission on Social Action to join in amicus briefs to strike down judicially such referenda and statutes.

Resolution Adopted by the Central Conference of American Rabbis 104th Annual Convention, 1993: Convening in States Denying Legal Protection of Civil Rights for Gays and Lesbians

WHEREAS, the CCAR has a longstanding commitment to civil rights of all individuals regardless of sexual orientation, and

WHEREAS, there is a concerted effort to block implementation of civil rights protection for gays and lesbians, evidenced by the passage of Amendment II by the voters of Colorado in November, 1992, and

WHEREAS, numerous ballot initiatives are currently being proposed in other jurisdictions, to similarly prevent the access to protection of civil rights laws, on the basis of sexual orientation, and

WHEREAS, the CCAR considers the principle in this instance to take priority over the transaction of business as usual.

THEREFORE BE IT RESOLVED, that the CCAR not hold regional or national meetings in any state, province, or municipality which has a law in effect on or after January 1, 1995, denying gays and lesbians legal protection of their civil rights. If a regional body cannot comply with this resolution within its own boundaries, it will be exempted.

Central Conference of American Rabbis 104th Annual Convention, "Resolution Adopted on Convening in States Denying Legal Protection of Civil Rights for Gays and Lesbians" (Montreal, 1993), http://www.ccarnet.org.

Resolution Adopted by the 63rd General Assembly of the Union of American Hebrew Congregations Biennial, 1995: Promoting Equal Employment and Leadership Opportunities for Lesbians and Gays in the Reform Movement

Background

Among our most sacred Jewish values is the fundamental principle that we are created in the image of the divine. All Jews, whatever their sexual orientation, are welcome in the Reform Movement.

Regardless of context, discrimination arising from apathy, insensitivity, ignorance, fear, or hatred is inconsistent with that principle and is morally wrong. Discrimination on the basis of sexual orientation is abhorrent.

The Union of American Hebrew Congregations is justly proud of its strong record in working to eliminate invidious discrimination in our society and is fiercely committed to continuing this effort. For example, in 1993 the UAHC resolved to oppose all anti-gay state ballot initiatives, and in certain circumstances boycott any community with such laws.

Within the Reform Movement, substantial progress has been made in demonstrating our commitment to equal opportunity regardless of sexual orientation. The UAHC has admitted and welcomed a number of congregations with a special outreach to lesbian, gay and bisexual Jews.

In 1987, the UAHC adopted a resolution that sexual orientation should not be a consideration for membership of, or participation in the activities of, any member congregation. This resolution urged its congregations and affiliates "to encourage lesbian and gay

---

Union of American Hebrew Congregations 63rd General Assembly, "Resolution Adopted on Promoting Equal Employment and Leadership Opportunities for Lesbians and Gays in the Reform Movement" (Atlanta, 1995), http://www.urj.org.

Jews to share and participate in the worship, leadership and general congregational life of all synagogues and to employ people without regard to sexual orientation."

In 1989, the UAHC reaffirmed its commitment to promoting full congregational membership opportunities for gay and lesbian Jews, as singles, couples, and families.

In 1990, the Central Conference of American Rabbis has affirmed that all graduates of the Hebrew Union College–Jewish Institute of Religion (HUC-JIR) will be admitted for membership regardless of sexual orientation.

In 1993, the UAHC called upon its congregations, the CCAR, and the HUC-JIR to extend the same benefits that are offered to the spouses of married staff members and employees to the partners of all staff members and employees living in committed lesbian and gay partnerships.

It is now appropriate to build upon this progress in support for our commitment to equal opportunities to all Reform Jews, and to enhance our efforts to promote equal employment and leadership opportunities within the UAHC, its affiliates and its congregations.

THEREFORE, the Union of American Hebrew Congregations resolves:
1. Not to discriminate on the basis of sexual orientation in matters relating to the employment of rabbis, cantors, educators, executives, administrators or other staff, or in matters relating to the appointment of lay leaders and to call upon all affiliates and member congregations to follow the same policy;
2. To call upon all placement arms of the Reform Movement to assist congregations in implementing this policy of non-discrimination;
3. To call upon all organizations affiliated with the Reform Movement to adopt written policies of non-discrimination; and
4. To commend the use of *Kulanu—A Program to Include Lesbian and Gay Jews in Our Temples*, a manual being published by the Task Force on Lesbian and Gay Inclusion, in conducting educational and other programs for the purpose of implementing this and previous related resolutions.

Resolution Adopted by the Central Conference of American Rabbis 107th Annual Convention, 1996: Gay and Lesbian Marriage

Background

Consistent with our Jewish commitment to the fundamental principle that we are all created in the divine image, the Reform Movement has "been in the vanguard of the support for the full recognition of equality for lesbians and gays in society." In 1977, the CCAR adopted a resolution encouraging legislation which decriminalizes homosexual acts between consenting adults, and prohibits discrimination against them as persons, followed by its adoption in 1990 of a substantial position paper on homosexuality and the rabbinate. Then, in 1993, the Union of American Hebrew Congregations observed that "committed lesbian and gay couples are denied the benefits routinely accorded to married heterosexual couples." The UAHC resolved that full equality under the law for lesbian and gay people requires legal recognition of lesbian and gay relationships.

In light of this background,

BE IT RESOLVED, that the Central Conference of American Rabbis support the right of gay and lesbian couples to share fully and equally in the rights of civil marriage, and

BE IT FURTHER RESOLVED, that the CCAR oppose governmental efforts to ban gay and lesbian marriage.

BE IT FURTHER RESOLVED, that this is a matter of civil law, and is separate from the question of rabbinic officiation at such.

Central Conference of American Rabbis 107th Annual Convention, "Resolution Adopted on Gay and Lesbian Marriage" (Philadelphia, 1996), http://www.ccarnet.org.

CCAR Responsum on Marriage after a Sex-Change Operation (1978)

Question

May a rabbi officiate at a marriage of two Jews, one of whom has undergone a surgical operation which has changed his/her sex?

Answer

Our responsum will deal with an individual who has undergone an operation for sexual change for physical or psychological reasons. We will presume (a) that the operation is done for valid, serious reasons, and not frivolously; (b) that the best available medical tests (chromosome analysis, etc.) will be utilized as aids; and (c) that this in no way constitutes a homosexual marriage.

There is some discussion in traditional literature about the propriety of this kind of operation. In addition, we must recall that tradition sought to avoid any operation which would seriously endanger life (Yoreh Deah 116; Chulin 10a). The *Mishnah* dealt with the problem of individuals whose sex was undetermined. It divided them into two separate categories, *Tumtum* and *Androginos*. A *Tumtum* is a person whose genitals are hidden or undeveloped and whose sex, therefore, is unknown. R. Ammi recorded an operation on one such individual who was found to be male and who then fathered seven children (Yev. 83b). Solomon B. Freehof has discussed such operations most recently; he *permits* such an operation for a *Tumtum*, but not for an *Androginos* (*Modern Reform Responsa*, pp. 128ff). The *Androginos* is a hermaphrodite and clearly carries characteristics of both sexes (M. Bik. IV.5). The former was a condition which could be corrected and the latter, as far as the ancients were concerned, could not, so the *Mishnah* and later tradition treated the *Androginos* sometimes as a male, sometimes as a female, and sometimes as a separate category. However, with regard to marriage, the *Mishnah* (Bik. IV.2) states unequivocally: "He can take a wife, but not be taken as a wife like men." If married, they were free from the obligation of bearing children (*Yad*, Hil. Yibum Vachalitsa 6.2), but some doubted the validity of their marriages (Yev. 81a; *Yad*, Hil. Ishut 4.11; also *Sh.A.*, Even Ha-ezer 44.6).

Central Conference of American Rabbis, "Responsum on Marriage after a Sex-Change Operation" (1978), http://www.ccarnet.org.

The *Talmud* has also dealt with *Ailonit,* a masculine woman, who was barren (*Yad*, Hil. Ishut 2.4; Nid. 47b; Yev. 80b). If she married and her husband was aware of her condition, then this was a valid marriage (*Yad*, Hil. Ishut 4.11); although the ancient authorities felt that such a marriage would only be permitted if the prospective husband had children by a previous marriage, otherwise, he could divorce her in order to have children (Yev. 61a; M. Yev. 24.1). Later authorities would simply permit such a marriage to stand.

We, however, are dealing either with a situation in which the lack of sexual development has been corrected and the individual has been provided with a sexual identity, or with a situation in which the psychological makeup of the individual clashed with the physical characteristics, and this was corrected through surgery. In other words, our question deals with an individual who now possesses definite physical characteristics of a man or a woman, but has obtained them through surgical procedure, and whose status is recognized by the civil government. The problem before us is that such an individual is sterile, and the question is whether under such circumstances he or she may be married. Our question, therefore, must deal with the nature of marriage for such individuals. Can a Jewish marriage be conducted under these circumstances?

There is no doubt that both procreation and sexual satisfaction are basic elements of marriage as seen by Jewish tradition. Procreation was considered essential, as is already stated in the *Mishnah*: "A man may not desist from the duty of procreation unless he already has children." The *Gemara* to this concluded that he may marry a barren woman if he has fulfilled this *mitzvah*; in any case, he should not remain unmarried (Yev. 61b). There was a difference between the Schools of Hillel and Shammai about what was required to fulfill the *mitzvah* of procreation. Tradition followed Hillel, who minimally required a son and a daughter, yet the codes all emphasize the need to produce children beyond that number (*Tos.*, Yev. 8; *Yad*, Hil. Ishut 15.16, etc.). The sources also clearly indicate that this *mitzvah* is only incumbent upon the male (*Tos.,* Yev. 8), although some later authorities would include women in the obligation, perhaps in a secondary sense (*Aruch Hashulchan*, Even Ha-ezer 1.4; *Chatam Sofer*, Even Ha-ezer, #20). Abraham Hirsh (*Noam*, vol. 16, pp. 152ff.) has recently discussed the matter of granting a divorce when one spouse has had a transsexual operation. Aside from opposing the operation generally, he also states that no essential biological changes have taken place and that the operation, therefore, was akin to sterilization (which is prohibited) and cosmetic surgery.

Hirsh also mentions a case related to our situation. A male in the time of R. Hananel added an orifice to his body, and R. Hananel decided that a male having intercourse with this individual has committed a homosexual act. This statement is quoted by Ibn Ezra in his commentary on Lev. 18:22. We, however, are not dealing with this kind of situation, but with a complete sexual change operation.

Despite the strong emphasis on procreation, companionship and joy also played a major role in the Jewish concept of marriage. Thus, the seven marriage blessings deal with joy, companionship, the unity of family, restoration of Zion, etc., as well as with children (Ket. 8a). These same blessings were to be recited for those beyond child-bearing age, or those who were sterile (Abudarham, *Birchot Erusin* 98a).

Most traditional authorities who discussed childless marriages were considering a marriage already in existence (*bedi-avad*) and not the entrance into such a union. Under such circumstances the marriage would be considered valid and need not result in divorce for the sake of procreation, although that possibility existed (*Sh.A.*, Even Ha-ezer 23; see Isserles' note on 154.10). This was the only alternative solution, since bigamy was no longer even theoretically possible after the decree of Rabbenu Gershom in the 11th century in those countries where this decree was accepted (Oriental Jews did not accept the *Cherem* of Rabbenu Gershom). Maimonides considered such a marriage valid under any circumstances (*Yad*, Hil. Ishut 4.10), whether this individual was born sterile or was sterilized later. The commentator, Abraham di Boton, emphasized the validity of such a marriage if sterility has been caused by an accident or surgery (*Lechem Mishneh* to *Yad*, Hil. Ishut 4.10). Yair Hayyim Bacharach stated that as long as the prospective wife realized that her prospective husband was infertile though sexually potent, and had agreed to the marriage, it was valid and acceptable (*Chavat Yair*, #221). Traditional *Halacha*, which makes a distinction between the obligations of men and women (a distinction not accepted by Reform Judaism), would allow a woman to marry a sterile male, since the obligation of procreation did not affect her (as mentioned earlier).

There was some difference of opinion when a change of status in the male member of a wedded couple had taken place. R. Asher discussed this, but came to no conclusion, though he felt that a male whose sexual organs had been removed could not contract a valid marriage (*Besamim Rosh*, #340—attributed to R. Asher). The contemporary Orthodox R. Waldenberg assumed that a sexual change has occurred, and terminated the marriage without a divorce (*Tsits Eli-ezer* X, #25). Joseph Pellagi came to a similar conclusion earlier (*Ahav Et Yosef* 3.5).

Perhaps the clearest statement about entering into such a marriage was made by Isaac bar Sheshet, who felt that the couple was permitted to marry and then be left alone, although they entered the marriage with full awareness of the situation (*Ribash*, #15; *Sh.A.*, Even Ha-ezer 1.3; see Isserles' note). Similarly, traditional authorities who usually oppose contraception permitted it to a couple if one partner was in ill health. The permission was granted so that the couple could remain happily married, a solution favored over abstinence (Moses Feinstein, *Igerot Mosheh*, Even Ha-ezer, #63 and #67, where he permits marriage under these circumstances).

Our discussion clearly indicates that individuals whose sex has been changed by a surgical procedure and who are now sterile may be married according to Jewish tradition. We agree with this conclusion. Both partners should be aware of each other's condition. The ceremony need not be changed in any way for the sake of these individuals.

Walter Jacob, *Chairman*
Solomon B. Freehof, *Honorary Chairman*
Stephen M. Passamaneck
W. Gunther Plaut
Harry A. Roth
Herman E. Schaalman
Bernard Zlotowitz

CCAR Responsum on Homosexual Marriage (1985)

Question

May a rabbi officiate at the "marriage" of two homosexuals? (Rabbi L. Poller, Larchmont, NY)

Answer

The attitude of our tradition and of Reform Judaism toward homosexuals is clear. For a full discussion, see the responsa by S. B. Freehof and W. Jacob (*American Reform Responsa*, #13, 14). The resolution of the Central Conference of American Rabbis on homosexuality deals exclusively with the civil rights and civil liberties of homosexuals and seeks to protect them from discrimination. It does not, however, understand it to be an alternative lifestyle which is religiously condoned.

Judaism places great emphasis on family, children and the future, which is assured by a family. However we may understand homosexuality, whether as an illness, as a genetically based dysfunction or as a sexual preference and lifestyle—we cannot accommodate the relationship of two homosexuals as a "marriage" within the context of Judaism, for none of the elements of *qiddushin* (sanctification) normally associated with marriage can be invoked for this relationship.

A rabbi can not, therefore, participate in the "marriage" of two homosexuals.

Central Conference of American Rabbis, "Responsum on Homosexual Marriage" (1985), http://www.ccarnet.org.

CCAR Responsum on Conversion and Marriage after Transsexual Surgery (1990)

She'elah

An applicant for conversion, X, received extensive therapy at a recognized psychiatric institution which offers a sex-change psycho-therapy program. Subsequently he underwent surgery; his male genitalia were removed and a cosmetic vagina was constructed. However, this having taken place, he had a change of heart and no longer desired to be a woman. Since he had never declared himself publicly or legally as a woman, he continued his status as a man and was later married in a civil ceremony to his fiancee, a Jewish woman who is satisfied to live with him permanently, despite his mutilated condition. She supports his desire to become a Jew. The couple have been attending Shabbat services regularly. (Rabbi's name withheld, in order to prevent identification of X)

Two questions:

1. Should we admit the 29-year-old person to the Jewish information course established jointly by the Reform congregations in our city, holding out the likelihood that in the end there would be religious conversion?
2. If X is converted, should the rabbi sanctify the civil marriage through a religious ceremony (*kiddushin*)?

Teshuvah

Traditional Considerations

1. **The question of conversion.** Deut. 23:2 states: "No one whose testes are crushed or whose member is cut off shall be admitted into the Congregation of the Lord." This would appear to exclude X from membership in the Jewish people, but already Isaiah (56:3 ff.) mitigated the application of this rule when he spoke of God having special regard for the eunuchs. Subsequently, rabbinic tradition understood the intent of "No one whose

testes are crushed . . ." to be that such a man should not marry an Israelite woman, while his status as a Jew was not affected.[1]

There is therefore no objection in principle to the conversion of a person whose genitalia are mutilated or missing altogether, even when he is a *seris adam*, one whose mutilation was effected by human hand and not by birth or illness (*seris chammah*). In these cases, immersion alone suffices for *giyur*, religious conversion.[2] We see no reason to depart from this view and therefore hold that X's desire to become a convert has to be treated on its own merits.

The question then arises whether X, with his history of identity problems, is qualified as a prospective convert. Should we not have some concern about the mental stability of a person who, having undergone this radical and irreversible operation, now desires to be a man after all?

The Rambam deals with a convert who had been admitted without proper examination or instruction in the mitzvot.[3] But since the error has been made, he says, his conversion is deemed valid ex post facto (*be-di'avad*) though one should be troubled about the person until his sincerity is fully established. Once conversion has taken place, the presumption is in favor of the convert.[4] But **before** the event (*lekhatchilah*) it is different, for the fitness of the prospective convert should be most carefully considered.

Rabbi Walter Jacob issued a *teshuvah* on the question how the mental competency of a convert might be assessed, and cautioned that "we cannot accept individuals who do not meet these prerequisites [of mental competency]."[5]

In the case before us, when could it be said that X has shown that his intention to become a Jew is firm and not likely subject to reversal? As a minimum we suggest a cautionary waiting period, like the traditional cycle of three Pilgrim Festivals (which waiting period applies in other cases[6]). Since the conversion program in X's city lasts for eight months, let him enter the course but let him also be informed that, upon conclusion of the program, there would be a further time span, say a year, after which the rabbinic court would rule on his admissibility to conversion.

(While this is the majority opinion of the Responsa Committee, some members disagree and would not admit X to the program at all. They would consider X as a person who has already shown his instability in a matter which fundamentally affects his physical identity. They would not wish conversion to be another stage of the person's psychi-

---

1. See Rashi and Ibn Ezra on Deut. 23:2. The prohibition against Ammonites and Moabites was applied only to men, while their women (like Ruth) were allowed to marry Israelite men. The matter is discussed in M. Yev. 8:2, and BT Yev. 76a and following.
2. Rosh, Yevamot 4:13; *Shulchan Arukh*, Yoreh De'ah 268:1.
3. *Yad*, Issurei Bi'ah 13:17.
4. The Mishnah (Git. 3:3) speaks of a man who desires to divorce his wife but, being old or ill, sends a messenger to represent him. The man is presumed alive at the time of *gittin* until the opposite is established (*bechezkat shehu'kayyam*). The same principle applies to an animal to be slaughtered. While alive it has the status of a forbidden object, for an *ever min ha-chay* may not be eaten; but once slaughtered, the presumption is that the *shechitah* was kosher until the opposite is established (*harei hee bechezkat hetteir*, Hul. 9a).
5. *American Reform Responsa*, ed. Walter Jacob (New York: CCAR, 1983), #67. The Rambam left the decision to the presiding judge; *Yad*, Hilch. Edut 9:9, and Hilch. Sanh. 2:1.
6. Such as the establishment of ownership of a lost object; see the Maggid Mishneh on the *Yad*, Issurei Bi'ah 13:17, who finds the case a confirmation of the uncomplimentary saying that "Converts are for Israel like a rash" (*safchat*, Lev. 13:2). See also M. B.M. 2:6 and commentaries.

atric meandering. The majority, as indicated, would leave the matter to the discretion of the *beit din*.)

2. **Should the rabbi officiate at X's marriage?** The question of admissibility to religious marriage is different from that of admissibility to conversion. In the latter, it is not necessary to deal with a presumption of X's maleness (*chezqat zakhar*), because in the Reform context which treats men and women as religious equals we convert X as a human being and not as either a male or a female. But in marriage differential gender has been the precondition.

First of all, let us briefly look at the admissibility of sex change altogether. Since the Halakhah regards the mitzvah of procreation as a chief purpose of marriage, the Rabbis forbade the removal of male genitalia in the hermaphrodite (*androginos*), the person who possesses both male and female genitalia.[7] Even more so would they forbid the removal of genitalia from an otherwise normally formed man who wishes to be a woman.[8]

Exceptions were made only occasionally. Thus, Rabbi Eliezer Waldenberg permitted transsexual surgery (from male to female) in the borderline case of an infant whose external genitalia were those of a female, though chromosome analysis and the presence of a testicle showed that the gender might be male.[9] According to Rabbi Waldenberg, the general rule is that the "visible, external organs" determine sexual identity, and in the case of X he would therefore not have allowed the surgery.

The issue before us is, however, not the permissibility of the surgery but rather, since it has already taken place, whether *kiddushin*, religiously sanctioned union, may now be celebrated.

There is a good deal of halakhic discussion of the question whether the marriage of a transsexual is still a marriage and whether—if it is contracted—religious divorce (*gittin*) is necessary or redundant. When the operation has already taken place, most follow Rabbenu Asher who says that a man whose genitalia have been removed is no longer able to contract a valid marriage—even though his sexual identity may not be affected and he is still considered a man.[10] The prohibition of the law in Deut. 23:2, as interpreted by Tradition, is deemed decisive.

Reform Perspectives

Are there reasons why Reform Judaism might reach a different conclusion? There might be, for it would likely view the biblical passage differently. It would see it as a time-bound response to a particular situation, namely the use of castrated men (*sarisim*) in society, and this original purpose of the law has fallen away.[11]

---

7. Based on Lev. 22:24; B. Shabbat 110b; Rambam. ibid. 16:10. See further the study by Moshe Steinberg in *Assiya*, vol. 1, pp. 142–145, and R. Gedaliah Felder's discussion of the way an *androginos* and *tumtum* are to be converted (*She'elat Yeshurun*, no. 23), both with extensive notes and a listing of the traditional decisors.
8. See Rabbi J. David Bleich, "Transsexual Surgery," in Fred Rosner and J. David Bleich, *Jewish Bioethics* (New York: Hebrew Publishing Company, 1983), p. 191, citing Lev. 22:24. Rabbi Solomon Freehof also says: "There seems to be no way in which Jewish tradition can permit it" [i.e., transsexual surgery, if people are born with normal genitalia]; see *Modern Reform Responsa* (Hebrew Union College Press, 1971), no 22.
9. Tzitz Eliezer, vol. 2, no. 78.
10. So *Besamim Rosh*, no. 340. (The work is ascribed to R. Asher ben Yechiel, known as the Rosh, but was probably not authored by him.)
11. This opinion is supported by *Yalkut Me'am Lo'ez*, Devarim 866.

In addition, Reform also would accept the findings of modern science, which holds that external genitalia may not reflect the true identity of the individual. Thus, analysts have distinguished five categories which can be said to identify biological sex. They are: chromosomal configuration; gonadal sex (presence of ovaries or testes); sex-based hormones (androgen or estrogen dominance); internal reproductive structure; and external genitalia.[12] Rabbi Solomon B. Freehof was therefore ambivalent and suggested that the rabbi be guided by the attitude of the community: if the state issues a license to a transsexual it may be assumed that his/her change has the recognition of the law and therefore *kiddushin* may take place.[13] Subsequently, a CCAR Responsa Committee which dealt with the matter in some detail also allowed sex change as a permissible procedure and did not object to *kiddushin*.[14]

Despite these precedents in our movement, we remain troubled about the matter. The questioner notes that X received the best available scientific and psychological advice before his transsexual surgery was effected. Should we therefore not assume that medical evidence showed X to possess a sufficient measure of the aforementioned female characteristics? In some institutions which deal with persons like him there is a period during which the patient receives hormonal treatment and lives for a while as a woman. Only when the results of this trial period are conclusive is the surgery performed.

Was this done in X's case and was his preference for femaleness physiologically founded? The answer is not available to us and may not be available to the rabbi either. Still, we have to believe that no reputable institution would have proceeded with the surgery had there not been sufficient indications that strong female characteristics were in evidence. We would therefore consider the presumption of X's maleness to have been seriously weakened, and X to fall into the category of *safek zakhar, safek nekevah*, meaning that his/her sexual identity is in doubt.[15] We would therefore advise the rabbi **not to proceed** with *kiddushin* in case X is converted to Judaism.

Of course, for those Reform rabbis who sanctify same-sex marriages, this part of our discussion is irrelevant. They will say: Here are two individuals who care for each other and who want a ceremony that recognizes their intent as holy. However, while individual rabbis have taken this position, the Reform movement as represented by the CCAR has refused to do so.

In any case, even though no religious wedding will be performed, we assume that X will be treated with all the compassion and concern which such a tormented individual desperately requires.

---

12. See John Money et al. in *Bulletin of the Johns Hopkins Hospital* 97 (1955), pp. 284–300; and the article "Sexual Identity" in the *Encyclopedia of Bioethics*, vol. 3.
13. *Reform Responsa for Our Time* (Hebrew Union College Press, 1977), no. 42.
14. See *American Reform Responsa*, #137, and *Contemporary American Reform Responsa*, # 199, both with extensive citations of source materials.
15. That uncertainty is repeatedly treated in the tradition; see *She'elat Yeshurun*, l.c.

CCAR Responsum on Homosexual Marriage (1996)

She'elah

May a Reform rabbi officiate at a wedding or "commitment" ceremony between two homosexuals? Does such a union qualify as *kiddushin* from a Reform perspective? (Rabbi Sidney M. Helbraun, Northbrook, IL)

Teshuvah

The majority of the members of this Committee respond in the negative to this *she'elah*. In our opinion, a Reform rabbi should not officiate at a ceremony of marriage between two persons of the same gender, whether or not this ceremony is called by the name *kiddushin*.

A minority of us, whose names are indicated at the conclusion of this *teshuvah*, disagree, holding that a Reform rabbi may officiate at a wedding or "commitment" ceremony for two homosexuals, although for important historical and theological reasons, that ceremony should perhaps not be called *kiddushin*.

This is, for us, an uncommonly long responsum. It is long because our discussion of this issue brought forth among us a number of profound disagreements, not only over the specific question of homosexual marriage but also over the nature of Reform Jewish religious discourse, at least as it is practiced among those of us committed to the responsa process and to the literature of liberal *halakhah*. In trying to talk to each other about this question, we discovered that we as a Committee had ceased to share the most elemental kinds of assumptions necessary for a common religious conversation. We were speaking different languages, languages that used similar words and terminology but which defined them in starkly and irreconcilably different ways. Hence, we discovered that we were no longer talking *to* or even arguing *with* each other; rather, we were conducting a series of parallel monologues in place of the dialogue of text and tradition that has served us so well in the past. We know that we are not alone in this experience, for we have noticed the same difficulties of communication in virtually all other discussions that have taken place within the Conference on this explosive subject.

We have decided therefore to depart from our normal practice, which is to present the decision of the Committee's majority and to register the dissents, should they

---

Central Conference of American Rabbis, "Responsum on Homosexual Marriage" (1996), http://www.ccarnet.org.

exist, in a note or in a separate opinion. We have thought it useful to reconstruct the "discussion" which took place within our Committee, to explain the positions of *both* points of view as carefully as we can. The point is not to reach some kind of synthesis between the two, for as we have indicated, such a meeting of the minds did not occur and shows no prospect of taking place in the near future. Nor is it to imply a sense of neutrality on our part as to the proper answer to this *she'elah*, for both our majority and our minority are quite confirmed in their particular opinion. We hope instead that through the very process of explanation we can describe with some adequacy the width and the depth of the chasm that divides us. We hope, too, that the thorough enunciation of our reasoning might help us to begin the recovery of that common language of discussion and argument which has deserted us and whose existence is the necessary precondition to our existence as a religious community. And finally, we hope that alongside the deep disagreements which no majority opinion can put to rest, our words might serve to remind us and our colleagues of those values and goals upon which we do agree and to whose attainment we stand committed.

Introduction

This question, currently one of the most controversial issues on the agenda of the Reform rabbinate, has been an extraordinarily difficult one for our Committee. This is not because we disagree as to its answer. Disagreement is commonplace among us, as it should be. Like the rabbis of old, we sometimes find *machloket* to be problematic,[1] but we accept its inevitability and indeed welcome it as a necessary and indispensable test of our ideas and presumptions. We do not shrink from argument. The difficulty in this case arises from the fact that argument itself, understood as the joint deliberative attempt to reach common ground through persuasive speech, has broken down and proven impossible.

In order for an argument to occur at even the most elementary level, its opposing sides must be able to express themselves in a language which both can speak fluently. That language, the vernacular of the interpretive community, consists of a set of shared intuitions and premises. These serve as the common starting points for reflection and debate; they are the values by which all participants in the conversation analyze and measure their assertions; they represent the standards of justification to which both sides appeal in their attempt to persuade the other. Although the existence of a common language of argument does not guarantee unanimity or even a predominant consensus among the members of the community, it at least offers the prospect that persuasion can take place. It is that prospect, and only that prospect, which makes argument meaningful and worthwhile. In the absence of a language common to all members of the community, a language through which each side of a debate might articulate its position in the reasonable hope of convincing the other of the rightness of its point of view, argument no longer makes sense, true conversation can no longer take place, and the continued existence of the community *as* a community, a collective whose members are united by a shared language with which to imagine and describe their deepest commitments, is imperiled.

---

1. "At first, there was but one *machloket* in Israel . . . but when the students of the schools of Hillel and Shamai became numerous and did not study sufficiently, the disagreements multiplied, and Israel was divided into two sects . . . which will not reunite until the coming of the Messiah"; *PT* Chagigah 2:2 (77d).

On this *she'elah*, we have discovered that we no longer share a language of argument. The presumptions and definitions, the techniques and approaches that customarily serve as starting points for our discussions have failed us in this case. We have split into two or more camps, each framing the issue in a language of argument which the other side finds foreign, indecipherable, and obtuse.

Let us illustrate. Under normal circumstances, we converse about the questions submitted to us in the language of "tradition," a language composed of the resources of the Jewish past, its sacred texts and the history of their interpretation. We comprehend this tradition, to be sure, as Reform rabbis who possess a liberal and liberating textual tradition of our own. And with the insight derived from that particular perspective, we work with the texts of the past, constructing answers which we think speak to our time and our community. On this question, however, "tradition" offers but the most uncertain guidance. We have been unable to reach a consensus as to whether Jewish tradition is at all relevant to our discussion, whether it can serve as a useful framework for our response. Some of us accord significant persuasive weight to the voice of tradition on the issue of sexual orientation, as we do on every issue. Others contend that the tradition has little of value to say to us, because its teachings about homosexuality reflect the long-since-abandoned assumptions and prejudices of ages past. One participant in our debate has suggested that the very concept of "tradition" be understood in a radically new way, that we identify it not with the literary corpus of sacred text but exclusively with those principles which, discoverable in those texts, lead us in the direction of justice and progress. According to this reading, we could reject the discrete holdings and teachings of the Jewish past and replace them with an entirely contradictory decision, all in the name of "tradition" itself. The language of "tradition," in other words, no longer unites us in a common conversation, for the simple reason that as a Committee we cannot agree as to what that language is, says, or means with respect to the question before us.

Our discussions are generally framed in other languages as well. Like Reform Jews generally, we ascribe great weight to considerations of justice and ethics, to the findings of science and human knowledge, and to the lessons we learn from history and contemporary culture. Each of these more "modern" discourses reflects our religious openness to the world and all that is in it, our eagerness to learn from the best that the human mind and experience can offer. While we seek, as a matter of general practice, to affirm the stance of tradition wherever possible, we are ready to abandon or to modify that stance when we find that it conflicts intolerably with our sense of the good and the just, when it would throttle the spirit of liberality to which we are committed. Yet these languages, too, like that of tradition, lead us in radically divergent directions. Put oversimply, while the voice of modernity (or, perhaps, of post-modernity) convinces some of us that homosexual couples deserve the right to Jewish marriage, most of us, with all respect, disagree; though we, too, are Jews of the contemporary world, committed to doing justice and to heeding the call of knowledge, it is far from obvious to us that the tide of the times sweeps us to say "yes." To say that we are "liberal" and "enlightened," that is, does not automatically answer this question for us, any more than does the simple assertion of our attachment to Jewish faith and tradition.

Again, the problem is not the fact that we disagree over the answer but rather that we lack any consensus as to how to go about reaching it. Each side appeals for support to particular conceptions of "tradition," "justice," "progress" and "Reform" which the other side does not accept. The result is that there is little ground for common persuasive discourse. Argument, in other words, has come to an end.

Given this state of affairs, although the majority of the members of this Committee respond in the negative to our *she'elah*, it is extraordinarily difficult for us to issue a decision, in the normal sense of that term, as we usually do. We shall indeed, as we usually do, tally the votes among us and express the majority viewpoint. With that, however, we are painfully aware that *as a Committee* we lack a shared conceptual approach to this issue and that in the absence of a common discourse it matters little that one side or the other holds a numerical advantage among us. No majority decision could ever dispose of a question when the minority rejects the very foundations upon which that decision rests. No positive contribution can be made toward the resolution of this debate when the reasons and arguments advanced by either side are greeted with indifference or acrimony by the other. When no conversation can occur, no real learning is possible. When no real learning is possible, teaching becomes irrelevant. And in a place where teaching is irrelevant, rabbis have no ground upon which to stand and to speak.

We want, rather, to turn our attention away from *ending* the debate and toward its satisfactory resumption. The task of this Committee, we believe, is not only to issue decisions but also, and perhaps more so, to *argue*, to justify those decisions in a language which helps unite us with other Reform Jews in the pursuit of religious understanding. As rabbis, we reveal our deepest Jewish and moral commitments precisely through the process of argument, in the language with which we justify and explain ourselves and our decisions. On this issue, until now, language has failed us because it has divided us; argument has deadlocked, community has vanished. And it is to this situation we feel compelled to respond. It is our hope as a Committee that, in discussing this *she'elah*, we might begin to recover the rudiments of a common language of argument and justification. If we can identify some lines of thought, however vague and general, which help us *as a community* to articulate and to argue our positions on the question before us, then we will feel that we have accomplished our most significant objective.

The goal of this responsum is therefore to describe, as carefully as possible, the impasse we have reached; to outline with precision the points of disagreement among us; and to suggest those grounds upon which we agree, which offer the hope of a common direction which we might pursue in our ongoing conversation.

I. Sexual Orientation, Homosexuality, and Jewish Tradition.

We begin with a consideration of how the topic of homosexuality is construed within the Jewish tradition in general and within our own Reform tradition in particular. We want to hear what these traditions have to say, even though their message does not, as we have indicated, answer this *she'elah* for us as a Committee.

The Torah explicitly condemns the practice of male homosexual intercourse. Leviticus 18:22 instructs: "do not lie with a male as one lies with a woman (*mishkevey ishah*); it is an abhorrence (*to'evah*)." In Leviticus 20:13, we read: "if a man lies with a male as one lies with a woman (*mishkevey ishah*), the two of them have done an abhorrent thing (*to'evah*). They shall be put to death;[2] their bloodguilt is upon them." In both cases, the prohibition appears as part of a list of forbidden sexual acts (incest; adultery; relations with a menstruating woman; sex with animals) associated with the customs of the Canaanite peoples

---

2. See *M.* Sanhedrin 7:4, *BT* Sanhedrin 54a–b, and *Yad*, Isurey Bi'ah 1:4: the penalty is *sekilah*, or "stoning" according to its particular halakhic form (*M.* Sanhedrin 6:4).

whose land is assigned by God to Israel.³ Indeed, the Canaanites have defiled the land by committing these abhorrent acts (*to'evot*; 18:26, 30) and the land, as it were, cooperates with God's plan by "spewing" out its offending inhabitants to make way for the Israelites (18:24ff; 20:22ff). The Torah admonishes Israel⁴ to keep far from these practices and instead to observe God's statutes, which are a source of life (18:5) and holiness (20:7–8, 26).⁵

Rabbinic literature adds relatively little to this legal material. The Talmud contains few mentions of overt homosexual acts and no reports of executions carried out as punishment.⁶ We cannot determine how prevalent homosexual behavior may have been in the society of the time. At any rate the rabbinic sources, which we utilize as the building-blocks of our own textual conversation, imply that the phenomenon was either not widespread or successfully hidden or suppressed. Thus, while Rabbi Yehudah forbids a lone unmarried male from pasturing a beast and two unmarried males from sleeping together under a common blanket, the *chakhamim* permit these practices, because "Jews are not suspected of homosexual relations and of buggery."⁷ On the other hand, "one who avoids even *yichud* (being alone together) with another man or a beast is deserving of praise."⁸ Some authorities hold that "in these days" of moral decline, it is essential to prohibit *yichud* between unmarried men.⁹ Others, however, do not believe that the breakdown of sexual mores in "our communities" warrants such a stringency.¹⁰

Female homosexual activity is not mentioned by the Torah, in all probability because, unlike the forbidden unions (*arayot*) of Leviticus 18 and 20, it does not involve actual intercourse. Rabbinic tradition on the subject is somewhat mixed. The Babylonian *amora* Rav Huna was of the opinion that "women who commit lewdness with each other" (*nashim hamesolelot zo bezo*) are forbidden to be married to a priest. This act, he thought, counted as a form of harlotry (*zenut*) which normally disqualifies a woman from marriage to a *kohen* (Lev. 21:7).¹¹ The final *halakhah*, however, took the view that since this act, though licentious (*pritzuta*), was not one of actual intercourse, these women were permitted to marry into the priesthood, though they remained subject to the corporal punishment customarily meted out to all who violate the standards of sexual propriety.¹² Female

---

3. Male homosexual intercourse features as one of the wicked deeds of the Sodomites (hence, "sodomy"; Gen. 19:5) and of the Benjaminites in Gibeah (Jud. 19:22). In addition, the *kadesh* or male prostitute (I Kings 14:24, 15:12; II Kings 23:7) proscribed in Deut. 23:18 may have provided male homosexual intercourse; thus, at any rate, is how the Talmud (*BT* Sanhedrin 54b) interprets the verse, although *Targum Onkelos* reads it differently.
4. However, rabbinic tradition affirms that male homosexual intercourse (*mishkav zakhar*), like the other *arayot*, is forbidden to Gentiles as well; *BT* Sanhedrin 58a–b; *Yad*, Melakhim 9:5.
5. The concept of holiness is here identified with that of *distinctness*, of separateness from other peoples and their way of life (20:24, 26), a theme to which we shall return below.
6. See, for example, the story of R. Yehudah ben Pazi, who discovers two men having intercourse in the attic of the house of study. They warn him to keep silent, since in court his own testimony would be outweighed by theirs; *YT* Sanhedrin 6:3(6), 23c.
7. *M.* Kiddushin 4:14; *BT* Kiddushin 82a; *Yad*, Isurey Bi'ah 22:2; *SA* EHE 24.
8. *Yad, loc. cit.*
9. R. Yosef Karo in *SA, loc. cit.* See *Be'er Hagolah*, no. 3: "these are his own words"; *i.e.*, an opinion not derived from sources or precedent.
10. *Bayit Chadash* to *Tur*, EHE 24; *Chelkat Mechokek* and *Beit Shemuel* to *SA, loc. cit.*; *Yam shel Shelomo*, Kiddushin 4:23; *Arukh Hashulchan*, EHE 24, par. 6. This applies in general. When a man has committed an act of homosexual intercourse, some require that he avoid all *yichud* with males in the future; see R. Chaim Pelaggi, *Ruach Chayim* EHE 24.
11. *BT* Shabbat 65a–b; *BT* Yevamot 76a, Rashi, *s.v. pesulot lekehunah*.
12. *BT* Yevamot 76a; *Yad*, Isurey Bi'ah 21:8; *SA* EHE 20:2.

homosexual behavior, if not one of the *arayot*, is nonetheless stigmatized as an example of "Egyptian practice" (*ma'aseh eretz mitzrayim*) which is prohibited to Jews under the broad sweep of the prohibitions of Leviticus 18. "And what is 'Egyptian practice'? For men to marry men, women to marry women, and for a woman to marry two men."[13]

To the extent that the sources offer a rationale for the Toraitic and rabbinic condemnation of homosexual behavior, we find that the concern over the breakdown of marriage, the bearing of children, and "normal sexuality," the proper and accepted relations between the genders, figures prominently. The Talmud explains that the prescription that the male shall "cleave unto his wife" (Gen. 2:24) comes explicitly to prohibit homosexual intercourse; that is to say, homosexual behavior threatens marriage and childbirth.[14] Bar Kaparah offers an agadic etymology for *to'evah*, the biblical term for "abhorrence": *to'eh atta bah*, "you go astray after it."[15] The fourteenth-century Spanish commentator R. Nissim b. Reuven Gerondi explains: "one abandons heterosexual intercourse (*mishkevey isha*) and seeks sex with males."[16] That is to say, since sexual union is traditionally expressed within the context of marriage, the indulgence in homosexual intercourse is destructive of this most basic unit of society and community.[17] This theme continues in the medieval *Sefer Hachinukh*, mitzvah 209:

> God desires that human beings populate the world He created.[18] Therefore, He has commanded that they not destroy their seed through acts of unnatural intercourse which do not bear fruit (*i.e.*, children). These acts violate not only the commandment of marital intercourse (*mitzvat onah*) but also every standard of sexual propriety, since by its nature homosexual intercourse is despised by every person of reason. Thus, the human being, who was created to serve his God, should not bring shame upon himself through such disgusting behavior. And for these reasons the rabbis prohibited a man from marrying a barren woman or one who is past childbearing years.[19]

All of this leads to the general impression that, in Jewish tradition, homosexual behavior is a transgression against the order of nature; it is "an offense against the foundations of the universe (*yesodot haberi'ah*) to lie carnally with another male."[20]

The search for the "reasons for the commandments" (*ta'amey hamitzvot*) has always been a controversial one in halakhic discourse. Ultimately, after all, Jewish tradition holds that a *mitzvah* is a *mitzvah*, a divine decree (*gezerat hamelekh*) whose authority does not diminish because of our inability to fathom its purpose.[21] Indeed, the example of King

---

13. *Sifra* to Lev. 18:3; *Yad, loc. cit.*
14. *BT* Sanhedrin 58a. Note Rashi's comment to the next part of the Genesis verse, "and they shall become one flesh": "a child is created by both male and female, and it is in the child that their flesh becomes one."
15. *BT* Nedarim 51a.
16. *Ran*, Nedarim 51a, *s.v. to'eh atta bah*.
17. See also *Gen. Rabah* 26:5 and *Lev. Rabah* 23:9: the generation of the Flood was destroyed because they wrote wedding contracts for males and animals.
18. See *BT* Gitin 41b and Arakhin 2b: the world was created only for the sake of the commandment "be fruitful and multiply," as it is said (Isaiah 45:18), "He did not create it for waste, but formed it for habitation."
19. *BT* Yevamot 61b–62b; *Yad*, Ishut 15:7. A dispute exists in the literature as to whether a man ought to continue to try to beget children even after he has fulfilled the Toraitic *mitzvah* of procreation. Rambam holds, at least as a matter of Torah law, that one who has fulfilled this commandment may then marry a woman who is not capable of bearing children.
20. *Torah Temimah* to Lev. 18:22, no. 70, on *BT* Ned. 51a.
21. *BT* Berakhot 33b; *Yad*, Tefilah 9:7.

Solomon's reliance upon the stated reasons for the laws of kingship in Deuteronomy 17:14–19 is traditionally cited to prove that the investigation of *ta'amey hamitzvot* leads to disobedience of the Torah.[22] Despite this fear, however, the rabbis recognized the value of discovering meaning in the *mitzvot* even when it was not readily apparent in the biblical text. The Rambam is the great example of one who devoted much of his intellectual energy to this search, as is evidenced by Part III of *Moreh Nevukhim* and by his programmatic statements in the *Mishneh Torah*.[23] And it is almost superfluous to remind ourselves that the search for *reasons*, the rationale and purpose of religious observance, has been a hallmark of Reform Judaism since its inception. When we find that biblical commandments and other traditional institutions no longer reflect our religious consciousness or speak to the felt needs of our times, we do not hesitate to set them aside. Reform Jews have justified their rejection of the old ways according to a number of doctrines—the spirit of prophetic Judaism, the belief in progressive revelation, the commitment to personal religious autonomy, to name but a few. What unites all of them, however, is an awareness that any religious observance or pattern of life, in order to fully express our sense of God and holiness, must correspond to our conception of morality and of appropriateness. Put differently, a *mitzvah* cannot oblige us unless it has a *ta'am*, a rationale, unless it makes *sense* to us in some fundamental way. And for many Reform Jews, including some of us on this Committee, the biblical and rabbinic tradition concerning homosexuality no longer makes that kind of sense, for several reasons.

1. It no longer makes sense to look upon homosexuality as a *to'evah*. That very term has become ambiguous given our religious world-view and our habits of speaking. The Torah, for example, labels three categories of actions as "abominations": idolatry (Deuteronomy 17:4), the eating of forbidden animal species (Deuteronomy 14:3), and the sexual prohibitions of Leviticus 18 and 20. What these sins share in common is decidedly not the fact that they violate what we would call the "moral law." Rather, they transgress against the biblical boundaries of holiness which are meant to distinguish Israel from the other nations. These are acts, in other words, which are not necessarily "immoral" but Jewishly inappropriate.[24]

The problems with this concept for contemporary Reform Jews are therefore obvious. We as a movement have long since done away with the dietary laws as an obligatory element of our religious practice. Although many Reform Jews observe *kashrut* or avoid the biblically-prohibited species, we surely do not say that those in our community who eat these foods are committing an "abomination" thereby. We still oppose "idolatry," but even though we may not accept the practices of other faith communities, we do not tend to label their religious traditions as *avodah zarah*. Our attitude toward the religions of our neighbors is one of tolerance, not "abhorrence." We continue, of course, to abhor many of the sexual unions proscribed in Leviticus 18 and 20, but we do so not so much because the Torah finds them abhorrent but because we see them as violations of our most cherished moral standards. We condemn incest, for example, because it inherently involves an abusive relationship between family members of unequal status and power; it is an act that is

---

22. *BT* Sanhedrin 21b.
23. See *Yad*, Me'ilah 8:8 and Temurah 4:13.
24. See *BT* Avodah Zarah 66a and 71a, and Rashi to Deut. 14:3: a *to'evah* is that which God declares "abominable" and not necessarily that which we, on the basis of our unaided reason or moral sense, would find to be so.

destructive of the healthy personality, one which inflicts deep emotional and psychological damage that might never be healed. We oppose adultery on the grounds that an adulterous act is a transgression against trust and moral commitment between wives and husbands. Even when a spouse knowingly tolerates the adultery of his or her partner, we oppose such behavior as destructive of the family unit.

But while "abhorrence" may be a proper reaction toward many of the forbidden sexual unions (*arayot*), it does not apply to the case of homosexuality, for the issues cited in the sources as rationales for the prohibition fail to strike us as convincing on moral grounds. This is especially true in that we, unlike our ancestors, are aware of the possibility of committed, stable, monogamous, and loving relationships between members of the same gender. This structure of human life, which parallels the institution of heterosexual marriage, does not produce moral evil; it neither abuses nor betrays the innocent. Nor can we seriously contend that it threatens the family unit and the bringing of children into the world. In a social climate of increasing tolerance, homosexual people are correspondingly more likely to resist entry into heterosexual marriage for the sake of appearance and propriety. An acceptance of homosexuality does not, therefore, augur the breakdown of a household that is less and less likely to exist in the first place. In addition, when homosexual couples are able to bring children into their lives by means of adoption and artificial insemination, it is not true that engaging in homosexual behavior inevitably means the abandonment of that Jewish ideal.

We of the minority do not wish to be misunderstood. We do not claim that the concept of *to'evah* is of no religious relevance. We, no less than our colleagues, are prepared to view an act as "abominable" when it offends our most basic sense of holiness and Jewish propriety. We simply wish to emphasize that Reform Jews are no longer persuaded to avoid a particular act merely *because* the Torah calls it a *to'evah*. For us to accept this designation, the act must be abhorrent to *us*; it must strike *us* as a transgression against the most basic standards of *kedushah* that the Jewish people are called upon to uphold. And we no longer view homosexuality as such a transgression.

2. It no longer makes sense to classify homosexual behavior as a sin, much less a *to'evah*, given our contemporary understanding of the nature of human sexual orientation.[25] This is not to imply that we "understand" fully just what causes a person to "be" a heterosexual or a homosexual or even that we as a society can come to any satisfactory consensus as to what those terms actually mean.[26] It is to say, rather, that we tend to regard homosexuality *as* an orientation, as the product of a complex of causational factors which render it, like heterosexuality, a part of one's psychological makeup rather than the result of a conscious choice on the part of the individual. With this reality in mind, we can conclude that

---

25. In this we part company from the opinion expressed by our teacher, R. Solomon B. Freehof, who in a 1973 responsum (*American Reform Responsa*, no. 13) clearly declares homosexuality to be in the category of "sin." We would note that his *teshuvah* makes no mention at all of the nature of homosexuality as a sexual orientation, a structure of psyche which is not the product of individual choice. As such, we feel that its message has lost much of its relevance for today.
26. We cannot, in this setting, enter into a detailed consideration of the vast scientific literature on the nature and causes of human sexual orientation. Nor, for that matter, are we qualified to judge the scientific accuracy of that material. The CCAR's Ad Hoc Committee on Homosexuality and the Rabbinate, reporting to the Conference in 1990 (*CCAR Yearbook* 100 [1990], 109–110), found that the scientific community lacked unanimity on this question and that the very definition of sexual orientation depends largely upon the interpretations and constructions which various disciplines and groups place upon that concept.

the biblical and rabbinic proscriptions of homosexual behavior do not speak to the situation as we know it today. The Torah, that is to say, punishes males who choose to perform homosexual intercourse; it is silent on the phenomenon of *homosexuality*, a constitutional orientation to seek sexual intimacy with those of one's own gender. In order to be punished for committing a sin, the act must be the outcome of the sinner's choice, whether that choice is made willfully and knowingly (*bemezid*) or accidentally (*beshegagah*). If, however, an individual commits an act under coercion and duress (*ones*), Jewish law exempts that person from punishment.[27] What we know about sexual orientation suggests that it is emphatically not a matter of choice. We also know that gays and lesbians are as capable as heterosexuals of establishing monogamous, stable, and loving relationships with their partners. The tradition, which portrays homosexual behavior as promiscuous and unnatural, clearly does not address reality as we know it to be. And Judaism has not survived and flourished for millennia by ignoring reality. On the contrary: it accepts it, deals with it, and changes its perceptions accordingly.

3. It no longer makes sense to treat homosexuality as a *to'evah* when many of us in all sincerity no longer respond to it with "abhorrence" or "abomination." This has much to do with our increased awareness of and exposure to gay and lesbian people in our culture. Those who were taught to despise homosexuals and their "lifestyle" have found their perceptions radically altered as they have worked alongside gays and lesbians in business and in school, in the professions and the arts. Gays and lesbians, too, are active members of our synagogues, colleagues in the rabbinate, and creative contributors to our religious and intellectual life. We have come to know homosexual people *as* people, as human beings who, despite their difference from the rest of us, share the hopes and dreams and human aspirations that are common to us all. All of this has helped to personalize what was once simply a "phenomenon" and a deviation from the norm. It is more difficult to abhor a person, a flesh-and-blood human being, than an idea in the abstract. We have put faces on the idea of homosexuality, and this has made us think deeply about how we have acted and ought to act in the face of that idea, that reality. We have come to realize that our former knee-jerk reactions were hasty, uninformed, out of place.

4. It no longer makes sense to single out homosexuals for distinctive treatment when we acknowledge that we are liberals, heirs to a tradition of thought which holds that a human being's most personal decisions are properly left to private discretion with a minimum of interference from the state or the community. We tend to believe that most matters of sexuality between consenting adults are the business of those adults and not of outside institutions. It is our Reform Jewish practice to speak of these issues in the language of civil rights, a rhetoric of political liberation rather than moral rebuke. Thus, in 1977, the Central Conference of American Rabbis (CCAR), noting its long-standing support for the civil liberties of "all people, especially for those from whom these rights and liberties

---

27. The rule is *ones rachmana petarei*, "one is legally exempt for acts committed under duress"; see *BT* Bava Kama 28a and parallels. A problem with this analysis is that *gilui arayot*, the commission of acts of intercourse forbidden in Lev. 18 and 20, is normally prohibited even on pain of death; *BT* Sanh. 74a. Moreover, *ones* in sexual cases applies only to the female or passive "partner;" the male or active "partner" by definition is said to perform intercourse with intention; see *BT* Yevamot 53b and *Yad*, Isurey Bi'ah 1:9. However, see *Yad*, Yesodey Hatorah 5:4: when a person commits any act, including *gilui arayot*, under duress, he or she does not suffer the Torah's prescribed punishment. Moreover, there are times when human nature "compels one to desire" an otherwise forbidden thing and thus mitigates the act from the law's point of view (*Yad*, Isurey Bi'ah 1:9). This can be said to apply to our case, where homosexual behavior results from an orientation which, whatever its cause, is beyond the control or the will of the individual.

have been withheld," called for legislation to decriminalize homosexual acts between consenting adults and to remove any and all vestiges of discrimination against homosexuals as persons.[28] Moreover, we have adopted this stance within our own ranks. We reject any suggestion that a candidate's homosexuality be used as a bar to deny automatically his or her entry into the rabbinate; we urge that "all rabbis, regardless of sexual orientation, be accorded the opportunity to fulfill the sacred vocation that they have chosen."[29] Our attitudes toward homosexual people have departed, radically so, from those which one might derive from the traditional sources.

5. Finally, it no longer makes sense, to some of us, to deny to homosexual people the spiritual satisfactions of Jewish marriage. The CCAR has already declared its support for "the right of gay and lesbian couples to share fully and equally in the rights of civil marriage."[30] This is generally understood to mean a broad endorsement of the goals of "domestic partner legislation," under which same-sex partnerships might qualify for the financial and social benefits which society accords to married couples: tax exemptions and deductions; health insurance coverage, and so forth. To this extent, the resolution accords with the *halakhah*, which permits individuals to make stipulations in matters of monetary law (*diney mamonot*) that contradict the financial arrangements set forth in the Torah itself.[31] A community may therefore decide to treat a homosexual couple as a married couple, at least from a monetary standpoint, determining its laws of taxation and social welfare accordingly. But implicit in this position, some of us feel, is the recognition that *marriage* as a social institution is a proper "fit" for homosexual relationships which, like the best heterosexual relationships, can and do embody the qualities of love, respect, and exclusive commitment. Put differently, marriage is arguably the best and most proper framework within which the adult Jew whose natural desire for intimacy is with members of the same gender can conduct his or her relationships.

For these reasons some of us believe that the time has come for us as rabbis and as a movement to extend this recognition of homosexual relationships to the sphere of religious marriage. We base this belief upon our understanding of Jewish tradition and of Reform Jewish precedent. We hold that homosexuality is no longer a *to'evah*; it is not a mental illness nor a social deviancy; it is not a perversion of the natural order. Homosexuality is not a choice or a preference; it is not something that one decides to do or to abstain from doing. It is, like heterosexuality, the way one is. It is not, in short, what is condemned by Leviticus 18:22 and 20:13. As such, it makes no sense on religious or moral grounds to differentiate between people on the basis of sexual orientation. As liberals, as Reform Jews, we no longer accept any of the theoretical rationales of the prohibitions against homosexual behavior. We partake of a religious culture which affirms the right and the duty of its members to set aside those aspects of the tradition which no longer reflect our consciousness of reality and morality. We therefore lack any defensible moral or religious grounds to withhold from gays and lesbians the opportunity to express

---

28. *CCAR Yearbook* 87 (1977), 86; *CCAR Yearbook* 100 (1990), 107.
29. *CCAR Yearbook* 90 (1990), 109 and 111. There, it is reported that the Hebrew Union College–Jewish Institute of Religion considers a rabbinical-school applicant's sexual orientation only within the context of that applicant's overall suitability for the rabbinate generally. The resolution as passed by the Conference endorsed this admissions policy.
30. *CCAR Yearbook* 106 (1996), 330.
31. See *BT* Bava Metzi'a 94a and *Yad*, Ishut 6:9. On this basis, a husband and wife can stipulate whatever financial arrangements they wish to govern their marital affairs; see *Yad*, Ishut 12:1ff.

the sanctity of those unions in precisely the way that heterosexual couples have always expressed it: through marriage.

And yet, despite their cogency, these arguments do not convince all of us, certainly not a majority of this Committee, to endorse rabbinic officiation at same-sex "marriage" or commitment ceremonies. We would point out that no resolution of the CCAR has expressed its approval of officiation. The very resolution which calls for gay and lesbian couples to be granted the benefits of civil marriage explicitly declares that "this is a matter of civil law, and is separate from the question of rabbinic officiation at such marriages." The Conference, in other words, does not take the final step of equating civil and religious marriage for homosexuals as do some of our colleagues. Indeed, to the extent that the Conference and its constituent committees have expressed an opinion on the subject, that opinion has been negative. This Committee has held that "however we may understand homosexuality . . . we cannot accommodate the relationship of two homosexuals as a 'marriage' within the context of Judaism," for none of the elements of *kiddushin*, of traditional Jewish marriage, can be invoked for that relationship.[32] And such was the position of the CCAR's Ad Hoc Committee on Homosexuality and the Rabbinate, whose majority stated in 1990:[33]

> In Jewish tradition heterosexual, monogamous, procreative marriage is the ideal human relationship for the propagation of the species, covenantal fulfillment, and the preservation of the Jewish people. While acknowledging that there are other human relationships which possess ethical and spiritual value and that there are some people for whom heterosexual, monogamous, procreative marriage is not a viable option or possibility, the majority of the committee reaffirms unequivocally the centrality of this ideal and its special status as *kiddushin*.

It is true that this *she'elah* asks us to reconsider all these precedents and that it is our right and our duty to do so. Yet it is at the least of some real significance that we as a rabbinate do not officially recognize homosexual relationships as marriage. Those of us who are not persuaded that the time has come to change this position wish to explain, as respectfully and cogently as we can, why we continue to adhere to our view.

1. We begin by suggesting that, in this argument, the burden of proof does not rest with us. This is no mere debaters' quibble. Frequently, in discussions of this sort in liberal circles such as ours, one hears the question posed as "why not?" That is to say, "why *shouldn't* we, as liberals who are open to new ideas, adopt this change?" To frame the issue in this way is to declare that, at least on this subject, the cumulative weight of millennia of Jewish tradition hardly counts. That tradition, as we have seen, condemns homosexual behavior in no uncertain terms, and even the Reform Jewish tradition has to date spoken negatively to the subject of our *she'elah*. As members of the Responsa Committee, we take tradition seriously and consider it prayerfully. Even on this subject, so often (and, to some of us, falsely) presented as a stark contrast between the values of the present versus those of an outdated past, tradition serves as our interpretive starting point. Those who

---

32. *Contemporary American Reform Responsa*, no. 200 (from 1985). See also *American Reform Responsa*, no. 14 (from 1981).
33. *CCAR Yearbook* 100 (1990), 110.

advocate a revolutionary transformation of Jewish marriage law and practice rightly shoulder the burden of proving that theirs is the better position.

We would add, parenthetically, this note concerning "tradition."[34] We do not form our moral beliefs out of thin air, as the result of some contemplative procedure carried on exclusively within ourselves. Nor do we derive them from some absolute source of moral truth that is accepted as determinative by all people everywhere. All our moral beliefs are socially constructed, rooted in the traditions and in the communities in which we participate. A community is the embodiment of a tradition, an ongoing, historically-centered argument about how a particular form of the ideal life is to be lived. A tradition, to be sure, can and does change; it develops as its members respond to new experiences which impel them to revise or modify their beliefs. For this reason, "argument" is a central and necessary feature of the life of any community. But this development and this argument always occur in reference to the beliefs, values, and accumulated experience of that community's past. Traditions, therefore, are inescapably particular; they are the record of a *particular* community's thought, experience, and struggle with circumstance and change.

What this teaches us is that the choice we face is not a decision between a particular Jewish tradition on the one hand and some set of universally-valid moral precepts on the other, because the latter does not exist in the real world. *All* evaluative concepts with which we measure and construct our moral universe—concepts such as "good," "evil," and "religious fulfillment"—are *particularly* determined. They emerge from specific traditions, from the historical religious experiences of specific communities. Our dilemma on this subject arises from the fact that we, as liberal Jews, belong to different communities, each with its own historically-centered tradition. The tradition of Western modernity—which, we point out, is no less "particular" or "historically-centered" than any other—lends itself to certain interpretations, and these affect us deeply. But we are also members of a religious community called Israel, and this means that among the particular vantage points from which we reflect upon our beliefs, the texts and sources of Jewish tradition must inevitably play a central role. We believe that our authority to act as rabbis, especially to officiate at weddings as *mesadrey kiddushin*, flows not from our perception of ourselves as "modern spiritual leaders" but from our standing as representatives and teachers of Torah and Jewish tradition. Our moral horizon is shaped, to a significant extent, by our interaction with Jewish literature and the Jewish past. It is so; it must be so; and we need not apologize when those sources call upon us to consider conclusions which differ from those seemingly demanded by the other particular traditions in which we partake.

2. Those who advocate homosexual marriage have not, in the opinion of our majority, met their burden of proof. That is, their arguments do not succeed in overcoming the opposition to this practice found in both the Jewish and the Western traditions.[35] We do not accept the suggestion that the ritual category of *to'evah* is irrelevant to the question under discussion. While we Reform Jews have departed from traditional practice in many

---

34. Readers will note the affinity between the ideas expressed in this paragraph and the works of such contemporary thinkers as Hans-Georg Gadamer, Alisdair MacIntyre, Michael Perry, Hillary Putnam and others. We are in no position to consider here whether these thinkers are "right" about the concept of tradition. We refer to them only as a reference point for a view we find persuasive: namely, that all moral thinking begins with tradition.

35. It bears emphasis that this *she'elah* is not a case of conflict between "Jewish tradition" on one side and "modernity" on the other. As of this writing, no "modern," "liberal" Western jurisdiction recognizes homosexual marriage as legally valid. This fact is evidence that the "modern Western tradition" is at least as divided as we are on this question and offers but uncertain support to the advocates of same-sex marriage.

areas, we continue to "abhor" virtually all of the sexual prohibitions listed in Leviticus 18 and 20 as destructive of the Jewish conception of a life of holiness and morality.[36] While it may be true that we as a community no longer look upon homosexual behavior, as we once did, as a revulsive act, the fact remains that no Jewish community has ever gone so far as to sanctify as marriage a sexual relationship which the Torah defines as *ervah*. Not even we, with all our liberality, have ever done this before.[37] To do so now would be a revolutionary step, one which would sunder us from all Jewish tradition, including our own, down to the most recent times.

At this point, we raise the delicate issue of Jewish unity. The extension of *kiddushin* to gays and lesbians would break so sharply with the standards of religious practice maintained by virtually all Jewish communities as to wreak havoc upon our relationships with most of them. A decision of this nature would continue a trend, which many Reform rabbis find quite troubling, of pushing the Reform movement toward the margins of our people, of the Jewish community as a whole. It would have dramatic and negative effects upon the standing of our Progressive colleagues in Israel and elsewhere. We know that the slogan "*kelal yisrael*" has often been used to intimidate us, to urge us to compromise our Reform Jewish principles to mollify those who will never compromise their own. We also know that the Ad Hoc Committee on Homosexuality and the Rabbinate has already addressed this issue, declaring that while we ought to be sensitive to this concern, we must make our decision independently of it, in the context of the North American situation, according to "the principles and practices of Reform Judaism."[38] Given, however, that our majority believe that the principles and practices of Reform Judaism do *not* require that we sanction marriage for homosexual couples, we would not set aside our concern for Jewish unity—which, we submit, is itself a "Reform Jewish principle."

3. Reform Judaism, as most of us understand it, does not mandate gay/lesbian marriage. Yes, we recognize that the attitudes of our community and society toward homosexuals and homosexuality have undergone a profound transformation in recent years. All of us are encouraged at the signs that a long history of repression and hatred is at last beginning to give way to a spirit of tolerance and inclusion. All of us stand as one behind the statement of the Ad Hoc Committee that "all human beings are created *betselem Elohim* ('in the divine image'). Their personhood must therefore be accorded full dignity. Sexual orientation is irrelevant to the human worth of a person."[39] But this affirmation, which demands that we work for full social and political equality for gays and lesbians, does not logically require that we must also support a Jewish religious "right" to homosexual marriage. From our acknowledgement of the right of gay and lesbian couples to arrange their financial affairs in the way they see fit, it does not logically follow that we must declare that their relationship partakes of the same religious sanctity as does traditional marriage. Similarly, we recognize that the understanding of homosexuality as an orientation rather

---

36. This is a point of vital significance. While the fact that Reform Judaism has departed from traditional standards of practice in one area suggests that we might abandon them in another, it does not logically *require* that we do so. Each issue has to be judged on its own particular merits.

37. The prohibition against sex with a *nidah*, or menstruating woman (Lev. 18:19), may be something of an exception. Though we have never "legalized" it, the subject is absent from virtually all discussions of sexual ethics in Reform Judaism. At any rate, the *halakhah* also distinguishes between the *nidah* and the other *arayot* in that *kiddushin* with the former, unlike with the latter, is recognized as valid; *BT* Yevamot 49b and *SA* EHE 61:1.

38. *CCAR Yearbook* 100 (1990), 110–111.

39. Ibid., 109.

than an intended choice (*ones* rather than *ratzon*) leads to the conclusion that the act of homosexual intercourse cannot be understood in traditional legal terms as a punishable sin. Again, however, the fact that a pattern of behavior is in some way involuntary does not necessarily mean we must sanctify it. Indeed, given the prevailing uncertainty as to the causes and development of sexual orientation—genetic or environmental? constitutional or socially constructed?—some of us are quite hesitant to draw the kinds of conclusions which need to be drawn in order to justify the institution of homosexual marriage.[40]

4. We are, all of us, committed to enabling gays and lesbians to live full Jewish lives within our communities. And, since we acknowledge that gays and lesbians are as capable as heterosexuals of forming monogamous, stable, and loving relationships, this commitment might—or might not—suggest a ritual response that reflects the spiritual reality which shapes the lives of these Jewish human beings. We shall consider this question in detail in Part III of this responsum. In itself, however, this commitment does not require that we endorse the creation of a religious institution of marriage for homosexuals when the entirety of Jewish tradition suggests that "marriage" is an exclusively heterosexual phenomenon. Again, it does not logically follow that our concern for gays and lesbians demands that we officiate at marriage ceremonies for them.[41]

From this discussion it should be obvious that the members of this Committee differ widely and deeply on the general subject of sexual orientation and on the specific issue of homosexuality and Judaism. We disagree fundamentally on the relevance of the Jewish, Reform Jewish, and Western traditions in addressing the issues raised by this *she'elah*. The moral and religious commitments that we do share lead us to radically differing conclusions. None of the moral languages we customarily speak when arguing our positions affords us sufficient common ground to arrive either at an answer or even at a consensus as to how the question is to be addressed.

II. *Kiddushin*, Reform Judaism, and Homosexuality.

There is, however, another way to frame the issue. Perhaps, we might say, we ought not to proceed from a consideration of our attitudes toward homosexuality and sexual orientation but rather from our conception of Jewish marriage. As our *sho'el* puts it: do homosexual unions "qualify as *kiddushin* from a Reform perspective"? That is to say, given that we recognize the existence of stable and committed gay and lesbian relationships, do these unions display enough of the major characteristics of marriage so as to deserve that title? To put the question in this way entails that we define, as carefully and as fully as we can,

---

40. See note 26. As the Ad Hoc Committee on Homosexuality and the Rabbinate notes, "the specific origin of sexual identity and its etiology are still imperfectly understood"; *CCAR Yearbook* 100 (1990), 109. In other words, we do not know with scientific certainty just what sexual orientation *is* or how a person develops one kind of sexual orientation as opposed to another. While we as individuals may believe that we are in possession of a clear understanding of the nature of sexual orientation, we *as a Committee* are unable to advance beyond the uncertainty expressed by the Ad Hoc Committee.

41. Similarly, while we must show love and concern for the intermarried couples in our midst, such a duty in no way *requires* that we as rabbis offer religious sanction to their unions. This analogy does not, of course, perfectly mirror the situation of homosexual couples. The differences and similarities will be discussed in Part III, below. It is cited here merely to demonstrate that compassion for human persons does not automatically entail that we offer ritual sanction their particular sexual relationships.

what we mean by "Jewish marriage." Does our definition of that institution allow for its extension to gay and lesbian couples? It is to this exploration we now turn.

It is important to note that, when we refer in this section to "marriage," we do not mean the idea of marriage in the abstract or marriage as a cross-cultural anthropological fact. We mean rather *Jewish* marriage as an aspect of the social and religious life of a particular historical community. Jewish marriage is an institution and a pattern of life with its own unique structure and history. It resembles, in many respects, other institutions of marriage, yet in many other ways it differs from them, and radically so. To say that a monogamous homosexual union is "like" a marriage does not prove, therefore, that it qualifies under the definition of *Jewish* marriage. Before we can ask whether to extend the possibility of marriage to gay and lesbian couples, we need first to understand the institutional nature of Jewish marriage and to consider the variations which Reform Judaism has introduced into the practice. It is in this way, and only in this way, that we can begin to consider whether homosexual couples can be included within the circumference of a "Reform perspective" on *kiddushin*.

What Is *Kiddushin?*

The word *kiddushin*, by which we designate Jewish marriage, is discussed as follows in an important Reform Jewish text:[42]

> Nothing clarifies the Jewish attitude toward marriage quite as well as the traditional name for the wedding ceremony, *Kiddushin*, derived from the Hebrew *kadosh* — holy — ... while all relationships, like all time and space, should be considered essentially sacred, certain relationships are especially exalted. In Judaism the Holy of Holies of all relationships, to which the poetic genius of the Hebraic spirit turned most often for the paradigm of the covenant between God and Israel, was and is the covenant between husband and wife.... A sacred entity comes into being in Jewish marriage. As in the *Kiddush* of Shabbat we set apart a period of *time* as holy, in *Kiddushin* the husband and wife set each other apart....
>
> *Kiddushin* is the rooting of the human in the realm of the sacred, with the goal that all our relationships become holy, bearing the blossom and the fruit of life.
>
> A Jewish marriage, then, takes place when a man and a woman [say] to [each] other: "Behold you are consecrated to me ... according to the tradition of Moses and Israel." It is as if each were saying to the other: "I will do everything that I can to make our relationship sacred."

This passage speaks the language of *agadah*, the evocative, lyrical, and metaphorical vernacular of Jewish lore. Taking as its point of departure a single word, *kiddushin*, it weaves a rich tapestry of religious ideas. What do we mean by "sacred," *kadosh*? What can it mean to call the institution of marriage a "sanctification"? How do the images, feelings, and responses we associate with the concept of holiness shed light upon the nature and purpose of the marital bond? To the extent that we adopt this agadic approach to the definition of *kiddushin*, then surely it is possible to make a place for gays and lesbians within the

---

42. R. Herbert Bronstein, in Rabbi Simeon J. Maslin, ed., *Gates of Mitzvah* (New York: CCAR, 1979), 123–124.

institution of marriage. For if *kiddushin*, like its Hebrew root, implies a "setting apart," the creation of a relationship of exclusive commitment and devotion similar to that which defines the relationship of Israel to its God, then homosexuals, who are as capable as heterosexuals of establishing exclusive and loving unions, deserve to be included.

Yet the *agadah* does not define *kiddushin*, any more than poets define marriage. True, *agadah* calls our attention to the most exalted possibilities inherent in the union of husband and wife. But it does not describe (because that is not its function) the nature of marriage as a legal institution, which it manifestly is.[43] That is to say, the full meaning of *kiddushin* cannot be conveyed by means of a homiletical treatise upon the etymology of that word. It is a complex of law and custom which, like "marriage" in every other social tradition, effects far-reaching transformations in the legal status of the parties involved. Our hearts soar at the mention of the aggadic aspects of *kiddushin*. But to ignore the legal, halakhic aspects of Jewish marriage is to distort what *kiddushin* really is and the way it functions in the fabric of traditional Jewish life.

Kiddushin is the rabbinic legal term for "Jewish marriage," which means first and foremost a marriage contracted between two Jews.[44] A marriage contracted with one of the *arayot*—a partner to whom one is prohibited by Leviticus 18—is invalid, and no *get* is required to permit the parties to remarry.[45] The legal bond of *kiddushin* (also called *erusin*) is created by a *ma'aseh kinyan*, an act of acquisition performed between the couple. In its accepted, customary form,[46] this act requires that, in the presence of two witnesses,[47] the man give the woman a ring or some other object of monetary value and declare, either in an explicit verbal formula or by behavior which clearly manifests his intent, that he wishes her to be his wife.[48] If she accepts the ring or object in a manner which indicates her freely-given consent to the marriage,[49] the couple are betrothed, though the marriage process is not completed until the ceremony of *chupah* or *nisu'in*.[50]

Kiddushin creates the following legal consequences.

---

43. We know that "Reform Jewish marriage" is often identified in the public mind as a purely "spiritual" endeavor, the legal aspects of the marital union being left to the control of the state. We regard this as an unfortunate historical error. In Jewish religious thought, marriage is a legal as well as a spiritual institution, and to understand marriage as a category of *Jewish* life requires that we take both its aspects seriously. That the legal implications of marriage are determined in practice by the civil law in most Western countries does not alter this elemental fact of history and religion.
44. *M.* Kiddushin 3:12. The *halakhah* recognizes the validity of a marriage between two Gentiles, in that the "children of Noah" are forbidden the *arayot*, the proscribed sexual practices of Leviticus 18, which include adultery. See also *Yad*, Ishut 1:1, where Rambam describes the law of marriage "before the Torah was given" and *Magid Mishneh ad loc*. However, the word *kiddushin* never designates non-Jewish marriage, and Jewish law is indifferent as to the ritual or ceremony by which Gentile traditions effect the marriage bond.
45. *M.* Kiddushin 3:12.
46. *M.* Kiddushin 1:1 lists three methods of effecting the *kinyan*: *kesef* (money); *shetar* (written document); or *bi'ah* (sexual intercourse). While any of these methods is halakhicly valid, the use of *kesef* is the universal custom; *Yad*, Ishut 3:21. Out of moral concern, the early Babylonian *amoraim* forbade the use of *bi'ah* as a method of contracting marriage; *BT* Kiddushin 12b.
47. *BT* Kiddushin 65b–66a; *Yad*, Ishut 4:6.
48. *BT* Kiddushin 5b–6a; *Yad*, Ishut 3:1. The wife is the passive party here; she neither gives the money nor recites the formula. If, however, *he* gives the money and *she* recites the formula, some authorities suggest the marriage may be valid. See *SA* EHE 27:8.
49. Marriage, unlike any other *kinyan*, requires the clear consent of the "acquired" party, the wife; *BT* Kiddushin 2b and Bava Batra 48b; *Yad*, Ishut 4:1.
50. *BT* Kiddushin 10a; *Yad*, Ishut 10:1.

1. The wife enters the husband's legal domain, or *reshut*, meaning that she is permitted sexually only to her husband. In so doing she becomes an *ervah* to all other men, and sexual intercourse between her and any of them is adultery. This, as far as the Talmud is concerned, is the original meaning of the word *kiddushin:* "he forbids her to all other men, as though she were *hekdesh* (consecrated property)."[51] The wife's status changes only at the dissolution of the marriage, upon the husband's death or upon divorce, at which time the woman "acquires herself" and re-enters her own *reshut*.[52]
2. The list of *arayot*, of forbidden sexual partners, expands to include the relatives of the spouse, as mentioned in Leviticus 18 and 20. The offspring of any of those prohibited unions, whether incestuous or adulterous, is a *mamzer*.[53]
3. Once the couple are betrothed, the laws of levirate marriage and release (*yibum* and *chalitzah*) go into effect. Should the husband die without having children, his widow is forbidden to remarry until her brother(s)-in-law perform either of these two rituals.[54]

All the other legal consequences of Jewish marriage, primarily those relating to the financial arrangements between the husband and wife, come into being at the ceremony of *nisu'in*.

Kiddushin, therefore, is a legal transaction which alters the conjugal status of the parties involved, making them subject to the laws of adultery, *arayot*, and *mamzerut*. The nature of *kiddushin* as a matter of legal experience is best summarized perhaps in the words of the blessing (*birkat erusin*) which the rabbis ordained for recitation at the time the transaction is carried out:[55]

> Praised are You, Adonai our God, sovereign of the Universe, Who has sanctified us through *mitzvot* and commanded us concerning the forbidden relations (*arayot*), Who has forbidden us to the betrothed (*ha'arusot*) and has permitted us to those whom we have married (*hanesu'ot*) by means of *chupah* and *kiddushin*. Praised are You, Adonai our God; You sanctify (*mekadesh*) Your people Israel by means of *chupah* and *kiddushin*.

In other words, Jewish marriage as a legal act establishes and transforms previously existing sexual boundaries. Two individuals who were previously forbidden to each other sexually are now permitted as husband and wife. Individuals who previously were potential marriage partners have now, due to their family relation to our spouse, become *arayot*, prohibited as incest. A formerly unmarried woman is now forbidden by the law of adultery to all men but her husband until he dies or the two of them are divorced.[56]

---

51. *BT* Kiddushin 2b. Tosafot, *s.v. de'asar*, notes that the use of *hekdesh* language in a secular transaction is unique to marriage; thus, perhaps, the sanctity of marriage lies at least in part in its essential un-likeness to every other kind of legal act.
52. *M.* Kiddushin 1:1 and Rashi, *s.v. vekonah et atzmah*.
53. *M.* Kiddushin 3:12.
54. Deut. 25; *Yad*, Yibum Vechalitzah 1:1.
55. *BT* Ketubot 7b. See *Yad*, Ishut 3:24, where the conclusion (*chatimah*) of the benediction is simply: . . . *mekadesh yisrael*, "Who sanctifies Israel."
56. And see Rashi, *BT* Ketubot 7b, *s.v. ve'asar lanu*: even the husband is forbidden to his betrothed wife, under rabbinic if not Toraitic law, until the time of *chupah* (*nisu'in*).

It is through reference to the *arayot*[57] that we can understand the meaning of *kiddushin* as a legal institution. It is a "sanctification," a "setting apart," the creation of an exclusive sexual relationship between husband and wife by which God sanctifies (*mekadesh*) Israel. Just as the early rabbis understood the commandment to "be holy" as a call to abstain from the *arayot*, so *kiddushin* rests upon a clear conception of the sexual relationships which the Torah has prohibited and permitted to the Israelite community. There is no such thing, in other words, as *Jewish* marriage in the absence of the prohibitions of the *arayot*, the recognition of the boundaries of permitted and prohibited sexual intercourse. And no marriage is a valid *Jewish* marriage if it is contracted between persons prohibited to each other as *arayot*.

Reform Judaism and *Kiddushin*

At this juncture we should ask ourselves whether and to what extent we continue to accept this halakhic notion of *kiddushin* in our Reform practice. For if our understanding differs substantially from that of the rabbinic tradition, we might have strong ground on which to claim that very different sorts of "marriage" qualify as *kiddushin* "from a Reform perspective."

Again, differing perspectives exist among us.

On the one hand, some of us would argue that Reform Jewish marriage is essentially different from the biblical and rabbinic institutions of *erusin* and *kiddushin*. We do not regard marriage as a *kinyan*, an act by which the woman is "acquired" by her husband and passes into his legal domain. We reject the association of marriage with the other "acts of acquisition"—of land, chattel, Hebrew and Canaanite slaves—redacted together in the first chapter of *Mishnah* Kiddushin. And the widespread custom among us for the bride to "sanctify" the groom, just as he "sanctifies" her, by offering him a ring and pronouncing the formula *harey attah mekudash li*, suggests that we have transformed marriage into an egalitarian, reciprocal reality which differs substantially from the structure of *kiddushin* in the halakhic tradition.

The tradition's linkage of marriage to the *arayot* is also problematic for us. It is a fact, first of all, that we no longer observe the laws of *yibum*, *chalitzah*, and *mamzerut*. And, as we discuss above, the very notion of *arayot* has been reconstructed in our discourse from a ritual to a moral problem. Thus, while we without any doubt acknowledge that numerous sexual relations remain forbidden, our primary concern is that the union between spouses be one that expresses our deepest moral conceptions of marriage, that it be one of exclusive sexual commitment. And there is no reason why gays and lesbians cannot establish such a union. When we stand under the *chupah*, we celebrate a joining together of two individuals in a relationship of equality and of love, one that promises emotional as well as sexual fulfillment, one which allows them to build a home that expresses Jewish values. This, in its essence, is what we mean when we call our marriages by the name *kiddushin*. If gay and lesbian couples, no less than their heterosexual counterparts can aspire to that kind of relationship, it would seem that *kiddushin* or "marriage," as *we Reform Jews* understand those terms, are fit names for it.

---

57. *Sifra* to Lev. 19:2, and see Rashi and Ramban *ad loc.*

Yet the majority of us would argue that this definition of Reform Jewish marriage, while accurate, is but part of a wider picture. The classical rabbinic conception of *kiddushin* retains much of its relevance for us. We note, first of all, that the language of *kinyan* or acquisition is the mechanism by which Jewish law creates legal obligations of any kind; thus, even if we no longer hold that the husband "acquires" the wife, both parties do indeed "acquire" from the other all the legal obligations which flow from the formation of marriage. In addition, we would claim that the reciprocal act of "sanctification" which takes place under a Reform Jewish *chupah* indicates the *strengthening* rather than the abandonment of the concept of *kiddushin*. It is our conviction that *both* bride *and* groom pass into the other's domain. The exclusivity of the marital relationship, the "setting apart" that lies at the heart of the idea of holiness and *kiddushin* itself, is now a mutual reality. We have not discarded the idea of *kiddushin*. On the contrary: we have extended its definition and its essence so that all its power and stringency apply to the husband as well as to the wife.[58]

The issue of *arayot*, too, remains central to our conception of marriage. It is certainly true that, when standing under the *chupah* on the day of their great joy, the bride and the groom in all likelihood do not think about the laws of incest, adultery, and divorce. Their minds and those of the community are rightly centered upon the more agadic and poetic elements of the union they are forming. Yet the legal facts of personal status continue to define the structure of Jewish marriage as we understand it. We may not discuss the *arayot* in our wedding sermons, but they are no less real to us on that account. We abhor incest[59] and marital infidelity, and we do not remarry either husband or wife until they have brought an end to their marriage by legal means.[60] The marital ceremony, as the *birkat erusin* teaches us,[61] comes to establish the contours of the *arayot*; it draws lines and sets boundaries which we continue to respect. *Kiddushin* is therefore more than an exalted moment of spirituality. It is as well a *legal* institution, whose structure and boundaries, no less than its feelings and emotions, are legitimate matters of rabbinic concern.

Given that the function of *kiddushin* has always been to draw lines that separate us (*i.e.*, "sanctify us") from the *arayot*, it is implausible to suggest that this legal act can actually permit a sexual relationship which the Torah and all of tradition so define.[62] Moreover, as we have noted, *kiddushin* effects a change in the legal status of the parties by making them

---

58. To refer again to the above citation from *Gates of Mitzvah*: "in *Kiddushin* the husband and wife set each other apart."
59. See the list of "Prohibited Marriages," both *de'oraita* and *derabanan*, in *Rabbi's Manual*, 235–236.
60. While the Reform movement in the United States accepts the validity of civil divorce (*Rabbi's Manual*, 244–246), the preponderant majority of our colleagues elsewhere require a *get* before remarriage. In addition, the American movement has explained its acceptance of civil divorce in traditional halakhic terminology: since divorce in Jewish law is regarded as a matter of monetary law (itself a controversial assumption), a divorce decree emanating from a civil court is valid at Jewish law under the doctrine of *dina demalkhuta dina*. In this sense, we continue to practice "Jewish divorce," since the secular courts act as our designated agents. On the history of Reform and the divorce question see *ARR*, no. 162, Solomon B. Freehof, *Reform Jewish Practice I*, 99–110, and Moses Mielziner, *The Jewish Law of Marriage and Divorce in Ancient and Modern Times*. Cincinnati: Bloch, 1884, 130–137. Moreover, the introduction of the Ritual of Release (*Rabbi's Manual*, 97–104) suggests that the movement is beginning to reconsider the necessity of some Jewish ritual procedure to mark the dissolution of a marriage.
61. It is true, but irrelevant, that the text of this *berakhah* in our *Rabbi's Manual*, 52–53, omits the prohibitions of *arayot* and *arusot*. Would anyone seriously argue that incest and adultery are thereby permitted? The omission may reflect the aesthetic concerns of the *Manual*'s liturgists, but its amended text does not describe our understanding of marriage as a legal institution.
62. We use the terms *ervah* and *arayot* here in their traditional Judaic context: they refer to those sexual unions which the Torah so classifies, and no Jewish marriage can take place between the two individuals involved. Whether we as individuals or as a group feel that any one of these unions is no longer "sinful" is a separate question and quite irrelevant to the point we are making here.

subject to the laws of adultery and divorce and by expanding the range of the prohibited incestual *arayot*. Whatever the potential of homosexual couples to establish loving and stable relationships, these laws do not apply to them. The partners in a homosexual union cannot legally commit incest with each other's relatives; they cannot legally commit adultery; and neither requires a divorce should he or she desire to enter into a Jewish marriage. It therefore makes little sense to use the term *kiddushin* to describe a union which involves none of these matters and does not alter the legal status of its participants.[63]

Most of the members of this Committee oppose the use of the term *kiddushin* to describe a gay or lesbian union, precisely because the historic definition of that term, its legal content and the notions of *kedushah* which lie at its foundations rule out its application to anything but heterosexual Jewish marriage. We accept the traditional understanding of *Jewish* marriage as that kind of marriage which recognizes and is contracted within the sexual boundaries set by the Torah's law of *arayot*. Even those of us who believe that *kedushah*, sanctity, can exist in gay and lesbian relationships and who would recognize those unions as a form of Jewish marriage concede that the word *kiddushin* is difficult to separate from its heterosexual connotations.

III. Gay and Lesbian Unions: Toward a Response.

Although the disagreements among us are real and deep, proceeding from radically different perspectives on homosexuality and Judaism and on the nature of Jewish marriage, there are some things—to be sure, basic and elementary things—on which we do see eye to eye. Therefore, before we rehearse our differences, let us acknowledge those assumptions we share in common. In the midst of divisiveness, these points of agreement may serve to remind us that, though we dispute the answers, we as rabbis are united by the questions we ask and by the religious commitments that stir us to ask them.

We agree that all human beings, regardless of sexual orientation, are created in the image of God and that it is the religious duty of Reform rabbis to treat all of them with respect and with love. This statement, we further agree, is more than a platitude; it is an aspiration which calls us to action. It demands of us that we receive all those who come before us with compassion and empathy. It demands that we hear them before we preach to them, that we listen to their stories of pain and exclusion, and that we respond to them as rabbis, as teachers of an ancient and honorable religious tradition.

And we agree that this response, first and foremost, must be one of invitation. Two centuries of modernity have brought us much progress, but they have exacted a price in the form of Jewish alienation. In our day, when so many Jews for so many reasons are spiritually exiled from Torah and from Jewish life, the *mitzvah* of outreach partakes of the age-old Jewish dream of *kibutz galuyot*. We must practice that *mitzvah* with all our strength.

What, then, do we say and how do we respond to the gays and lesbians in our midst who join together in committed relationships and seek to build a home and a life according to a pattern that expresses Jewish values? What does the duty of compassion and empathy, the *mitzvah* of outreach require us to do?

---

63. Some suggest that we institute divorce procedures for gay and lesbian couples and that we prohibit sexual infidelity among them as though these were adultery and incest. This would have the effect of making homosexual unions fully parallel to traditional marriage. The problem, of course, is that these boundaries and requirements would be entirely our own creation; they are not what the Torah considers "adultery," "incest," and "divorce." It is the Torah's definition of *arayot*—and *not* our own—which is central to the traditional conception of *kiddushin*.

For some of us, that duty requires the institution of wedding ceremonies for homosexual couples. To include gay and lesbian Jews as equal members of our communities means that we must advance far beyond mere toleration of their presence. They should rather be encouraged, like their heterosexual counterparts, to find partners and to form monogamous, stable, and hopefully permanent relationships. We do not believe that, in so doing, we either promote homosexuality or lead more heterosexuals to become homosexuals; we believe, rather, that we will be reducing the number of gay and lesbian couples who are living in unstable or promiscuous fashion.

More than that: the fact that gay and lesbian Jews are seeking to hold ceremonies establishing their relationships formally and celebrating them is not a threat to the traditional Jewish values of marriage and family but a supreme tribute to them. When two Jews marry, they do not seek only to legitimize their sexual relations and their offspring. They link themselves to the Jewish past, present and future and to a series of concentric circles of family, friends, community, and *kelal yisrael* around them. The wedding ceremony is that moment of magical transformation when two individuals become a *bayit beyisrael*. These layers of meaning do not disappear when the individuals are homosexual.

The ritual format by which Jewish tradition affirms this transformation is the wedding. Since we know that sexual orientation is both unalterable and irrelevant to the capacity of an individual to form a loving and stable relationship with another; and since it is our business and our calling to promote the formation of Jewish households which affirm Jewish values, we should offer wedding ceremonies to gay and lesbian Jewish couples. Some Reform rabbis will call these ceremonies *kiddushin*, while others may prefer a different term that carries less historical baggage. Some will structure a ceremony filled with the rituals and choreography of the traditional Jewish wedding (*chupah*, wine, the breaking of a glass, the reading of a *ketubah*, and so forth); others may prefer to create new ceremonies whose imagery does not so obviously mirror that of the traditional wedding of bride and groom. But in either case, we will be fulfilling our rabbinic responsibilities to Jewish people in our time, in the world and the culture in which we live.

The majority of the members of this Committee, however, do not interpret our responsibility as rabbis to warrant officiation at weddings or wedding-like "commitment ceremonies" for gay and lesbian couples. We hold that we are empowered to "officiate" only and exclusively at *Jewish* marriage ceremonies, and we know of no form of "Jewish marriage" other than *kiddushin*. We understand *kiddushin*, in both its traditional and its Reform Jewish manifestations, as an institution whose legal essence excludes homosexual relations. The performance of a ceremony that resembles but is not *kiddushin* does not qualify as a Jewish marriage, even if the couple regard it as such.[64]

It is true that we Reform Jews are accustomed to creating new liturgies and rituals all the time, so that we might substitute another language and another kind of wedding ceremony for *kiddushin* should we for whatever reason deem the latter unsuitable for gay and lesbian unions. Yet so long as we hold that "heterosexual, monogamous, procreative marriage is the ideal human relationship for the propagation of the species, covenantal fulfillment, and the preservation of the Jewish people,"[65] we believe that, however we respond

---

64. The operative concept here is *ein kiddushin tofsin*: "Jewish marriage is impossible" between these two persons; see *M*. Kiddushin 3:12.
65. See above, at note 32.

to those whose relationships do not adhere to this ideal, the public ceremony which celebrates Jewish marriage should correspond to it as closely as possible.

It is also true that not all Jewish marriages realize this ideal. Not all Jewish marriages, for example, are procreative. According to *halakhah*, a marriage between a man and a woman who cannot have children, while certainly to be discouraged as long as the man has not fulfilled his obligation to "be fruitful and multiply," is nonetheless valid.[66] To this we would say, first, that the Jewish tradition has tended to view this situation as one of sadness and even tragedy, and second, that the marriage of an intentionally childless couple, if not ideal from the rabbinic perspective, does not transgress the biblical *arayot*. No power which we feel we possess as rabbis is sufficient to declare any of the relationships prohibited in Leviticus 18 and 20 to be a Jewish marriage.

It is true, moreover, that gay and lesbian couples are capable of establishing stable and committed relationships—marriages in fact if not in law. The same is true of couples of mixed religious identity. We are well aware of the pressures placed upon rabbis to officiate at mixed marriages, on the grounds of outreach, compassion, a desire to include the couple within the Jewish fold. We accept those values; we do not wish to turn the intermarried couple away from the Jewish community. But we as a Conference and as a Committee have resolved that these concerns do not warrant our officiation at mixed marriages, for among other reasons because we cannot define mixed marriage as *Jewish* marriage, the only kind of marriage we as a community are empowered to provide. We are deeply concerned that, by granting recognition to gay and lesbian unions, we will be unable in the future to defend our position on mixed marriage. Our congregants will wonder, with some justification, why we officiate at one kind of marriage that Torah finds unacceptable but not at another.

The two cases, of course, are not exactly parallel. The non-Jewish partner in a heterosexual relationship has the option to convert to Judaism. Jewish marriage is a real possibility for that couple, and the rabbi can say: "I am not turning you away; I offer you the option of Jewish marriage as this community understands it. Should you not accept that option according to its inherent rules, that is *your* choice. You have by your own free will rejected Jewish marriage; the community has not rejected you."[67] So long as we recognize sexual orientation as unalterable, the element of "choice" does not apply. If we do not offer them marriage, there *is* no other religious option available for gay and lesbian couples. Moreover, when both partners in a homosexual union are Jews, their household will by definition be a Jewish one, something we cannot say in the same way for a religiously-mixed couple. A rabbi who officiates at wedding ceremonies for two Jewish homosexuals can therefore explain with consistency and justification why he or she does not also officiate at mixed marriages.

With all of that, however, we continue to live in a world where appearances count and where impressions can make all the difference. When a rabbi conducts a commitment ceremony for a homosexual couple, we cannot expect that the community will *not* learn from that act that Judaism, as represented by the rabbi, sanctions this union as a marriage, even though

---

66. *Yad*, Ishut 1:7; Isserles, *EHE* 1:3, and *Resp. Rivash* (R. Yitzchak b. Sheshet, 14th-cent. Spain/North Africa), no. 15: while the ideal (*lekhatchilah*) standard is to require a man to marry a fertile woman, it is "no longer customary for the courts to exercise coercion over this."
67. In a similar way, we do not offer religious sanction to the relationship of an unmarried couple. They can choose to accept the sanction we do offer: Jewish marriage. If they reject that option, it is not our responsibility to make a "better offer."

Jewish law and tradition do not recognize it as such. Distinctions between one kind of "non-Jewish marriage" and another, if obvious to the rabbi, will not be so clear to the community. Inevitably, the rabbi will be placed under ever-increasing pressure to officiate at mixed marriages, which are *also* unions between loving and committed persons which Jewish tradition does not recognize as marriage. And even if that individual rabbi can withstand the pressure, the Reform rabbinate as a whole will be buffeted by what many in our community will consider justified outrage. When some Reform rabbis depart from tradition to the extent that they conduct "weddings"—by whatever name—for gays and lesbians, many of our congregants will ask, quite reasonably, why they and other Reform rabbis refuse at the same time to abandon tradition to marry religiously-mixed couples.

That most of us are disinclined to conduct wedding ceremonies for gay and lesbian couples does not imply that we can make no positive ritual response to their presence within our communities. On the contrary: so long as we welcome them into our midst, it is our duty as rabbis to accompany them, as we seek to accompany all our people, along the path of Jewish life. How might we do this, if we do not recognize homosexual unions as marriages?

We might begin by acknowledging that, whether or not we define them as "marriages," homosexual unions are *households*, the nuclear social and family units which compose our communities and whose strength and stability is a primary Jewish religious concern. To speak of a gay or lesbian union as a household does not imply that we offer ritual sanctification to their sexual union or, indeed, that we must say anything about it. It is to recognize that, however we understand the nature of *kiddushin*, we are dealing here with a Jewish home, the classic environment of the Jewish experience. These individuals have formed a union bonded together by cords of love, and *that*, without any question, is a positive Jewish value.

This recognition quite properly brings any number of ritual responses in its wake. We are all familar with ceremonies, traditional and creative, which speak to the life of the Jewish household. Families dedicate their homes, and they celebrate significant moments in the lives of their members. The ceremonies which mark these occasions are as appropriate for gay and lesbian households as for all others. In addition, even though most of us are hesitant to sanction actual wedding ceremonies for gays and lesbians, there is no reason why a community cannot offer a ceremony of welcome for any new household which joins their ranks. A number of us, too, see no reason why homosexual couples might not observe their personal *semachot* at the synagogue as do other Jews, perhaps by sponsoring a *kiddush* or an *oneg shabbat*. If words of Torah are spoken on these occasions, they may take on the character of a religious festivity, a *se'udat mitzvah*. To accept homosexual couples as households, in other words, is to invite them to express that identity according to the full range of possibilities afforded by the Jewish ritual tradition.

We realize that those who favor rabbinic officiation at homosexual weddings may view the ritual recognition of gay and lesbian households as an inadequate substitute. Yet they may concede that, viewed against the backdrop of sacred text and Jewish history, the declaration by a rabbinic body that gays and lesbians can form a household and constitute a family represents a remarkable transformation in Jewish religious thought. To say that the community ought to accept gay and lesbian couples as households in every respect, if not a totally satisfactory solution to the problem before us, can still do much to focus our people's attention and energies upon its most essential aim: the strengthening of Jewish life for *all* Jewish families. And this may help restore a sense of community that seems at times to have disappeared in the controversy surrounding this issue.

IV. Conclusion.

To summarize, we note the following points.

1. We as a Committee acknowledge that our beliefs concerning the nature of human sexual orientation differ significantly from those of the past, even the recent past. The majority of us, however, are not persuaded that this transformation in our attitudes requires that we recognize and institute a system of homosexual marriage within our congregations and communities.
2. The majority of this Committee define "Jewish marriage" as *kiddushin*. That concept, whether understood according to its traditional terms or its Reform interpretation, is a legal institution whose parameters are defined by the sexual boundaries which Jewish law calls the *arayot*. Homosexual relationships, however exclusive and committed they may be, do not fit within this legal category; they cannot be called *kiddushin*. We do not understand Jewish marriage apart from the concept of *kiddushin*, and our interpretation of rabbinic authority does not embrace the power to "sanctify" any relationship that cannot be *kiddushin* as its functional equivalent. For this reason, although a minority of us disagree, our majority believes that Reform rabbis should not officiate at ceremonies of marriage or "commitment" for same-sex couples.
3. Our duty of outreach and our concern for all Jews require that rabbis and communities consider other ritual and social means by which homosexual couples might express their identity as households and families within the wider community of Israel.

In presenting this responsum, we have sought to outline the various positions held by our members as completely and as honestly as we can. The result is a *teshuvah* which, because it speaks several different languages of argument, expresses in literary form the deep divisions which split us and all our colleagues in the Conference. Though we have arrived at a majority opinion, we have failed to reach a consensus as to how we as a community ought to understand and talk about this question. Some day, history may permit us as a movement or a Conference to reach that consensus. Some day, the controversy over the Jewish religious status of gay and lesbian unions may be resolved to the satisfaction of all. Given, however, that such a day is yet far off, we do not believe that anything of value can be accomplished by declaring through majority vote that one position or the other is the official policy of the Conference. A resolution at this juncture would do little to bring us together. It would persuade no one; it would change no minds. On the contrary: it would stifle the possibility of genuine conversation among us, serving but to enrage and to embarrass the adherents of the losing side. We urge our colleagues to refrain from taking that step.

What do we advocate in its stead? We call upon our colleagues to do what we have so haltingly attempted to do in this responsum: to talk; to explain; to justify and to argue. Our goal should be the recovery of a common discourse on this most divisive of subjects. To achieve it will take much time, a great deal of patience, and no little faith in each other. And it will require that we renew each day our commitment to conduct our discussion in an atmosphere of mutual respect. No disagreement that occurs among us, however heated, and no controversy that divides us, however intractable, should cause us to doubt or to denigrate the religious sincerity of those who take the opposing view. As rabbis, we owe each other the presumption that all of us are students and lovers of Torah, whose intentions are honorable even though our arguments do not always succeed in persuading. We know that mutual respect does not guarantee that we will reach a solution satisfactory to all. Yet we also know that, in its absence, no solution and no learning are possible.

C.C.A.R. Responsa Committee
Mark Washofsky, Chair
Joan S. Friedman
David Lilienthal
Bernard Mehlman
W. Gunther Plaut
Richard S. Rheins
Jeffrey K. Salkin
Daniel Schiff
Faedra L. Weiss

Joan S. Friedman and Bernard Mehlman side with the minority position as expressed in this responsum.

Moshe Zemer agrees with the conclusion and the decision of the majority of the Committee that same-sex unions do not qualify as *kiddushin* and that Reform rabbis should not officiate at wedding or commitment ceremonies for gay or lesbian couples. He will append a separate responsum.

Resolution Adopted by the 64th General Assembly of the Union of American Hebrew Congregations Biennial, 1997: Civil Marriage for Gay and Lesbian Jewish Couples

Background

In 1987, the Union of American Hebrew Congregations (UAHC) reaffirmed its commitment to welcoming gay and lesbian Jews into its congregations and encouraging their participation in all aspects of synagogue and communal life. In 1993, Rabbi Alexander M. Schindler, President of the UAHC, called upon the Reform Movement to support the right of gay and lesbian couples to adopt children, to file joint income-tax returns, and to share in health and death benefits provided to heterosexual couples by federal, state, and local governments and by both large and small corporations. Following Rabbi Schindler's call, the UAHC, in 1993, resolved that full equality under the law for gay men and lesbians requires legal recognition of monogamous domestic gay and lesbian relationships.

In 1990, the Central Conference of American Rabbis (CCAR) adopted a position paper encouraging rabbis and congregations to treat with respect and to integrate fully all Jews into the life of the community regardless of sexual orientation and acknowledging the need for continuing discussion regarding the religious status of monogamous domestic relationships between gay men or lesbians and the creation of special ceremonies. In April 1996, the CCAR adopted a resolution supporting the right of gay and lesbian couples to share fully and equally in the benefits of civil marriage....

In the years since first the UAHC and subsequently the CCAR gave their support for full equality for gay men and lesbians in congregational life, gay men and lesbians have increasingly come forward to participate in the life of Reform Judaism on national, regional, and local levels. No less than heterosexual couples, gay men or lesbians living in monogamous domestic relationships have demonstrated, like their counterparts, love for one another, compassion for the sick, and grief for the dead.

Union of American Hebrew Congregations 64th General Assembly, "Resolution Adopted on Civil Marriage for Gay and Lesbian Jewish Couples" (Dallas, 1997), http://www.urj.org.

The UAHC has for decades provided moral leadership to the Jewish community and to our nation, recognizing our differences and diversity, but acknowledging that we are but one family, equal before God. In this spirit, the UAHC must now move more forcefully to support the monogamous domestic relationships of gay men and lesbians. . . .

THEREFORE, the Union of American Hebrew Congregations resolves to:
1. Support secular efforts to promote legislation which would provide through civil marriage equal opportunity for gay men and lesbians;
2. Encourage its constituent congregations to honor monogamous domestic relationships formed by gay men or lesbians; and
3. Support the efforts of the CCAR in its ongoing work as it studies the appropriateness of religious ceremonies for use in a celebration of commitment recognizing a monogamous domestic relationship between two Jewish gay men or two Jewish lesbians.

Resolution Adopted by the Central Conference of American Rabbis 111th Annual Convention, 2000: Same Gender Officiation

Background

Over the years, the Central Conference of American Rabbis has adopted a number of positions on the rights of homosexuals, on homosexuality in the rabbinate, and advocating changes in civil law pertaining to same gender relationships.

In 1977, the CCAR adopted a resolution calling for legislation decriminalizing homosexual acts between consenting adults, and calling for an end to discrimination against gays and lesbians. The resolution called on Reform Jewish organizations to develop programs to implement this stand.

In 1990, the CCAR endorsed the report of the Ad Hoc Committee on Homosexuality and the Rabbinate. This position paper urged that "all rabbis, regardless of sexual orientation, be accorded the opportunity to fulfill the sacred vocation that they have chosen." The committee endorsed the view that "all Jews are religiously equal regardless of their sexual orientation." The committee expressed its agreement with changes in the admissions policies of the Hebrew Union College–Jewish Institute of Religion, which stated that the "sexual orientation of an applicant [be considered] only within the context of a candidate's overall suitability for the rabbinate," and reaffirmed that all rabbinic graduates of the HUC-JIR would be admitted into CCAR membership upon application. The report described differing views within the committee as to the nature of *kiddushin*, and deferred the matter of rabbinic officiation.

A 1996 resolution resolved that the CCAR "support the right of gay and lesbian couples to share fully and equally in the rights of civil marriage," and voiced opposition to governmental efforts to ban gay and lesbian marriages.

In addition to these resolutions, two CCAR committees have addressed the question of same gender officiation. The CCAR Committee on Responsa addressed the question of whether homosexual relationships can qualify as *kiddushin* (which it defined as "Jewish marriage"). By a committee majority of 7 to 2, the committee concluded that "homosexual

---

Central Conference of American Rabbis 111th Annual Convention, "Resolution Adopted on Same Gender Officiation" (Greensboro, NC, 2000) http://www.ccarnet.org.

relationships, however exclusive and committed they may be, do not fit within this legal category; they cannot be called *kiddushin*. We do not understand Jewish marriage apart from the concept of *kiddushin*." The committee acknowledged its lack of consensus on this question.

The Ad Hoc Committee on Human Sexuality issued a report in 1998 which included its conclusion, by a committee majority of 11 with 1 abstention, that "kedushah may be present in committed same gender relationships between two Jews and that these relationships can serve as the foundation of stable Jewish families, thus adding strength to the Jewish community." The report called upon the CCAR to support all colleagues in their choices in this matter, and to develop educational programs.

Resolution

WHEREAS justice and human dignity are cherished Jewish values, and

WHEREAS, in March of 1999 the Women's Rabbinic Network passed a resolution urging the Central Conference of American Rabbis to bring the issue of honoring ceremonies between two Jews of the same gender to the floor of the convention plenum, and

WHEREAS, the institutions of Reform Judaism have a long history of support for civil and equal rights for gays and lesbians, and

WHEREAS, North American organizations of the Reform Movement have passed resolutions in support of civil marriage for gays and lesbians, therefore

WE DO HEREBY RESOLVE, that the relationship of a Jewish, same gender couple is worthy of affirmation through appropriate Jewish ritual, and

FURTHER RESOLVED, that we recognize the diversity of opinions within our ranks on this issue. We support the decision of those who choose to officiate at rituals of union for same gender couples, and we support the decision of those who do not, and

FURTHER RESOLVED, that we call upon the CCAR to support all colleagues in their choices in this matter, and

FURTHER RESOLVED, that we also call upon the CCAR to develop both educational and liturgical resources in this area.

Same Gender Officiation: A Statement by Rabbi Eric Yoffie (2000)

This afternoon the Central Conference of American Rabbis, meeting in Greensboro, NC, adopted a resolution by an overwhelming vote stating, in part, that "the relationship of a Jewish, same gender couple is worthy of affirmation through appropriate Jewish ritual."

It is important to note what the resolution on same gender unions does and does not say. It does not compel any rabbi to officiate at such a ritual, and indeed supports the right of a rabbi not to officiate. It does not specify what ritual is appropriate for such a ceremony. It does not say that the ceremony performed should be called a "marriage."

Nonetheless, the historical and religious significance of this resolution is indisputable. For the first time in history, a major rabbinical body has affirmed the Jewish validity of committed, same gender relationships.

What do the members of UAHC congregations think about this resolution? It is impossible to know for certain. Some have told me of their strong support, while others have indicated their opposition. Still others have said that they are sympathetic to the ideas expressed but felt no resolution was necessary at this time.

Over the last quarter century, the UAHC Biennial Assembly has spoken out strongly in support of human and civil rights for gays and lesbians. We have admitted to membership a number of congregations that offer special outreach to gay and lesbian Jews, and called upon Reform synagogues to welcome gay and lesbian Jews as singles, couples, and families, and not to discriminate on the basis of sexual orientation in matters related to employment and volunteer leadership. And the UAHC has initiated vigorous education programs to heighten awareness of discrimination and to achieve fuller acceptance of gay and lesbian Jews in our midst.

The Union, however, has always refrained from addressing the issue of rabbinic participation in same gender weddings or commitment ceremonies. As a congregational body, it is our task to provide guidance on issues of congregational policy that are normally decided by synagogue boards. But performance or non-performance of a same gender commitment ceremony is a rabbinical matter, to be determined by each rabbi according to his or her conscience and understanding of Jewish tradition. Therefore, while our synagogue members have felt free to present their views to their own rabbis, and many have done so vigorously, the Union as an organization has appropriately remained silent on the CCAR resolution, and took no part in the many months of debate prior to the convention.

Union of American Hebrew Congregations, "Same Gender Officiation: A Statement by Rabbi Eric Yoffie" (Greensboro, NC, 2000), http://www.urj.org.

But I too am a rabbi, of course, and I was present at Greensboro. And I would like you to know that, voting as an individual, I cast my ballot in favor the resolution. I did so because of my belief that our gay and lesbian children, relatives, and friends are in great need of spiritual support; that the Torah's prohibition of homosexuality can reasonably be understood as a general condemnation of ancient cultic practice; that loving, permanent homosexual relationships, once difficult to conceive, are now recognized as an indisputable reality; and that in these relationships, whether or not we see them as "marriages" it is surely true that God and holiness can be present.

I know that many disagree. But whatever one thinks on the commitment ceremony question, I assume that we will respect those who believe otherwise, and remember what unites us in this debate: our responsibility to welcome gays and lesbians into our synagogues. Because this I know: if there is anything at all that Reform Jews do, it is to create an inclusive spiritual home for all those who seek the solace of our sanctuaries. And if this Movement does not extend support to all who have been victims of discrimination, including gays and lesbians, then we have no right to call ourselves Reform Jews.

Resolution Adopted by the Executive Board of the Commission on Social Action of Reform Judaism, 2003: Support for the Inclusion and Acceptance of the Transgender and Bisexual Communities

Background

Throughout the Reform Movement's history, we have worked tirelessly to fight discrimination, support equality, and strengthen the rights of minorities and women. Similar to past systemic injustices that prevented a litany of minority communities from realizing equal rights, so too have the transgender and bisexual communities in North America been condemned to live as second-class citizens.

The transgender community has had an especially difficult experience in North America due to the community's unique needs which are overlooked or ignored by society. The barriers the transgender community faces have led to a high incidence of mental illness and an especially high suicide rate. Transgendered individuals are frequent victims of hate crimes and employment discrimination. Transgenderism remains a virtually unspoken and unaccepted element within our society; this has led to discrimination in health care and insurance coverage, access to public facilities, police, paramedic, and other emergency services and a variety of as yet fully unexplored legal issues ([See the] "Introduction," by Jamison Green to *Transgender Equality: A Handbook for Activists and Policy Makers*, by Paisley Currah and Shannon Minter, the Policy Institute of the National Gay and Lesbian Task Force [www.thetaskforce.org]).

The bisexual community has also suffered discrimination. Victims of workplace discrimination and hate crimes, bisexuals are consistently left unprotected by legislation created to protect America's minorities from xenophobia.

As currently defined by the National Gay and Lesbian Task Force, transgendered people are individuals of any sex whose identity or behavior is perceived to be gender atypical or falls outside of stereotypical gender norms. Biblical tradition teaches us that all human beings are created *b'tselem Elohim*—in the Divine image. As it says in Genesis 1:27, "And God created humans in God's image, in the image of God, God created them; male and female God created them." From this bedrock principle stems our commitment to defend any individual from the discrimination that arises from ignorance, fear, insensitivity, or hatred. Knowing that this community is often singled out as victims of discriminatory violence and has a high suicide rate, we are reminded of the Torah's injunction, "do not stand idly while your neighbor bleeds" (Leviticus 19:16).

The Written Torah initially seems very exclusionary in this regard (see, for instance, Deuteronomy 23:2, which would exclude from the Jewish community one whose genitalia have been disfigured or removed). However, this position already was tempered by the time of Isaiah (56:3 ff.), and even more so by the rabbis of the Talmud, who argued that one's status as a Jew in such cases was not changed.

Two key Reform responsa lay the groundwork for the inclusion and acceptance of transgender and bisexual communities in accordance with Jewish tradition. A 1990 responsum (CCAR 5750.8) affirmed that transgenderism alone is not grounds to deny someone conversion to Judaism. A 1978 responsum affirmed that a rabbi may officiate at the wedding of two Jews if one partner has transitioned from one gender to another ("Marriage After a Sex-Change Operation" in *American Reform Responsa*, Vol. LXXXVIII, 1978, pp. 52–54).

The UAHC 1987 resolution entitled "Support for Inclusion of Lesbian and Gay Jews" states: "Sexual orientation should not be a criterion for membership or for participation in an activity of any synagogue. Thus all Jews should be welcome, however they may define themselves."

THEREFORE, BE IT RESOLVED that the Commission on Social Action of Reform Judaism:

1. Applies all aspects of the policy created by the Union of American Hebrew Congregations in 1977 in its "Human Rights of Homosexuals" resolution to the transgender and bisexual communities;
2. Supports legislation that both opposes discrimination based on gender identity and allows individuals to be treated under the law as the gender by which they identify;
3. Urges all UAHC congregations to continue or develop inclusive policies toward all Jews regardless of sexual orientation and gender identity; and
4. Invites the Central Conference of American Rabbis and the American Conference of Cantors to engage in discussion regarding ritual participation of and for transgender Jews within the Reform Movement.

Countering the Family Values Monopoly

Rabbi David Ellenson

In his State of the Union address, President Bush signaled his intent to make "family values" a centerpiece of the 2004 presidential campaign.

His belief that "the sanctity of the family" needs to be defended from the "threat" that gay and lesbian couples ostensibly pose to heterosexual family units is hardly surprising. After all, when asked about same-sex unions after a court decision that affirmed the constitutionality of same-sex marriage, the president commented, "We are all sinners."

The very language the president employed then indicates that his religious views play a significant role in the public-policy position he has adopted on this matter, and the role that religious fundamentalism has played in setting the terms for this debate in the public square is unquestionably considerable. In taking the stance he did, President Bush displayed the impact that the Traditional Values Coalition and allied conservative religious groups—including Jewish ones—that have long been at the forefront of the fight against the advancement of rights and options for gays and lesbians in our society has had upon him. I regret that this is so and I feel obliged to speak out lest religious literalists claim a monopoly in speaking on behalf of religion on issues concerning gay and lesbian rights in our country.

These religious literalists justify their refusal to accord full rights to gays and lesbians by pointing to Leviticus 18:22, which condemns male homosexual intercourse as an "abomination," and there is little doubt that the influence of this biblical verse has been decisive in shaping the attitudes of many in our society toward this question of gay and lesbian rights—including the president. Yet, such a reading of this text represents the most literal interpretation possible of this passage. This reading also completely removes this scripture from an ancient social context that could not envision the possibility or appreciate the reality of loving same-sex relationships.

I see no reason why such negative judgments regarding gays and lesbians should go unchallenged from a religious perspective. As the Catholic feminist scholar Elizabeth Schussler Fiorenza has maintained in her powerful "In Memory of Her," the divinity of any passage in Scripture that diminishes the humanity of another—as this one does—can surely be questioned. The thrust of one such passage should not override an overarching

---

David Ellenson, "Countering the Family Values Monopoly," *Jewish Journal of Greater Los Angeles*, Spring 2004, 9.

biblical ethos that teaches us that God loves and affirms the full humanity of each human being.

As a Jew, I feel this even more strongly. After all, Judaism does not base its religious teachings on the Protestant doctrine of *Sola Scriptura* (Scripture alone). Instead, Judaism asserts that moral truths emerge out of an interpretive process that requires Jews to recognize that God has called on the Jewish people to serve as covenantal partners in the unfolding expression of divine truths, and this obligation can only be fulfilled through an ongoing exegesis of the written text. This notion allowed the rabbis of the Talmud to declare in one instance that the "stubborn and rebellious son" identified in Deuteronomy 21:18–21 "never was and never will be" (Sanhedrin 71a) and in another instance this process caused the talmudic sage Johanan ben Zakkai to assert (Sotah 9:9) that as a result of contemporaneous conditions, a woman accused of adultery would no longer be subject to the "ordeal of bitter waters" (Numbers 5:11–31). In these ways, great rabbis—depending upon their own wisdom and in light of their own judgments regarding social and ethical contexts—either muted or obviated the application of teachings found in the Written Law.

All Jews should recognize that this interpretive approach characterizes our tradition, and we should assert that this is so within the Jewish community as well as in the public square. This approach has allowed Reform and Reconstructionist Judaism to ordain gays and lesbians as rabbis, and has led to a vigorous discussion of this issue in Conservative Judaism. Such Jewish understandings have also permitted a number of rabbis to perform same-sex unions. From these perspectives, legislation against same-sex unions can be viewed as not only discriminating against gays and lesbians. It also discriminates against those of us whose religious beliefs mandate us to perform same-sex weddings.

In Dickens' "Oliver Twist," when young Oliver approaches the wardens of the orphanage where he was housed and, after a scant meal, asks for "more," the wardens are scandalized. Yet, as one commentator upon this passage has pointed out, Oliver said "more" when what he "really meant was this: 'Will you just give me that normal portion which is necessary for a boy my age to live.'"

As a religious Jew, I assert that the gay community today seeks nothing more than Oliver Twist—the "normal portion" required to live a life of dignity and equality. Our society should be ashamed that gays and lesbians are subjected daily to indignity and prejudice in legal as well as social arenas, and religious persons must declare that position loud and clear in order to influence public opinion on this matter.

When I was a teenager, I was moved, as were millions of other people, by the vision Dr. Martin Luther King Jr. expressed when he dreamed of a just world where people would be judged by the content of their character. This vision was inspired by the Bible and extends to express a simple truth—all persons, regardless of sexual orientation, are equally beloved by God and are equally entitled to life, liberty and the pursuit of happiness.

The desire that full rights be extended to lesbians and gays reflects the Jewish belief that gays and lesbians are human beings created in the image of God. The time has come for that truth to guide our culture, and religious Jews should not be hesitant in saying so.

Until the day arrives that our gay and lesbian friends enjoy full rights, we who are religious should not rest. When that day of liberty and freedom arrives, justice will at long last roll down like waters and righteousness like a mighty stream.

NER-CCAR Passes Resolution in Support of Marriage Ruling; Opposes Efforts to Undermine Equality for Same-Sex Couples

(January 20, 2004) On January 14, 2004, the Northeast Region of the Central Conference of American Rabbis (NER-CCAR) unanimously passed a resolution supporting equal marriage rights for same-sex couples. The resolution voices support for the Massachusetts Supreme Judicial Court's ruling in *Goodridge v. Dep't of Public Health* that excluding gay and lesbian couples from marriage violates the state Constitution. The resolution further affirms equal access to civil marriage regardless of sexual orientation, opposes legislative efforts to create a separate and unequal legal status solely for same-sex couples, and opposes attempts to enshrine discrimination against same-sex couples into either state or federal constitutions.

NER-CCAR is a regional organization of over 100 Reform rabbis serving congregations, schools and organizations in Massachusetts, Maine, New Hampshire, Vermont, Connecticut, Rhode Island and upstate New York. Rabbi Mark Dov Shapiro, Regional President, stated, "Our tradition teaches us to pursue justice. We believe that the Court's ruling is an important step towards that goal of justice, and call upon elected officials to make real the promise of equality for same-sex couples by removing all legal impediments to their marriage."

Additionally, Rabbi David Wolfman, Director of the Union for Reform Judaism Northeast Council, stated, "The Reform Movement has long been on record as standing by the Gay and Lesbian members of our communities by advocating full and equal inclusion in our congregations and communities. As a Reform rabbi, I am proud that the Reform rabbinate has spoken with one voice to call for full legal status of same gender marriage. We have long stood by the sanctity of same sex marriage: now we call for its legalization. May this be the first step to full equality in marriage."

The resolution reads as follows:

Background

The Reform Jewish Movement has long been committed to welcoming gay and lesbian Jews and their children into our synagogues and communal life. For too long, much of the world has treated them as "strangers." Our Scriptures teach us: "You shall not oppress a stranger, for you know the feelings of a stranger, having yourselves been strangers in the land of Egypt" (Exodus 23:9). The Central Conference of American Rabbis has thus consistently supported full equality for lesbians and gays in society, adopting resolutions in 1977 encouraging the decriminalization of same-sex intimacy between consenting adults and prohibiting discrimination against gays and lesbians as persons, and in 1996 supporting the right of gay and lesbian couples to share fully and equally in the rights of civil marriage.

As rabbis, we believe it is our obligation as people of faith to defend vigorously the dignity of every human being, consistent with the principle that each of us is created in the Divine image. (Genesis 1:27). While we respect those who may be single, we uphold the values of marriage and family. Marriage, imbued with the values of exclusivity, permanence, intimate companionship, and love, provides fulfillment for each partner and adds to the common good of the community. We affirm that every human being has an absolute right to such fulfillment, and that the loving, committed relationships of same-sex couples have the same potential for holiness as those of heterosexual couples.

At the same time, we recognize that not all people of faith and not all clergy share our affirmation. We respect their right to hold opposing views. Still, we contend that the civil rights of some should not be denied because of the religious beliefs of others. Government should treat all people equally and fairly under the law.

THEREFORE BE IT RESOLVED that the Northeast Region of the Central Conference of American Rabbis applauds and supports the Massachusetts Supreme Judicial Court's ruling in *Goodridge v. Department of Public Health*—that denying same-sex couples access to civil marriage violates the constitutional guarantees of liberty and equality—as a step toward ensuring the right of gay and lesbian Americans to share in the joys, privileges, and responsibilities of marriage afforded in law to heterosexuals, and

BE IT FURTHER RESOLVED that, as citizens, we call upon the legislators of all states to affirm civil marriage rights of every person regardless of sexual orientation, and

BE IT FURTHER RESOLVED that we oppose legislative efforts to substitute a separate and lesser legal status, such as civil unions, for the full marriage equality same-sex couples deserve, and

BE IT FURTHER RESOLVED that we unequivocally oppose attempts to amend the constitution of any state or the Constitution of the United States in order to discriminate against same-sex couples and their families.

Resolution Adopted by the Executive Board of the Commission on Social Action of Reform Judaism, 2004: The Proposed Federal Marriage Amendment to the United States Constitution

The Reform Jewish Movement has deep respect for the United States Constitution. The lofty vision it articulates for our nation has much in common with the prophetic teachings of Judaism, and its wise principles of governance have allowed our communities to flourish. In the 1960's, in the 1970's and again in the 1980's, the Union for Reform Judaism and the Central Conference of American Rabbis spoke about the importance of this foundational text of our nation and warned of the dangers of tampering with it. We are particularly concerned about changes which would codify discrimination or limit the protection of religious liberties.

Just as strongly, our Movement has long worked to ensure that the promise of equality put forward by the Constitution, and commanded by Jewish tradition, is extended to gay, lesbian, bisexual and transgender individuals. The Union for Reform Judaism and the Central Conference of American Rabbis have clear policy supporting full civil marriage equality for gay men and lesbians. We applaud the Canadian provinces of Ontario and British Columbia for removing the barriers to gay and lesbian civil marriage there, and we hope that Canada's policies can serve as a model for the United States.

THEREFORE, the Commission on Social Action of Reform Judaism resolves to:

1. Reaffirm our commitment to upholding the integrity of the United States Constitution, particularly concerning its prohibitions against discrimination and its safeguarding of religious liberties;
2. Reaffirm our commitment to pursuing full civil marriage rights for gay, lesbian, bisexual and transgender individuals; and
3. Oppose any proposal to amend the United States Constitution to limit these rights.

Resolution Adopted by the Central Conference of American Rabbis 115th Annual Convention, 2004: Proposed Federal Marriage Amendment to the United States Constitution

Background

At its 1996 Convention in Philadelphia, PA, the Central Conference of American Rabbis (CCAR) resolved to "support the right of gay and lesbian couples to share fully and equally in the rights of civil marriage" and to "oppose governmental efforts to ban gay and lesbian marriage." At its 2000 Convention in Greensboro, NC, the CCAR recognized the legitimacy of same-gender unions and affirmed its support for rabbis who choose to officiate at such ceremonies.

These positions reflect Torah's fundamental principle that all human beings are created in the divine image, and the Reform rabbinate's commitment to welcoming and fully including lesbian and gay couples in all aspects of Jewish life. As we have grown in our knowledge and experience of same-gender couples establishing Jewish homes and raising Jewish children, we have learned to admire their courage, integrity and commitment despite the bigotry and discrimination that confront them daily in the larger society.

Moreover, as Reform rabbis, we have a deep and abiding respect for the United States Constitution. The lofty vision it articulates has much in common with the prophetic teachings of Judaism, and its wise principles of governance have allowed our communities to flourish. For decades, the Central Conference of American Rabbis has emphasized the importance of this foundational text and warned of the dangers of tampering with it. Having worked to ensure that the promise of equality put forward by the Constitution, and commanded by Jewish tradition, is extended to all, we are particularly concerned about the proposed changes to it which would codify discrimination, consign some in our

---

Central Conference of American Rabbis 115th Annual Convention, "Resolution Adopted on Proposed Federal Marriage Amendment to the United States Constitution" (2004), http://www.ccarnet.org.

society to permanent second-class status, and limit the protection of religious liberties. Moreover, we applaud the Canadian provinces of Ontario, Quebec and British Columbia and the Commonwealth of Massachusetts for removing the barriers to civil marriage for same-gender couples, and hope that those constituencies' policies can serve as a model for the entire United States and Canada.

THEREFORE, the Central Conference of American Rabbis resolves to:

1. Reaffirm our commitment to upholding the integrity of the United States Constitution, particularly concerning its guarantee of equal protection for all citizens, its prohibitions against discrimination and its safeguarding of religious liberties;
2. Reaffirm our commitment to pursuing full civil marriage rights for same-gender couples; and
3. Oppose any proposal to amend the United States Constitution or any state constitutions, or any state legislation that would limit these rights; and
4. Call upon CCAR members to play a leadership role on the federal, state and local levels on this issue, and to join coalitions and other efforts in local communities.

Excerpt on Same-Sex Marriage from Rabbi Eric H. Yoffie's Regional Biennial Speech, 2004–2005

And there is one issue in particular on which we will not bend.

It is hardly a secret that the Christian right has made a conscious effort to expand its ranks by bashing gays. It has come to believe that prejudice against gays runs so deep in America that if it champions the anti-gay cause, millions of Americans will flock to its banner. And it is not entirely wrong. Thirteen states have passed bans on same-sex marriage, and we have an administration that advocates writing anti-gay prejudice into the U.S. constitution.

But the fact that gay marriage is widely unpopular in some places cannot obscure the fact that it is morally momentous and morally right. Liberals once lost elections for supporting civil rights and now look back on those losses as badges of honor. And we must do no less. Since young people are far more supportive of gay marriage than their parents, the day will come when conservatives will apologize for trying to deny yet another group of Americans their full human rights.

And in the meantime, we need to educate our fellow citizens. Yes, many Americans have religious reservations about homosexuality, and they are entitled to that. But they can still be made to understand that America does not mistreat people because of what they are. And they can understand too that the right to have the benefits that others have when they make a lifelong commitment to a loved one is not a "special right." It is simply a component of equal citizenship.

Therefore, we Reform Jews will fight this battle, even if others in the Jewish community choose not to join us. Most of the Orthodox community opposes gay marriage, and others in our community who have spoken out for gays and lesbians have done so far more gently than we would like.

But if that is the case, then so be it. We will raise our voices as we have so many times before, and we will stand behind our gay brothers and sisters—Jew and non-Jew—no matter what the dangers and no matter what the cost.

And in the end we will win. Because history is moving toward more tolerance and liberty, and because Americans, despite the battles that lie ahead, still aspire to be united in a sense of high national purpose and common cause.

Excerpted from Rabbi Eric H. Yoffie, "Regional Biennial Speech, 2004–2005," http://www.urj.org.

And as religious leaders and Reform Jews we see it our task to further that purpose and advance that cause; we see it our task to do what God and Torah demand of us; we see it our task to help heal the soul of America, this great country in which we live.

It is no easy matter, this enterprise of being Jewish; it summons us to be fired by a very broad vision. But as leaders of the synagogue we expect no less. As leaders of the synagogue, we are destined to be healers and fixers and pursuers of justice, and thus to be a blessing to all humankind.

Glossary

biological sex: This can be considered our "packaging" and is determined by our chromosomes (XX for females; XY for males); our hormones (estrogen/progesterone for females; testosterone for males); and our internal and external genitalia (vulva, clitoris, vagina for females; penis and testicles for males). About 1.7 percent of the population can be defined as intersex (intersexual/intersexed)—born with biological aspects of both sexes to varying degrees and, at times, different chromosomal combinations. So, in actuality, there are more than two sexes.

biphobia: Irrational fear or hatred of individuals who identify as bisexual. This fear may stem from a belief that the bisexual identity is not an authentic queer identity, resentment at the bisexual's heterosexual privileges, or a concern that the bisexual is harbinger of disease from queer communities into the heterosexual communities.

birthsex: The sex indicated on the birth certificate, which does not necessarily reflect gender identity.

bisexual: Someone who has emotional, romantic, and/or physical attraction or behavior with men and women (though not necessarily at the same time). However, since not everyone has had the opportunity or desire to act on their sexual/romantic attractions, some people prefer a looser definition; for instance, that a bisexual is a person who—in his or her own estimation—feels *potentially* able to have such attraction. This could be anyone who has erotic, affectionate, or romantic feelings for, fantasies of, and/or experiences with both men and women. A bisexual may be attracted to one gender/sex more than the other, attracted equally to both, or find people's gender/sex unimportant. The strength of their attractions to men and women may vary over time.

bisexuality: The capacity for emotional, romantic, and/or physical attraction or behavior directed toward more than one sex or gender.

Note: Some definitions were adapted from two sources, while others were developed from the editors' research. Sources include: GLSEN for GLSEN Lunchbox Resource (Jan. 14, 2003), from Warren J. Blumenfeld, co-author of *Looking at Gay and Lesbian Life*, and editor of *Homophobia: How We All Pay the Price* (http://www.glsen.org/cgi-bin/iowa/all/library/record/1278.html) and the Oregon State Pride Center Frequently Asked Questions, Terms and Definitions (http://oregonstate.edu/pridecenter/resources/faq.php#7d).

civil union: Formal recognition of committed lesbian and gay relationships by the states of Vermont, New Jersey, and Connecticut. Civil unions confer upon same-sex couples the same rights available to married couples under the law in such areas as state taxes, medical decisions, and estate planning. North American Reform Movement organizations have passed resolutions in support of civil marriage/union for gay men and lesbians.

coming-out: The process of coming to terms with one's sexual and/or gender identity or identities. It can describe an internal process, describing the internal decisions to take on a sexual or gender identity. It can be an external process, describing the process of disclosing sexual and gender identity to friends, family, coworkers, etc. Coming-out is a lifelong process—in each new situation a person must decide whether or not to come out. Coming-out can be difficult for some, because reactions vary from complete acceptance and support to disapproval, rejection, and violence.

coming-out (of the closet): To be "in the closet" means to hide one's sexual and or gender identity. Many GLBT people are "out" in some situations and "closeted" in others.

cross-dressing: Adopting the dress of another gender. Cross-dressers are mainly heterosexual men, but can also be men of other sexual orientations and gender identities. Cross-dressers differ from transsexuals in that they do not necessarily wish to change their sex.

domestic partnership: A civil or legal contract recognizing a partnership or a relationship between two people, which sometimes confers limited benefits to them. Such a partnership can be formed by lesbians or gay men, by unmarried heterosexual life partners, or by others making a home together.

drag: The adoption of clothing and roles of another gender for the purposes of play, entertainment, or eroticism. This term was originally used to refer to "drag queens," who are men dressed as women, but there are also now "drag kings," who are usually women dressing as men. Drag performers are not cross-dressers, who adopt the clothing of another gender outside of the context of entertainment or performance.

DSM-IV: *The Diagnostic and Statistical Manual of Mental Disorders*, published by the American Psychiatric Association, is the handbook used most often in diagnosing mental disorders in the United States. On December 15, 1973, the Board of the American Psychiatric Association voted 13–0 to remove homosexuality from its official list of psychiatric disorders.

dyke: A derogatory word for people who are lesbians. This term is sometimes reclaimed in younger generations as a symbol of pride to empower lesbian communities.

fag, faggot: A derogatory term for gay men.

faygele: The derogatory Yiddish word for gay men. Literally, it translates to "little bird."

female-to-male: Abbraviated FTM or F2M. Usually said aloud as "F to M." Most commonly refers to female-to-male transsexuals. A person who was born in a female body but whose gender identity is male. It can also refer to those assigned female at birth, in the case of intersex people, whose gender identity is male. Many but not all female-to-male transsexuals will seek hormonal and/or surgical treatment in order to live successfully as a man in society. This term is sometimes also used by others who are born in female bodies and who move toward masculine or male presentation without hormones or surgery.

gay: Someone who is man-identified who seeks to be emotionally, spiritually, and/or physically involved with other people who are man-identified. It is also used as a generic or umbrella term to include both lesbians and gay men.

gay lifestyle: A term often used by those who are anti-gay and who link this term to a variety of negative behaviors. The phrase is also used to suggest that sexual orientation is a choice and can be changed. Just as there is no one "heterosexual lifestyle," there is no one lesbian or "gay lifestyle."

gender: A person's expression and/or presentation of some combination of socially constructed ideas defining masculine and/or feminine characteristics.

gender binary: The prevalent construction of boyness and girlness; the concept that there are only two genders.

gender dysphoria: This term was coined by Dr. Harry Benjamin to describe a symptom of being profoundly uncomfortable with one's birth sex and the belief that one is actually the other sex. In the medical and psychological communities, the term "gender identity disorder" is currently used to encompass the larger disorder of which gender dysphoria was one symptom. See the *DSM-IV* definition for "gender identity disorder" or the Harry Benjamin International Gender Dysphoria Association's "Standards of Care for Gender Identity Disorders."

gender expression: Refers to the ways in which people externally communicate their gender identity to others through behavior, clothing, haircut, voice, and emphasizing, deemphasizing, or changing their bodies' characteristics. Typically, transgender people seek to make their gender expression match their gender identity, rather than their birth-assigned sex. Gender expression is not necessarily an indication of sexual orientation.

gender identity: Our innermost concept of self as male, female, or another identity that is neither male nor female. What we perceive and call ourselves. Individuals are conscious of this beginning between the ages of eighteen months and three years. Most people develop a gender identity that matches their biological or birth-assigned sex. For some, however, their gender identity is different from their biological or birth-assigned sex.

gender identity disorder: A mental disorder as determined by the *Diagnostic and Statistical Manual of Mental Disorders*, published by the American Psychiatric Association. According to the *DSM-IV* definition, there are two components of gender identity disorder, both of which must be present to make the diagnosis. There must be evidence of a strong and persistent cross-gender identification, which is the desire to be, or the insistence that one is of the other sex (Criteria A). This cross-gender identification must not merely be a desire for any perceived cultural advantages of being the other sex. There must also be evidence of persistent discomfort about one's assigned sex or a sense of inappropriateness in the gender role of that sex (Criteria B). The diagnosis is not made if the individual has a concurrent physical intersex condition (e.g., androgen insensitivity syndrome or congenital adrenal hyperplasia) (Criteria C). To make the diagnosis, there must be evidence of clinically significant distress or impairment in social, occupational, or other important areas of functioning (Criteria D).

gender queer: A mindset of viewing gender as having more than two options, that is, an understanding that is not gender binary in its construction. Individuals who identify as "gender queer" may prefer not to identify as either "male" or "female"; may see themselves as outside of the binary gender box; may feel restricted by gender labels, categories, and pronouns; or may be themselves comfortable identifying as "male" or "female," while recognizing that these categories do not fit everyone.

gender role: The set of roles and behaviors assigned to females and males by society. Western culture recognizes two basic gender roles: masculine (having the qualities attributed to males) and feminine (having the qualities attributed to females).

hermaphrodite: A medical, mythological, zoological, and botanical term describing aspects of ambiguous genitalia and/or biological sex. When applied to a person in a social setting, it is now considered antiquated and or offensive. See **intersex**.

heteronormativity: A concept whereby practices, social policies, and institutions are perceived to support and privilege heterosexuality. It is the belief that heterosexual relationships are the normal and natural state and, by extension, that anything outside this state is an unnatural variant.

heterosexism: The assumption that all people are heterosexual and that heterosexuality is right, correct, and normal. It is also the power to enforce policies, practices, and structures against gays, lesbians, bisexuals, and transgender people.

heterosexual: A person who seeks emotional, physical, and/or spiritual relationships with a person of the opposite sex or gender expression.

hir: Pronounced "here." Hir is a third person possessive or objective pronoun that is used in lieu of "him/his" and "her/hers" by some people who identify as transgender. One should not use this pronoun to refer to someone unless you have been asked to do so.

HIV/AIDS: HIV stands for human immunodeficiency virus. HIV is communicable only through direct contact with blood, semen, cervical/vaginal secretions, and breast milk. It is *not* communicable through social kissing, hugging, or inanimate objects like toilet seats. **AIDS** stands for acquired immunodeficiency syndrome. According to the Center for Disease Control (CDC), "acquired" means that the disease is not hereditary but develops after birth from contact with a disease-causing agent (in this case, HIV). "Immunodeficiency" means that the disease is characterized by a weakening of the immune system. "Syndrome" refers to a group of symptoms that collectively indicate or characterize a disease. In the case of AIDS, this can include the development of certain infections and/or cancers, as well as a decrease in the number of certain cells in a person's immune system.

homophobia: An irrational fear or hatred of people who identify as homosexual. This fear may stem from the out-of-date belief that homosexuality is a mental illness, from personal religious beliefs, from the incorrect belief that homosexuals are responsible for AIDS, etc.

homosexual: A person who seeks emotional, physical, and/or spiritual relationships with another person of the same gender/sex.

hormone replacement therapy: The process of taking hormones to achieve the secondary sex characteristics of the desired sex. "T" is common shorthand or slang for the male hormone testosterone.

internalized homophobia, internalized transphobia, internalized biphoba: Self-hatred at one's own identity as a result of "believing" or internalizing the negative stereotypes of one's identity.

intersex: An individual whose biological sex does not correspond with conventional expectations of male or female anatomy or genetics. Approximately 1.7 percent of the population is intersex. Some intersex individuals identify themselves as transgender, which is a social or gender identity, and some do not. Other related terms and usages include **intersexed** and **intersexual**.

in the closet: A term used to refer to people who have not revealed their sexual or gender identity/identities either to themselves or others.

lesbian: A woman-identified person who seeks emotional, spiritual, and/or physical relationships with other woman-identified people.

LGBTQQIA: Acronym for lesbian, gay, bisexual, transgender, queer, questioning, intersex, ally.

male-to-female: Abbrevatiated MTF or M2F. Usually said aloud as "M to F." Most commonly refers to male-to-female transsexuals. A person who was born in a male body but whose gender identity is female. It can also refer to those assigned male at birth, in the case of intersex people, whose gender identity is female. Some, but not all female-to-male transsexuals will seek hormonal and/or surgical treatment in order to live successfully as a woman in society. This term is sometimes also used by others who are born in male bodies and who move toward feminine or female presentation without hormones or surgery.

MSM (men who have sex with men): Men, regardless of their sexual identity or orientation, who engage in sexual activity with men.

oppression: A state or experience when one is denied rights and/or acceptance based on one's gender, sexual orientation, race, nationality, or other characteristic.

outing: The act of publicly revealing another person's sexual orientation.

perceived gender: What another person assumes one's gender is in a given interaction. Some people's gender expressions can be misinterpreted or confused and perceived as different from the person's identity.

prejudice: Inaccurate and negative beliefs about another group and its members without basis in fact. It is often based on stereotypes and can occur on a conscious or subconscious level.

queer: Historically, a negative term used against people perceived to be GLBT. More recently, "queer" has been reclaimed by some people as a positive term describing all those who do not conform to rigid notions of gender and sexuality. The term is often used in a political context and in academic settings to challenge traditional ideas about identity ("queer theory"). Caution: for older gay men and lesbians, this term may still be considered offensive.

questioning: Refers to people who are uncertain as to their sexual orientation or gender identity. They are often seeking information and support during this stage of their identity development. It can refer to someone who is exploring his or her queer potential.

rainbow flag: Historically, there have been several rainbow flags that are unrelated to the gay liberation movement. In 1978, artist Gilbert Baker designed the first rainbow flag to symbolize gay pride and diversity. It was originally designed with eight stripes: pink (sexuality), red (life), orange (healing), yellow (sun), green (nature), blue (art), indigo (harmony), and violet (spirit). However, the colors pink and indigo were eventually taken out, partially for production availability reasons, and the current rainbow flag has remaining six colors.

same-gender officiation: The act of presiding over rituals of union for same-gender couples. In March 2000, the Central Conference of American Rabbis (CCAR), the rabbinic arm of the Reform Movement, adopted a resolution stating that "the relationship of a Jewish, same gender couple is worthy of affirmation through appropriate Jewish ritual." The resolution supported "those who choose to officiate" at same-gender ceremonies and "those who do not" choose to officiate at such ceremonies.

sex: In its biological sense, a concept or classification of people as male or female. At birth, an infant's sex is determined or assigned based on a combination of bodily characteristics, including chromosomes, hormones, internal and external reproductive organs, and genitalia. Sex is generally thought of as dichotomous—male or female—but with a greater knowledge of intersex conditions, this understanding is revealed to exclude a number of people who do not conform to the "either/or" classification. See also **biological sex**.

sex reassignment surgery: Formerly called a "sex change." Surgery for the purpose of having a body more consistent with one's gender identity. There are a variety of sex reassignment surgeries. People in the process of transitioning (see definition) may choose to have some of these surgeries or none at all as part of that transition. These surgeries can be quite costly, and not everyone who desires sex reassignment surgery has equal access.

sexual behavior: Describes an individual's behavior in sexual attachments or relationships. However, sexual behavior does not determine one's sexual orientation. For example, a celibate lesbian (one who does not have sex at all) is still a lesbian, and men who have sex with men (MSM) in prison or in general may not identify their sexual orientation as gay.

sexual identity: This is a construction of how we perceive ourselves and what we call ourselves regarding who we have as physical, sexual, and/or emotional partners. Such labels include "lesbian," "gay," "bisexual," "queer," "questioning," "heterosexual," and "straight."

sexual orientation: The gender or genders of the people to whom one is attracted and forms romantic, emotional, and spiritual relationships and sexual, physical attachments. Sexual orientation is influenced by a variety of factors, including genetics as well as unknown environmental factors. The origins of it are not completely understood. Sexual orientation and gender identity are very different; transgender people can have a sexual orientation of gay, lesbian, straight, queer, bisexual, or other label as they determine it.

social privilege: A right, advantage, or immunity granted to or enjoyed by certain people beyond the common advantage of all others. In many cases, it is an exemption from certain burdens or liabilities that those without the privilege must still bear.

sodomy laws: Term for various state laws against specific sexual acts. Sodomy is not synonymous with lesbian or gay sex, although sodomy laws are usually used to prosecute lesbians and gay men. The legal definition of sodomy is different in each state and often applies to certain sexual acts practiced by non-gay people. See the Lambda Legal Defense and Education Fund, http://www.lambdalegal.org/

standards of care (SOC): Organizational professional consensus document about the psychiatric, psychological, medical, and surgical management of gender identity disorders (GID). Professionals use this document to understand the parameters within which they may offer assistance to those diagnosed with GID. People with gender identity disorders and their families use the SOC to understand the current thinking of professionals. See http://www.hbigda.org/soc.htm.

straight ally: Any non-GLBT person who supports and stands up for the rights of GLBT people.

third gender: A term used to describe a gender-variant person whose gender identity is neither male nor female, some combination of genders, or between or beyond genders.

tokenize: The policy or practice of making only a symbolic effort. For example, you are the only (out) queer student in your class, and your professor, to create the illusion of a diverse discussion, asks you to fill in the gay parts of a discussion on Oscar Wilde.

transgender: The term was coined or popularized along with "transgenderist" by Virginia (Charles) Prince, Ph.D. (in pharmacology), a married heterosexual, full-time cross-dresser. She wanted to differentiate between those individuals like herself, who chose to live in the opposite gender role without surgery, from those who chose sex reassignment surgery (SRS) and were known as transsexuals. Ironically, given Prince's strong views against SRS and her attempts to create separate categories, over time the term has become an umbrella to describe a wide range of identities and experiences, including female-to-male transsexuals (FTMs), male-to-female transsexuals (MTFs), cross-dressers, drag queens, drag kings, gender queers, and others, each of whom is likely to have a very different experience of their actual gender identity, despite all being lumped into one category.

Today, those who embrace a transgender label are those individuals whose gender identity and/or gender expression differs from the biological sex they were born as or were assigned at birth. Identifying as "transgender" (sometimes shortened to "trans") says nothing about sexual orientation, as gender identity and sexual orientation are different constructs. Transgender people can have a sexual orientation of gay, lesbian, straight, queer, bisexual, or none of the above.

transitioning, transition: The process of ceasing to live in one gender role and starting to live in another, undertaken by transgender and transsexual people. Transitioning usually happens before any sex reassignment surgery, and in some cases even before any hormone replacement therapy. Transitioning often marks the start of the real-life experience that is usually required for sex reassignment surgery.

Many people also use the term "transitioning" to refer to the entire transgender/transsexual process (from living 24/7 in the original gender role to after surgery). The beginning of the real-life experience is then often called "going fulltime" (i.e., starting to live 24/7 in the opposite gender role).

Transitioning can involve sex reassignment therapy, name changes, wearing clothing seen as gender appropriate, or the use of makeup, and generally coming out of the closet. It is a complicated, multistep process that may take years to complete and can start and stop at a variety of places and with different activities along the process.

transphobia: The irrational fear or hatred of people who identify as transgender. This fear may stem from the incorrect belief that transgender people have a psychological disorder or are confused. Transphobia is manifested in a number of ways, including violence, harassment, and discrimination.

transsexuals: Individuals who do not identify with their biological or birth-assigned sex and who wish to alter their bodies surgically and or hormonally to be congruent with how they experience themselves. See also **transitioning**.

transvestite: A person who dresses and acts in a style or manner traditionally associated with the opposite gender. In some cases, the person derives emotional or sexual gratification from doing this. Transvestites differ from transsexuals in that they do not necessarily want to alter their bodies. In the United States, the term is considered by many to be offensive, but the usage and connotation vary internationally. See **cross-dresser**.

two-spirit: A term developed by Native Americans to describe the specific traditional and cultural gender identities in many Native American nations, but not all, of a person in which the male and female spirit coexisted in one body and who exhibited the characteristics of both spirits. Each nation had their own name for this person in its native language. The older generic term "berdache" was developed by Europeans and anthropologists; based on its origins, many Native Americans now consider it offensive.

zie: Pronounced "zee." Zie is a third person subjective pronoun that is used in lieu of "she" and "he." One should not use this pronoun to refer to someone unless you have been asked to or well understand a person's gender identity.

Resources

This series of three annotated resource lists was compiled from sources on the Jeff Herman Virtual Resource Center (JHVRC). The JHVRC is a Web-based educational environment for all those interested in learning about Judaism, sexual orientation, and gender. It is a project of the Institute for Judaism and Sexual Orientation (IJSO) and the National Department of Distance Education at Hebrew Union College–Jewish Institute of Religion (HUC-JIR).

The JHVRC also contains hundreds of links to Web sites on the intersection of Judaism and GLBT topics as well as general GLBT information sites. They are not included here as Web resources, and since Web addresses change faster than print material, it is best to access them live.

The Web site can be accessed at http://www.huc.edu/IJSO/jhvrc.

The first list is an annotated bibliography separated into the following categories:

- Experiences and issues around the intersection of Judaism and GLBT topics
- Israel and GLBT topics
- GLBT parents, kids, and families and their heterosexual parents, kids, and families
- Gay Holocaust literature

The second list is GLBT education resources for schools.

The third list includes two annotated bibliographies, compiled from COLAGE (Children of Lesbians and Gays Everywhere), for children ages 0–12 and for those ages 12 and up.

Annotated Bibliography

Jewish and Gay, Lesbian, Bisexual, and Transgender (GLBT) Sources

Allen, Mariette Pathy. *The Gender Frontier*. Heidelberg, Germany: Kehrer Verlag, 2003. Photographer Mariette Pathy Allen captures a remarkable range of frontier genders including a transsexual cop, a Stonewall veteran, gender-fluid NYU students, Capitol Hill lobbyists, scientists, intersex activists, icons, and factory workers. Allen has been questioning the "mysterious essence" of human existence for over two decades and using her camera to offer multiple interpretations.

Alpert, Rebecca T. *Like Bread on the Seder Plate: Jewish Lesbians and the Transformation of Tradition*. New York: Columbia University Press, 1997.
Both a feminist and a lesbian, Rabbi Rebecca Alpert demonstrates that the Jewish faith is constantly evolving and therefore transformational. The book received the 1998 Lambda Literary Award in the spirituality/religion category and the 1999 Award for Scholarship from the Jewish Women's Caucus of the Association for Women in Psychology.

Alpert, Rebecca T., Sue Levi Elwell, and Shirley Idelson. *Lesbian Rabbis: The First Generation*. New Brunswick, NJ: Rutgers University Press, 2001.
This is a collection of thoughtful essays by eighteen groundbreaking rabbis from the Reform, Reconstructionist, and Conservative Movements.

Balka, Christie, and Andy Rose, eds. *Twice Blessed: On Being Lesbian or Gay and Jewish*. Boston: Beacon Press, 1989.
Groundbreaking book that includes essays by Rebecca Alpert, Martha Ackelsberg, Eric Rofes, Judith Plaskow, Sue Levi Elwell, and many others. This is an original collection of articles and essays on Jewish lesbian and gay life.

Beck, Evelyn Torton, ed. *Nice Jewish Girls: A Lesbian Anthology*. Boston: Beacon Press, 1989.
Collection of essays, stories, poetry, and photographs about women's experiences straddling the Jewish and lesbian worlds. Includes pieces on mother-daughter relations, Israel, and anti-Semitism in the lesbian community.

Beck, Gad. *An Underground Life: Memoirs of a Gay Jew in Nazi Berlin*. Madison: University of Wisconsin Press, 2000.
Gad Beck was born to a dual-faith couple in Weimar, Germany. He recounts gay life in Berlin prior to and after the rise to power of the Nazis. Beck tried to save gay friends and Jews from concentration and deportation camps by forging documents, hiding people, and even in one case donning a Hitler youth uniform to deceive the Gestapo to attempt to help his lover. There is also an online exhibit of his wartime diary produced by the United States Holocaust Memorial Museum at http://www.ushmm.org/museum/exhibit/online/doyourememberwhen/co/co.htm.

Bornstein, Kate. *Gender Outlaw: On Men, Women and the Rest of Us*. New York: Routledge, 1994.
This book includes cultural criticism, a play, and autobiographical writings by the author on gender, orientation, and desire. She asserts that gender is a cultural phenomenon and explores the possibilities beyond this social construction.

Boyarin, Daniel, Daniel Itzkovitz, and Ann Pellegrini, eds. *Queer Theory and the Jewish Question*. New York: Columbia University Press, 2003.
The construction of Jewish and queer identities are "bound up with one another in resonant ways," even extending to modern discourses of anti-Semitism and homophobia, according to the editors. They present seventeen essays approaching the topic from the field of cultural studies. Topics include the way gender is represented by the Jewish

character played by Barbra Streisand in the film *Funny Girl*, and the sexualized aspects of Chaucer's portrayal of "the vicious murder of a saintly Christian child by perverse Jews" in *The Canterbury Tales*.

Brettschneider, Marla. *The Family Flamboyant—Race Politics, Queer Families, Jewish Lives*. Albany: SUNY Press, 2006.
Through personal accounts as well as political analysis, the author examines how families are affected by their relation to race, gender, sexuality, and one shaped by a Jewish lens.

Brown, Angela, ed. *Mentsh: On Being Jewish and Queer*. Los Angeles: Alyson Books, 2004.
Over thirty queer Jewish contributors from around the world (including Israel, Serbia, and Australia) reveal their surprising, poignant, and sometimes hilarious experiences in ways that offer a staggering perspective on issues of identity, institutions, and culture from the viewpoint of the queer outsider struggling to belong.

Dickson, Deborah, director. *Ruthie and Connie: Every Room in the House* (film). 2002.
They're Jewish, they're grandmothers, and they're lesbians. This documentary shares the lives of Ruth Berman and Connie Kurtz, who first met in Brooklyn in 1959 as young married women raising their young children. After becoming good friends, they fell in love in 1974 and decided to leave their marriages and children for one another. The film includes their struggles and joys, including their fight against the New York City Board of Education for domestic partner benefits and their establishment of a PFLAG chapter for retirees in Florida.

Dubowski, Sandi Simcha, director. *Trembling Before G-d* (film). 2001.
Built around intimately told personal stories of Chasidic and Orthodox Jews who are gay or lesbian, the film portrays a group of people who face a profound dilemma—how to reconcile their passionate love of Judaism and the divine with the drastic biblical prohibitions that forbid homosexuality.

Fayngold, Irena, director. *Hineini: Coming Out in a Jewish High School* (film). 2005.
Hineini (Hebrew for "Here I am") chronicles the story of one student's courageous fight to establish a gay-straight alliance at a Jewish pluralistic high school in the Boston area and the transformative impact of her campaign on everyone involved. Using interviews with Shulamit, her family, teachers, and other students—both those who support her campaign and those who oppose it—the film allows the members of this community to tell their own story as it unfolds. What emerges is a potent story of Jewish pluralism and a community navigating the crosscurrents of Jewish tradition and social change. For more information: http://www.boston-keshet.org/hineini/index.html.

Feinberg, Leslie. *Stone Butch Blues*. Ithaca, NY: Alyson Books, 1993.
A novel about lesbian Jess Goldberg, who, coming of age in the 1950s/60s pre-Stonewall, attempts to come to grips with her identity as a butch lesbian, undergoing transformations, including hormone treatments, along the way. Leslie Feinberg is also the author of *Trans Liberation: Beyond Pink or Blue* and *Transgender Warriors* and is a noted activist and speaker on transgender issues.

Galford, Ellen. *The Dyke and the Dybbuk*. Seattle, WA: Seal Press, 1998.
A work of humorous fiction filled with Jewish folklore about a London taxi driver, film critic, and lesbian named Rainbow Rosenbloom, and the Dybbuk Kokos, who must hunt Rainbow down to fulfill an ancient curse.

Gluck, Robert, ed. *Homosexuality and Judaism: A Reconstructionist Workshop Series*. Jenkintown, PA: Jewish Reconstructionist Federation, 1993.
A compilation of eight workshops designed for use by congregations or small groups to study the issue of inclusivity and becoming a welcoming community. This work includes extensive references to biblical sources. This resource is only available from the Jewish Reconstructionist Federation at http://www.jrf.org/pub/cat-papers.html.

Greenberg, Steven. *Wrestling with God and Men*. Madison: University of Wisconsin Press, 2005.
This book is about Rabbi Greenberg's ten-year struggle to reconcile his homosexuality with Orthodox Judaism. Employing traditional rabbinic resources, Greenberg presents readers with surprising biblical interpretations of the Creation story, the love of David and Jonathan, the destruction of Sodom, and the condemning verses of Leviticus. In so doing, he draws on a wide array of nonscriptural texts to introduce readers to occasions of same-sex love in Talmudic narratives, medieval Jewish poetry and prose, and traditional Jewish case law literature.

Heschel, Susannah, and Danya Ruttenberg, eds. *Yentl's Revenge: The Next Wave of Jewish Feminism*. Seattle, WA: Seal Press, 2001.
This collection of essays by twenty young Jewish feminists and includes an exploration of Jewish transgender issues.

Hutchins, Loraine, and Lani Kaahumanu, eds. *Bi Any Other Name: Bisexual People Speak Out*. Boston: Alyson Books, 1991.
An anthology written by bisexuals who tell their stories of acceptance and understanding from a perspective that helps the reader better relate to the spirit and essence of what it is like to have affections for multiple genders. Many of the stories reflect hardship in coming to terms with bisexuality, and rejection from both the heterosexual and gay communities. Stories written by Jewish bisexuals in the anthology include Rebecca Gorlin and David Lourea.

Kaplan, Dana Evan, ed. *Contemporary Debates in American Reform Judaism: Conflicting Visions*. New York: Routledge, 2001.
A collection of essays that explore a range of issues and questions currently confronting American Reform Judaism. Rabbi Denise L. Eger contributed the essay "Embracing Lesbians and Gay Men: A Reform Jewish Innovation," which traces the evolution of the Reform Movement's inclusion of gay men and lesbians. Hinda Seif also has a chapter entitled "'Where Kosher Means Organic and Union Label': Bisexual Women Re-embrace Their Jewish Heritage."

Kaye, Melanie, ed. *The Tribe of Dina: A Jewish Women's Anthology*. Boston: Beacon Press, 1986.
This book is a collection of essays, poetry, fiction, and artwork and includes a number of stories of Jewish women who are also lesbian exploring identity, discrimination, and

bridging cultures. This is an expanded and updated version of materials published in 1986 as a special issue of the journal *Sinister Wisdom.*

Klepfisz, Irena. *Dreams of an Insomniac: Jewish Feminist Essays, Speeches, and Diatribes.* Portland, OR: Eighth Mountain Press, 1990.
This book examines issues the author considers "central to my experience as a feminist and lesbian, as a Jew sorting out my identity and my relationship to Jewish history, as an American Jew defining my relationship to events in the Middle East."

Kolodny, Debra R., ed. *Blessed Bi Spirit: Bisexual People of Faith.* New York: Continuum Publishers, 2000.
Over thirty contributors from a variety of religious traditions and spiritual paths—including Buddhist, Hindu, pagan, 12-step, Christian, and Jewish—speak about the intersections of their faith practice and their bisexuality.

Kroeger, Brooke. *Passing: When People Can't Be Who They Are.* New York: Perseus Publishing, 2004.
These are stories about people who "pass," as black for white, gay for straight, and in other ways. Two stories relate to gay and lesbians passing for straight. One, entited "Leviticus 18:22," is about a gay, conservative seminarian. The other is about a lesbian naval officer. There is also an interesting story about a straight, Latina Jew-by-choice.

Lebow, Alisa, and Cynthia Madansky, directors. *Treyf* (film). 1998.
Treyf means "not kosher" in Yiddish. This is an unorthodox documentary by and about two Jewish lesbians who met and fell in love at a Passover seder. With personal narration, real and imagined educational films, and haunting imagery, the filmmakers examine the Jewish identity of their upbringings and its impact on their lives.

Lewin, Ellen. *Recognizing Ourselves: Ceremonies of Lesbian and Gay Commitment.* New York: Columbia Press, 1998.
This book was written by an anthropologist whose commitment ceremony took place at Congregation Sha'ar Zahav in San Francisco in 1992. The book looks at the personal, ritual, ethical, and religious factors that lead same-gender couples to undertake public recognition of their relationships and how they embrace that recognition. Several Jewish wedding ritual adaptations and additions are included in the book.

Mass, Lawrence D. *Confessions of a Jewish Wagnerite: Being Gay and Jewish in America.* New York: Cassell Academic, 1999.
A collection of autobiographical essays, the book looks at "the interconnectedness of gay, Jewish and musical cultures in post-World War II America, against a backdrop of resurgent anti-Semitism." Mass comes to terms with his internalized anti-Semitism and gay identity through his friendship with the great-grandson of the composer Richard Wagner and his life-partnership with a fellow gay activist and Jewish-American writer.

Nestle, Joan. *A Fragile Union: New and Selected Writings.* San Francsico: Cleis Press, 1998.
This collection of the author's essays explores gender, class, sexuality, politics, and more. It brings together history, critical review, and analysis on the lives of lesbians and women in general.

———. *A Restricted Country*. Ithaca, NY: Firebrand Books, 1987.
A proud working-class woman and an "out" lesbian long before the rainbow revolution, Joan Nestle has explored struggles for freedom from the McCarthy era to the present day. This collection recounts the lesbian, feminist, and civil rights movements through personal essays and has been recently reissued.

Ochs, Robyn, and Sarah E. Rowley, eds. *Getting Bi: Voices of Bisexuals Around the World*. Boston: Bisexual Resource Center, 2005.
This book is a compilation of stories and individual experiences of bisexuals from around the world. It includes a story by Jonathan Daniel Hoffman, a graduate student at Hebrew University in Jerusalem. Jonathan has formed a group in Israel called BIS (Bisexuals in Israel) to bring the bisexual agenda to the GLBT and heterosexual communities. Has a great bisexual bibliography.

O'Hearn, Claudine Chaiwei, ed. *Half and Half: Writers on Growing Up Biracial and Bicultural*. New York: Pantheon, 1998.
A collection of eighteen essays, edited by Claudine Chaiwei O'Hearn, recounts the life stories and musings of individuals who grew up not only biracial, but bicultural as well. Their life stories are also about adjusting to life in the American landscape, which can sometimes be insensitive to or obsessed with race and identity. Of interest to Jewish readers is the story entitled "What Color Is Jesus," by James McBride. Both his biological father and stepfather were African American, while his mother is a Polish Jew, the eldest daughter of an Orthodox rabbi.

Raphael, Lev. *Dancing on Tisha B'Av*. New York: St. Martin's Griffin, 1991.
A collection of nineteen stories that probe the challenges of being gay and Jewish. The author explores the experiences of concentration camp survivor parents and their gay children, a sister admiring her brother's devotion to Orthodoxy and then understanding his struggle to accept his gay identity, and other characters striving to reconcile seemingly mutually exclusive feelings, desires, and values.

———. *Journeys and Arrivals: On Being Gay and Jewish*. Boston: Faber & Faber, 1996.
Prize-winning author Lev Raphael (*Dancing on Tisha B'Av*) writes for the first time in nonfiction form about the themes of gay and Jewish identity that permeate his work. He is the child of Holocaust survivors, which gives him a unique perspective and is the subject for one of his chapters, "Empty Memory? Gays in Holocaust Literature."

Rapoport, Chaim. *Judaism and Homosexuality: An Authentic Orthodox View*. Portland, OR: Mitchell Vallentine & Company, 2004.
This extensively researched book presents an Orthodox response to homosexuality. From his tradition, the author, rabbi of London's Ilford United Synagogue and a member of the cabinet of the Chief Rabbi of the United Kingdom, applies sensitivity while still adhering to halachah.

Schimel, Lawrence, ed. *Found Tribe: Jewish Coming Out Stories*. Santa Fe, NM: Sherman Asher Publishing, 2002.
This book contains seventeen personal essays by well-known Jewish personalities, who reflect, in a kind of "midrash," on sex and sexuality and finding a sense of community

within Jewish life. Through their words and actions, they explain what it is like to be both gay and Jewish in contemporary times. Essayists include by David Bergman, Gabriel Blau, David Ian Cavill, Edward M. Cohen, Rabbi Steve Greenberg, Daniel M. Jaffe, Arnie Kantrowitz, Gabriel Lampert, Andrew Martin, Jesse G. Monteagudo, Julian Padilla, Lev Raphael, Andrew Ramer, Phillip Ritari, David Rosen, Lawrence Schimel, and Jonathan Wald.

Shneer, David, and Caryn Aviv, eds. *Queer Jews*. New York: Routledge Press, 2002.
A collection of essays written by GLBT Jews, exploring "the conflict between the desire to integrate into established Jewish communities, changing them from within and the comforts of creating and maintaining 'separate' spaces for queer Jews."

Shokeid, Moshe. *A Gay Synagogue in New York*. Philadelphia: University of Pennsylvania Press, 2002.
This book speaks to the heart of organizing from scratch what is now the largest gay and lesbian synagogue in the United States. There were many trials and tribulations, as well as many rewards, along the way. It is a great way to see the inner workings of establishing a temple and to learn how the visions of the founders made it into the final congregation.

Silin, Jonathan. *My Father's Keeper: The Story of a Gay Son and His Aging Parents*. Boston: Beacon Press, 2006.
The author, an early childhood educator and Jewish, gay, middle-aged man learns to care for his elderly parents after a series of life-threatening illnesses forced them to make the difficult transition from being independent to being reliant on their son. Their new needs and unrelenting demands brought parents and child into intimate daily contact and radically transformed what had been a distant and emotionally fraught relationship.

Simkin, Ruth. *Like an Orange on a Seder Plate: Our Lesbian Haggadah*. Canada: Privately Printed, 1999.
This Haggadah is lesbian centered and woman oriented.

Tucker, Naomi S., ed. *Bisexual Politics: Theories, Queries, and Visions*. New York: Harrington Park Press, 1995.
This book contains thirty-five essays, interviews, and poems that explore the history, strategies, and theory of bisexual political activism in the United States. They discuss the movement's beginning in the 1970s and its current state, sexuality, coalition building, visions for the future, and the radical right. There are several Jewish-related chapters in the book, including "If Half of You Dodges a Bullet, All of You Ends Up Dead."

Warshow, Joyce, director. *Hand on the Pulse* (Film). 2002.
This documentary film is a biography of Joan Nestle, a teacher, writer, and founder of the Lesbian Herstory Archives. Nestle has done major work towards furthering society's understanding of gender and female sexuality. Using photos, archival footage, and interviews, director Joyce Warshow allows viewers to peek into Nestle's life.

Weiner, Nancy H. *Beyond Breaking the Glass: A Spiritual Guide to Your Jewish Wedding.* New York: Central Conference of American Rabbis, 2001.

A book that includes guidance for same-gender couples planning weddings. Rabbi Wiener explains Reform Judaism's approach to wedding customs and preparations, offers practical information about ceremonies, and provides contemporary, gender-inclusive prayers and rituals.

Woog, Dan, ed. *Friends and Families: True Stories of Gay America's Straight Allies.* Los Angeles: Alyson Books, 1999.

This book is a compilation of profiles of people from many walks of life who all share a common theme: being proactively supportive of GLBT issues. Each story is interesting in and of itself, although there are two that are of particular interest to Jewish readers: "Every Day the Rabbi Helps Gays" by David Horowitz, and "The Holocaust Still Haunts Her" by Roxanne Pappenheimer.

Wythe, Douglas, Andrew Merling, Roslyn Merling, and Sheldon Merling. *The Wedding: A Family's Coming Out Story.* New York: Avon Books, 2000.

This is a true story told in four voices (two grooms and the parents of one of them) of how a Jewish family in Montreal takes on the upcoming wedding of their Jewish son, living in New York. Initially, there is shock and then a slow process of coming to terms with all that is involved in having a gay son and accepting gay marriage.

GLBT Issues in Israel

Alexander, Ilil, director. *Keep Not Silent (Ortho-Dykes)* (film). 2004.

Winner of the Israeli Oscar for Best Documentary, as well as eight international awards, this film documents the clandestine struggle of three women fighting for their right to love within their beloved Orthodox communities in Jerusalem. All three are pious, religiously committed women. All three are lesbians and members of a secret support group called the "Ortho-Dykes."

Dubowski, Sandi Simcha, director. *Trembling Before G-d* (film). 2001.

This documentary is built around intimately told personal stories of Chasidic and Orthodox Jews who are gay or lesbian, some of whom live in Israel. Overall, the film portrays a group of people who face a profound dilemma: how to reconcile their passionate love of Judaism and the divine with the drastic biblical prohibitions that forbid homosexuality.

Fox, Eytan, director. *Walk on Water* (film). 2003.

Eyal, an Israeli Mossad agent, is given the mission to track down and kill the very old Alfred Himmelman, an ex-Nazi officer, who might still be alive. Pretending to be a tourist guide, he befriends Himmelman's grandson, Axel, in Israel to help him visit his sister, Pia. The two men set out on a tour of the country, during which Axel challenges Eyal's values as a gay man.

Fox, Eytan, Amir Harel, and Gal Uchovsky, directors. *Yossi and Jagger* (film). 2002.

This film is a homosexual love story about an Israeli army platoon commander and a company commander in an outpost on the Lebanon border. Jagger, the platoon commander, is the open and extroverted one, and ready for his coming-out. Yossi, the company commander, is introverted and inhibited. The film deals explicitly with romantic love between these two commanders.

Freedman, Marcia. *Exile in the Promised Land: A Memoir*. Ithaca, NY: Firebrand Books, 1990.
This is a first-person account of the experiences of Marcia Freedman, a U.S.-born feminist who became a founding member of Israel's women's movement and a member of the Knesset. Freedman came out as a lesbian to her husband and young daughter after thirteen years of marriage. Making *aliyah* in 1967, Freedman returned to the United States in 1981, convinced her lesbianism and peace activism could not be tolerated in Israel.

Moore, Tracy, ed. *Lesbiot: Israeli Lesbians Talk About Sexuality, Feminism, Judaism and Their Lives*. New York: Cassell, 1999.
A collection of essays/interviews with twenty-one Israeli lesbians who share their family histories, personal biographies, reflections on the lesbian experience, and opinions on political and social issues.

Press, Jacob, and Amir Sumakai Fink, eds. *Independence Park: The Lives of Gay Men in Israel (Contraversions: Jews and Other Differences)*. Stanford, CA: Stanford University Press, 1999.
Independence Park in Tel Aviv and Independence Park in Jerusalem are well-known meeting places for gay men in Israel. The book also picks up independence as the theme of the collection of narratives told by twelve gay men from a cross-section of contemporary Israeli society. The speakers are Jewish and Arab, ranging in age from twenty-two to seventy-two, and speak about their family backgrounds and early childhood memories, including their first understanding of sexuality and responses to those feelings.

Shadmi, Erella, and Chava Frankfort-Nachmias, eds. *Sappho in the Holy Land: Lesbian Dilemmas and Existence*. Albany: State University of New York, 2005.
This unique collection examines the experience of lesbians in Israel, providing insight into some of the institutions that have helped shape that experience. The book analyzes and interprets how culturally specific political, ideological, and social systems construct lesbian identities, experiences, and dilemmas, and it also explores how a specific society is seen, understood, and interpreted from a lesbian perspective.

Walzer, Lee. *Between Sodom and Eden: A Gay Journey Through Today's Changing Israel*. New York: Columbia University Press, 2000.
This work is based on interviews with over one hundred Israelis, as well as Palestinians. Lee Walzer explores how, within a decade, Israel evolved from a society that marginalized homosexuals to one that offers some of the most extensive legal protections in the world. Examining the interplay between Judaism and homosexuality, he traces the political, religious, and social factors that make Israel a gay rights trendsetter.

Yosef, Raz. *Beyond Flesh: Queer Masculinities in Israel Cinema.* New Brunswick, NJ: Rutgers University Press, 2004.
Raz Yosef explores Israeli cinema's role in the creation of national identity and the complex ways the marginalization of queerness became necessary to that goal.

Family Issues: GLBT and Straight Parents and Children

Bernstein, Robert A. *Families of Value: Personal Profiles of Pioneering Lesbian and Gay Parents.* New York: Marlowe & Company, 2005.
This book is a collection of short stories of real families telling of gay parents' struggles to raise their children in a society that is often hostile to their lifestyle. The stories compiled range from a gay Protestant minister to two lesbian police officers hoping to extend death benefits to each other.

———. *Straight Parents, Gay Children: Inspiring Families to Live Honestly and With Greater Understanding.* New York: Thunder's Mouth Press/Nation Books, 1999.
Personal account of a man coming to terms with his daughter's lesbianism, his understanding of the challenges she faces, and the work he and other parents of gay children have on behalf of acceptance of gay men and lesbians.

Boenke, Mary, ed. *Trans Forming Families: Real Stories About Transgender Loved Ones.* New Castle, DE: Oak Knoll Press, 2003.
The first of its kind, this book features forty authors who share their personal journeys from the initial shock or resistance when learning their loved ones (or they, themselves) were struggling with gender problems, through the various feelings, to final acceptance. Arlene Ishtar Lev, noted trans-therapist, has written a lucid foreword, and Jessica Xavier's introduction documents the constant public interest in trans-family relationships. Boenke is the mother of an adult MTF son, chair of PFLAG's Transgender Network, a trans activist, and a retired psychotherapist.

Brettschneider, Marla. *The Family Flamboyant— Race Politics, Queer Families, Jewish Lives.* Albany: SUNY Press, 2006.
Through personal accounts as well as political analysis, the author examines how families are affected by their relation to race, gender, sexuality, and one shaped by a Jewish lens.

Feinberg, Leslie. *Transgender Warriors: Making History from Joan of Arc to Dennis Rodman.* Boston: Beacon Press, 1997.
Leslie Feinberg uncovers persuasive evidence that there have always been people who crossed the cultural boundaries of gender. *Transgender Warriors* is an eye-opening jaunt through the history of gender expression and a powerful testament to the rebellious spirit.

Gillespie, Peggy, ed. Gigi Kaeser, photographer. *Love Makes a Family: Portraits of Lesbian, Gay, Bisexual, and Transgender Parents and Their Families..* Amherst: University of Massachusetts Press, 1999.
A revealing photography book with autobiographical text of GLBT families, which include a gay dad who is a cantor and a lesbian couple who struggled with their temple

to accept them and their children as a family. The book accompanies a traveling photo-text exhibit for K–12, colleges, businesses, and religious institutions. For information: Peggy Gillespie and Gigi Kaeser, Family Diversity Projects, www.familydiv.org; 413-256-0502.

Gottlieb, Andrew R., ed. *Side by Side: On Having a Gay or Lesbian Sibling*. New York: Harrington Park Press, 2005.
A compilation of stories written by siblings who have a gay or lesbian brother or sister about how this has impacted their lives. This book is an easy and enjoyable read, offering insight ranging from shock and denial to acceptance, support, and understanding. Many of the stories are quite touching and show the special relationships that often evolve out of the heartfelt emotions that involve the difficult coming-out process. It has been suggested that this is an excellent book for classroom discussion.

Howey, Noelle, and Ellen Samuels, eds. *Out of the Ordinary: Essays on Growing Up with Gay, Lesbian and Transgender Parents*. New York: St. Martin's Press, 2000.
A collection of essays, edited by Noelle Howey and Ellen Samuels, that talk from the heart about the experience of growing up with gay, lesbian, and transsexual parents. Some of the stories are easy to relate to, while others really make us think about what it means to be an inclusive family. In the chapter "Rites of Passage," by Daniel Belasco, the Jewish teenage author talks about his lesbian mom, her partner, a rabbi, and how they all integrated into Jewish society at large and within their own family.

Jennings, Kevin, and Pat Shapiro. *Always My Child: a Parent's Guide to Understanding Your Gay, Lesbian, Bisexual, Transgendered or Questioning Son or Daughter*. New York: Fireside, 2003.
This guide will help parents navigate the challenges of connecting with a GLBTQ child and becoming an integral and supportive part of that child's life. The book is especially notable for its chapters on transgender issues and multicultural issues. There is also a chapter on youth questioning their sexuality (straight and gay and in-between), and how parents can be supportive in that as well.

Kessler, Susanne. *Lessons from the Intersexed*. New Brunswick, NJ: Rutgers University Press, 1998.
This is a cutting-edge and radical book on gender and the experiences of intersex people. Well researched, with extensive resource material.

Mastoon, Adam. *The Shared Heart: Portraits and Stories Celebrating Lesbian, Gay, and Bisexual Young People*. New York: William Morrow, 1997.
Photographs of affirming images of lesbian, gay, and bisexual young people in high schools, colleges, and workplaces.

Snow, Judith. *How It Feels to Have a Gay or Lesbian Parent: A Book by Kids for Kids of All Ages*. New York: Harrington Park Press, 2004.
This paperback book is written by kids for kids. It reflects the "thoughts, feelings, and experiences of children, adolescents, and young adults who have a gay or lesbian

parent." They openly discuss what it is like to learn of their parents' sexual orientation and the impact this has at home, school, and with friends and other family members. Issues such as homophobia, discrimination, shame, and struggle in coping with being different are common themes, and each kid has a different important and valuable story to tell.

Gays and the Holocaust

Beck, Gad. *An Underground Life: Memoirs of a Gay Jew in Nazi Berlin.* Madison: University of Wisconsin Press, 2000.
Gad Beck was born to a dual-faith couple in Weimar, Germany. He recounts gay life in Berlin prior to and after the rise to power of the Nazis. Beck tried to save gay friends and Jews from concentration and deportation camps by forging documents, hiding people, and even in one case donning a Hitler youth uniform to deceive the Gestapo to attempt to help his lover. There is also an online exhibit of his wartime diary produced by the United States Holocaust Memorial Museum at http://www.ushmm.org/museum/exhibit/online/doyourememberwhen/co/co.htm.

Epstein, Rob, and Jeffrey Friedman. *Paragraph 175* (film). A Telling Pictures Production, 2000.
This movie is set in 1920s Berlin, known as a homosexual Eden, where gay men and lesbians lived relatively open lives. With the rise of the Nazis, all this changed. Between 1933 and 1945, one hundred thousand men were arrested for homosexuality under Paragraph 175. Some were imprisoned, others were sent to concentration camps. Of the latter, only about four thousand survived. In 2000, fewer than ten of these men were known to be living. Five of them told their stories for the first time in the film. The Web site, http://www.tellingpix.com/outreach/index.html, under Educational Outreach Program, has an online study guide that is downloadable as well as a resource guide.

Heger, Heinz. *The Men with Pink Triangles: The True Life-and-Death Story of Homosexuals in Nazi Death Camps.* Translated by David Fernbach. Los Angeles: Alyson Books, 1994.
This is a life-and-death story of homosexual prisoners in the Nazi concentration camps of World War II. Very little has been written before on this subject, as discrimination against homosexuals continued into the 1970s, and many prisoners, once released from the camps (if lucky enough to have survived them), were reimprisoned. It is a graphic book, but important reading of those nightmarish years. *The Advocate* rated this "One of the Ten Best Books of the Year."

Plant, Richard. *The Pink Triangle: The Nazi War Against Homosexuals.* New York: Owl Books, 1998.
A comprehensive book about the conditions that led up to the persecution of homosexuals in Germany, their capture, and subsequent internment in Nazi SS camps. It gives many personal accounts of what happened to survivors of the camps and, through their tales, stories of the far greater who did not survive.

Sherman, Martin. *Bent.* New York: Applause Books, 1979.
This play (also later a movie) is about Max, who is a gay man in Nazi Germany. Max is sent to Dachau concentration camp under the Nazi regime. He tries to deny he is gay

and gets a yellow label (the one for Jews) instead of pink (the one for gays). In camp he falls in love with his fellow prisoner Horst, who wears his pink label with pride. *Bent* debuted onstage at the Royal National Theatre in 1979, with Ian McKellen starring in the London production and Richard Gere in its later Broadway version. The play raised awareness about how Hitler used Paragraph 175, a largely ignored German law making homosexuality a criminal offense. The movie of the play can be rented or purchased.

GLBT Education Resources*

The following resources have been used successfully to introduce GLBT issues or conduct GLBT education in schools.

Jewish GLBT Curricula

The Anti-Defamation League's A World of Difference. *Combating Homophobia and Heterosexism: A Training Program for the Jewish Community.*
This curriculum explores sources of bias, the nature of homophobia, the impact of homophobia and heterosexism, and the links between homophobia and anti-Semitism. It teaches tolerance. Though the curriculum is not designed specifically for Jewish educational settings, it has been used for teacher training.

Angel, Camille, and Shifra Teitelbaum, 1994. *Intimate Connections: Integrating Human Love with God's Love: Using Jewish Values to Sensitize Students of All Ages to the Lesbian and Gay Experience.*
This curriculum moves beyond tolerance to teach inclusive community. In an integrated and thorough treatment of GLBT issues from the perspective of Jewish values, the curriculum covers human diversity; holiness in relationships; myths and stereotypes; anti-Semitism and homophobia; Jewish and GLBT visibility; homosexuality, and Torah through the concept of progressive revelation; taking action; and creating inclusive community.

Additional Curricula

Bowles, Norman, and Mark Rosenthal. *Cootie Shots: Theatrical Inoculations against Bigotry for Kids, Parents, and Teachers.* New York: Theatre Communications Group, 2001. Plays, poems, and songs to prevent discrimination and stereotyping.

The Gay, Lesbian, and Straight Education Network. "History Match Up." N.p.: The Gay, Lesbian, and Straight Education Network, 2003. A card game in which students learn about seventeen GLBT historical figures. Available at www.glsen.org.

---

*This list was originally created in 2002 by Rachel Timoner (now a third-year rabbinical student at Hebrew Union College–Jewish Institute of Religion) when she was a consultant to the LGBT Education Collaborative, a San Francisco Bay Area organization comprising representatives of Jewish Family and Children's Services, the Jewish Community Federation, LGBT Alliance, the Bureau of Jewish Education, Congregation Emanuel, and Congregation Sha'ar Zahav that was formed to build the capacity of Jewish schools to include GLBT people and topics in their learning environments in lasting and meaningful ways. The list has been updated by the editors.

Goodman, Jane, Kim Klausner, Lynn Levey, Eric Heins, and Terri Massin. *Preventing Prejudice: Lesbian/Gay/Bisexual/Transgender Lesson Plan Guide for Elementary Schools.* N.p.: Lesbian & Gay Parents Association, Buena Vista Lesbian and Gay Parents Group, 1999. Fifteen ready-to-use, age-appropriate lesson plans for grades K–5.

How-To Guides

Bass, Ellen, and Kate Kaufman. *Free Your Mind: The Book for Gay, Lesbian, and Bisexual Youth and Their Allies.* New York: Harper Perennial, 1996.
How-to chapter on making schools safe.

Brickley, Margie, Aimee Gelnaw, Hilary Marsh, and Daniel Ryan. "Opening Doors: Lesbian and Gay Parents and Schools." Washington, DC: Family Pride Coalition, 1999.
A short how-to guide for parents and educators from the perspective of lesbian and gay parents. Available at www.familypride.org.

Perrotti, Jeff, and Kim Westheimer. *When the Drama Club Is Not Enough: Lessons from the Safe Schools Program for Gay and Lesbian Students.* Boston: Beacon Press, 2001.
The authors give examples of inclusive language for use in the classroom, give examples of how teachers can come out to parents and discuss GLBT issues in the classroom, provide a primer on faculty workshops, and devote a chapter on how a school can handle controversy.

Project Io. "Name Calling in the Classroom: We can Do Something About It." Amherst, MA: Equity Institute.
Exercises for establishing classroom rules and a code of discipline.

Youth Leadership and Action Program of COLAGE. "Tips for Making Classrooms Safer for Students with LGBT Parents." San Francisco: COLAGE: Children of Lesbians and Gays Everywhere, 2002.
Ideas from the children's perspective for making classrooms inclusive. Available at www.colage.org.

Teacher Training

The Gay, Lesbian, and Straight Education Network. "Attitudes Toward Difference Survey: The Riddle Scale." New York: The Gay, Lesbian, and Straight Education Network, 2003.
This scale is a useful tool for raising awareness among faculty and administration about their views on GLBT issues. Available at www.glsen.org.

———. "From Denial to Denigration: Understanding Institutionalized Heterosexism in Our Schools." New York: The Gay, Lesbian, and Straight Education Network, 2002.
An introductory article on heterosexism for educators. Available at www.glsen.org.

———. "Homophobia 101." New York: The Gay, Lesbian, and Straight Education Network, 1999.
Beginning faculty trainings on GLBT issues that have been successfully conducted at more than 400 schools. Available at www.glsen.org.

———. "Homophobia 201." New York: The Gay, Lesbian, and Straight Education Network, 1999.
Intermediate faculty training on GLBT issues that have been successfully conducted at more than four hundred schools. Available at www.glsen.org.

———. *Teaching Respect for All*. New York: The Gay, Lesbian, and Straight Education Network, 1996.
A faculty training video by Kevin Jennings, the founder of the Gay, Lesbian, and Straight Education Network and former teacher. Available at www.glsen.org.

Lesbian and Gay Parents Association. *Overcoming Homophobia in the Elementary Classroom: A Workshop for Educators and Administrators*. San Francisco: Lesbian and Gay Parents Association, 1996.
A training program geared for elementary school educators for use in conjunction with the film *Both of My Moms' Names Are Judy*. Includes instructions for the presenters, pre- and post-workshop surveys, teacher handouts, sample lesson plans, and resource materials.

Exhibits and Films

Chasnoff, Debra and Helen Cohen. *It's Elementary: Talking about Gay Issues in School*. Women's Education Media, 1996.
A funny, heartwarming exploration, from the children's perspective, of gay issues at school. Shot in first through eighth grade classrooms across the United States.

———. *That's a Family!* Women's Educational Media, 2000.
Designed for elementary school kids, this film about family diversity profiles the lives of mixed race, adoptive, blended, single-parent, and GLBT families from the kids' perspectives.

Dubowski, Sandi Simcha, director. *Trembling Before G-d*. 2001.
A documentary of intimately told personal stories of Chasidic and Orthodox Jews who are gay or lesbian. The film portrays a group of people who face a profound dilemma—how to reconcile their passionate love of Judaism and the Divine with the drastic biblical prohibitions that forbid homosexuality.

Kaeser, Gillespie. *Love Makes a Family: Portraits of Lesbian, Gay, Bisexual, and Transgender People and Their Families*. Amherst: University of Massachusetts Press, 1999.
A traveling photo and text exhibit of GLBT families, which includes a gay dad who is a cantor and a lesbian couple who struggled with their synagogue to accept them and their children as a family. For information: Peggy Gillespie and Gigi Kaeser, Family Diversity Projects, www.familydiv.org; 413-256-0502.

Lesbian and Gay Parents Association. *Both of My Moms' Names Are Judy*. Lesbian and Gay Parents Association, 1994.
A ten-minute film interviewing children with lesbian and gay parents about their experiences at school. Sweet, touching, inspiring.

Symons, Johnny. *Daddy and Papa*. In association with Independent Television Service, 2002.
A documentary film about the personal, cultural, and political impact of gay men who are raising children themselves.

Additional Resources

Bigelow, Bill. *Rethinking Our Classrooms: Teaching for Equity and Justice*, vol. 1. Milwaukee, WI: Rethinking Schools, 1994.
A collection of articles and guides by teachers about creating inclusive and justice-based environments in the classroom.

———. *Rethinking Our Classrooms: Teaching for Equity and Justice*, vol. 2. Milwaukee, WI: Rethinking Schools, 2001.

COLAGE: Children of Lesbians and Gays Everywhere. "Books for Children." San Francisco: COLAGE: Children of Lesbians and Gays Everywhere.
List and description of twenty books for young children on GLBT families and anti-bias topics. Available at www.colage.org.

———. *Our Stories*. San Francisco: COLAGE: Children of Lesbians and Gays Everywhere, 1995.
A collection of thirty first-person accounts by children with lesbian, gay, bisexual, and transgender parents.

———. "Transgender Family Resources." San Francsico: COLAGE: Children of Lesbians and Gays Everywhere.
Internet resources, support groups, movies, books, publications, and scholarship information for children with transgender parents. Available at www.colage.org.

The Gay, Lesbian, and Straight Education Network. *Sexual Orientation, Our Children, and the Law*. San Mateo County, CA: The Gay, Lesbian, and Straight Education Network, 2000.
A guide to the responsibilities and obligations of California schools under the California Student Safety and Violence Prevention Act of 2000, A.B. 537.

Ponton, Lynn. *What Does Gay Mean?* National Mental Health Association.
A brochure for parents about how to talk to children about sexual orientation. Available at www.nmha.org.

Child and Youth Bibliography from COLAGE: Children of Lesbians and Gays Everywhere

http://colage.org/resources/kids_books.htm

Books for Ages 0-12

Aldrich, Andrew. *Daddy, Papa and Me: How My Family Came to Be*. Oakland, CA: New Family Press, 2003.
The story of a young African-America boy's adoption by his Daddy and Papa, who happen to be Caucasian, with the message that families are made up of people who love each other. Simple sentences and big, bold playful illustrations. **Ages 4–8.**

Alexander, Earl, Sheila Rudin, and Pam Sejkora. *My Dad Has HIV*. Minneapolis, MN: Fairview Press, 1996.
A young girl whose father has HIV learns about the virus and is proud of her dad for trying to stay healthy. This book is very easy to read, with simple, colorful illustrations. **Ages 5–8.**

Black, L., and J. Lovvorn. *My Family, Our Family, Your Family*. 2004.
A fabulous coloring book depicting a diverse variety of GLBT families doing mundane things like going shopping, eating dinner, and playing games together. **Ages 2–7.**

Charbonnet, Gabrielle, and P. Lindenbaum. *Else-Marie and Her Seven Little Daddies*. New York: Henry Holt, 1991.
In this Swedish tale, Else-Marie has seven little daddies instead of one big one and a mom, and she worries how the other children will react when her daddies come to pick her up at afternoon playgroup. **Ages 4–8.**

Considine, Kaitlyn Taylor. *Emma and Meesha My Boy: A Two Mom Story*. N.p.: Xlibris, 2004.
A little girl learns to treat her cat gently. **Ages 2–7.**

Coville, Bruce. *The Skull of Truth: A Magic Shop Book*. San Diego, CA: Harcourt Brace, 1997.
A boy who is forced through magic to tell the truth faces issues of his uncle's homosexuality and friend's cancer. Especially appealing to reluctant readers. **Ages 9–12.**

de Haan, Linda, and Stern Nijland. *King and King*. Berkeley, CA: Tricycle Press, 2002.
A prince who is reluctant to marry any of the princesses his mother invites to the castle finally finds love with another prince in this charming, colorful, and exuberantly collaged story. **Ages 5–8.**

———. *King and King and Family*. Berkeley, CA: Tricycle Press, 2004.
In this sequel to *King and King*, the two kings go on a honeymoon trip to the jungle, where they see lots of animal families and return home with a surprise of their own. **Ages 5–8.**

de Paola, Tomie. *Oliver Button Is a Sissy*. New York: Voyager Books, 1997.
A little boy must come to terms with being teased and ostracized because he'd rather read books, paint pictures, and tap-dance than participate in sports. **Ages 4–8.**

Edmonds, Barbara Lynn, and M. Danielle. *Mama Eat Ant, Yuck*. Eugene, OR: Barby's House Books, 2000.
This book, told in the form of a funny poem, is about the family life of one-year-old Emma, her Mama and Mommy, and her siblings. One day Emma is delighted when her mother receives a surprise in her raisins. **Ages 4–8.**

Fierstein, Harvey. *The Sissy Duckling*. New York: Simon & Schuster, 2002.
Actor and author Fierstein creates an alternative Hans Christian Andersen tale. Elmer, a happy duckling who loves to bake cookies and stage puppet shows, must deal with a

Papa Duck who wants him to play baseball and be a school bully. He runs away but returns to save the day while staying true to his identity. **Ages 4–8.**

Garden, Nancy. *The Case of the Stolen Scarab (Candlestone Inn Mystery #1)*. Ridley Park, PA: Two Lives Publishing, 2002.
When the Taylor-Michaelson family, Nikki and Travis and their two moms, buy an old inn in Vermont, they neither expect their first visitor to be the local sheriff with news of a robbery nor their second to be a bedraggled hiker with amnesia! Soon Nikki and Travis find themselves trying to solve a mystery that steadily grows more complicated—and perhaps dangerous as well. **Ages 8–12.**

———. *Holly's Secret*. New York: Farrar, Straus and Giroux Inc., 2000.
When Holly's family moves to a new town, she decides to take on a new identity at her new middle school and lies about her two moms, hoping that she'll fit in. She learns that her true friends will stand by her and that love is the most important thing. **Ages 7–12.**

———. *Molly's Family*. New York: Farrar Straus Giroux, 2004.
When Molly draws a picture of her family for kindergarten Open School Night, one of her classmates makes her feel bad because he says "you can't have a mommy and a mama." After talking to her teacher and her parents, she feels better knowing there are all different kinds of families, even in her own class. **Ages 4–8.**

Greenburg, Keith. *Zack's Story: Growing Up with Same-Sex Parents (Meeting the Challenge)*. Minneapolis, MN: Lerner Publishing Group, 1996.
A photo-story about an eleven-year-old boy who describes life as part of a family made up of himself, his mother, her lesbian partner, and his younger sister along with his father, stepmother, and their baby. **Ages 8–12.**

Jordan, Marykate. *Losing Uncle Tim*. Niles, IL: Albert Whitman, 1989.
A touching and beautifully illustrated story about a young boy who must deal with the fact that his beloved uncle Tim is dying of AIDS. **Ages 7–12.**

Kennedy, Joseph. *Lucy Goes to the Country*. Los Angeles: Alyson, 1998.
The story of Lucy the cat and her two "big guys" who travel to the country every weekend and run into a little bit of trouble. Contains many queer characters, including a lesbian couple with a daughter. **Ages 5–7.**

Newman, Leslea. *The Boy Who Cried Fabulous*. Berkeley, CA: Ten Speed Press, 2004.
This rhymed book tells the story of a young boy who marvels at everything around him and is constantly late, upsetting his parents until they realize how truly fabulous their son is. **Ages 5–8.**

———. *Felicia's Favorite Story*. Ridley Park, PA: Two Lives Publishing, 2002.
This book tells Felicia's favorite bedtime story of how Mama Nessa and Mama Linda adopted her, with a read-along style and charming watercolor illustrations. **Ages 4–7.**

———. *Heather Has Two Mommies*. Los Angeles: Alyson Publications, 1991.
One of the first books of its kind tells the story of three-year-old Heather and her two moms. **Ages 4–7.**

———. *Saturday Is Pattyday*. Norwich, VT: Women's Press: 1993.
Frankie used to live with his two moms, Allie and Patty, but they have separated. Frankie brings Doris Delores Brontausaurus to visit Allie in her new apartment and learns that Allie will always be part of his life. **Ages 4–9.**

———. *Too Far Away to Touch*. New York: Clarion Books, 1999.
This is the story of Zoë and her relationship with her uncle as he grows sick from AIDS. Zoë's uncle explains to her that when he dies he won't be close enough to touch but, like the stars, close enough to see. **Ages 5–9.**

Parnell, Peter, and Justin Richardson, New York: *And Tango Makes Three*. Simon & Schuster Children's Publishing, 2005.
This GLBT-reaffirming book is based on a true story about a penguin family living in New York City's Central Park Zoo. Two male penguins, named Roy and Silo, are "a little bit different" and what we would call "partners." With a little help from the zookeepers, Roy and Silo are given an egg to hatch and become proud parents. Their family is still on display at the zoo today, reaffirming that there are many kinds of families. **Ages 4–8.**

Parr, Todd. *The Family Book*. New York: Little, Brown, 2003.
A book celebrating all kinds of families, including our own. **Ages 4–8.**

Snow, Judith. *How it Feels to Have a Gay or Lesbian Parent: A Book by Kids for Kids of All Ages*. New York: Harrington Park Press, 2004. **Ages 7+.**

Valentine, Johnny. *The Duke Who Outlawed Jelly Beans and Other Stories*. Los Angeles: Alyson Publications, 2004.
This is a collection of five original fairy tales: "The Frog Prince," "The Eagle Rider," "The Dragon Sense," "The Ogre's Boots," and "The Duke Who Outlawed Jelly Beans." Embedded within the stories are a cast of gay and lesbian characters. **Ages 5–10.**

———. *One Dad, Two Dads, Brown Dad, Blue Dads*. Los Angeles: Alyson Books, 2004.
Two children—one with blue dads, one from a more traditional family—compare notes in this lighthearted book about parents who are different. In the end, of course, they discover that blue dads aren't really that different from other dads. Except for one thing. **Ages 3–6.**

Vigna, Judith. *My Two Uncles*. Morton Grove, IL: Albert Whitman, 1995.
Elly is upset when her grandfather refuses to invite her uncle and his partner to a family party. **Ages 7–10.**

Wilhoite, M. *Daddy's Roommate*. Boston: Alyson Publications, 1991.
Meet a boy, his gay dad, and his dad's partner in this Lambda Literary Award–winning book. **Ages 2–9.**

Wilson, Barbara. *A Clear Spring*. New York: Feminist Press, 2002.
During her stay with Aunt Ceci and her partner, Janie, who is a naturalist, Willa learns about environmentalism, gets to know more about her family, and solves a mystery. **Ages 7–12.**

Withrow, Sarah. *Box Girl*. Buffalo, NY: Groundwood Publishing, 2001.
Gwen's father is gay, and her mother left years ago. Despite her struggles at school and with finding friends with whom she can be open about her family, her father and his boyfriend, Leon, provide Gwen with love and hope. **Ages 10–12.**

Books for Ages 12 and up

Bass, Ellen, and Kate Kaufman, eds. *Free Your Mind: The Book for Gay, Lesbian, and Bisexual Youth*. New York: HarperCollins, 1996.
A great resource for anyone with an interest in GLBT youth issues. **Ages 14 and up**.

Bauer, M. Dane, ed., *Am I Blue? Coming Out from the Silence*. New York: HarperCollins, 1995.
A fantastic anthology of stories by well-known children's authors, each on the theme of growing up gay or lesbian, or with gay or lesbian parents or friends. **Ages 12 and up.**

Bechard, Margaret. *If It Doesn't Kill You*. New York: Viking Children's Books, 1999.
It comes as a shock to Ben and his mother when Ben's father announces he is gay and leaves home to move in with his boyfriend. Ben is not overly sympathetic at first, but must learn to confront his emotions. **Ages 14 and up.**

Bloch, Francesca Lia. *Girl Goddess #9: Nine Stories*. New York: HarperCollins, 1996.
This collection of short stories is focused on girls who discover that the world is not a simple place and that there is more than one way to live. Included in the book is "Dragons in Manhattan," the story of a girl with lesbian mothers who goes looking for her father. **Ages 14 and up.**

Carroll, Rebecca, ed. *Sugar in the Raw: Voices of Young Black Girls in America*. New York: Three Rivers Press, 1997.
A powerful collection of first-person narratives based on interviews conducted by the author; includes a story of a bisexual homegirl. **Ages 13 and up.**

Day, Angie. *The Way to Somewhere*. New York: Simon & Schuster, 2002.
The story of tomboy Taylor's journeys and struggles as she grows up. Her parents divorced when her father came out of the closet, and Taylor is searching for a plan for her life that will get her where she wants to be. **Ages 13 and up.**

Donoghue. Emma. *Stir-Fry*. New York: HarperCollins, 1994.
Seventeen-year-old Maria lives with a lesbian couple in her first flat away from home. A touching coming-of-age story. **Ages 16 and up.**

Durbin, Peggy. *And Featuring Bailey Wellcom as the Biscuit*. Port Orchard, WA: Little Blue Works, 1999.
    A novel featuring twelve-year-old Bailey Wellcom, who has just moved to the small town of Lucien, New Mexico, with her lesbian mother. Bailey goes on to come to terms with her mother's new girlfriend and the frightening event of a hate crime. **Ages 12–16.**

The Family Letter Project. *Beloved Daughter*. San Bruno, CA: Mandarin Asian Pacific Islander Lesbian/Bisexual Network (MAPLBN), 1999.
    A wonderful collection of letters written by Asian immigrants about their queer family member. In Chinese and in English. To order, email http://www.labrys.org/family. **Ages 14 and up.**

Garner, A. *Families Like Mine: Children of Gay Parents Tell It Like It Is*. New York: HarperCollins, 2004.
    This book interweaves the author's personal experiences of growing up with a gay father and straight mother, with those of other adult children of GLBT parents, based on eight years of activism and over fifty interviews. Included are the topics of coming-out, breakups, cultural queerness, second-generation queers, family definitions, and HIV/AIDS. **Ages 13 and up**.

Halpin, Brendan. *Donorboy: A Novel*. New York: Villard, 2004.
    A comic novel sharing the story of fourteen-year-old Rosalind, who develops a relationship with her sperm donor after the death of her lesbian moms. **Ages 13 and up**.

Hartinger, Brent. *The Geography Club*. New York: Harper Tempest, 2003.
    Russel and other gay students at his high school get together under the guise of a geography club. "We just choose a club that's so boring, nobody in their right mind would ever in a million years join it. We could call it Geography Club!" **Ages 13 and up.**

Hines, Sue. *Out of the Shadows*. New York: Avon Tempest, 2000.
    Rowanna is a sixteen-year-old girl growing up in contemporary Australia. Rowanna has a secret. Her mother was a lesbian, but was killed by a drunk driver, and she now lives with her mother's partner, whom she must learn to accept. **Ages 14 and up.**

Homes, A. M. *Jack*. Random House, 1990.
    Bond with fifteen-year-old Jack as he struggles to redefine the word "family" when his divorced father announces that he is gay. **Ages 14 and up.**

Howey, Noelle, and Ellen Samuels, eds. *Out of the Ordinary: Essays on Growing Up with Gay, Lesbian, and Transgender Parents*. New York: St. Martin's Press, 2000.
    A collection of essays, edited by Noelle Howey and Ellen Samuels, that talk from the heart about the experience of growing up with gay, lesbian, and transsexual parents. Some of the stories are easy to relate to, while others really make us think about what it means to be an inclusive family. In the chapter "Rites of Passage," by Daniel Belasco, the Jewish teenage author talks about his lesbian mom, her partner, a rabbi, and how they all integrated into Jewish society at large and within their own family. **Ages 14 and up.**

Peters, Julie. *Luna*. New York: Little, Brown, 2004.
Told from the eyes of his younger sister, a transgender boy goes through his senior year of high school and wants to transition to a girl. **Ages 14 and up.**

Ponton, Lynn. *What Does Gay Mean? How to Talk with Kids about Sexual Orientation and Prejudice*. National Mental Health Association, 2002.
This booklet is part of an anti-bullying program and provides resources and tips for parents talking with kids about sexual orientation and homophobia. Anti-gay prejudice affects straight kids, too. Studies show that for every gay, lesbian, and bisexual student who reported being harassed, four straight students said they were harassed because they were perceived as being gay or lesbian. **Ages preschool and up.**

Rafkin, Louise, ed. *Different Mothers: Sons and Daughters of Lesbians Talk about Their Lives*. Pittsburgh, PA: Cleis Press, 1990.
This book includes memoirs by thirty-eight "kids" (ages five to forty) about their experiences in their lesbian families. From peer pressure to custody issues, from coming-out to extended families, these writers cover it all! **Ages 13 and up.**

Ripslinger, Jon. *How I Fell in Love and Learned to Shoot Free Throws*. Brookfield, CT: Roaring Brook Press, 2003.
When seventeen-year-old Danny falls for Angel McPherson, the best female basketball player in school, they both have to come to terms with their family secrets. **Ages 15 and up.**

Romero, Melissa. *Long Way Home*. Port Orchard, WA: Windstorm Creative Limited, 2000.
Eleven-year-old Veronica is involved in a custody battle between her abusive father and her mother, who has recently come out as a lesbian. As a result she is caught between the two feuding households. **Ages 14 and up.**

Shannon, George. *Unlived Affections*. Los Angeles: Alyson Publications, 1995.
The story of an eighteen-year-old boy who loses his grandmother, only to uncover a family secret in old letters. The story tells of how Willie comes to terms with his father's homosexuality. **Ages 14 and up.**

Siegel, Laura, and Nancy Lamkin Olson, eds. *Out of the Closet into Our Hearts: Celebrating Our Gay/Lesbian Family Members*. San Francsico: Leyland Publications, 2001.
Stories and poems written by families of gay and lesbians. Includes interesting accounts from children as well as a diversity of other family members. **Ages 12 and up.**

Snow, Judith. *How it Feels to Have a Gay or Lesbian Parent: A Book by Kids for Kids of All Ages*. New York: Harrington Park Press, 2004.
This paperback book is written by kids for kids. It reflects the "thoughts, feelings, and experiences of children, adolescents, and young adults who have a gay or lesbian parent." They openly discuss what it is like to learn of their parents' sexual orientation and the impact this has at home, school, and with friends and other family members. Issues such as homophobia, discrimination, shame, and struggle in coping with being differ-

ent are common themes, and each kid has a different important and valuable story to tell. **Ages 12 and up.**

Velásquez, Gloria. *Tommy Stands Alone*. Houston, TX: Arte Publico Press, 1995.
The story of a young Mexican-American gay teenager and his struggle to overcome homophobia in his relationships with his family and friends. **Ages 12–16.**

Warren, Patricia Nell. *Billy's Boy*. Beverly Hills, CA: Wildcat Press, 1997.
This book tells the story of twelve-year-old John William Seden, the son of dead gay track star Billy Sive. His mother is a closeted lesbian. Billy is beginning to find out about his own sexuality as he comes of age. This books discusses coming out to friends and family, tolerance in schools, and some Christian, right-wing attitudes toward queers and queer families. **Ages 14 and up.**

Woodson, Jaqueline. *From the Notebooks of Melanin Sun*. New York: Point Signature, 1995.
The story of a thirteen-year-old-boy who is dealing with his mother's interracial lesbian relationship. **Ages 13 and up.**

———. *House You Pass on the Way*. New York: Putnam, 2003
A lesbian coming-of-age story about a young woman growing up in an interracial family. **Ages 11–14.**

Woog, Dan, ed. *Friends and Family: True Stories of America's Straight Allies*. Los Angeles: Alyson Books, 1999.
A collection of stories of straight allies, from children to high school teachers, and their battle to fight for queer rights. **Ages 12 and up.**

General GLBT Internet Links

The CCAR and the URJ provide these links for information purposes only and do not necessarily endorse the views expressed by any particular link on the following list.

www.aclunc.org/lesbian-and-gay	ACLU Northern California
www.civilmarriage.org	California Freedom to Marry Coalition
www.law.ucla.edu/williamsinstitute/home.html	The Williams Institute on Sexual Orientation Law and Public Policy
www.eqca.org	Equality California
www.glaad.org	Gay and Lesbian Alliance Against Defamation
www.glad.org	Gay and Lesbian Defenders
www.hrc.org	Human Rights Campaign
www.dontamend.com	Information and Action on Defeating the Federal Marriage Amendment
www.lgrl.sitestreet.com	Lesbian and Gay Rights Lobby of Texas
www.laglc.org	Los Angeles Gay and Lesbian Center Public Policy Department
www.lambdalegal.org	Lambda Legal Defense and Education Fund
www.meca.org	Marriage Equality California
www.marriageequality.org	Marriage Equality New York and California
www.nbjcoalition.org	National Black Justice Coalition
www.nclr.org	National Center For Lesbian Rights
www.freedomtomarry.org	National Freedom to Marry Coalition
www.thetaskforce.org	National Gay and Lesbian Task Force
www.nlgla.org	National Lesbian and Gay Law Association
www.transsexual.org	Transsexuality
www.pflag.org	Parents, Families, and Friends of Lesbians and Gays
www.buddybuddy.com	Partners Task Force

Biographies of Contributors

Rabbi Victor Appell, a native New Yorker and the product of a small congregation, grew up in the Reform Movement. Rabbi Appell was ordained from HUC-JIR in 1999. For four years he served as assistant and then associate rabbi of Temple Jeremiah in Northfield, Illinois. For two years, Rabbi Appell served at Temple Emanu-El in Edison, New Jersey. In July of 2005, Rabbi Appell joined the staff of the Union for Reform Judaism as the Small Congregations Specialist in the Department of Synagogue Management.

Rabbi Bradley Shavit Artson (http://www.bradartson.com) is the dean of the Ziegler School of Rabbinic Studies and vice president at the University of Judaism in Los Angeles, where he teaches ancient and medieval Jewish philosophy, as well as senior homiletics. He is the author of six books, most recently *Gift of Soul, Gift of Wisdom: Spiritual Resources for Mentoring and Leadership*, and a weekly e-mail commentary on the Torah portion that goes to almost 12,000 subscribers. He served as a congregational rabbi in Southern California for ten years. During that time, his synagogue grew from 200 to almost 600 membership units, and he helped over 200 people convert to Judaism. Rabbi Artson is on the faculty of the Wexner Heritage Foundation and speaks frequently for UJA/Federation communities.

Ali Cannon, a transgender man who identified as a butch dyke for almost twenty years, is a writer of short stories, poetry, and theater pieces. He appeared in and is the assistant producer of the film *It's a Boy: Journeys from Female to Male*. His writing is published in the anthology of *Secret Sisters: Stories of Being Lesbian and Bisexual in a College Sorority*. Most importantly, Ali celebrates his life as a newlywed; he is still *kvelling* over his marriage to his beautiful bisexual wife, Jessica, who has been an amazing supportive partner in his transition process.

Robert Kenneth Dixon III graduated magna cum laude from Loyola Marymount University with a degree in communication studies. At Loyola Marymount University, Robert cofounded a multicultural organization, Club Fusion, and was the president of the Business Law Society. Also at Loyola Marymount University, Robert, as Dr. Arthur Gross-Schaefer's research assistant, wrote the article included in *Kulanu* and planned and coordinated the Pacific Southwest Legal Studies in Business annual conference. Currently, he is embarking on his second year of law school, where he is the president of Street Law and the academic co-chair of the Black Law Students Association.

Rabbi Lisa A. Edwards, Ph.D., has been rabbi of Beth Chayim Chadashim in Los Angeles since her ordination from HUC-JIR in 1994. She also teaches "Introduction to Judaism" and "Gender and Judaism" at the University of Southern California and at HUC-JIR. Rabbi Edwards holds a Ph.D. in literature from the University of Iowa. She is a coeditor of URJ's *Introduction to Judaism: A Sourcebook* and has articles in several anthologies, including *Lesbian Rabbis: The First Generation* and the foreword to *Mentsh: On Being Jewish and Queer*. She lives in Los Angeles with her partner, Tracy Moore. Lisa and Tracy stood under a chuppah in 1995, on their tenth anniversary together, at a ceremony officiated by two Reform rabbis.

Bobbi and David Fishback are members of Temple Emanu-El of Kensington, Maryland, and are very proud of their two gay sons.

Seth W. Goren from Oreland, Pennsylvania, is a candidate for rabbinic ordination at HUC-JIR in May 2007. He received his B.A. and M.A. in Linguistics from the University of Pennsylvania, and his J.D. from the University of Pennsylvania Law School. He has worked at the Israeli Ministry of Justice and at the Jerusalem Open House, Jerusalem's LGBTQ center, and has served as a rabbinical student fellow with both the Jewish Council on Urban Affairs and the Jewish Funds for Justice. In the United States, he has done outreach work on GLBT issues on behalf of the Union for Reform Judaism and served on the board of Congregation Beth Ahavah, a predominantly GLBT synagogue in Philadelphia.

Rebecca Gorlin was born in New York City in 1961 and moved to Boston in 1980 for college; she has lived there ever since. Her major activities include singing with and being the archivist of Voices Rising, a women's chorus; writing music and literature; and political activism when she has the time and energy. She married Kim in 1994 in a Jewish wedding and legally in 2003 in Toronto; she has spent years fighting to make and keep same-sex marriage legal. Four crazy but lovable cats also demand much of her time, but save her sanity.

Rabbi Arthur Gross-Schaefer, J.D., C.P.A., is the chair of the Department of Marketing and Business Law at Loyola Marymount University in Los Angeles, California. He received a J.D. from Boston University in 1976 and was ordained by HUC-JIR in 1984. He is a consultant to the California State Library System on issues of legal resources and diversity and is a consultant to several schools and school boards on issues surrounding religion in the public schools. He also works with law firms, helping them to more ethically practice office law. He has created a pamphlet for the California State Library System explaining the criminal legal system to new immigrants that has been translated into over twelve languages. His ethics decision model and audit has been widely distributed to non-profit institutions, and he has been published in numerous publications.

John E. Hirsch, Ph.D., was the founder and chair of Temple Beth-El's Gay and Lesbian Inclusion Committee, as well as chair of the Union for Reform Judaism—Greater New York Council Gay & Lesbian Resource Committee. In 2004, John and his partner Herbert were Grand Marshals of the Long Island Gay Pride March in Huntington, Long Island.

Lani Ka'ahumanu is a bisexual, feminist, biracial (Hawaiian/Irish) writer and activist. She is the coeditor with Loraine Hutchins of *Bi Any Other Name: Bisexual People Speak Out* (Alyson, 1991), a groundbreaking anthology.

Biographies of Contributors

Rabbi Yoel Kahn, Ph.D., is currently the director of the Taube Center for Jewish Life at the Jewish Community Center of San Francisco. He served as the rabbi of Congregation Sha'ar Zahav from 1985 to 1996. Rabbi Kahn has been involved in a variety of community, interfaith, and municipal organizations and committees. Ordained at the HUC-JIR in 1985, he received his Ph.D. through the Center for Jewish Studies at the Graduate Theological Union, Berkeley, California, in 1999. He is a former director of curriculum at Synagogue 2000, an institute for the synagogue of the twenty-first century, the executive director of Hillel at Stanford University, and a teacher at the Graduate Theological Union and the University of California, Davis. A specialist in the history of prayer books and liturgy, Rabbi Kahn advises clergy, ritual committees, and congregations on liturgical innovation and renewal and works directly with groups who are editing or creating new prayer books or liturgical materials.

Inbal Kashtan has an M.A. in Jewish studies from the Graduate Theological Union. Her master's thesis, "Fissures, Hermeneutics, and Ideology: Reading Women in Rabbinic Midrash," explores texts about women from *Sifrei Bamidbar*. She is also the Parenting Project coordinator at the Center for Nonviolent Communication (NVC) and leads public workshops as well as trainings in schools and organizations. Her work most recently appeared in *Mothering* magazine, and she is currently working on a book on parenting. She and her partner, Kathy Simon, are mothers of a vibrant son, Yannai.

Rabbi Elliot Kukla was ordained by HUC-JIR in 2006 and is currently the rabbi of the Danforth Jewish Circle in Toronto, Canada. He has been involved in transgender activism and education since 2000 and teaches about the spiritual implications of gender diversity for men, women, and everybody else. He is currently co-creating a transgender resource library for *Jewish Mosiac: National Center for Gender and Sexual Diversity* (www.jewishmosaic.org) and helping to launch a Web site of educational and liturgical resources (www.transtorah.org). Elliot's essays on gender are published in a number of magazines and will appear in *Righteous Indignation: A Jewish Call for Justice* (Jewish Lights, September 2007).

Rabbi Richard N. Levy is the director of the School of Rabbinic Studies on the Los Angeles campus of HUC-JIR. He completed a two-year term as the president of the Central Conference of American Rabbis and was the architect of the "Statement of Principles for Reform Judaism" (the "Pittsburgh Principles") overwhelmingly passed at the May 1999 CCAR convention. He is the author of the book *A Vision of Holiness: The Future of Reform Judaism*, published by URJ Press.

Rabbi Jane Rachel Litman has consulted with the National Council of Churches, the Metropolitan Community Church, and numerous Jewish institutions on religious education for alternative families including GLBT, interfaith, multiracial, and single-parent families. She is the rabbi/educator at Congregation Beth El in Berkeley, California. Prior to that, she served gay outreach congregations Kol Simcha and Sha'ar Zahav for eight years. She has taught religious and women's studies at California State University Northridge and Loyola Marymount College. She is the coeditor of *Lifecycles 2* and a regular columnist on gender issues for *Beliefnet.com*.

TJ Michels is an editor and writer living in Washington, D.C., whose articles have appeared in both the Jewish and gay presses. In addition to teaching classes on transgender theory for the Harvey Milk Institute in San Francisco, she has presented academically on topics relating to dyke masculinity, feminism, and queer theory.

Harriet Perl is a longtime member of Congregation Beth Chayim Chadashim (BCC), and at age eighty-five, a revered elder in her community. Harriet was not only an early member of the National Organization for Women (NOW) but she also stood up as an open lesbian. It was during the activism of the early 1970s that Harriet came to BCC as one of its earliest members. She volunteered for the position of secretary, then vice president. As the congregation grew and moved to its current location on Pico Boulevard, she served on the BCC board, edited the *G'vanim* newsletter, cochaired one of the first international conferences of gay and lesbian Jewish organizations (forerunner of today's World Congress), served on three rabbinic search committees, and—as one of her greatest legacies—spearheaded, along with member Jesse Jacobs (z"l), the effort to degenderize BCC's English prayer book liturgy in 1974.

Bernard Schlager, Ph.D., is director of national outreach for the Center for Lesbian and Gay Studies in Religion and Ministry (CLGS) in Berkeley, California. In addition, he teaches in the Certificate in Sexuality and Religion Program (CSR) at Pacific School of Religion, serves as an editorial consultant for the CLGS/Pilgrim Press Book series, and directs the Center's national OutFront workshop program. He also is coordinator for the Bay Area Coalition of Welcoming Congregations.

Rabbi Burt Schuman was rabbi at Temple Beth Israel in Altoona, Pennsylvania. He has now moved to Poland to serve at Beit Warzawa, the first Progressive synagogue in Poland since the Holocaust.

Dr. David Shneer, a cofounder of Jewish Mosaic, is an associate professor of history and director of the Center for Judaic Studies at the University of Denver. His work concentrates on modern Jewish culture, Soviet Jewish history, and Jews and sexuality. Shneer and Caryn Aviv are coauthors of the forthcoming textbook *American Queer, Now and Then* (Paradigm Publishers, 2006) and coedited the groundbreaking anthology *Queer Jews* (Routledge, 2002). As a board member of Jewish Mosaic and as a scholar, Shneer speaks widely about issues of Jews and sexuality, most recently giving talks about the role of GLBT Jews in advancing Jewish culture at "Rejewvenation: The Future of Jewish Cultures," a conference held at the University of Toronto in October 2005. Shneer earned his Ph.D. in history at the University of California, Berkeley.

Rabbi Sharon Sobel was ordained from HUC-JIR in New York, in May 1989. She was the assistant rabbi at Holy Blossom Temple in Toronto until July 1995, and from August 1995 to June 2000, she served as the rabbi of Temple Sinai in Stamford, Connecticut. In July 2000, she was appointed executive director of the Union for Reform Judaism's Canadian Council for Reform Judaism and ARZA Canada. She has done extensive traveling on behalf of the Reform Movement to other parts of the world, including going both to South Africa and to the former Soviet Union. She has published numerous papers and articles, and in 1994, Vision TV produced a documentary on Rabbi Sobel's rabbinate, shown many times on Canadian national television.

Neil Spencer Welles has been a member of Temple Micah, a Reform congregation, in Washington, D.C., since 1988. He has served on the synagogue's social action committee, on its board of directors, and as the coordinator for the activities of *Kulanu*, Micah's GLBT gateway group. The first *simchah* celebrated in the sanctuary of the shul's newly dedicated building in 1995 was his marriage to his former husband, Harlan Messinger. In 2002, he addressed the UAHC mid-Atlantic conference held in Greensboro, North Carolina, on the topic of how a synagogue can make outreach efforts to become more welcoming and inclusive to its GLBT members and potential GLBT congregants. He is a member of the Arlington Gay and Lesbian Alliance, and of Equality Virginia, and currently practices consumer law and bankruptcy law at the law firm of Robert A. Ades & Associates, in Springfield, Virginia. He resides in Arlington, Virginia with his partner, Juan Pedro Villagrana.

Rabbi Margaret Moers Wenig has served simultaneously as a congregational rabbi and a teacher at HUC-JIR since her ordination in 1984. She is both a teacher of liturgy and an innovative liturgist; both a challenging and widely published preacher and a teacher of preaching. *New York Jewish Week* named Rabbi Wenig one of "45 for Tomorrow: A New Generation of Young Jewish Leaders to Take the New York Jewish Community into the 21st Century," for she is often among the pioneers in endeavors that the mainstream Jewish community subsequently undertakes.

Rabbi Nancy H. Wiener is currently the fieldwork coordinator and instructor of pastoral care and counseling at the HUC-JIR. She manages the College-Institute's fieldwork program. Rabbi Wiener also serves as the rabbi of Pound Ridge Jewish Community in Pound Ridge, New York; the bereavement group co-leader of the National Center for Jewish Healing/Jewish Board of Family and Children's Services in New York; and volunteers as a grief counselor at the Names Project of the AIDS Memorial Quilt. Rabbi Wiener received her doctor of ministry in pastoral counseling in 1994 and her rabbinic ordination in 1990 from HUC-JIR. She received her chaplaincy certification from the National Association of Jewish Chaplains and a certificate in pastoral counseling from the Postgraduate Center for Mental Health in 1993.

Laura Wolfson is a temple educator at Anshe Chesed, a Reform congregation in Canada. She is married to her partner, Tish, and they are mothers of Hannah.

Reuben Zellman is a candidate for rabbinic ordination at HUC-JIR in 2008. He was the Cooperberg-Rittmaster Rabbinic Intern at Congregation Beth Simchat Torah in New York city and is currently the rabbinic intern at Congregation Sha'ar Zahav in San Francisco. He received his B.A. in linguistics from UC Berkeley and worked in disability services before doing his post-baccalaureate work in music theory and classical voice at San Francisco State University. He has been involved with transgender activism since 1999 and writes and teaches about transgender and intersex issues and Judaism.

Biographies of Editors

Rabbi Richard F. Address, D.Min., joined the URJ staff in 1978 after pulpit work in California. He served as regional director of the Pennsylvania Council of the URJ from August 1978 through December 2000. He was named director of Jewish Family Concerns on July 1, 1997. Rabbi Address was ordained from HUC-JIR (Cincinnati) in 1972 and received his honorary doctor of divinity from HUC-JIR in 1997. In May 1998 he received a certificate in pastoral counseling from the Postgraduate Center for Mental Health in New York, and in May 1999 he received his doctor of ministry from HUC-JIR in New York. Rabbi Address teaches classes on Jewish family issues at HUC-JIR in New York. He is married to Jane Travis-Address, and they have three children.

Joel L. Kushner, Psy.D., is the first director of the Institute for Judaism and Sexual Orientation (IJSO) and the Jeff Herman Virtual Resource Center (JHVRC) for Sexual Orientation and Gender Issues in the Jewish Community at HUR-JIR. He has multiple graduate degrees in counseling and clinical psychology from Columbia University and Rutgers University in New Jersey. Prior to working for HUC, Dr. Kushner was a behavioral health-care consultant advising clients like Pepsi, Nordstrom, and the City of Los Angeles on critical incident stress debriefing, employee performance, supervision training, and policy development. Dr. Kushner has a lifelong commitment to pastoral care and bereavement work, originally developed at the New College, University of Edinburgh, Scotland. In the mid-1980s, Dr. Kushner volunteered for Gay Men's Health Crisis (GMHC) in New York, conducting outreach and training in several of the first AIDS education programs. In California, Dr. Kushner co-led bereavement groups for adults at St. John's Medical Center for eight years. He has a loving and supportive husband and two beautiful children.

Rabbi Geoffrey Mitelman was ordained at the HUC-JIR in June 2007. He graduated from Princeton University in 2000 with a degree in religion and Jewish studies and was awarded multiple prizes for biblical and Judaic scholarship. Before entering HUC, he spent a year volunteering in Israel through Project Otzma and a year working on teacher training and curriculum development at the nonprofit educational organization Facing History and Ourselves. As a second-year student at HUC-JIR in 2003, he represented the school at an international interfaith program in Krakow, Poland, entitled "Building Towards the Future," exploring Catholic and Jewish responses to the Holocaust in Germany, Poland, and the United States. For two years, he was the student rabbi at

Temple Oheb Shalom in Sandusky, Ohio, and for one year he traveled monthly to Grand Forks, North Dakota to be student rabbi at Congregation B'nai Israel. His rabbinic thesis is entitled "Rabbinic Thought Through the Lens of Emotional Intelligence," and it was his interest in the intersection between Judaism and psychology that led him to his internship at the URJ Department of Jewish Family Concerns. He has been published in *Reform Judaism, Jewish Education News,* and *D'var Acher.*